Perspectives
on Social Network Research

Proceedings
of the Mathematical Social Science Board's
Advanced Research Symposium on Social Networks
Held at Dartmouth College, Hanover, New Hampshire,
September 18-21, 1975

This is a volume of
Quantitative Studies in Social Relations
Consulting Editor: Peter H. Rossi, University of Massachusetts,
Amherst, Massachusetts

A complete list of titles in this series appears at the end of this volume.

Perspectives on Social Network Research

edited by

Paul W. Holland

Educational Testing Service
Princeton, New Jersey

Samuel Leinhardt

School of Urban and Public Affairs
Carnegie-Mellon University
Pittsburgh, Pennsylvania

ACADEMIC PRESS
A Subsidiary of Harcourt Brace Jovanovich, Publishers

New York   London   Toronto   Sydney   San Francisco
1979

Reproduction, translation, publication, use, and disposal by and for the

United Stated Government and its officers, agents, and employees acting

within the scope of their official duties, for Government use only, is

permitted.

This material was prepared with the support of National Science

Foundation grant No. SOC70-02316 A04. Any opinions, findings,

conclusions or recommendations expressed herein are those of the

authors and do not necessarily reflect the view of the National

Science Foundation.

ACADEMIC PRESS, INC.
111 Fifth Avenue, New York, New York 10003

United Kingdom Edition published by
ACADEMIC PRESS, INC. (LONDON) LTD.
24/28 Oval Road, London NW1 7DX

Mathematical Social Science Board's Advanced Research
    Symposium on Social Networks, Dartmouth, 1975.
    Advances in social network research.

    (Quantitative studies in social relations)
    Papers prepared for presentation at the Mathematical
Social Science Board's Advanced Research Symposium on
Social Networks, held at Dartmouth College, Hanover, N.H.,
Sept. 18–21, 1975.
    Includes index.
    1. Sociology—Methodology—Congresses.   2. Social
structure—Congresses.   3. Sociometry—Congresses.
4. Sociology—Mathematical models—Congresses.
I. Holland, Paul W.   II. Leinhardt, Samuel.   III. Ti-
tle.
HM24.M2984 1975   301'.01'8   78-4813
ISBN 0-12-352550-0

PRINTED IN THE UNITED STATES OF AMERICA

79 80 81 82   9 8 7 6 5 4 3 2 1

Contents

v

Contributors
and Symposium Participants

Numbers in parentheses indicate the pages on which authors' contributions begin.

ROBERT P. ABELSON (239), Department of Psychology, Yale University, New Haven, Connecticut

BO ANDERSON (453), Department of Sociology, Michigan State University, East Lansing, Michigan

JOHN A. BARNES (403), Faculty of Sociology, Churchill College, Cambridge University, Cambridge, England

H. RUSSELL BERNARD (165), Department of Sociology and Anthropology, West Virginia University, Morgantown, West Virginia

SCOTT BOORMAN, Department of Sociology, University of Pennsylvania, Philadelphia, Pennsylvania

DORWIN CARTWRIGHT (25), Department of Psychology, University of Michigan, Ann Arbor, Michigan

JAMES S. COLEMAN (257), University of Chicago, National Opinion Research Center, Chicago, Illinois

ANTHONY P. M. COXON (489), Faculty of Sociology, University College, University of Wales, Wales, United Kingdom

JAMES A. DAVIS[1] (51), National Opinion Research Center, University of Chicago, Chicago, Illinois

PATRICK DOREIAN (201), Department of Sociology and Program in Environmental Systems Engineering, University of Pittsburgh, Pittsburgh, Pennsylvania

CLAUDE FLAMENT (187), Laboratoire de Psychologie Sociale, Université de Provence, Aix-en-Provence, France

[1] Present address: Department of Sociology, Harvard University, Cambridge, Massachusetts.

OVE FRANK (319), Department of Statistics, University of Lund, Lund, Sweden

MARK GRANOVETTER (501), Department of Sociology, SUNY at Stony Brook, Stony Brook, New York

FRANK HARARY (25), Department of Mathematics, University of Michigan, Ann Arbor, Michigan

FRITZ HEIDER (11), Department of Psychology, University of Kansas, Lawrence, Kansas

PAUL W. HOLLAND (1, 63), Educational Testing Service, Princeton, New Jersey

JOHN E. HUNTER (223), Department of Psychology, Michigan State University, East Lansing, Michigan

PETER D. KILLWORTH (165), Department of Applied Mathematics, University of Cambridge, Cambridge, England

EDWARD O. LAUMANN (379), Department of Sociology, University of Chicago, Chicago, Illinois

SAMUEL LEINHARDT (1, 63), School of Urban and Public Affairs, Carnegie-Mellon University, Pittsburgh, Pennsylvania

JOEL H. LEVINE (349), Department of Sociology, Dartmouth College, Hanover, New Hampshire

JOHN M. LIGHT (85), Department of Sociology, Princeton University, Princeton, New Jersey

J. CLYDE MITCHELL (425), Faculty of Anthropology, Nuffield College, Oxford University, Oxford, England

NICHOLAS C. MULLINS (85, 519), Department of Sociology, Indiana University, Bloomington, Indiana

ROBERT NORMAN, Department of Mathematics, Dartmouth College, Hanover, New Hampshire

CHARLES H. PROCTOR (301), Department of Statistics, North Carolina State University, Raleigh, North Carolina

ANATOL RAPOPORT (119), Department of Mathematics, University of Toronto, Toronto, Ontario, Canada

EVERETT M. ROGERS (137), Institute for Communication Research, Stanford University, Stanford, California

RICHARD C. ROISTACHER[1] (471), Department of Sociology and Center for Advanced Computation, University of Illinois, Champaign-Urbana, Illinois

WILLIAM S. ROY (349), Norris Cotton Cancer Center, Dartmouth College, Hanover, New Hampshire

D. GARTH TAYLOR[2] (257), University of Chicago, National Opinion Research Center, Chicago, Illinois

DOUGLAS WHITE, Department of Anthropology, University of California, Irvine, California

HARRISON C. WHITE, Department of Sociology, Harvard University, Cambridge, Massachusetts

NORMAN WHITTEN, Department of Anthropology, University of Illinois, Campaign-Urbana, Illinois

Several other individuals attended the symposium. They included: **Nancie Gonzalez** (NSF-Anthropology), **Grace Heider, David Heise** (University of North Carolina), **Charles Hubbell** (California State University), **Kenneth Land** (University of Illinois), **Donald Ploch** (NSF-Sociology), **Walter Sedelow** (NSF-Computing), **Kazuo Seiyama** (Harvard University), **Stanley Wasserman**, and **Christopher Winship** (Harvard University). The symposium was also open to members of the Sociology Department, Dartmouth College.

[1] Present address: Bureau of Social Science Research, 1990 M Street, NW, Washington, D. C. 20036

[2] Present address: Department of Political Science, University of Chicago, Chicago, Illinois

Preface

The chapters in this volume were originally prepared for presentation at the Mathematical Social Science Board's Advanced Research Symposium on Social Networks held at Dartmouth College, Hanover, New Hampshire, September 18–21, 1975, under the codirection of Samuel Leinhardt and H. Russell Bernard.[1] The thirty-one invited participants included sociologists, psychologists, anthropologists, mathematicians, and statisticians representing a variety of institutions in the United States, Canada, Great Britain, France, and Sweden. The symposium was made possible by a National Science Foundation grant to the Mathematical Social Science Board. The Center for Advanced Study in the Behavioral Sciences, Stanford, California, administered the grant.

Many people were involved in running the symposium and producing this volume. Richard Dietrich and Christine Visminas-Clark helped make the symposium a smoothly run and well-organized affair. Joel Levine played a singularly important role in establishing and maintaining a network of connections to the Sociology Department, College Administration, Hanover Inn, and the Amos Tuck School of Business Administration at Dartmouth. Mary Kuiper, Linda Aldridge and Robert Jameson provided editorial assistance. Marjorie Farinelli faced many a frustrating and exasperating moment with editors and authors but managed nonetheless to maintain the sense of purpose and dedication needed to coordinate the typing and proofing of this volume.

The original idea for the symposium occurred during a conversation between Samuel Leinhardt and James A. Davis. Hubert A. Blalock suggested applying to the MSSB for funding. Kenneth Land acted as advocate with the MSSB and, once the project was off the ground, Preston Cutler saw to the establishment of semblance of fiscal order. Editorial staff at Academic Press provided the continuing encouragement and support that was necessary to bring this project to a successful conclusion.

We are indebted and grateful to all.

Paul W. Holland
Samuel Leinhardt

[1]Chapter 6 is an exception to this statement. It does not derive from a symposium presentation.

CHAPTER 1

THE ADVANCED RESEARCH SYMPOSIUM ON SOCIAL NETWORKS

Paul W. Holland

Educational Testing Service

Princeton, New Jersey

Samuel Leinhardt

School of Urban and Public Affairs

Carnegie-Mellon University

Pittsburgh, Pennsylvania

I. PURPOSE

The symposium was called to survey research on social networks, to review and criticize major research thrusts involving
network studies of social behavior and to specify promising directions for future research activities. In the first half of
the twentieth century network notions and methods were introduced
by a few social and behavioral scientists (e.g., Simmel, Moreno,
Radcliffe-Brown) to help describe and measure regularities in
social relationships. By 1975, network terms, models and methods
were being applied by a very large number of social scientists in
diverse ways. Research was appearing on topics as varied as
cognition, attitude formation, social and economic mobility,
diffusion of innovations, communication, corporate and community
organization, interpersonal behavior, political behavior and non-

human social behavior.[1] Network ideas were being used to improve theoretical formulations, designs for data collection, and
frameworks for data analysis. An obvious question to ask in the
face of this explosion of activity and breadth of application
was whether any significant new insights were being generated.
The symposium was called to provide an opportunity for determining whether useful new results were being obtained and at what
level.

II. MATHEMATICS AND SOCIAL NETWORKS

Part of the explanation for the ubiquity of network concepts
in contemporary social research seems to rest in the central role
that structure has come to play in modern social and behavioral
theory. While the theoretical importance of structure is not new,
over the past two decades there has been a significant change in
the way in which structural ideas are employed. Older applications were primarily metaphorical and, while such usage has its
value in the development of perspectives and in focusing attention on outstanding problems, modern applications evidence a
greater concern for precision and analytic depth. Presumably, a
principal advantage of network ideas rests in their ability to
represent the essential features of what is meant by the term
structure, to do so parsimoniously and to permit the use of the
powerful, deductive analytic features of structural mathematics
in stating and in testing theory. Networks and network variables
seem to be especially amenable to formulation in modern algebraic

[1]For a selection of articles on social network research see
Leinhardt (1976). Two journal issues have been dedicated to
social network research, The Journal of Mathematical Sociology,
volume 5, number 1, 1977, edited by S. Leinhardt, and Sociological
Methods and Research, volume 7, number 2, November, 1978, edited
by R. Burt.

and graph theoretic terms. Such formalization often yields a new level of clarity in the statement of issues and the development of arguments about social structure because thinking in mathematics rather than words often leads to discoveries that are not otherwise obvious or readily obtained. We don't mean to suggest that networks are the only area in sociology or anthropology where mathematization is purposeful or possible. It just seems that when networks are brought into the discussion mathematical representation is a natural and easily defended means of making statements and developing arguments. (For a discussion of this role of mathematics in social science see Simon, 1977.) Indeed, network research is one of the few areas in sociology where mathematical theorems have contained important substantive content, and, conversely, substantive results have had implications for mathematical developments. The symposium, in the process of creating an opportunity for the critical review of accomplishments, allowed a group of experienced network researchers to confront the specific issue of whether the formal, analytic approach had proven especially effective.

Of course, the advantages that network mathematics and statistics provide are not without cost. Indeed, one might well argue that the process of abstracting social behavior so as to permit it to be expressed in terms of network or graph theoretic concepts involves so extreme a reduction in conceptual richness that essential features are lost and, consequently, theory construction and empirical research become trivial and irrelevant. There is, in this argument, the thread of a classic dispute over the general advisability of using mathematical tools to study social behavior. The editors' own joint research activities clearly demonstrate their personal belief that formal methods applied to the study of social structure will provide the greatest gains in terms of important and reliable results. Nonetheless, it is clear that the graph theory, topological

algebras, stochastic processes and other mathematical and statistical tools now employed in network studies of social organization do require a vast simplification of reality. For example, a
typical application of network ideas may require conceptualizing
a highly complex relationship such as friendship in terms of a
simple binary code that records only whether each of two individuals claims the other as a "friend". The acceptability of such a
reduction depends on its ultimate practical utility in terms of
leading to models that are good at explaining and predicting aggregate or individual behavior. In this vein, the questions of
degree of abstraction and level of mathematization are practical
issues relating to the usefulness of tools and are not directly
related to how well the model replicates the known richness of
social behavior. The use of mathematics in social science is
never meant to imply that social behavior lacks complexity any
more than an equation in physics implies physical reality is
simple. What we social scientists need to discover is which abstractions successfully capture the necessary components of social
behavior and how to express these in sufficient detail to permit
us to learn more about the relationships among the components.
When the tools of abstraction are amenable to mathematical manipulation the gain in analytic power can be enormous. In much current thinking, the appeal of networks and network variables results from their potential to allow us to exploit recent advances
in mathematical and stochastic theories of structure and, as a
consequence, break through to a much enhanced understanding of
social behavior.

      While the objectives of quantification and formal represen-
tation bias our own approach to the study of social behavior,
ours is not the only way in which social networks are appreciated. This volume presents a variety of alternative views.
Nonetheless, it is fair to say that the chapters are dominated by
a perspective which emphasizes the utility, precision and conceptual clarity of mathematical and statistical approaches.

III.   THE FUTURE OF SOCIAL NETWORK RESEARCH

Research involving social network ideas has thrived in the
period since the symposium was held and the future will doubtless
witness increased activity. A new journal, *Social Networks,* which
is self-described as "an international journal of structural
analysis", began to be published in 1978. Sessions on social
networks have begun to be held on a regular basis at the annual
meetings of major scientific associations and a separate association, the International Network for Social Network Analysis,
has come into being. Thus, except for the extraordinary diversity
of substantive interests, theoretical approaches and empirical
methods, social network research would appear to have all the
trappings of a bonafide research subspecialty. Current research
activities are reasonably well represented by the chapters in
this volume although research on social cognition, community
organization and political behavior are underrepresented.[2]

Contemporary research on social structure invariably involves
qualitative or quantitative network notions and the appearance
of studies emphasizing practical applications of social networks
research would suggest that we know much more than we actually
do. Network ideas are being used to enhance theory construction,
facilitate study design, and direct data collection procedures
and data analysis methods in so many research contexts that it is
really impossible to catalog them exhaustively. This undoubtedly
means that network methods and models have been generally
accepted as respectable modes for organizing and motivating
research on structured regularities in social behavior. In this
vein social network research is now simply research on social
structure in which a network framework is employed because, in

[2]*Clinton DeSoto, Herbert Menzel and Elihu Katz were originally invited to the symposium but were unable to attend. It
is likely that had they done so this underrepresentation would
not have occurred.*

a practical sense, it is an effective way of formulating structural concepts and of understanding structural data.

Future research activities will no doubt see an even broader
range of application as this integration with the central topics
of social science continues. In the immediate future the most
vigorous disciplines of application will probably remain sociology
and anthropology although activities in political science, educational research, social psychology and social psychiatry are increasing. The problems of improving the richness of mathematical
models, of developing reliable data collection and sampling
designs, of performing inferential tests for empirically estimated parameters and of formulating computer routines for efficient
data management are likely to be leading issues. Three areas
seem ripe for near term breakthrough quality work; all relate to
increasing the conceptual richness of network models to enable
them to provide more accurate predictions of social behavior.
These directions involve time, simultaneous relationships and
valued relationships. Currently, most models are cross sectional,
handling only single, binary ties at one moment in time and are
obviously in need of generalization. A fourth major research
area likely to be actively pursued involves open-ended networks
with ill-defined boundaries and membership. Such networks are
important in community level research and usable models must be
available if research on macro social structure is to advance.

Some work on these topics has begun to appear but, interestingly, the technical sophistication of the modeling procedures
seems to have outpaced the development of relevant substantive
theory. Here, again, is another classic dilemma in the study of
social behavior. Theorists rarely have precise, clear empirical
results about which to theorize while empiricists usually have
few explicit, well formulated (i.e., capable of being discon-
firmed) theoretical statements to test. Indeed, it would appear
that the theory of social structure is still at a very primitive

level even though social network methods seem well advanced from
a technical standpoint. This does not imply, however, that
methodological development should be halted to give theorists an
opportunity to catch up. Advanced methods can and do lead to
advances in substantive understanding especially at the preliminary stages of conceptual penetration of a phenomenon.

While scientists have been systematically observing social
systems for many years, it is becoming clear that the complexity
of the phenomenon requires levels of precision in measurement
and complexity in modeling that are yet to be developed. Thomas
(1979), writing on the life sciences, has observed that perhaps
the most important discovery biologists have made in the twentieth century is that even with the numerous achievements of the
discipline, our ignorance of nature remains enormous. The
research reported and discussed in the chapters that follow
demonstrate that social scientists have also begun to shed their
naivete and to face up to the fact that social structure is
extraordinarily complicated and that its ultimate comprehension
requires mastery and application of very advanced procedures.

IV.   ORGANIZATION OF THE VOLUME

The original design of the symposium called for a mix of
three activities. One involved participants in the presentation
of reviews of major research thrusts or application areas,
another involved the presentation of new research results or
theoretical developments, and a third involved commentary in the
form of discussion related to earlier presentations or in the
form of a review of extant publications.

In the organization of this volume, we have deviated from the
original presentation sequence in two ways. On the one hand,
we have grouped the chapters by similarity of form (e.g., review,
new work or commentary). On the other, we have tried to group

chapters by the similarity of their substantive focus (e.g., small-scale social systems, macro-structure, the symposium itself). Clearly, these two principles can and did yield conflicts within and among chapters. We applied them leniently, and when conflicts arose we strove to maintain the integrity of the overall organization.

Part I contains surveys and overviews. It is, perhaps, the most cohesive part. This results in large measure from the fact that close historical, theoretical and methodological ties interconnect the first five chapters. Chapter 6 is unique in this collection in the sense that it is not a direct derivative of a symposium presentation. The symposium did include a presentation by Ronald Breiger on the blockmodeling research of Harrison C. White and his co-workers which was published elsewhere (Breiger, 1976). The absence of a manuscript on blockmodeling threatened to leave this volume without a discussion of an extremely important method of structural analysis. At our suggestion, Phipps Arabie, Scott Boorman and Paul Levitt agreed to provide one. The result of their collaboration, however, while useful, was too large for inclusion in this volume and was eventually published elsewhere (Arabie, Boorman and Levitt, 1978). A draft manuscript by John Light and Nicholas Mullins, on the other hand, struck us as perfect in breadth of scope and level of detail and after revision it became Chapter 6. Two additional symposium presentations are not included in the volume: Scott Boorman's (1977) and Douglas White's (1975). The remainder of Part I consists of a discussion of biased nets, a report on networks and information diffusion, and a broadly based critique of the process of constructing mathematical models of social networks.

Part II consists of chapters in which the author's primary objective is the presentation of new ideas, empirical results or methodological advances. A wide variety of topics are covered with an equally diverse set of methods. The first five chapters

are substantively focused, i.e., they relate theoretical or empirical results bearing upon our understanding of aspects of
cognitive and social behavior. The remaining four chapters concentrate on the presentation of methods.

Part III consists of commentaries in which the authors engage
in critical discussion of the objectives and methods of social
network research. The last three chapters in this part, unlike
the other chapters in the volume, were meant primarily as reflec-
tions on the symposium.[3] The final chapter, by Nicholas Mullins,
is unique both in terms of the other chapters and in terms of
symposium presentations generally. It contains a study of the
network of social network researchers, at least as the field was
represented by the symposium's participants. In preparation for
this study, vitae of all the invited participants were sent to
Mullins prior to the symposium's commencement. Additional data
on sociometric and institutional ties were collected during the
symposium.

REFERENCES

Arabie, P., Boorman, S. A., & Levitt, P. R.   Constructing
    blockmodels: How and why, *Journal of Mathematical Psychol-
    ogy,* 1978, *17,* 1, 21-63.
Boorman, S. A. A combinatorial optimization model for trans-
    mission of job information through contact networks, *Bell
    Journal of Economics,* 1975, *6,* 216-249.
Breiger, R. L. Career attributes and network structure: A
    blockmodel study of a bio-medical research specialty,
    American Sociological Review, 1976, *41,* 117-135.

[3]*Norman Whitten and Robert Norman participated in the
symposium as discussants but prepared no written material.*

Leinhardt, S. *Social Networks: A Developing Paradigm,* New York:
    Academic Press, 1976.

Simon, H. *Models of Discovery,* Dordrecht, Holland: R. Reidel
    Publishing Co., 1977.

Thomas, L. *Medussa and the Snail,* New York: Viking Press,
    1979.

White, D. Avoidance in social networks, presented at the
    MSSB Advanced Research Symposium on Social Networks,
    Hanover, New Hampshire, 1975.

CHAPTER 2

ON BALANCE AND ATTRIBUTION

Fritz Heider[1]

Department of Psychology

University of Kansas

Lawrence, Kansas

Before talking about the early developments of the idea of balance, I should say that, in my thinking, the problems of balance and the problems of attribution are so closely connected that indeed I cannot completely separate the two, and I have to talk about both. Both groups of problems have roots going back to my early life. I will try to be brief, but in order to get a better perspective on the later developments, I must at least mention these more personal beginnings.

One of the roots was an early concern with perception, which had its origin in an interest in art. I grew up in Austria where painting was, at least at that time, a favorite hobby. Most of my relatives painted or sketched, and I got my first sketch book before I was 7 years old. I still think that attempts to sketch, that is, to put on paper pictorial representations of the

---

[1]*Present address: 1801 Indiana Street, Lawrence, Kansas 66044.*

environment, is the best introduction to the remarkable processes involved in the perception. It leads to an intimate familiarity with and a know-how about perception. One would probably not be far wrong to say that such a know-how may provide the soil on which good theories of perception can flourish.

A second early concern that led to later theorizing was an interest in interpersonal relations. As far as I remember, my interest developed gradually, but it was certainly very much intensified by the situation right after World War I, when life in Austria became difficult due to grave shortages in food, heat, and illumination. This led to an atmosphere thick with quarrels and irritability; people easily became touchy and petulant.

My early concern with perception, which grew out of painting and sketching, and with human relations, which was stimulated by a stressful social climate, soon merged and led into thoughts of what is now called person perception. In an environment of discord and petty squabbles, often we are confronted with troubling interpersonal situations. For instance, two people who are close and dear to us may come into conflict with each other. Each one thinks that only his interpretation of the issue is the right one. We listen to one of them, we are sympathetic, and we think, yes, that seem plausible. Then we listen to the other one and his view also seems justified. Thus, we experience conflict in ourselves. One resolution is to intellectualize everything, to realize that people often have very egocentric views of the events that concern them and that personal perspective may distort the truth. In short, such experiences make us reexamine person perception and make us more aware of relations and events between other people. Anyway, this is how my experiences affected me, and already by 1920 or 1921 I had given a talk on person perception to a group of people who were interested in science. That was in Graz, the Austrian city in which I had grown up. The talk fell flat; I was not sure whether it was my fault or the fault of the audience.

I should remind you at this point that there seem to be two different kinds of problems within the field of social psychology. One deals with questions in which the concept of a group is prominent. Objects of study are relations between groups or relations between a group and individuals. For instance, how does being part of a group influence the individual person, his beliefs, motivations, and achievements? Until 10 or 15 years ago, what was called social psychology dealt almost exclusively with problems involving groups. The second big class of problems, namely those that treat interpersonal relations, relations between one person and one or very few other persons, was considered only rarely. At present, however, the field of interpersonal relations is growing very rapidly and has been accepted as another part of social psychology. The difference between these two parts of social psychology has some important consequences. First, the very rich folklore of common sense psychology is mainly concerned with interpersonal problems and is much less specific about groups. Second, the study of relations between a few individuals soon leads one to consider questions of person perception and attribution.

Returning to the origin of the balance idea, I want to mention three papers that I published in the 1940s that trace a continuous development. The first paper, prepared with Marianne Simmel, tried to show the importance of attribution and person perception. It appeared in 1944 and I will call it the "film paper." The second one, also from 1944, deals with some factors responsible for attribution and actually discusses cases of balance, though balance was not yet explicitly presented. I will refer to it as the "phenomenal causality paper." The third paper, published in 1946, contains the explicit formulation of the balance hypothesis.

The film paper describes a little experiment with an abstract film. It has its origin in an attempt to study person perception. In 1930 I had come to the Research Department of The Clarke School for the Deaf in Northampton, Massachusetts. One of our projects was an investigation of the problem-solving processes of young deaf children who as yet could hardly speak. How was it possible for them to think without the help of words? We tried giving the children a number of language-free tests. One test that seemed especially interesting used a form board which required fitting tiles of different geometrical forms into the appropriate openings. It was fascinating to watch the children work on them. One had the feeling that it was possible to follow a child's thinking as he picked up a piece, tried to fit it into different gaps without success, then picked up another piece, and so on. We made some films of this process, and soon found that we could dispense with photographing the child's face and concentrate on the movements of the child's hands carrying the pieces. This observation led to the idea of a film in which the geometric pieces move around by themselves--one could show how they try to find their proper places, how they attempt to fit themselves into their beds, to get a snug fit, and so on. That would be a film in which just the movements and some geometric forms portray thought and purposive behavior. Such a film might give clues to the main problem of our concern: Namely, how do we perceive thought in another being? How do we get information about the so-called mental processes? How do we perceive intention, wishes, abilities, and so on?

Developing the idea still further, I thought of a little story, a succession of interpersonal events told by the motion of geometric figures with no similarity to human beings. That is the origin of the film that I made with Marianne Simmel in which a circle and two triangles move around in different ways. The subjects who saw the film were asked to describe it and to answer

a number of questions about it. Most of them perceived the action
in the film in terms of some kind of give and take between persons. As a matter of fact it was rather difficult to describe the
events in purely spatial geometric terms, avoiding any "anthro-
pomorphizing."

A study of the subjects' responses made one realize the great
importance that attribution plays in person perception, where
attribution is understood to be the connection between a perceived
change and a person conceived of as causing this change by some
action. Attribution has the effect of connecting the perceived
change with the significant environment, and especially with its
more invariant features. The relation to nonperson perception and
to constancy phenomena is also mentioned in the film paper:
"phenomenal movements *per se* are comparable to reduction colors,
and acts of persons are comparable to object colors [1944a,
p. 256]." It is also suggested that a hypothesis of unit-
formation might help us understand this organization in which
movements are seen as actions of persons, and the question is
asked: "Does this unit-formation follow some of the laws of
purely figural unit-formation? [1940a, p. 257]."

The paper on phenomenal causality carries out the suggestion
from the end of the film paper that deals with the way in which
Wertheimer's laws of unit-formation influence attribution of
actions to persons. Wertheimer (1923) says that parts of the
visual field that are close together or that are similar to each
other will be seen as belonging together, as forming one unit.
Thus, proximity and similarity are unit-forming factors, and he
enumerates a number of others.

It is tempting to take a further step, namely to assume that
the Wertheimer factors (similarity, proximity, etc.) not only
bring about phenomenal belongingness but that they can also bring
about phenomenal causation. In other words, when two parts of the
cognitive field are similar (or proximal, etc.), this similarity

can induce attribution; that is, one of these parts is likely to
be seen as the origin or cause of the other part. For instance,
a bad action will easily be seen as committed by a person who
already has a bad reputation. The paper indicates that the opposite phenomenon has also been reported in the literature, that
is, attribution can induce apparent similarity. A familiar case
would be the prestige suggestion: The evaluation of utterances
or artistic products can depend on the prestige of the person to
whom they are attributed. This attribution can influence not
only the value of the product, but may even change its meaning.

   The first paragraph of the third paper treats the idea of
balance as a logical continuation of the previous paper on phenomenal causality--as if one only needed to sit down and think
through what is said about attribution and figural unit-formation,
generalize a little, and out comes balance. One might also suppose that the balance idea came about by way of the *prägnanz* idea,
which was very familiar to me and which is closely related to balance. Both are manifestations of a tendency toward simplicity or
order, toward a distinguished state. We want to have our cognitive food prepared so that it is easy to swallow, to assimilate.
But that was actually not the way in which I came to balance. I
came to it, one might say, empirically though not through experimental results, rather through informal observations and through
Spinoza, the old rationalist, who had collected very shrewd observations about life and about liking and loving, and who had
tried to systematize these observations. He thought he could
put them into some kind of logical order a la Euclid in the
fashion of geometry.

   I was greatly attracted by Spinoza, first because he treated
important interpersonal phenomena (e.g., loving and hating), and
second because he attempted to build a coherent theory about
them. However, when I studied closely what he had to say and
tried to think through all of his propositions and derivations,

I came to the conclusion that he did not quite succeed and that in the end his attempt was very unsatisfactory. Nevertheless, these propositions seemed to contain some kind of system. When one listed them and looked them over, they definitely did not give the impression of a random, chance medley. One had the feeling that there was some order in them, as if one were confronted with a kind of cipher. I cannot resist this opportunity to paraphrase some propositions from Book III of Spinoza's *Ethics*, and in doing so I will simplify them a bit. I will use the letters *p, q*, and *o* for persons and *x* and *y* for nonpersonal entities.

Proposition Number 16 states:

If *p* likes *x*, and *y* is similar to *x*, *p* will like *y*.

Number 22:

If *p* likes *o*, and *q* benefits *o*, *p* will like *q*.

Number 33:

If *p* loves *o*, he will try to make *o* love *p*.

Number 45:

If *p* likes *o*, and *q* dislikes *o*, *p* will dislike *q* .

I pored over the propositions. I tried all sorts of graphic representations, looked at them from different points of view, and with different central concepts in mind—but for a long time they refused to disclose their pattern. It was tantalizing, since I had the conviction that all the information necessary for the solution of the problem was right in front of my eyes. Then, one afternoon, I realized that I had to bring in Wertheimer's unit-forming factors and that I had to treat unit relations on the same plane with attitudes. I do not remember whether I understood right away all of the implications of this conception—but anyway, I had the feeling that the puzzle was solved. I stopped work and went for a walk.

Looking back now, it seems strange that it took me so long to consider units as relevant to my problem, since I had used this idea in the paper on phenomenal causality. Probably at that time I still thought that attitudes such as "to love" or "to like" belonged in a compartment different from that in which unit-formation belonged. The mental blinders of "textbook psychology" imply that attitudes belong to social psychology while units belong to perception, and such artificial separations can often make trouble. Now I conceive of attitudes as interacting with unit-formation. But it was clear to me right away that a breakthrough had occurred, the kind of reorganization that gestalt psychologists talk about.

It would be worthwhile to spell out in greater detail what this reorganization involved. Two facts are important. First, Spinoza uses a number of different expressions to characterize the relevant connections, for instance, love, hate, benefit, similarity. The relations between these expressions are not specified. In contrast to that, the connections in the balance formulation form two large groups, the positive connections and the negative connections. Second, the relation between these two groups is clear and one can put them together in a quasi-mathematical calculus, for instance, by multiplication. On the other hand, it would be impossible to multiply "p loves o" with "o dislikes p". This means that the balance calculus is based on a classification that considers as equivalent apparently different and incommensurable connections. Not only are different kinds of attitudes treated as equivalent--at least in the first approximation--but also positive attitudes are treated as belonging to the same class as positive unit relations.

There is one other aspect of the balance calculus that does not appear in Spinoza's formulations, and that is the importance of the loop arrangement or the "cycle" as Cartwright and Harary (1956) called it. Why is the cycle necessary? I am puzzled

by it and I have suspicions that it is in some way akin to the
mathematical concept of a group, in which cycle arrangements
also play important roles.

I will now go back to the paper on phenomenal causality and
explain what was meant earlier when I mentioned the implicit presentation of balance in that paper. Recall that one of the main
results of the article was that similarity and proximity (or
other Wertheimer factors) favor the attribution of acts to persons. This means that if the relation of a certain act a to a
certain person p is one of similarity, then there is a tendency
to attribute a to p, that is, to connect a with p by a causal
relation as well. Or, in terms of balance, if a has one positive
relation to p, there is a tendency to connect the two by another
positive connection. Two relations of the same sign between two
items are "path balanced" in the terminology of Cartwright and
Harary. It appears that what the paper on phenomenal causality
really treats is the influence of the balance tendency on
attribution.

We have here a case of two different formulations of the same
observations, one formulation given in the paper on phenomenal
causality and the other in terms of balance. The first does not
allow one to go much beyond oneself; it leads to a more restricted view, while the second suddenly makes many new considerations
possible. Unsuspected new relations, similarities, categories,
or possibilities of combinations are brought to one's attention.
They have been inaccessable and invisible--now they abruptly come
within reach.

The difference between the two formulations can probably best
be shown by an example. Let us take the statement: "Bad actions
will often be attributed to people thought of as bad." In the
formulation of phenomenal causality this means that similarity
seems to induce attribution. One would not expect that this
statement is in any way related to the statement that a person

will generally try to meet people that he likes. The formulation
in terms of balance would be the following: Both similarity and
attribution refer to positive relations, and one positive relation will often tend to bring about another positive relation.
We see right away the equality in structure of "similarity produces attribution," and of "liking produces proximity."

I must add another point in regard to the role balance plays
in the paper on phenomenal causality. Attitudes (like and dislike) are not considered, but only interactions between unit relations, that is, between causal units and other units are discussed. Examples include how the appearance of a causal unit
may be induced by similarity and how a belief in a causal unit
may induce phenomenal similarity. As long as the focus is on
causal unit relations, no new questions are raised. But according to the new formulation in the paper on balance we now consider it possible to treat any unit relation as functionally
equivalent to any other (at least to some degree). This leads
right away the question of whether there exist interactions
between other unit relations, for example, between similarity
and proximity, which are comparable to the interactions between
similarity and causal connections.

During the last years, I have followed up this idea off and
on and have come to the conclusion that there is indeed a tendency toward balance that concerns arrangements of unit relations
alone, without attitudes. I have collected numerous examples
and so far, in my notes, I have spoken of the tendency toward
coinciding unit formations. Usually, when unit factors coincide
we have the impression of an orderly set-up, and when a pair of
items is connected with one unit factor often the appearance of
a second is induced. Things that are similar to each other
often seem to be closer to each other than dissimilar things, and
vice versa; there is often an influence of proximity on similarity. I do not have the time to go into that--I only want to

remind you of what it means to "make order": Usually it means to make the factor of proximity coincide with the factor of similarity; we tend to put similar things together.

Whether or not we include attitudes in our considerations, it is probably safe to say that the tendency toward harmony is not merely reactive, that it is not only a matter of repairing the disturbances and attempting to get back to a state of restful peace. Often it implies a reaching out, a changing of more and more parts of the cognitive field and of the environment to bring them into consonance with important seminal ideas and attitudes. This acquisitive growth spreads out a network of relations over the environment which are in balance with the founding source relation.

A good illustration of this growth is the process that starts with a fortunate love affair. The original attitude is like a seed in a crystal formation. If, for instance, a man, A, loves a girl, B, he will try to bring about that B loves A, in case this symmetrical attitude did not arise simultaneously with A's love. If the mutual love between A and B is once established, they will both work toward adding more positive relations since these are in harmony with the seed attitude. They will want to be together as much as possible, they will want to start sexual relations, to live together, to marry. Then a host of common relations to other people and things will develop. They may acquire common property, which both like; their tastes and values may become more and more alike; they may have children to whom they are connected by blood relation and by love; they have friends in common; they share many experiences and have a stock of common memories, and so on. In short, a great many attitude and unit relations are clustered around the original seed element. Each of these relations combines in cycles that are in harmony with the original attitude, and therefore in harmony with each other.

If the mutual sentiment of *A* and *B* changes from love to dislike or hate, then the whole network of relations becomes at once
discordant in all its parts.   *A* and *B* will feel that all the
unit formations that grew up in harmony with love are fetters
that tie together two persons who repel each other. They will
try to separate, and the separation will lead to many difficulties because it is in conflict with the developed cluster. They
will want to cut the bands of common property, divide up the
children, etc.

The fact that the change in sign of just one relation can
produce such a massive disharmony seems to speak against the
assumption that "the amount of balance...can be measured by the
number of lines...whose sign must be changed in order to achieve
balance [Harary, Norman, Cartwright, 1965, p. 348]." At the same
time, this case makes one skeptical about the hypothesis that
balanced structures can always be learned more easily than imbalanced ones (DeSoto, 1960). True enough, ease of learning and
redundancy go together, and balance represents one kind of redundancy. However, imbalance can also be redundant, as is shown by
the cluster of relations that becomes imbalanced when the seed
relation changes.

The significant feature of this kind of network of relations
is that one relation, namely the relation of *A* to *B* is part of
many cycles. One might speak here of a polycycle relation. Then,
of course, this relation is a factor in the balance of all the
cycles, and one would assume that it has much greater influence on
the amount of balance than a relation that is part of only one
cycle.

In conclusion, I want once more to describe briefly the roles
that attribution and balance play in our cognitive makeup. Attribution is a relative of perception. It serves to anchor our
impressions and the perceived changes in the conception of the

more invariant sphere of relevant entities. It serves to make happenings understandable and to extract from them as much useful information about the environment as possible. Attribution often means a unit formation, a relation of belonging together between an event and a person.

The tendency toward balance is a tendency of the parts of the cognitive field not to quarrel with each other, to be accommodating, and to make up a harmonious family. Parts that are connected in some way should fit each other, should be concordant, and so it is very plausible that parts that are connected as cause and effect will also be seen as fitting each other. Balance deals with relations of relations, and dyadic arrangements in which the relations of the two items are all positive or all negative will be harmonious.

REFERENCES

Cartwright, D., & Harary, F. Structural balance: A generalization of Heider's theory. *Psychological Review,* 1956, *63,* 277-293.

DeSoto, C. Learning a social structure, *Journal of Abnormal and Social Psychology,* 1960, *60,* 417-420.

Harary, F., Norman, R., & Cartwright, D. *Structural Models: An introduction to the theory of directed graphs.* New York, Wiley, 1965.

Heider, F. Social perception and phenomenal causality, *Psychological Review,* 1944, *51,* 358-374.

Heider, F. Attitudes and cognitive organization. *Journal of Psychology,* 1946, *21,* 107-112.

Heider, F., & Simmel, M. An experimental study of apparent behavior, *American Journal of Psychology,* 1944, *57,* 243-259.

Wertheimer, M. Untersuchungen zur lehre von der gestalt, II. *Psychologische Forschung,* 1923, *4,* 301-350.

CHAPTER 3

BALANCE AND CLUSTERABILITY: AN OVERVIEW

Dorwin Cartwright[1]

Frank Harary[2]

University of Michigan

Ann Arbor, Michigan

This chapter summarizes the application of graph theory to the study of balance and clusterability and discusses some open questions for future research.

Interest in balance and clusterability among social scientists was initiated by the work of Heider (1946, 1958) on cognitive structures that contain subjective representations of social relationships, and by the work of Newcomb (1953) on structures of objective interpersonal relationships. The possibility of employing graph theory in such research was noted by Cartwright and Harary (1956), who formalized the concepts employed by Heider and Newcomb and provided a basic characterization of

[1]*Present address: 643 Island View Drive, Santa Barbara, California 93109.*

[2]*Present address: Department of Mathematics, University of Michigan, Ann Arbor, Michigan 48106.*

balanced structures. Subsequent investigators have employed the
graph theory concepts of balance and, more recently, of clusterability in research on a great variety of empirical structures.

The term *empirical structure* is used here to refer to a set
of empirical elements together with an empirical relation between
pairs of these elements. Given such a structure, its *digraph D*
is obtained as follows: The set of points of *D*, denoted $V =$
$\{v_1, v_2, \ldots, v_p\}$, corresponds to the set of empirical elements
and there is an arc (directed line) from v_i to v_j if and only if
the corresponding ordered pair of elements is in the specified
empirical relation. If this relation is symmetric, the corre-
spondinging abstract structure is *graph G* whose (undirected) lines
represent symmetric relationships.

An indication of the various kinds of empirical structures
that can be analyzed graphically is provided by Table I. Seven
classes of empirical elements are identified, and several possible kinds of relationships are indicated for each. A specified
set of elements of any particular class, together with an appropriate relation on this set, constitutes an empirical structure
having an associated graph or digraph. The findings of graph
theory are applicable to all such structures.

In the social sciences some of the different types of empirical structures that have been subjected to analysis using graph
theory include: *cognitive structures* composed of subjective
representations of people or attitude objects joined by affective or unit relationships (Heider, 1958); *interpersonal structures* containing people joined by affective bonds (Newcomb,
1963; Taylor, 1970); *social networks* made up of people linked by
characteristic modes of interaction (Mitchell, 1969; Barnes,
1972); *role structures* consisting of "kin roles" linked by interpersonal relationships among role occupants (Carroll, 1973);

TABLE I. Types of Realization of Graphs and Digraphs

Points	Lines
A. Cognitive elements	Cognitive relationships

people
  attitude objects
  propositions
  attributes
	affection
	  unit
	  implication
	  preference

B. Persons	Interpersonal relationships

	sociometric choice
	  communication
	  interaction: helping, gift
	    giving, social visiting, etc.
	  power and influence

C. Social roles, positions	Interrole relationships

	legitimate authority
	  mobility of personnel
	  interpersonal relations among
	    role occupants

D. Groups, organizations	Intergroup relationships
	alliance/warfare common membership
E. Nations	International relationships
	alliance/warfare trade
F. Tasks	Intertask relationships
	precedence facilitation/hindering
G. Variables	Covariation
	dependence correlation

intergroup structures of subtribes and bonds of traditional warfare or alliance (Hage, 1974); *international structures* of nations linked by friendship or hostility (Harary, 1961); *task structures* composed of tasks and precedence relationships (Oeser and Harary, 1962); *variable structures* consisting of variables and relationships of covariation (Roberts, 1971).

In graph theory, the concept of balance refers to *signed graphs,* or *signed digraphs,* all of whose lines have either a positive or a negative sign. Its use in empirical research thus requires some appropriate rule for identifying those empirical relationships that are to be considered as being positive or negative. Unfortunately, no such rule has yet been explicitly formulated, but certain requirements can be specified. In the theory of signed graphs, the signs of lines satisfy the principle of *antithetical duality,* which states that when the dual (or opposite) is applied twice to a sign, the original sign is obtained (Harary, 1957). This holds since the antithetical dual of a positive sign is a negative one, and its dual is positive. The first requirement for the assignment of signs to a pair of empirical relations, then, is that the assignment satisfy the principle of antithetical duality. The relations of "liking" and "disliking" appear to meet this requirement, since there is common agreement that the opposite of "liking" is "disliking" and that its opposite is "liking." There are, however, empirical relations, such as "interacts with," where it is not immediately obvious which relation, if any, is its antithetical dual.

Given a pair of relationships that satisfy the antithetical duality principle, the problem of establishing signs remains. For most relations that have been employed in research on balance, the solution has been intuitively obvious--everyone agrees, for example, that "liking" is positive and that "warfare" is negative. On the other hand, it is not so evident what sign should be given to "joking hostility" or "does not speak to." It should be possible to empirically determine the evaluative signs of social relationships as viewed by the participants within a particular

culture. With or without a particular context the decision to
sign a relation is always critical since it determines which particular structures will be classified as balanced.

   It should be kept in mind that, strictly speaking, balance
and clusterability are characteristics of abstract structures and
are applicable to empirical structures only when the terms *point*
and *signed line* are associated with concrete elements and signed
relationships. Given such an interpretation, theorems about balance or clusterability in signed graphs become true statements
about their associated empirical structures. Whether a particular
structure will display a tendency toward balance (or clusterability) and how this tendency will manifest itself are empirical
questions that can be answered only by empirical research. Graph
theory can assist such research by identifying balanced structures
and their respective properties, by providing measures of the
degree of balance, and by indicating which relationships are
likely to change; however, these results cannot, in themselves,
answer questions about the existence of empirical processes.

I.   THEOREMS CONCERNING BALANCE

   The cognitive structures originally considered by Heider
(1946) consist of three entities (three people, denoted *p, o, q,*
or two people *p, o* and an attitude object *x*) that are joined by
affective relationships or unit relationships. If we consider
only affective relationships in *p-o-q* structures and assume that
the affective relation is symmetric, then the eight possible
configurations yield the eight signed graphs shown in Figure 1,
where solid lines are taken to be positive (liking) and dashed
lines negative (disliking). The structures are grouped in Figure
1 so that those classified by Heider as balanced are in the top
row. These eight structures, described symbolically by Heider
using relational notation, can be regarded graphically as cycles

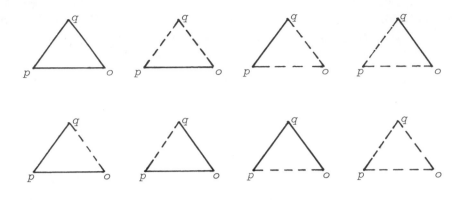

Fig. 1.

of length 3.   Building on this observation, Cartwright and
Harary (1956) proposed the following definitions.   The *sign of a*
cycle of a signed graph is the product of the signs of its lines.
Thus, every positive cycle has an even number of negative lines.
A signed graph S is *balanced* if every cycle of S is positive.
This definition of balance clearly agrees with Heider's clas-
sification and applies to signed graphs of any size.

   Some of the basic properties of balanced structures that have
been identified by graph theory research can be given in theorem
form.   The first theorem provides a characterization of balanced
signed graphs (Harary, Norman, & Cartwright, 1965, p. 342).

   Theorem 1.   The following conditions are equivalent for a
signed graph S:
   (1)   S is balanced: every cycle is positive.
   (2)   For each pair of points   u, v of S, all paths joining
u *and* v *have the same sign.*
   (3)   There exists a partition of the points of S into two sub-
sets (one of which may be empty) such that every positive line
joins two points of the same subset and every negative line joins
points from different subsets.

This theorem shows that if a signed graph satisfies one of three conditions, it necessarily satisfies the other two. Thus, any one of the conditions could serve as the definition of balance. In retrospect, it seems that the third condition probably best captures Heider's intuitions about the nature of balanced structures, and we shall see that it provides the link between the concept of balance and the more general concept of clusterability.

The most obvious method for ascertaining whether a given signed graph is balanced is to check the signs of its cycles, but this procedure is cumbersome when the number of cycles is large. This task can be simplified when it is known that the signed graph is complete (or, in other words, that every pair of points is joined by a line) by simply checking the signs of its cycles of length 3.

Corollary 1a. A signed complete graph S is balanced if and only if every triangle of S is positive.

Another simplifying procedure defines a *cut point* of a connected graph as one whose removal disconnects the graph. A signed graph is then said to be *balanced at a point v* if every cycle containing *v* is positive.

Theorem 2. Let S be a connected signed graph. If S has no cut points, then S is balanced if and only if it is balanced at any one point. Otherwise, S is balanced if and only if it is balanced at every cut point.

Thus, if *S* has no cut points, one need only test the signs of the cycles through any one point. In particular, if there is one point lying on fewer cycles than other points, it is only necessary to verify the signs of these cycles. If, on the other hand, S has cut points, one need only ascertain the signs of the cycles through these cut points.

When a structure has a large number of elements, it may contain cycles of considerable length. It would seem reasonable to assume that the signs of very long cycles might be inconsequential for balance. In order to deal with this possibility, we define a signed graph S as n-balanced if every cycle of length at most n is positive. Obviously, S is balanced if and only if it is N-balanced, where N is the length of a longest cycle in S. But it is possible for a signed graph that is not balanced to be n-balanced, for some n less than N.

It is possible to provide a matrix criterion for both n-balance and balance. Given a signed graph S, its adjacency matrix A has an entry of +1, -1, or 0, depending on whether the corresponding pair of points is joined by a positive line, a negative one, or neither.

Theorem 3. A signed graph S is n-balanced if and only if the diagonal entries of every matrix A^k, with $k \leq n$, are zero or positive. Thus, S is balanced if and only if the diagonal entries of every matrix A^k, $k \leq N$, are zero or positive.

A. Measures of the Degree of Balance

If two signed graphs are not balanced, it is natural to ask whether one is more balanced than the other. For such a question to be meaningful, we need a measure of the "amount" of balance. Two kinds of measures have been proposed: a line index and a cycle index.

1. Line Index. Any signed graph that is not balanced can be converted into a balanced one by changing the signs of some of its lines or by removing some. And it would seem reasonable to say that a signed graph is more balanced, the smaller the

number of lines that need to be altered in this way. The results
given in the next theorem (Harary, 1959, p. 322) provide the
basis for an index of the amount of balance that is consistent
with this observation.

  *Theorem 4. Given a signed graph S, the minimum number of
lines whose negation (change in sign) results in a balanced signed
graph is equal to the minimum number whose deletion results in
balance. Each minimal set Y of lines whose deletion results in
balance can also be negated, and moreover, any subset of the lines
of Y can be deleted and the others negated.*

  Based on this theorem, an *alteration/minimal* set *Y* of lines of
a signed graph S can be defined as a set whose alteration (either
deletion or negation) leaves *S* balanced, but the alteration of
any proper subset of *Y* does not. The *line index of balance*
is then defined as the number of lines in an alteration/minimal
set. As noted by Abelson and Rosenberg (1958), a principle of
"least effort" would suggest that the relationships corresponding
to the lines in such a set should be most susceptible to alteration whenever there is a tendency toward balance.
  Although the identification of alteration/minimal sets in
relatively small signed graphs is not especially difficult, it
would be desirable to have a general method of identifying these
sets. Unfortunately, no such method is known except for a topol-
ogically special class of graphs. A graph *G* is *planar* if *G* can
be drawn in the plane so that no two lines intersect. Schwenk
(to appear) has recently developed an algorithm for specifying the
alteration/minimal sets of lines in such signed graphs. Various
criteria for planarity of a graph are presented in Harary (1969,
Chap. 11).
  2. Cycle Index. The second measure of degree of balance
makes direct use of the definition of balance. The *cycle index*

of balance is the ratio β of the number of positive cycles of a
signed graph S to its total number of cycles. Thus, β is the probability that a cycle chosen at random from S is positive. Obviously, β = 1 if and only if S is balanced. It can be shown that
β = 0 if and only if S has at least one cycle and each block of
S is either a negative cycle or a line (where a *block B* of a
graph is a maximal connected subgraph having no point v such that
B-v is disconnected). The index β can be calculated by means of
matrices following a procedure developed by Cartwright and Gleason
(1966).

The cycle index for balance can be modified in several ways to
reflect the intuitive feeling that shorter cycles may have greater
influence in an empirical structure than longer ones. In a signed
graph S, there are no cycles of length 2 by definition of a graph.
Therefore, for $n \geq 3$, let c_n be the number of n-cycles and let c_n^+
be the number of positive n-cycles. In order to obtain a general
formulation of weighting systems for different cycle lengths, we
define for $n \geq 3$ a weight w_n, $0 \leq w_n \leq 1$ with $w_3 \neq 0$. It is also
assumed that $w_3 \geq w_4 \geq w_5 \ldots$ With such a sequence of weights
w_n, the *weighted cycle index of balance* is given by the ratio

$$\frac{w_3 c_3^+ + w_4 c_4^+ + \ldots}{w_3 c_3 + w_4 c_4 + \ldots} \quad .$$

Harary (1959) and Norman and Roberts (1972) have presented various
methods for assigning values to the weights w_n. It remains an empirical problem, however, to determine which of the possible
weighting systems is most appropriate for a particular empirical
structure.

II. BASIC THEOREMS CONCERNING CLUSTERING

Condition (3) of Theorem 1 shows that a structure is balanced if and only if its elements can be partitioned into at most
two subsets such that all positive relationships join elements in
the same subset and all negative relationships join elements of
different subsets. The hypothesis that a structure will display
a tendency toward balance thus implies that it will tend to form
at most two clusters of positively related elements. Likewise,
if it contains any negative relationships, it will tend to "polarize" into exactly two clusters that are negatively related to
each other.

In considering these implications for social relationships,
Davis (1967) noted that sociometric structures do appear to form
clusters of this sort but that they often contain more than two.
This observation led Davis to formulate a characterization of
signed graphs that are clusterable but not necessarily balanced.
Cartwright and Harary (1968), noting that the problem of clusterability is intrinsically related to the classic problem of color-
ability of graphs (where "clusters" are called "color sets"), have
provided certain extensions of Davis's work.

The principal graph theory findings concerning clusterability
are presented in the next three theorems. We shall say that a
signed graph S has an *n-clustering,* or is *n-clusterable,* if its
points can be partitioned into n subsets, called *clusters,* such
that each positive line joins two points of the same cluster and
each negative line joins two points from different clusters.
Clearly, S is balanced if and only if it has a 2-clustering.
Every balanced signed graph is clusterable, but there are clusterable signed graphs that are not balanced. Thus, for example,
the all negative triangle of Figure 1 is 3-clusterable but not
balanced. It is also interesting to note that this structure was
considered problematic by Heider (1946).

Theorem 5 provides a characterization of clusterable signed
graphs, where the *positive components* of a signed graph *S* are defined as the components of the spanning subgraph obtained by
removing all negative lines from *S*.

*Theorem 5. The following conditions are equivalent for a
signed graph S.*
(1) S has a clustering.
*(2) S has no negative line joining two points in the same
positive component.*
(3) S has no cycle with exactly one negative line.

The concept of the boundary of a subset of the points of a
graph leads to an interesting observation about clusterable signed
graphs. Given a subset *Z* of the points of a signed graph *S*, the
liasons of *Z* are the lines of *S* that join a point of *Z* to one
not in *Z*. The *boundary* of *Z* is the subgraph of *S* induced by the
liasons of *Z*. Thus, if *S* is clusterable and *Z* is one of its clusters, then the points in the boundary of *Z* are all the points of
Z that have "direct contact" with the environment of *Z*. Corollary
5a shows that all of these contacts, if any, must be negative.

*Corollary 5a. A signed graph is clusterable if and only if
the boundary of the set of points in each of its positive components is either empty or contains only negative lines.*

It should be noted that a clusterable signed graph may have
more than one clustering. In this case, its clusters are not
uniquely determined. An example of a signed graph with more
than one clustering is given in Figure 2. It can readily be
seen that this graph has two clusterings: $\{v_1, v_2\}\{v_3, v_4\}\{v_5\}$
and $\{v_1, v_2, v_3, v_4\}\{v_5\}$. We shall say that *S* has a unique

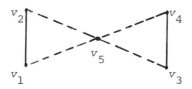

Fig. 2.

clustering if there is only one partitioning of its points into
clusters. The next theorem provides useful information about a
common class of signed graphs that are uniquely clusterable.

*Theorem 6. The following conditions are equivalent for a
complete signed graph S.*
  (1) S has a clustering.
  (2) S has a unique clustering.
  (3) S has no triangle with exactly one negative line.

A general characterization of uniquely clusterable signed
graphs may now be given. For this purpose, we define the conden-
sation S^* of a signed graph S as that signed graph obtained by
shrinking each positive component of S to a single point. Thus,
every line of S^* is negative.

*Theorem 7. The following conditions are equivalent for a
clusterable signed graph S.*
  (1) S has a unique clustering.
  (2) S^* is complete.
  *(3) For each pair of points, u, v exactly one of the fol-
lowing conditions holds: either there exists an all positive
path joining u and v or there exists a u-v path with just one
negative line.*

This last condition is shown by Cartwright and Gleason (1967) to be an important step in establishing a matrix criterion for unique clusterability of signed graphs.

Measures of the degree of clusterability, analogous to those for balance, are readily formulated. Extending Theorem 4, we can define the *line index of clusterability* as the minimum number of lines whose alteration is required to achieve clusterability. Clearly, this index has as an upper bound the number of negative lines of S that join two points in the same positive component. The *cycle index of clusterability* is 1 minus the ratio of the number of cycles with exactly one negative line to the total number of cycles.

A closely related measure of the tendency toward clusterability in a signed graph has been proposed by Peay (1970). If S is a clusterable signed graph, then it follows from Condition (2) of Theorem 5 that no two points of S are joined both by an all positive path and by a negative line. If, on the other hand, S displays no tendency toward clusterability, the occurrence of an all positive path and that of a negative line between any two points are completely independent. Thus, if one constructs a 2 × 2 contingency table for the pairs of points of S in which these pairs are partitioned according to whether or not they are joined by an all positive path and whether or not they are joined by a negative line, the descriptive statistic χ^2 calculated from this table provides a measure for the given signed graph of its tendency toward clusterability.

III.   OPEN QUESTIONS

In the remainder of this chapter, we consider some unsolved problems in applying the concepts of balance and clusterability to social structures. These will suggest some promising leads for future research both by mathematicians and by social scientists.

A. *Tendencies Toward Clustering or Balance*

Most of the research on signed structures conducted by social scientists has been guided by the hypothesis that such structures display an empirical tendency toward balance. But now that it is recognized that balance is a specific instance of clusterability, it is evident that two separate questions should be distinguished. What conditions bring about a tendency toward clustering? What determines the number of clusters that will be formed?

Although these questions can be answered only by empirical research, certain graph theory considerations may be helpful. First, it is obvious that a signed graph is 1-clusterable if and only if it contains no negative lines whatsoever. Thus, a tendency to form just one cluster would seem to reflect a general aversion toward negative relationships, and such a tendency would be expected for all empirical relations having this property.

If, however, negative relationships are tolerated in a structure, then any tendency toward clustering reflects a constraint on their location. Condition (2) of Theorem 5 asserts that a signed graph is clusterable if and only if it contains no negative line joining two points in the same positive component. Corollary 5a shows that all negative lines of a clusterable signed graph must lie in the boundary of some positive component. These facts suggest two requirements for the existence of a tendency toward clustering: (a) that those relationships considered as positive be of such a nature as to provide a basis for grouping elements into empirically meaningful *subparts*, or units, of the structure, and (b) that those considered as negative serve to segregate a subpart from its environment. There is considerable evidence that interpersonal relationships such as friendship usually do provide a basis for subgroup formation and that relationships of enmity are usually located in the boundary of such subgroups, but no generalizations about the kinds of relations that satisfy these two requirements have yet been derived.

The question of what determines whether a clusterable structure will form two rather than some larger number of clusters has
received little attention in the empirical literature. Some insight into this problem can be gained, however, by considering
the properties of balance signed graphs that distinguish them
from other clusterable ones. One such property is that given as
Condition (2) of Theorem 1, namely that all paths joining any two
points have the same sign. If a clusterable signed graph containing some negative lines satisfies this condition, then it
must have exactly two clusters, and if it does not satisfy this
condition, it must have at least three. This observation suggests that the signs of paths, or more specifically the consistency of these signs for each given pair of points, may be critical for the existence of a tendency to form just two clusters.

Let us suppose, for example, that the lines of a signed
graph correspond to links of communication by which "messages" of
some kind are transmitted from one element to another within a
structure. Let us further assume that these messages are of such
a nature that each has a unique opposite and that the opposite
of the opposite is the original message. Then if we assume that
a message remains unchanged when transmitted via a positive link
and is converted into its opposite when transmitted via a negative one, it follows that a message originating at an element u
will be in its original form upon reaching an element v when it
traverses a positive path and will be in its opposite form when
it traverses a negative one. The requirement that all paths between any two points have the same sign thus guarantees a sort of
communicative consistency within a structure, and the desirability
of such consistency would appear to be one possible source of the
tendency to form at most two clusters.

A rather different view of this problem can be taken when
dealing with complete structures in which every pair of elements

is joined by either a positive or negative relationship. Let S be a clusterable signed complete graph containing some negative lines. Then, by Theorem 6, S has no triangles with exactly one negative line. By Corollary 1a, S can have two clusters if and only if it has no triangle with three negative lines. It follows, then, that a complete structure is clusterable into two clusters if and only if it contains at least one triangle with some negative relationships and all such triangles contain exactly two. This last condition for 2-clusterability can be viewed as a requirement for a kind of "signed transitivity" such that any two points joined by a path with two negative lines must themselves be joined by a positive line. As noted by Davis (1967), this requirement, when stated in terms of interpersonal relations of friendship or enmity, implies adherence to the principle that "an enemy of an enemy must be a friend" or, in other words, that "any two enemies of the same person must be friends." A more general statement of the types of signed relations that display this kind of signed transitivity has yet to be established.

B. *Balance and Stability*

A common assumption underlying most discussions of the theory of balance has been that balanced structures are more stable than unbalanced ones, and this hypothesis has received some support in research on cognitive structures of attitudes and interpersonal relationships. Theoretical work by Roberts (1974) suggests, however, that there are situations in which this assumption may not be justified.

In the approach adopted by Roberts, signed digraphs represent covariance among a set of real variables x_1, x_2, x_3, ... Here, the points of S are coordinated to variables, and there is a positive arc from x_i to x_j if x_j increases as x_i increases (or

decreases as x_i decreases) and a negative one if x_j decreases as
x_i increases (or increases as x_i decreases). Thus, the adjacency
matrix A of S has entries of 0, +1, -1.

In order to quantify the effects of these variables on one
another, Roberts defines the *pulse* at x_j at time t with starting
point x_i as the i, j entry of A^t, that is, the number of positive
walks from x_i to x_j of length t minus the number of such negative
walks. The *value* of x_j at time t with starting point x_i is given by
the sum of the pulses at all times from 1 through t. A signed
digraph is *value stable* if this value does not become infinite as
t approaches infinity for any x_j. Roberts has shown that if S
is nonvacuously *cycle-balanced* (that is, if all of its directed
cycles are positive), then S is value unstable, or in other words,
the values of its points approach infinity through time. Although
Roberts has provided a criterion for the value stability of a
signed digraph in terms of the eigenvalues of a matrix, the discovery of a structural criterion for this kind of stability remains an unsolved, and perhaps intractable, problem.

C. Quantitative Relationships and Ambivalence

Research of the past two decades has demonstrated that signed
graphs can contribute significantly to an understanding of the
phenomena of clustering in a variety of empirical structures, but
it is important to recognize that they also possess certain inherent limitations. The qualitative value system for signed
graphs requires that every relationship be classified merely as
positive or negative and does not permit the representation of
gradations in strength, nor does it provide a means for dealing
with relationships such as ambivalence, which simultaneously contain both positive and negative components.

In order to overcome the first of these limitations, Peay
(1970) has devised a method by which signed graphs can be used

to study clustering in structures whose relationships vary quantitatively. This method rests on two assumptions: that every two elements in a structure can be assigned a "distance" between them, and that two elements can be conceived as being positively related if this distance is sufficiently small and negatively related if sufficiently large. Applied to interpersonal relationships, this second assumption captures the intuitive notion that friends are "close" whereas enemies are "distant."

Given such a measure of interelement distances, it is then possible to construct a *family* of signed graphs for a specified structure by establishing various pairs of cut-points on the rank order of these distances. Let us denote the distance between elements v_i and v_j by d_{ij} and the lower and upper cut-points by d_0 and f_0, respectively. For any pair of cut-points, one can then construct a signed graph in which points v_i and v_j are joined by a positive line if $d_{ij} < d_0$ and by a negative line if $d_{ij} \geq f_0$. Obviously, the number of positive and negative lines thus obtained depends on the values d_0 and f_0, and the resulting graph is complete if and only if $d_0 = f_0$.

Having obtained such a family of signed graphs for a given structure, one can then examine the tendency toward clustering in each. A systematic comparison of these graphs reveals which cut-points yield a maximum tendency toward clusterability. This procedure thus simultaneously provides a basis for classifying quantitative relationships as positive, negative, or neither, and for evaluating the tendency toward clustering in structures containing such relationships.

Peay's method clearly provides more information about a structure than that contained in a single signed graph, but it does not solve the problem of ambivalence. It would seem that the solution to this problem requires the use of a more complex value system than that employed by signed graphs. More specifically, such a value system should (*a*) permit the representation of gradations in the degree of positivity or negativity of a relationship, (*b*) allow for the simultaneous existence of various degrees of positivity or negativity in the same relationship, and (*c*) allow relationships of indifference.

A value system satisfying these requirements has been devised independently by Cartwright and Harary (1970) and Kaplan (1972). In this system, each relationship is conceived as consisting of various combinations of two atomic elements: a positive component and a negative one. By letting p be a measure of the amount of positivity contained in a relationship x, and letting n be a measure of its negativity, we may define three interrelated measures of a relationship x: the *value* of x, denoted $m(x)$, is expressed as the ordered pair, $m(x) = (p, n)$; the *resultant* r is defined by the equation, $r = p - n$; and the *intensity* i is given by the equation, $i = p + n$. If we assume that p and n vary continuously between 0 and 1, then it follows immediately that r varies between +1 and -1 and i varies between 0 and 2. And if we construct two perpendicular axes (a positive and a negative one), then the collection of values $m(x) = (p, n)$ is given by the closed unit square shown in Figure 3.

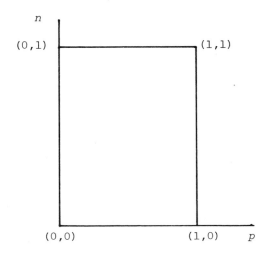

Fig 3.

The essential difference between this approach and that employed by signed graphs may be grasped by considering the discrete value system obtained when p and n are required to be either 0 or 1. We let $p = 1$ if and only if the relationship contains a critical amount of positivity, and let $n = 1$ if it contains a critical amount of negativity. The resulting values for $m(x)$ are the vertices of the unit square shown in Figure 3. In addition to the two familiar positive and negative relationships, whose values are now denoted by $m(x) = (1, 0)$ and $m(x) = (0, 1)$, respectively, we have one of ambivalence, $m(x) = (1, 1)$, and one of indifference, $m(x) = (0, 0)$. It can readily be seen that the resultants are +1 and -1 for the positive and negative relationships, respectively, and are 0 for both ambivalence and indifference. These latter two are distinguished, however, by the fact that ambivalence has an intensity, $i = 2$, whereas, indifference has an intensity, $i = 0$.

In considering how this new value system can be employed to investigate the phenomena of balance and clusterability, Cartwright and Harary (1970) have proposed that the theory of networks provide a suitable mathematical model. A *network* consists of a set of points, together with a value assigned to every ordered pair of points (directed line) in the relation. Viewed in this perspective, a signed digraph is an irreflexive network whose set of values is limited to +1 and -1. But since no restriction is placed on the values assigned to the lines of a network, the value system described previously can be employed for networks. In order to do so, however, some procedure must be specified for deriving the value of a walk from the values of its lines. Cartwright and Harary (1970) have shown how one such procedure can be used to derive several theorems concerning balance in networks of this sort, but the empirical applicability of these results remains to be demonstrated.

D. Consistency Theory

All of the research considered thus far has been concerned
with structures in which signs (or values) are assigned to relationships. There are, however, empirical situations where the
elements themselves have an intrinsic positive or negative quality. In order to provide an appropriate mathematical model for
situations of this sort, we define a *marked graph M* as one in
which each point is given either a positive or a negative sign.
Then, analogous to balance in signed graphs, we say that a marked
graph is *harmonious* if every cycle is positive (has an even number of negative points). In order to present a basic result on
harmonious marked graphs, in accordance with Beineke and Harary
(to appear), we require a concept concerning connectedness. A
graph *G* is *3-connected* if *G* is connected, has no cut-points, and
there are no two points *u, v* such that *G-u-v* is disconnected.

Theorem 8. *No harmonious marked graph with both positive and
negative points is 3-connected*.

This result is illustrated in Figure 4, which shows the smallest possible 3-connected graph K_4. It can readily be seen that
it is impossible to mark the points of this graph positive and
negative so that the resulting marked graph is harmonious.

K_4:

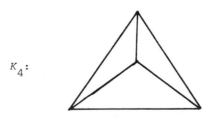

Fig. 4.

Both signed graphs and marked graphs are special cases of *nets*. A *net N* is obtained from a graph *G* when both the points and lines of *G* are given signs. The *sign of a cycle of a net* is the product of the signs of its points and of its lines. A net *N* is *consistent* if all of its cycles are positive.

Let *S*(*N*) be the signed graph obtained from *N* by ignoring the signs of its points, and let *M*(*N*) be the marked graph obtained from *N* by ignoring the signs of its lines. It is obvious that if *S*(*N*) is balanced and *M*(*N*) is harmonious, then the net *N* is consistent. But it is easily seen that the converse does not hold. If, however, *N* contains only positive points, then *N* is consistent if and only if *S*(*N*) is balanced. Thus, the results concerning balanced signed graphs immediately generalize to consistent nets all of whose points are positive.

Nets provide a formulation for precisely handling a great variety of cognitive consistency theories (see Abelson, *et al.*, 1968; Gollob, 1974). And they should also be useful in dealing with any empirical structure where it is meaningful to give signs to both relationships and elements. The study of consistent nets would seem to constitute one of the most promising topics for both mathematical and empirical research.

IV. CONCLUDING COMMENTS

The work of the past 20 years has produced a body of mathematical theory that is increasingly comprehensive and, at the same time, more capable of dealing with the full complexity of empirical reality. The demonstration that balanced signed graphs are specific instances of clusterable graphs has placed the topic of balance in a much broader context and has posed a number of new problems for empirical research. The recognition that the qualitative value system for signed graphs is a specific instance of the more general system for networks has provided a means for

representing gradations in the strength of relationships and for
dealing with the phenomena of ambivalence and indifference. The
quite recent extension of the concept of a signed graph to that
of a net allows for the representation of structures in which both
elements and relationships have signs. This concept provides the
basis for generalizing the concepts of balance and clusterability
to that of consistency. In view of these developments, it may be
expected that mathematical research in the near future will provide an elaborated theory of consistent nets and that this theory
should have a wide range of empirical applicability.

REFERENCES

Abelson, R. P., & Rosenberg, M. J. Symbolic psycho-logic: A
     model of attitudinal cognition. *Behavioral Science,* 1958, *3,*
     1-13.
Abelson, R. P., *et al.* (Eds.). *Theories of cognitive consistency:
     A sourcebook.* Chicago: Rand McNally, 1968.
Barnes, J. A. Social networks. *Addison-Wesley Modular Publica-
     tions,* 1972, *26.*
Beineke, L. W., & Harary, F. Harmonious graphs with signed points.
     In press.
Carroll, M. P. Applying Heider's theory to Levi-Strauss.
     Sociometry, 1973, *26,* 285-301.
Cartwright, D., & Gleason, T. C. The number of paths and cycles
     in a digraph. *Psychometrika,* 1966, *31,* 179-199.
Cartwright, D., & Gleason, T. C. A note on a matrix criterion for
     unique colorability of a signed graph. *Psychometrika,* 1967,
     32, 291-296.
Cartwright, D., & Harary, F. Structural balance: A generalization
     of Heider's theory. *Psychological Review,* 1956, *63,* 277-293.
Cartwright, D., & Harary, F. On the coloring of signed graphs.
     Elemente der Mathematik, 1968, *23,* 85-89.

Cartwright, D., & Harary, F. Ambivalence and indifference in generalizations of structural balance. *Behavioral Science,* 1970, *15,* 497-513.

Davis, J. A. Clustering and structural balance in graphs. *Human Relations,* 1967, *20,* 181-187.

Gollob, H. F. The subject-verb-object approach to social cognition. *Psychological Review,* 1974, *81,* 286-321.

Hage, P. A graph theoretic approach to the analysis of alliance structure and local grouping in highland New Guinea. *Anthropological Forum,* 1974, *3,* 280-294.

Harary, F. A structural analysis of the situation in the Middle East in 1956. *Journal of Conflict Resolution,* 1961, *5,* 167-178.

Harary, F. Structural duality. *Behavioral Science,* 1957, *2,* 255-265.

Harary, F. On the measurement of structural balance. *Behavioral Science,* 1959, *4,* 316-323.

Harary, F. *Graph theory.* Reading, Massachusetts: Addison-Wesley, 1969.

Harary, F., Norman, R. Z., & Cartwright, D. *Structural models: An introduction to the theory of directed graphs.* New York: Wiley, 1965.

Heider, F. Attitudes and cognitive organization. *Journal of Psychology,* 1946, *21,* 107-112.

Heider, F. *The psychology of interpersonal relations.* New York: Wiley, 1958.

Kaplan, K. J. On the ambivalence-indifference problem in attitude theory and measurement: A suggested modification in the semantic differential technique. *Psychological Bulletin,* 1972, *77,* 361-372.

Mitchell, J. C. *Social networks in urban situations.* Manchester: Manchester University Press, 1969.

Newcomb, T. M. An approach to the study of communicative acts. *Psychological Review,* 1953, *60,* 393-404.

Newcomb, T. M. Stabilities underlying changes in interpersonal attraction. *Journal of Abnormal and Social Psychology,* 1963, *66,* 376-386.

Norman, R. Z., & Roberts, F. S. A derivation of a measure of relative balance for social structures and a characterization of extensive ratio systems. *Journal of Mathematical Psychology,* 1972, *9,* 66-91.

Oeser, O. A., & Harary, F. A mathematical model for structural role theory, I. *Human Relations,* 1962, *15,* 89-109.

Peay, E. R., Jr. Extensions of clusterability to quantitative data with an application to the cognition of political attitudes. Unpublished doctoral dissertation, University of Michigan, 1970.

Roberts, F. S. Signed digraphs and the growing demand for energy. *Environment and Planning,* 1971, *3,* 395-410.

Roberts, F. S. Structural characterizations of stability of signed digraphs under pulse processes. In F. Harary and R. Bari (Eds.), *Graphs and combinatorics.* Berlin: Springer-Verlag, 1974, Pp. 330-338.

Schwenk, A. J. An algorithm for determining the line index of a planar signed graph. In press.

Taylor, H. F. *Balance in small groups.* New York: Van Nostrand Reinhold, 1970.

CHAPTER 4

THE DAVIS/HOLLAND/LEINHARDT STUDIES: AN OVERVIEW[1]

James A. Davis[2]

National Opinion Research Center

University of Chicago

Chicago, Illinois

In all the plastic blather associated with our national bicentennial, it has escaped the attention of the media that 1976 is also the twentieth anniversary of the Cartwright and Harary paper (1956) on balance theory. The oversight is regrettable. It is hardly extraordinary for a nation to endure 200 years, but two decades is a remarkable span of life for a social science theory.

[1] *Over the years, this research has received support from N.S.F. grants (Nos. GS-1286, GP-8774, GS-2044X, GS-39778, and GJ-1154X2) as well as fellowship support for Davis (NIMH) and Leinhardt (SSRC). Dartmouth College, Carnegie-Mellon University, and the National Bureau of Economic Research Contributed generous computer support for the project.*

[2] *Present address: Department of Sociology, Harvard University, Cambridge, Massachusetts.*

Whether this conference celebrates the theory's coming of age
or its retirement remains to be seen; but I will seize the coincidence of the date and the conference to review how far we have
come in two decades in the hope this may tell us where we might
be going.

Properly, of course, I can speak only for the research done
by me and my long-term friends and collaborators, Samuel Leinhardt
and Paul Holland, and not for the many other lines of work that
have been influenced by that seminal article. But, I feel com-
fortable in starting from Cartwright and Harary (1956) since I
view our work as a generalization and extension of their theory--
one of the extensions being to try to find out whether it is true.
(Strictly speaking, we are sure it is not, but more on that
later.)

While the Davis/Holland/Leinhardt papers are highly technical
and apparently methodological, my own interest has always been
theoretical and didactic. In plain English, I first stumbled on
balance theory when looking for teaching materials for a night
school course in social psychology at the University of Chicago
Graduate School of Business. As we all know, social psychology
involves the most interesting stuff, but it is packaged in the
form of isolated, highly contrived experiments. Thus, for teacher
and students, it has the general character of a bucket of artificial diamonds. To me, and I hope for the students, balance
theory provided a nifty way to pull together all those isolated
shimmering facts about college freshmen.

Now, when I say nifty, I have definite criteria in mind. A
nifty theory is one that is falsifiable, nonobvious, and simple.
We are all aware that the requirement of falsifiability is a
stiff one. If one were to apply it rigorously, most courses in
sociological theory could be shortened to about a week and a half,
including historical background. Having said we think simple
structural balance theory is wrong, we clearly believe it to be

falsifiable. The other two requirements are a bit more aesthetic.
Since we are all people functioning reasonably well in society,
we all are good amateur sociologists, and it is painfully rare for
beginning social science students to say, "By golly, I never in
the world would have thought of that." This is not the case for
balance theory. One starts with apparently innocent propositions
about points and lines--and then, whammo, out of the blue, we get
cliques. Now, it is not that students are unaware of cliques,
but I have yet to find one who had already figured out that they
have anything to do with even numbers of negative relationships.
Balance theory clearly has the nifty property of being nonobvious.
Furthermore, it is simple in the sense that persons with a limited
mathematics background can grasp the major working parts and key
theorems. (I am aware that in pure mathematics, graph theory is
part of topology and topology is far from simple--but in social
science applications so far, simplicity holds.)

As a bonus, the Cartwright and Harary version (but not
Heider's, 1944, original discussion) is very sociological. It is
about group structures and dyadic relations, not about individual
psyches. So many sociological propositions are merely fluffed
out psychology or economics that structural models have a special
appeal for sociologists.

So, even in 1956 the Cartwright and Harary version of Heider
was a full blown nifty sociological theory. In fact, my first
paper on the topic (Davis, 1963) was simply a list of the many
discrete propositions in sociology that come together when
translated into balance theory.

Why didn't I quit when I was ahead?

Again, it was a classroom episode. One day when I was
teaching at Johns Hopkins, a student asked, "Well, what would
happen if a group had three cliques?" Since he had been re-
working the Coleman high school data and had located some hundred

cliques per high school, it was not an unreasonable question--
but it had me stumped. After more days and weeks than I care to
remember, I worked out the answer which appears in the "cluster
theorem" paper, (Davis, 1967).

And this led to those damn triads. Since Flament (1963) had
shown triad properties sufficient to assess balance *and* Davis
(1967) showed the same for clustering, *and* the transitivity of a
tournament turns on triads, it seemed to me that "threezies"
were the key to the whole thing.

I wish I could say the triad business stems directly from
Simmel (1950) and his pioneer analysis of the sociological importance of the jump from pairs to trios. I do find this gambit
useful in getting sociological editors--who tend to be high
priests of ancestor cults--to accept my papers, but the truth is
this: if the key theorems had involved five points, the Davis/
Holland/Leinhardt papers would all be about quintets.

So, by 1967, only one piece was missing--the empirical
evidence.

I am by training and proclivity a "survey analyst," not an
experimental social psychologist. Survey analysts tend to think
big, at least in terms of cases, if not magnitudes of relationships. Furthermore, I was lucky enough in the late 1960s to
receive an NIMH fellowship that provided my salary but no funds
for research. It thus became almost inevitable that my strategy
for empirical testing would involve (*a*) statistical trends in
many sociomatrices rather than the study of a single group, and
(*b*) hunting and gathering other people's data rather than collecting new data.

This notion was parlayed into an NSF grant that enabled me to
hire a research assistant to do the dirty work. Sam Leinhardt
got the job and doubled the proportion of the world's social
scientists interested in the statistical study of triads. Under
this grant, we sniffed out some 1000 sociograms, rigged a crude

statistical test for triad surpluses and deficits, and discovered
to our amazement that choices are not always reciprocated.

Sam, Paul, and I have sometimes been accused of an obsession
with demonstrating the hierarchical character of sociometric
choices. In fact, Moreno (1934) demonstrated that regularity
years and years ago, and we were dragged into the problem because we had to do something with the asymmetric choices in our
data bank.

The upshot was an unanticipated further extension of the
mathematical model (Davis and Leinhardt, 1972).[3] The ideal
typical Davis/Leinhardt group--yet to appear in real data--may
be thought of as a sort of socioemotional "high rise," with
floors ordered in terms of popularity and each floor partitioned
into cliques.

And, as you might expect, we showed a group must have this
structure if and only if a mere 7 out of 16 possible triad types
never occur.

What never? Well, hardly ever...

When the data bank matrices were shoveled into the Dartmouth
computer the following clear cut, but equivocal results emerged:

(1) The Davis/Leinhardt model worked, in the sense that the
vast majority of the groups supported the vast majority of the
triad predictions, that is, the undesirable seven generally turn
up at less than chance levels of frequency.

(2) The triad that diagnoses balance as opposed to clusterability (the 0-0-3 in our terminology) was not at all shy. It
turned up at about chance levels. Thus we concluded that the

[3]The paper was completed in 1968, but only appeared in print
in 1972 because of publication problems for the symposium volume
to which is was submitted.

Cartwright/Harary model is not valid in its strict form, though
the pattern of results clearly supported their more general
hypothesis of cliquing.

(3) Two of the seven critical triad types, the hated and
feared "2-1-0," and the insidious "0-1-2" simply are not rare.
(See Holland and Leinhardt for definitions of all 16 triad types.)
We had obtained our good over-all predictions by being very
right about five triads and severely wrong about two.[4]

And there we were with strong empirical evidence for 5/7 of
a theorem.

Quickly persuading ourselves that 71.4% is not a bad average
for a seven-proposition social science theory, Leinhardt and I
published the results with as much upbeat interpretation as
decency would allow.

Around this time our research dyad expanded to become a
triad with the inclusion of Paul Holland. At the 1968 American
Sociological Association meetings, Leinhardt presented our paper,
and a mathematical statistician, Paul Holland, was the dis-
cussant. It turned out that Holland was not wholly opposed and
he soon joined us, the first fruits being a method to handle the
triad statistics the right way(Holland and Leinhardt, 1970).

Since, alas, the right statistics gave about the same results
as our first crude statistics, we were still stuck with the
0-1-2s and the 2-1-0s.

Holland and Leinhardt managed to knock out 0-1-2s with the
fist of a priori reasoning. In an undeservedly neglected paper,
Holland and Leinhardt (1971) presented our most general deterministic model for group structures. Their notion of "partially ordered clusters" allows one to come up with models that

---

[4]In fact, Leinhardt (1968) demonstrated that 0-1-2s were
inevitable in any group that had at least two independent
hierarchies, a common occurrence in children's groups.

incorporate strict balance, clustering, and ranked clusters in a
scheme that permits 0 1-2s to run around free. In a study of 118
children's groups, Leinhardt (1972) lent support to this model
and suggested that its importance increases with age.

Six down, and one to go.

But it would not go. That blasted 2-1-0 triad (two mutual
positive relationships and one asymmetric) was clearly not rare
(in fact, it tends to occur at higher than chance levels in our
data bank matrices), and we have simply been unable to find a
plausible ideal type group structure where 2-1-0s exist.

When painted into a corner, social scientists tend to leap to
freedom by grasping the agreeable assumption they were done in by
measurement problems. Taking that escape route, I argued (Davis,
1970) that if we could represent choices on an interval scale
instead of 0-1 categories, pair *sums* would show clustering and
pair *differences* would form a hierarchy. This pretty conceit
does paper over most of the cracks in the results for triad frequencies, but it never caught on and has an unfortunate, artificial character. I, for one, have a hard time grasping the sort
of social structure that would generate these patterns.

Therefore, Holland and Leinhardt (1971) presents the
high water mark of our sociologism and our theoretical use
of ideal typical graph models. [5] Starting from a boldly

[5] *Which may be just as well, since a Dartmouth student, Mr.
Tom Hynes, in "The Last Triad Paper," an Honors Thesis in Mathematical Social Science, June 5, 1975, generates persuasive simulation results showing that ideal typical structures other than
clusterability can generate our patterns of triad surpluses and
deficits! In particular, Mr. Hynes gets nice clusterability from
a model where people are spread out evenly in a two dimensional
space and each chooses his closest neighbor, as for example,
students seated at desks in a class room.*

sociological perspective, we have been drifting back toward
psychology, forced into retreat, without ever making it to four
people, much less entire groups! And all because of those
2-1-0's. Our psychology is not the sort that Freudians and
Jungians would call "rich," but Professor Heider would accept
it as psychology, since the cast of characters includes our old
friends, *p*, *o*, and *x*, appearing under the stage names of *i*, *j*,
and *k*.

This retrogressive progress stems from the concept of transitivity. Holland and Leinhardt (1971) prove that the entire family
of models we have postulated may be viewed as transitive graphs,
the subtypes being produced by various assumptions about symmetry
and asymmetry of pair relations.

Now, transitivity is a property of ordered *triplets*, not of
triads. That is, the triplet *i-j-k* is transitive if $(i \rightarrow j)$ and
$(j \rightarrow k)$ implies $(i \rightarrow k)$. Thus, a triad--the set of all choices among
three persons--may be viewed as a collection of six distinct or-
dered triplets. Holland and Leinhardt (1972) provide pretty
persuasive evidence for transitivity as a pervasive effect in
sociometric data.

The transitivity approach goes a long way toward solving the
2-1-0 mess because 2-1-0's have a fat total of five transitive
triplets, which presumably increase its frequency plus one
intransitive triple which creates a bit of friction, so it isn't
endemic.

But, transitivity is only one of many possible configurations
for triplets, just as structural balance is only one of many
possible configurations for graphs. Holland and Leinhardt (1976)
develop a virtually brand new method for analyzing micro-
sociometric data. Acting on the insight that transitivity is
merely one of many possible linear combinations of triad

frequencies, they develop a general scheme for testing any hypothesis that can be formulated in terms of triplets. So far, transitivity looks like the most promising, but a number of possibilities remain to be explored.

Which brings us from 1956 to 1976.

What does it all add up to?

I am happy to say I don't know, since we do not believe our work is done and most of the lurches in our party line could not be foreseen even a few months ahead. Nevertheless, treating our experiences so far as a case in the history of social science, I would draw the following conclusions.

First, I think we were lucky to have stumbled on the idea of a sociometric data bank. Obviously larger N's are preferable to smaller N's, but the effects have been more subtle than that. For one thing, it has kept us on the main course. If you "do a study" the obvious step is to do some other study when you have completed the first. But when you own some 1000 sociograms, it never occurs to you to move on to some new topic, since it seems to be impossible to exhaust the information in our vaults. I think the data bank is the main reason our papers show a degree of logical and substantive coherence. Furthermore, the data bank has persuaded me that our findings are "really true." While it is not exactly the case I believe my non-data-bank research is a pack of lies, one has a certain diffidence in interpreting results from a single case. We are so frightened of "type I errors" and worried that samples of slightly different populations would give different results, most of us have less faith in our research than we should. However, when definite patterns turn up in dozens and hundreds of sociograms from the most diverse populations, in studies using a variety of measurements (mostly sloppy, see Holland and Leinhardt, 1973, for a discussion of just how sloppy), one really begins to believe there is "something there."

Second, I have become even more committed to a statistical
rather than deterministic approach. Granted that the most bril-
liant work on networks has been deterministic, I am struck by
this fact: While the vast majority of our matrices show agreeable
triads, no more than one or two of the matrices in our collection
show perfect structures, even in terms of the ultrarelaxed graph
models we developed. Whether sociometric data are more error
laden than other social science observations, I do not know; but
I do feel that when even the most talented regression analysts
come up with R^2's of .5 and less, network researchers must learn
to live with error.

Now for some less self-congratulatory conclusions.

I regret our slide from global structure to microanalysis. I
don't think it is wrong. I think we were led there by the facts.
Nevertheless, I wish we had been able to move upward to say things
about groups as a whole instead of retreating to a perspective
from which a *triad* looks as large and complicated as intergalactic
space. Given a choice, I would rather be right than sociological,
but I would prefer not to be forced into the choice.

Finally, I wish we had gained a lot more insight into what is
really going on. According to the textbook models of science, our
group has not been unsuccessful. We have built models, tested
them against the data, revised the models on the basis of our
findings and have generally found better a match with the facts
in our later models. Nevertheless, after a decade of matrix
grinding, I have no more idea of why triads are transitive than I
did when I began. In fact, my insight has been eroded to the extent that I am no longer so sure that what we get is a noisy reflection of total group structures. Furthermore, I not only
don't understand it, but I am somewhat opposed to it. That is,
if I were free to choose a group to join, the last thing in the
world I'd like would be one divided into tight cliques and
arranged in an iron pecking order of popularity. I think it is

no coincidence that when we tabulate our parameters against the
age of the group members, there is a tendency to get the best
fit with junior high school students. To have devoted a substantial fraction of my career to showing most groups have a
touch of preadolescence is not entirely gratifying.

What has been gratifying, however, have been the rich
rewards of working with affable and stimulating collaborators,
of seeing that the textbook rules for scientific work do occasionally apply in social science, and the recurrent feeling--
which the three of us share--that, by golly, maybe this new model
will crack the thing wide open.

REFERENCES

Cartwright, D., & Harary, F. Structural Balance: A generalization
    of Heider's theory. *Psychological Review,* 1956, *63,* 277-293.
Davis, James A. Structural balance, mechanical solidarity, and
    interpersonal relations. *American Journal of Sociology,* 1963,
    68, 444-463.
Davis, James, A. Clustering and structural balance in graphics.
    Human Relations, 1967, *20,* 181-187.
Davis, James A. Clustering and hierarchy in interpersonal rela-
    tions: Testing two theoretical models in 742 sociograms.
    American Sociological Review, 1970, *35,* 843-852.
Davis, James A., & Leinhardt Samuel The structure of positive
    interpersonal relations in small groups in J. Berger (Ed.),
    Sociological Theories in Progress, Vol. 2. Boston: Houghton-
    Mifflin, 1972.
Flament, C. *Applications of graph theory to group structure.*
    Englewood Cliffs, New Jersey: Prentice-Hall, 1963.
Heider, F. Social perception and phenomenal causality. *Psycho-
    logical Review,* 1944, *51,* 358-374.

Holland, Paul W., & Leinhardt, Samuel. A method for detecting structure in sociometric data. *American Journal of Sociology,* 1970, *70,* 492-573.

Holland, Paul W., & Leinhardt, Samuel. Transitivity structural models of small groups. *Comparative Group Studies,* 1971, *2,* 107-124.

Holland, Paul W., & Leinhardt, Samuel. Some evidence on the transitivity of positive interpersonal sentiment. *American Journal of Sociology,* 1972, *72,* 1205-1209.

Holland, Paul W., & Leinhardt, Samuel. The structural implications of measurement error in sociometry. *Journal of Mathematical Sociology,* 1973, *3,* 85-111.

Holland, Paul W., & Leinhardt, Samuel. Local structure in networks. D. Heise (Ed.), *Sociological Methodology, 1976,* San Francisco: Jossey-Bass, in press.

Leinhardt, Samuel. The development of structure in the interpersonal relations of children, Ph.D. Thesis, University of Chicago, 1968.

Leinhardt, Samuel. Developmental change in the sentiment structure of children's groups. *American Sociological Review,* 1972, *37,* 202-212.

Moreno, J. L., *Who shall survive?* Washington, D.C.: Nervous and Mental Disease Publishing Co., 1934.

Simmel, Georg. *The sociology of Georg Simmel.* Glencoe, Illinois: The Free Press, 1950.

CHAPTER 5

STRUCTURAL SOCIOMETRY[1]

Paul W. Holland
Eductional Testing Service
Princeton, New Jersey

Samuel Leinhardt
Carnegie-Mellon University
Pittsburgh, Pennsylvania

I. INTRODUCTION

Our objectives in this chapter are to review our approach to the analysis of sociometric data (Holland and Leinhardt, 1970, 1971) as we have elaborated it (Holland and Leinhardt, 1975) and to introduce some new empirical results. We address the traditional type of sociometric data raising the question of whether or not they contain anything of interest to social scientists. There is no *a priori* reason why sociometric data should interest social scientists. Sociometry was invented by a psychiatrist,

[1]*This chapter is part of a continuing research series and reports work that is collaborative in every respect. The order of authorship is alphabetical. Originally prepared for presentation at: The Mathematical Social Science Board Advanced Research Symposium on Social Networks, Hanover, NH, September 18-21, 1975. Research supported in part by NSF Grant SOC 73-05489 to Carnegie-Mellon University.*

Jacob L. Moreno, and most extant sociometric data have been collected by educators. Still, there is something about a small
group of individuals and data on their interrelationships that
seems to elicit a Pavlovian response in students of social structure. A principal objective of our research program over the past
few years has been to determine whether or not this response is
warranted. Our criterion for evaluating this is the observation
of sufficiently strong empirical deviations from randomness in
sociometric data. In this chapter we ellucidate what we mean by
this criterion and use it to determine whether 384 sociograms
possess any sociologically interesting qualities.

II. NOTATION AND PRELIMINARIES

   Before proceeding, we introduce some notation. We restrict
our attention to sociometric data that can be represented by a
single digraph. The digraph nodes (individuals) are denoted by
i, j, k, ..., and $i \rightarrow j$ means that i "chooses" j where "choice"
is interpreted broadly to mean any binary relation.
   As is customary (e.g., see Harary, Cartwright, and Norman,
1965), we use the zero-one matrix representation of digraphs.
The sociomatrix, X, is the basic data structure and is defined
as

$$X_{ij} = \begin{cases} 1 & \text{if } i \rightarrow j, \quad i \neq j, \\ 0 & \text{otherwise.} \end{cases} \tag{1}$$

For a group of size g, X is a g by g matrix.
   We ignore self-loops and set $X_{ii} = 0$. We always deal with
labeled digraphs in which the individuals are distinguished so
the sociomatrix X is equivalent to the digraph. Important derived
statistics of the graph may be expressed in terms of X. As examples, for each individual we have:

$$X_{i+} = \sum_{j} X_{ij} = \text{out-degree of } i = \text{choices made by } i, \qquad (2)$$

$$X_{+j} = \sum_{i} X_{ij} = \text{in-degree of } j = \text{choices received by } j, \qquad (3)$$

$$\text{for } i, j = 1, \dots, g.$$

The in- and out-degree distributions can be summarized by their respective means and variances. The means are both equal to the number of choices made per individual, and are given by:

$$\overline{X} = \frac{1}{g} \sum_{i} X_{i+} = \frac{1}{g} \sum_{j} X_{+j}. \qquad (4)$$

The variances are, respectively:

$$V(\text{in}) = \frac{1}{g} \sum_{j} (X_{+j} - \overline{X})^2 \qquad (5)$$

and

$$V(\text{out}) = \frac{1}{g} \sum_{i} (X_{i+} - \overline{X})^2. \qquad (6)$$

For a "fixed choice" sociogram $V(\text{out}) = 0$, whereas $V(\text{out}) > 0$ for a "free choice" sociogram. Two other statistics related to $\overline{X}$ are the total number of choices, X_{++}, and the choice density,

$$CDY = \overline{X}/(g - 1) \qquad (7)$$

which is the number of choices made per ordered pair of individuals.

The in- and out-degrees are *nodal properties* in the sense that they describe characteristics of the digraph at each node. The out-degrees reflect individual "expansiveness" or possibly experimental constraints (e.g., when $V(\text{out}) = 0$). The in-degrees are often interpreted as measures of status or of individual popularity. Both expansiveness and popularity are individual characteristics

describing properties that individuals may possess regardless of
the properties possessed by other individuals.

The distributions of the in- and out-degrees do not distinguish between reciprocated and unreciprocated choices. Since
friendship is a property of *pairs* of individuals we need to go
beyond the level of individual nodes to obtain information about
it, to the level of pairs. The number of mutual, asymmetric, and
null dyads in the digraph are given by:

$$M = \sum_{i < j} X_{ij} X_{ji},\tag{8}$$

$$A = \sum_{i \neq j} X_{ij}(1 - X_{ji}),\tag{9}$$

$$N = \sum_{i < j} (1 - X_{ij})(1 - X_{ji}),\tag{10}$$

respectively.

The essential issue of any notion of structure is how the
components are combined, not the components themselves. In our
approach to sociometric data this issue amounts to the proposition
that the lowest interesting level of structure in a digraph is
the level of triples of nodes--the triadic level. At this level
one can begin to raise the sociologically relevant questions of
how the pairs are *combined* in the whole digraph and how this combination is affected by the in- and out-degrees.

While we regard nodal and dyadic quantities as *components*
rather than as structure, they do constrain the *structure* and
this point leads us to ask a basic question. Is there anything
in sociometric data *besides*:

(1)   experimental constraints (fixed versus free choice),
(2)   differential popularity, and
(3)   a tendency for choices to be reciprocated?

If sociometric data were simple and fell into neat patterns, we could answer this question positively. But no adequate model for sociometric data has yet been formulated and the question remains open.

III. RANDOM DIGRAPHS IN SOCIOMETRY

The notion of random graphs (defined here) provides us with a precise definition of a graph that defies description, or equivalently, one that has no structure. Comparing observed features of a sociogram with the predictions of a random graph is as old as sociometry itself. Moreno's "sociodynamic effect" (Moreno, 1934) states that the observed distribution of choices received $\{X_{+j}\}$ is more variable than that predicted by chance-- there are more "stars" and "isolates," than expected in a random graph. We show subsequently how $V(in)$ can be used to measure this effect. It is also well established that M exceeds its chance expectation--that is, choices tend to be reciprocated.

We now discuss the notion of a random graph in more detail. There are really several types of random graphs that are relevant; each is a probability distribution on the set of all labeled digraphs with g nodes.

A. The Uniform Distribution

This is the basic distribution. In the uniform distribution, all labeled digraphs on g nodes are equally likely. It is easy to generate the sociomatrix for the uniform distribution because the X_{ij} are all independent zero-one variables with

$$P\{X_{ij} = 1\} = 1/2 \quad i \neq j .$$

By conditioning on particular statistics of the digraph we can derive all the other distributions discussed here.

B. The $U|\{X_{++}\}$ Distribution

This is a conditional distribution based on the uniform distribution. X_{++} is the number of directed edges in the digraph. $U|\{X_{++}\}$ is the uniform distribution conditional on X_{++} such that all labeled digraphs with the specific value of X_{++} are equally likely. This distribution is easily generated by selecting at random and without replacement X_{++} of the $g(g - 1)$ possible ordered pairs of nodes and allocating the X_{++} directed edges to them. In the uniform distribution X_{++} is a binomial random variable whereas in $U|X_{++}, X_{++}$ is a specified value. The $U|X_{++}$ distribution has been used by Erdös and Rényi (1960) to study the evolution of random graphs.

C. The $U|\{X_{i+}\}$ Distribution

This is the uniform distribution conditioned by the out-degrees. All labeled digraphs with the specified out-degrees are equally likely. To generate X from this distribution, observe that all the rows of X are statistically independent and that in the ith row we merely need to choose X_{i+} columns randomly and without replacement (excluding X_{ii}, of course) for the ones, and set the rest equal to zero. This distribution is the first of those mentioned that has statistical utility in the study of empirical digraphs. It is the one that provides the usual baseline for establishing Moreno's sociodynamic effect and the excess of mutuality over its chance expectation. In particular we observe that

$$E[M|\{X_{i+}\}] = \left(\frac{g}{g-1}\right)\left(\frac{(\bar{X})^2}{2}\right) - \left(\frac{g}{(g-1)^2}\right)\left(\frac{V(\text{out})}{2}\right) \tag{11}$$

and

$$E[V(\text{in})|\{X_{i+}\}] = \bar{X} - \frac{(\bar{X})^2}{g-1} - \left(\frac{g-2}{(g-1)^2}\right)\left(V(\text{out})\right). \tag{12}$$

The derivations of these formulas are straightforward using indi-

cator variables and, consequently, we omit them. The "sociodynamic effect" of Moreno may be verified by comparing $V(\text{in})$ with
its expected value given in Eq. (12), and "choice reciprocity"
may be shown by comparing M with its expectation given in Eq. (11).
We point out that both of the expectations given in Eqs. (11) and
(12) depend on $\{X_{i+}\}$ only through the mean $\overline{X}$ and variance $V(\text{out})$.
Note that for the $U|\{X_{i+}\}$ distribution the value of X_{++} is fixed
since $X_{++} = \sum_i X_{i+}$ and the individual X_{i+} are fixed.

D. The $U|M,A,N$ Distribution

In this distribution all labeled digraphs with the specified
values of $M,A,$ and N are equally likely. We have discussed this
distribution at length elsewhere (Holland and Leinhardt, 1970,
1975) and in most of our earlier work this is the type of random
graph we dealt with. It is easy to generate X from this distribution by sampling the pairs of nodes randomly and without replacement. Again, $X_{++} = 2M + A$ is fixed since M and A are fixed.
In Holland and Leinhardt (1975) we give results that facilitate
certain theoretical calculations using the $U|M,A,N$ distribution.

E. The $U|\{X_{i+}\},\{X_{+j}\}$ Distribution

In this distribution all labeled digraphs with the specified
values of both $\{X_{i+}\}$ and $\{X_{+j}\}$ are equally likely. This is a
nontrivial distribution and to our knowledge there is no known
practical way of generating random graphs from it. Katz and
Powell (1954) discuss some theoretical aspects of this distribution, as do Harary and Palmer (1966).

F. The $U|\{X_{i+}\}$, M Distribution

This combines the conditioning of both $U|M,A,N$ and $U|\{X_{i+}\}$.
Note that fixing M and $\{X_{i+}\}$ also fixes A and N because $A = X_{++} -$
$2M$ and $N = \binom{g}{2} - M - A$. This is also a nontrivial distribution
and there is no known practical way for generating random digraphs
from it. We know of no theoretical work on this distribution,
either.

G. The $U \mid \{X_{i+}\}$, $\{X_{+j}\}$, M *Distribution*

In this distribution all digraphs with the specified values
of $\{X_{i+}\}$, $\{X_{+j}\}$, and M are equally likely. Again, there is no
known way of generating random graphs from this distribution,
nor can we calculate expectations of interesting statistics from
it.

What is the point of introducing all these different kinds of
random graphs? In our search for sociometric structure these
conditional uniform distributions are what we mean by controlling
for choices-made, choices-received, and degree of mutuality. It
is also necessary to control for these nonstructural effects in
the assessment of structure. Random graphs with excessive numbers of mutual dyads can look cliqued if the definition of a
clique is sufficiently weak. Surprisingly, the need to control
for lower order effects in determining whether sociometric data
exhibit complex structure is not generally appreciated. If we
were comparing the income for two groups--say men and women--every-
one would agree that the comparison would be misleading if it
did not adjust for the confounding effects of other variables
such as occupation, age, and education. In sociometry, adjustment is just as necessary. Nonstructural constraints, like those
discussed earlier, can influence what we observe in sociograms
and should be taken into account by sociometric analysis procedures.

The presence of nontrivial structure in sociometric data can
be assessed by comparing functions of the observed sociomatrix
with their expected values under a random digraph. In a random
digraph there is no structure, only component parts pasted together in a haphazard fashion. The component parts are the
statistics of the digraph that we condition on.

It should be clear from the previous discussion that of the
types of random digraphs mentioned earlier, only $U \mid \{X_{i+}\}, \{X_{+j}\}$,
M will be satisfactory for this purpose. The others are not
sufficiently conditional. As previously mentioned, this distri-

bution is exceedingly difficult to work with. The solution requires that we lower our sights, deal with a simpler function of the digraph instead of the whole digraph, and use a somewhat lower level of conditioning.

IV. THE TRIAD CENSUS

In a digraph there are $\binom{g}{3}$ distinct unlabeled subgraphs formed by each of the possible subsets of three nodes and their corresponding edges. These subgraphs can be classified by their isomorphism type. Let T_u denote the number of these subgraphs of isomorphism type u where u ranges over the 16 triad types given in Figure 2 of Holland and Leinhardt (1975). The 16 dimensional vector

$$\underset{\sim}{T} = (T_u)$$

is called the triad census of the digraph. The triad census is a special case of the more general notion of a subgraph census, but it occupies an important position among subgraph censuses in that it is manageable and, as we show, contains a substantial amount of information about the original digraph.

We should note that the triad census is a real reduction in information when $g > 5$ since X then contains more than 16 elements of data. In general, knowing the triad census does not uniquely determine the digraph.

What information does the triad census provide? First, we have

$$\sum_u T_u = \binom{g}{3} \tag{13}$$

allowing the number of nodes, g, to be recovered. Other linear combinations of the triad frequencies yield useful information.

For example, X_{++}, M, A, and N may all be expressed as linear combinations of the triad frequencies. More interestingly, $V(\text{in})$ and $V(\text{out})$ can be expressed as a linear function of the triad frequencies minus the term $\overline{X}(\overline{X}-1)$. The details of these expressions are given in Holland and Leinhardt (1975). Hence, we see that from the triad census $\underset{\sim}{T}$, we can obtain:

1. the mean, $\overline{X}$, and variance, $V(\text{out})$, of the out-degree distribution, $\{X_{i+}\}$,

2. the mean, $\overline{X}$, and variance, $V(\text{in})$, of the in-degree distribution, $\{X_{+j}\}$, and

3. the number of mutual, M, asymmetric, A, and null, N, dyads in the digraph.

Thus, much of the *nonstructural* information described in Section II can be obtained directly from the triad census. The next question is whether or not any sociologically relevant *structural* information can also be obtained from it.

In Holland and Leinhardt (1971) we showed that many of the proposed "ideal type" models of social structure assume that the digraph is *transitive* with different models adding certain other constraints. By a transitive digraph we mean one in which

$$\text{when } i \rightarrow j \text{ and } j \rightarrow k \text{ then } i \rightarrow k . \tag{14}$$

For example, clustering (Davis, 1967) corresponds to transitivity with no asymmetry. Balance (Cartwright and Harary, 1956), ranked clusters (Davis and Leinhardt, 1972), quasi-series, and linear orders can be expressed in similar fashion.

Since many notions of structure in sociometry involve transitivity we are lead to consider enumerating the number of *intransitivities* that occur in a digraph. An intransitivity is an ordered triple, (i,j,k), in which

$$i \rightarrow j \text{ and } j \rightarrow k \text{ but } i \not\rightarrow k . \tag{15}$$

If IT denotes the number of intransitivities in the digraph then

$$IT = \sum_{u} (IT)_u \; T_u \; , \qquad\qquad (16)$$

where $(IT)_u$ is the number of intransitivities in triads of isomorphism type u. Hence, we see that IT is also a linear combination of triad frequencies. The values of $(IT)_u$ and other interesting linear combinations of triad frequencies are considered
in Holland and Leinhardt (1975).

We are thus lead to consider *all* linear combinations of the
triad frequencies. If $\underset{\sim}{\ell}$ denotes a vector of linear weights then
$\underset{\sim}{\ell}^t \underset{\sim}{T}$ is the linear combination of triad frequencies that corresponds to $\underset{\sim}{\ell}$ (where t denotes the operation of vector or matrix
transpose).

From this perspective, IT is merely one of an infinite number
of possible linear combinations of the triad frequencies. It is
distinguished from the others in that many "ideal type" models
for sociometric structure predict that IT will be zero. Thus, IT
is a natural single degree of freedom that we may associate with
structure in sociometric data.

An assessment of structure in sociometric data requires obtaining the mean vector,

$$\underset{\sim}{\mu} = E(\underset{\sim}{T}) \qquad\qquad (17)$$

and convariance matrix,

$$\underset{\sim}{\Sigma} = \text{Cov}(\underset{\sim}{T}) \; , \qquad\qquad (18)$$

for $\underset{\sim}{T}$ under an appropriate distribution that conditions on the
relevant nonstructural components of the digraph.

Suppose we have $\underset{\sim}{\mu}$ and $\underset{\sim}{\Sigma}$ computed appropriately. A test statistic for the null hypothesis of randomness, given the relevant
nonstructural components of the digraph for the linear combina-

tion $\underset{\sim}{\ell}^t \underset{\sim}{T}$, is:

$$\tau(\underset{\sim}{\ell}) = \frac{\underset{\sim}{\ell}^t \underset{\sim}{T} - \underset{\sim}{\ell}^t \underset{\sim}{\mu}}{\sqrt{\underset{\sim}{\ell}^t \underset{\sim}{\Sigma} \underset{\sim}{\ell}}} .$$

(19)

If ℓ is the weighting vector for intransitivity, large negative
values of $\tau(\underset{\sim}{\ell})$ indicate that the observed sociogram has fewer intransitivities (i.e., is more transitive) than predicted by the
nonstructural characteristics of the digraph. Earlier (Holland
and Leinhardt, 1972), we gave a histogram of values of $\tau(\ell)$ using
the $U|M,A,N$ distribution for intransitivity for several hundred
sociograms from diverse sources. While those values of $\tau(\ell)$ were
generally negative, the gnawing suspicion lingers that perhaps
$U|M,A,N$ is not sufficiently conditional since it does not control
for experimental constraints and differential popularity.

The need for a more highly conditional distribution than
$U|M,A,N$ motivates our current work. We have developed an approach
based on two levels of approximation. First, since we cannot work
with the entire set of in- and out-degrees, we content ourselves
with conditioning on the mean and variance of each of these dis-
tributions--$\overline{X}$, $V(in)$, and $V(out)$. Second, we assume the distri-
bution of T under $U|M,A,N$ is approximately multivariate normal
and we use well-known formulas for conditioning a multivariate
normal vector on linear combinations of its entries. More precisely, μ and Σ are the mean vector and covariance matrix for T
under $U|M,A,N$. These values can be computed with our FORTRAN
program using the tables given in Holland and Leinhardt, (1975).
Let $\underset{\sim}{L}$ be the 2 X 16 matrix whose 2 rows are the weighting vectors
for $V(in)$ and $V(out)$ given in Holland and Leinhardt, 1975).
The approximate conditional distribution of T given M,A,N, $V(in)$,
and $V(out)$ is then normal with mean vector given by

$$E(\underset{\sim}{T}|\underset{\sim}{L}\underset{\sim}{T}) \doteq \underset{\sim}{\mu} + \underset{\sim}{\Sigma} \underset{\sim}{L}^t (\underset{\sim}{L}\underset{\sim}{\Sigma}\underset{\sim}{L}^t)^{-1} \underset{\sim}{L} (\underset{\sim}{T}-\underset{\sim}{\mu}) = \underset{\sim}{\mu}^*,$$

(20)

and covariance matrix

$$\mathrm{Cov}(T \,|\, LT) \doteq \underset{\sim}{\Sigma} - \underset{\sim}{\Sigma}L^t(L\underset{\sim}{\Sigma}L^t)^{-1}L\underset{\sim}{\Sigma} = \underset{\sim}{\Sigma}^*. \tag{21}$$

These approximations give us means, variances and covariances for T under the $U\,|\,\overline{X}$, $V(out)$, $V(in)$, M distribution. While this is not as highly conditional as $U\,|\,\{X_{i+}\},\{X_{+j}\}$, M, it is the best we can obtain with current knowledge. If μ^* and Σ^* given in Eqs. (20) and (21) are substituted for $\underset{\sim}{\mu}$ and $\underset{\sim}{\Sigma}$ in $\tau(\ell)$ in Eq. (19), we obtain a test statistic for structure that controls for the effects of expansiveness, $\overline{X}$, and $V(out)$, popularity, $V(in)$, and choice reciprocity, M.

V. APPLICATION TO DATA

This extra conditioning can be employed to form the associated τ's for intransitivity. In this section we give results for a randomly selected set of 384 sociomatrices from the (Davis and Leinhardt, 1972) sociometric data bank. These are sociograms from a wide variety of sources that represent a fair sampling of the type of sociometric data that was collected before 1968.

-36	7	-15	83
-35	5	-14	9877620
-34		-13	100
-33		-12	43330
-32		-11	997632000
-31		-10	97644320
-30		- 9	98886110
-29		- 8	976554443211
-28	5	- 7	99887754211110000
-27	6	- 6	99887777655332222100
-26	93	- 5	99987777777544443333222222211100000000
-25		- 4	999998888777776666666555555554442211000
-24	9	- 3	888888887777776666666444433333322222211111111100000
-23		- 2	998888887777666666666655555444333333222211111100
-22	4	- 1	99999888876666555544443333222221110000
-21	5	- 0	99999888877766655555554443322221111000
-20		0	00111334556677777999
-19	8321	1	019
-18	5440	2	5
-17	975511	3	
-16	8431	4	12

Fig. 1. τ(Intransitivity) under $U\,|\,M,A,N.$

Figure 1 contains a stem-and-leaf display[2] of τ for intransitivity under the $U|M,A,N$ distribution. The median of the distribution is -4.0. It is clearly skewed to large negative values of τ. Fifty percent of the computed τ values lie between -1.98 and -7.04. Thus, for approximately 75% of the sociograms, τ under $U|M,A,N$ is statistically significant at the 5% level. This result and display is similar to our earlier presentation (Holland and Leinhardt, 1971). While the set of sociomatrices examined differs, the general finding and the shape of the distribution of τ values are comparable. We next raise the question of whether this apparent empirical tendency toward nonrandom, higher level structure is due to the inability of the $U|M,A,N$ distribution to effectively control for the influence of nodal and pair properties on the digraph. Figure 2 contains a stem-and-leaf display of τ for intransitivity computed using our techniques to obtain the $U|X,V(\text{out}),V(\text{in}),M$ distribution.

The two distributions of τ are clearly different. With the higher level of conditioning the range of τ has been reduced

[2]This form of display was introduced by Tukey (1972). It is similar to a histogram in the sense that it provides a graphic representation of the shape of a distribution. However, unlike a histogram, it retains information on individual values. The stems are the values arrayed in the left-hand column. In this case they range from -36 to 4 and contain information on the integer components of the 384 τ values. The leaves are arrayed in rows to the right of the stems. Each digit in a row is a leaf. Each leaf represents the first digit in the decimal portion of a value of τ. Thus, there are as many leaves as τ values. A value of τ is retrieved from the display by combining a stem with any of its leaves. For example, the most negative value of τ in the display is $(-36)+(-.7)$ or -36.7. The most positive value is 4.2.

```
-22    7
-21
-20
-19
-18
-17
-16    92
-15
-14
-13
-12    98
-11    86543310
-10    90
- 9    99886643
- 8    999876664322211000
- 7    86655332221
- 6    987666655432100
- 5    999888876666654443333211111000
- 4    999988877776655555544444433333322222222110000
- 3    999988888777777776655555444444443333332222221111100000
- 2    999988877766666554444443333332222222221111000
- 1    999888888887776666666655444433333333222111111111100000
- 0    999999888888777777766666655544444444443333222211100000
  0    11122233344577788899
  1    001112344456689
  2    11457
  3    9
  4    04
```

Fig. 2. τ(Intransitivity) under U|X̄,V(out),V(in),M.

and the median has become less negative at -3.39. Fifty percent
of the distribution now lies between -1.01 and -5.03. The proportion of sociomatrices with τ significant at the 5% level has
fallen to 60%. This means that employing the higher level of
conditioning revealed that, at least in some cases, what was previously thought to be structure was spurious, the result of lower
level constraints operating on the digraphs. This overall shift
in the distribution of τ can be easily seen in Figure 3.

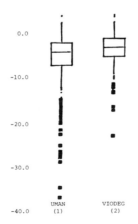

Fig. 3. τ under U|M,A,N (1) and U|X̄,V(out), V(in), M (2).

This figure contains box plots,[3] displays that allow us to place
summaries of the distributions side by side. Here, the general
shift in τ associated with increased conditioning is clear.

These graphic displays help us contrast overall patterns in
the two distributions, but they do not permit us to determine
what happens to individual digraphs when the level of conditioning is altered. To pursue this we present a scatter plot of the
paired τ values in Figure 4. Each point of the scatter plot
represents one of the 384 digraphs. Read the τ value obtained
from $U|M,A,N$ on the x-axis and that obtained from $U|\bar{X},V$(out),
V(in),M on the y-axis.

To facilitate understanding this plot, recall that more
positive values of τ are associated with a lower index of structure. Thus, the points gathered in the upper right-hand corner
of the plot are from digraphs that do not register as significant
under either level of conditioning. Those points in the upper
area of the plot represent digraphs that registered deviations
under $U|M,A,N$ but that had this indication of structure reduced
under the higher conditioning level of $U|\bar{X},V$(out),V(in),M. In
some instances this reduction is extraordinary, as in the case of
the digraph that had the most negative τ under $U|M,A,N$, ap-
proximately -36, generating a τ under $U|\bar{X},V$(out),V(in),M of ap-
proximately -10. However, there is a large section of the plot,
the dense area toward the right along a 45° line emanating from
the origin, which is not very strongly affected by conditioning

[3] This is another graphic display due to Tukey (1972). The
boxes encapsulate the middle 50% of the distribution. The bar
within each box identifies the median. Solid lines reach from
the boxes to points determined by a robust estimate of spread
covering values that are not exceptionally distant from the central section of the distribution. The reamining points and small
boxes identify specific values that are relatively distant from
the central portion.

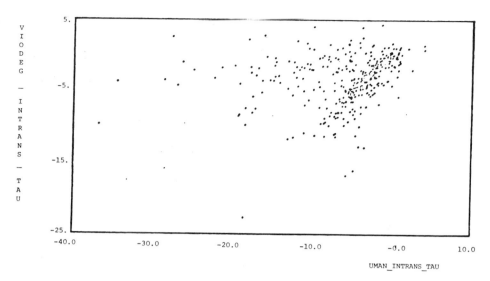

Fig. 4. Individual τ values.

level. The indicated structure of these digraphs was not due to
lower order properties. In a few instances, digraphs that did
not give evidence of structure under $U|M,A,N$ do so under
$U|\bar{X},V(\text{out}),V(\text{in}),M$.

These results indicate that the level of conditioning matters.
In many instances as the level of conditioning increases, what
first appeared to be structure is revealed to be no more than
what one would expect given the nodal and pair properties of the
digraph. The additional conditioning has not made any real structure disappear. It acts instead as a filter with a finer mesh to
keep back digraphs that had passed earlier. Sixty percent of
the sociomatrices still pass; they have a level of organization
that cannot be explained on the basis of the lower level nodal
and pair properties of the digraph. On the other hand, in 40% of
the sociomatrices, there is no structure. All we need to predict
their triadic structure are their nodal and pair properties.
This is what we mean when we say a group has no social structure.

While we have emphasized the reduction in apparent structure that accompanies increased conditioning, we should not overlook the fact that the indexes of many digraphs are not affected by the level of conditioning, and others, while affected, continue to exhibit significant tendencies toward structure. In some cases, in fact, τ remains extremely negative indicating that very large deviations from random expectation occur. Assuming that these data are representative of human groups, this finding implies that nontrivial structure exhibited by unaccountably high deficits of intransitivities is a fact of social life.

VI. DISCUSSION[4]

We began this chapter by asking whether or not sociometric data possess any qualities which make them relevant to the study of social structure. To be relevant, we reasoned, the structure of sociometric data had to demonstrate strong deviations away from randomness. Thus, we were placed in a position of defining what we meant by randomness in a digraph and of developing techniques with which to gauge deviations. Structure was taken to mean the shape or patterned way in which social relations are joined together into larger aggregations. We defined randomness in a precise fashion, one that allowed us to focus on variation in these aggregations that was not due to the nature of a digraph's components and used this definition to create measures of structure. In the data analysis of Section V we discovered that the level of conditioning is important. Different conclusions regarding the prevalence of social structure in interpersonal relations result when different levels of conditioning

[4]This section has benefited from the remarks made by Mark Granovetter on the version of this chapter delivered at the symposium.

are employed. Much of the data we explored exhibited unusually strong deviations from randomness defined in terms of $U|M,A,N$. But occasionally, the deviations disappeared when randomness was defined in terms of $U|\bar{X},V(\text{out}),V(\text{in}),M$. Thus, at times, what was presumed to be structure represented nonstructural factors. The higher level of conditioning increased our precision in discriminating between those digraphs that had structure and those that had none.

The digraphs that were not structured were explained without recourse to sociological phenomena. This means that, for 40% of the digraphs examined, given the lower order properties of the digraph, we were able to predict higher order properties. We could not, however, explain the structure of 60% of the digraphs using only their lower order properties. These digraphs remain as evidence that sociometric data are relevant to the study of social structure. They are relevant because something else besides nodal and pair properties, something structural, operates within them. This concept of explanation requires some elucidation. When we construct a contingency table from survey data we usually test a variety of models. These models can be hierarchically arranged with each successive model requiring more factors to explain the data, that is, predict the cell frequencies. We normally seek the simplest model, one that explains or permits us to reproduce the table with the fewest factors. When we reproduce the table from the marginals we have a simple explanation for the structure of the table. This is precisely what we mean in the case of structure in digraphs. When we can generate the distribution of higher order aggregates from lower, we explain the digraph's structure without recourse to concepts such as structural tendencies in social relations. When we cannot explain the data in this way then we have evidence for the existence of structural processes.

Does this mean that lower order properties are not important? Considering the impact nodal and pair properties have on the individual participants, the people and social relations that give rise to sociometric data, the answer is certainly no. Clearly, when one person likes another and this liking is not reciprocated, the consequences of the presence of an asymmetric rather than a mutual pair can be important. But this is not an issue of social structure. The question we address is the fundamental question of social structure: whether or not the pairs, the asymmetrics, the mutuals, or the nulls are organized in a systematic fashion. To raise questions of structure, we ought not be concerned with the quality of pairs or the character of nodes, but rather, with how the whole is arranged. The techniques we have developed permit investigators to raise such questions in a precise fashion. The data analytic results we have presented indicate that social structure does exist--some of the time. But these methodological techniques can only tell us when structure is present. We now need tools with which to estimate the strength of tendencies toward structure, to determine how structure develops over time, and to explore how other variables influence this development. We have begun work on these problems (see Holland and Leinhardt, 1976). Our ultimate objective is an empirically grounded formal theory of social structure.

REFERENCES

Cartwright, D., & Harary, F. Structural balance: A generalization of Heider's theory. *Psychological Review,* 1956, *63,* 277-293.
Davis, J. A. Clustering and structural balance in graphs. *Human Relations,* 1967, *20,* 181-187.

Davis, J. A., & Leinhardt, S. The structure of positive inter-
personal relations in small groups. In J. Berger (Ed.),
Sociological theories in progress, Vol. 2 Boston: Houghton-
Mifflin, 1972.

Erodös, P. & Renyi, A. On the evolution of random graphs. *Proceedings of the Mathematical Institute of the Hungarian
Academy of Sciences, 1961, 5A,* 17-61.

Harary, F., & Palmer, J. Enumeration of locally restricted digraphs. *Canadian Journal of Mathematics, 1966,* 18, 853-860.

Holland, P. W., & Leinhardt, S. A method for detecting structure in sociometric data. *American Journal of Sociology,*
1970, *70,* 492-513.

Holland, P. W., & Leinhardt, S. Transitivity in structural
models of small groups. *Comparative Group Studies,* 1971, *2,*
107-124.

Holland, P. W., & Leinhardt, S. Some evidence on the transitivity
of positive interpersonal sentiment. *American Journal of
Sociology,* 1972, *72,* 1205-9.

Holland, P. W., & Leinhardt, S. Local structure in social networks. In D. R. Heise (Ed.), *Sociological Methodology-1976.*
San Francisco: Jossey-Bass, 1975.

Holland, P. W., & Leinhardt, S. A dynamic model for social networks. *Journal of Mathematical Sociology,* 1976, *5.*

Katz, L., & Powell, J. H. The number of locally restricted
directed graphs. *Proceedings of the American Statistical
Association,* 1954, *5,* 621-626.

Moreno, J. L. *Who Shall Survive?* Washington, D.C.: Nervous and
Mental Disease Publishing Co., 1934.

Tukey, J. W. Some graphic and semigraphic displays. In T. A.
Bancroft (Ed.), *Statistical papers in Honor of G. W.
Snedecor.* Ames, Iowa: Iowa State University Press, 1972.

CHAPTER 6

A PRIMER ON BLOCKMODELING PROCEDURE[1]

John M. Light

Department of Sociology

Princeton University

Nicholas C. Mullins

Department of Sociology

Indiana University

I. INTRODUCTION

Blockmodeling is a technique for structural analysis that uses social network principles. It was introduced in two some-what complicated expository papers (Boorman & White, 1976; White, Boorman, & Breiger, 1976) and two papers devoted to methods (Breiger, Boorman, & Arabie, 1975; Heil & White, 1976). Now there are other descriptions and applications of blockmodeling (Groeneveld, 1974; Breiger, 1976; Hecht, 1977; Mullins, 1977; Mullins *et al.*, 1977; Arabie *et al.*, 1978).

Although blockmodeling has generated considerable interest among sociologists, the quantity and unfamiliarity of ideas

[1]*NCM was supported in part by a fellowship from the Institute for Advanced Study. We used examples from data gathered under NSF grant SOC 74-24537.*

involved has made it inaccessible to many. Blockmodeling essentially compounds social relationships to form an algebraic
structure, conceptualization of which is difficult; moreover,
several procedures exist for carrying out blockmodeling. As a
result, the would-be blockmodeler may not know what procedure to
follow, when to deviate from accepted practice, and what practices
are and are not accepted (e.g., Schwartz, 1977).

The original papers by White and his associates contain more
detail on some ideas, and more examples. We discuss in detail
only the most important concepts. Our purpose is to clarify
topics that received insufficient emphasis in the original papers.
Because many of the ideas used in blockmodeling are new and unfamiliar, we have provided a glossary of terms in an appendix.

II. BASICS

A. *Blockmodeling and Social Networks*

Blockmodeling uses information on relations between units of
a social system.[2] The raw information for each relation is
reported as a sociomatrix, which is simply a square matrix containing 0s and 1s. The ith row and column represent one
person, and the (i,j)th entry of the matrix is 1 if person i is
in a particular type of social relationship with person j; otherwise, it is 0.

A blockmodel analysis typically begins with a set of k sociomatrices that represent the patterns formed by k different kinds
of ties among n people. The ties that are analyzed in any given
study are those that the researcher believes to be substantively
important; typical ties are reports of interaction (see often,
work with), obligation (owe money, receive orders), and

[2]*Blockmodeling can be done on systems in which the initial
units are not people but entities such as organizations, geographical areas, etc. See also Section VI.*

structural relation (teacher of, member of the same group). Each
tie is represented by a different sociomatrix.

B. The Algebraic Approach

Instead of dealing with relations among people, the blockmodeler first partitions the population into a set of "structurally equivalent" subgroups, or blocks, such that the people in a
block have approximately the same pattern of relations with themselves and with people in other blocks. The partitioning yields a
set of k "image" matrices (one for each type of tie in the study),
which are only m by m, where m equals the number of blocks
produced by the partitioning. The blocking algorithm must rearrange the rows and columns of all k sociomatrices so that people
with the same relational profiles appear together along the
columns (and, thus, along the rows, too). Figure 1 shows the partitioning of a hypothetical sociomatrix into structurally equivalent subgroups. We assign a 1 or 0 to each submatrix (intersection between blocks) depending on the density of 1s or 0s in
the corresponding permuted submatrix. Thus in the image matrix
we assign a 1 to the (i,j) th entry for tie r if people in subgroup
i usually have relation r with people in subgroup j; otherwise,
the entry is 0.[3]

Note that the focus now is no longer on persons. We are not
concerned about, say, person 1's individual relationship with
person 4. Instead, we are concerned with the relationship of
block 1 (persons 1,2, and 3) with either itself, or block 2
(persons 4 and 5) or block 3 (persons 6 and 7). The concept of
structural equivalence is essentially the same as the structuralist concept of a social role (Boorman and White, 1976, pp. 1388-
1393). Thus a block empirically defines a social role. By

---

[3] *Assignment of 1s and 0s is discussed in Section III.A.*

A. *Partitioned sociomatrix*

	1	2	3	4	5	6	7
1	0	1	1	0	0	0	0
2	1	0	1	0	0	0	0
3	0	1	1	0	0	0	0
4	0	0	0	0	1	0	0
5	0	0	0	1	0	0	0
6	1	1	0	1	0	0	0
7	0	0	1	0	1	1	1

B. *Image matrix*

	I	II	III
I	1	0	0
II	0	1	0
III	1	1	1

Fig. 1. Partitioning of a sociomatrix and the corresponding image matrix.

dealing with ties between roles instead of individuals, block-modeling (1) incorporates an often-used element of sociological theory, the social role, to discuss aspects of group structure, and (2) enables researchers to analyze relationships in larger groups.[4]

1. *Compounding.* Compounding relations by matrix multiplication is an old sociometric technique. Katz (1947) recommended it as a way to discover cliques, and Coleman (1961) used it in a connectivity analysis of a sociomatrix of choices in a junior high school. White (1963) developed compounding further by using

[4]*See Section IV.*

it with different types of ties; this conception enabled him to
use compounds as representations of complex relations, whether
direct or very indirect.

Boolean matrix multiplication of images is the way compounding
is implemented in blockmodeling. This is simply ordinary (inner
product) matrix multiplication, with the added proviso that if the
result of taking the inner product of the *ith* row of the first
matrix, and the *jth* row of the second matrix is nonzero, the compounded matrix has an $(i,j)th$ entry of 1; otherwise, this entry
is 0. Figure 2 shows two image matrices from a study of scientific
specialities (Mullins *et al.*, 1977). The compound of the two
images is also shown. Notice that since the matrices B and C are
$m \times m$, the compound BC is also $m \times m$. The 1 in the first row and
second column of BC indicates that people in block I of this
research speciality area tend to know well people in at least one

	I	II	III	IV			I	II	III	IV
I	1	1	0	0		I	1	1	0	0
II	1	0	0	0		II	1	1	0	0
III	0	0	0	0		III	0	0	0	0
IV	0	0	0	0		IV	0	0	0	0

Know well (B)   *Coauthor (C)*

	I	II	III	IV
I	1	1	0	0
II	1	1	0	0
III	0	0	0	0
IV	0	0	0	0

Compound (B*C)

*Fig. 2. Two image matrices, and their compound, obtained by
Boolean Matrix multiplication (Mullins et al., 1977).*

of the blocks, who in turn coauthor papers with people in block II; other 1s are similarly interpreted.

2. *The Role Structure*. Blockmodeling represents role structure in a "semigroup." Formally, a semigroup is a set S, and an associated binary relation "*" defined on pairs of S. S must be closed under the * operation; that is, for every a, b, in S, $a*b$ is also in S. In addition, * must be associative; that is, for every a, b, c in S, $(a*b)*c = a*(b*c)$. The semigroup of interest (which we denote by R) contains the k $m \times m$ matrices, called generators, and all the *unique $m \times m$* products of Boolean matrix multiplication. The set S will therefore have only a finite number of elements (though this number may be uncomfortably large). The associated relation * will be the compounding operation.

The semigroup R is generated by creating all possible words (generators, compounds of generators and other words, etc.). R can be represented by strings of compounded generators; for example, if we use "1" and "2" as our generators, the set of all possible words consists of such elements as: 1, 2, 2*1, 1*2, 1*2*2, and so forth. There are infinitely many such distinct strings, even with only one generator; for example, 1, 1*1, 1*1*1, and so on. However, there will not be infinitely many different matrix representations of the various compounds. If blocking yields image matrices that are $m \times m$, there can be at most 2^{m^2} distinct image matrices (e.g., for $m = 4$, 65536); and, depending on the original generator, they could consist entirely of 0s. We can still create an infinite number of words, but they all will have the same image matrix. In that case, our role structure R would have but one element, the zero matrix. Thus in general, R is created by using the set of generator matices and the compounding operation, forming new words (new matrices) until the matrices associated with those words create no new matrices. R then consists of the set of unique $m \times m$ matrices that result, and the compounding relation.

TABLE I. Three Image Matrices (Generators) from the study of Connections among Members of a Scientific Specialty[a]

	I	II	III	IV			I	II	III	IV
I	1	1	0	0		I	1	1	0	0
II	1	0	0	0		II	1	1	0	0
III	0	0	0	0		III	0	0	0	0
IV	0	0	0	0		IV	0	0	0	0

Know well (B)   *Coauthor (C)*

	I	II	III	IV
I	1	0	0	0
II	1	1	1	1
III	1	0	0	0
IV	1	0	0	0

Student of (D)

[a]*From Mullins et al. (1977).*

A less trivial example of a role structure is shown in Figure 3. The three generators (see Table 1) B (know well), C (coauthor), and D (student of) generate a role structure with four additional distinct 4 x 4 binary matrices, for a total of 7. Figure 4 shows part of a "multiplication table" for the semigroup R. It shows what happens when we apply the compounding operation to all pairs of matrices in R. The (i,j) th entry of the table is the matrix resulting from $i*j$. Of course, if R has a large number of elements, it is not possible to display the actual matrices either along the rows and columns, or in the body of the table. In practice, as R is generated one assigns a new identifier (letter or number) to each new matrix produced by compounding previously existing words (Figure 3). By convention,

x	B	C	D	DB	BD	CD	U
B	C	C	BD	C	CD	CD	CD
C	C	C	CD	C	CD	CD	CD
D	DB	DB	D	DB	U	U	U
DB	DB	DB	U	DB	U	U	U
BD	C	C	BD	C	CD	CD	CD
CD	C	C	CD	C	CD	CD	CD
U	DB	DB	U	DB	U	U	U

(a)

x	1	2	3	4	5	6	7
1	2	2	5	2	6	6	6
2	2	2	6	2	6	6	6
3	4	4	3	4	7	7	7
4	4	4	7	4	7	7	7
5	3	3	5	3	6	6	6
6	3	3	6	3	6	6	6
7	4	4	7	4	7	7	7

(b)

Fig. 3. Two alternative representations of the role structure multiplication table created by the three generators shown
in Table I. (a) Letter products (B = know well, C = coauthor,
D = student of; others are all compounds. (b) Numerical
products (1 = know well, 2 = coauthor, 3 = student of).

	1 1 0 0	1 1 0 0	1 0 0 0	
x	1 0 0 0	1 1 0 0	1 1 1 1	. . . .
	0 0 0 0	0 0 0 0	1 0 0 0	
	0 0 0 0	0 0 0 0	1 0 0 0	

1 1 0 0	1 1 0 0	1 1 0 0	1 1 1 1	
1 1 0 0	1 1 0 0	1 1 0 0	1 0 0 0	. . . .
0 0 0 0	0 0 0 0	0 0 0 0	0 0 0 0	
0 0 0 0	0 0 0 0	0 0 0 0	0 0 0 0	
1 1 0 0	1 1 0 0	1 1 0 0	1 1 1 1	
1 1 0 0	1 1 0 0	1 1 0 0	1 1 1 1	. . . .
0 0 0 0	0 0 0 0	0 0 0 0	0 0 0 0	
0 0 0 0	0 0 0 0	0 0 0 0	0 0 0 0	
1 0 0 0	1 1 0 0	1 1 0 0	1 0 0 0	
1 1 1 1	1 1 0 0	1 1 0 0	1 1 1 1	. . . .
1 0 0 0	1 1 0 0	1 1 0 0	1 0 0 0	
1 0 0 0	1 1 0 0	1 1 0 0	1 0 0 0	
.	.	.	.	
.	.	.	.	
.	.	.	.	
.	.	.	.	

Fig. 4. Partial multiplication table for role structure shown in Fig. 3. If there were room, one could represent semigroup elements as matrices in any multiplication table. The compact symbolic forms of Fig. 3 are more practical.

generators are often given the numbers 1 through k (or k different
letters), and additional words (matrices) are labeled by larger
consecutive integers (or other letters). Also, by convention, if
letters are used to identify generators, new words are named by
the *first* set of generators that produce a matrix with a new
pattern of 0s and 1s. Thus in Figure 3a, DB is a new word
(matrix), the first instance of that word in this role structure.

Notice that the multiplication table for this role structure
demonstrates the closure of R under compounding. We could use
Figure 3 (either representation) to form compounds of any length
whatever, and the result would always be found somewhere in the
body of the table. Because in addition the compounding operation
is associative, the R of Figure 3 is indeed a semigroup.

C. Available Programs and Texts.

Four main programs, with assorted auxiliaries, are available.
These programs are titled BLOCKER, GENSG, JNTHOM, and CONCOR.
At the moment, all programs are written in VM 370 APL, for the
IBM 370 time-sharing system.[5] CONCOR, though, can be simulated
with any correlation program.

CONCOR, described in Breiger, Boorman, and Arabie (1976), will
block the initial input data inductively. Listings of CONCOR
are available from Breiger. BLOCKER is described in Heil and
White (1976), which gives a complete listing. This program will
create blockings based on initial hypotheses about block configuration. GENSG (which will generate the role-structure semigroup)
and JNTHOM (which compares role structures) are currently
available only from Harrison White and his colleagues at Harvard.

[5] *APL as APLUM is available for the CDC 6000 series. There
may be other versions.*

III.   PROCEDURE

A.   *The Process of Blocking*

   Figure 5 shows different ways to block data. BLOCKER might
be termed "deductive." It takes as input a set of hypothesized
images, which the investigator expects to find on the basis of
some theoretical considerations. The program then looks for
permutations of the original matrices that could fit the blocking.
The analyst can specify constraints like the minimum number of
people that might be in one block, and the number of blocks.
Examples of BLOCKER are in Heil and White (1976) and White, *et al.*
(1976). The difficulty with a deductive procedure is that often
(or even typically), the investigator has no hypotheses about the
composition of blocks. We suggest that as more experience is
gained with blockmodeling, it will become easier to form such
hypotheses, however.
   Other techniques are inductive. The CONCOR algorithm takes
as input the set of all k sociomatrices. For purposes of input,
these matrices are stacked one on top of the other, into what
amounts to a kn x n matrix (assuming n people in the group under
study). The column vectors of the stacked matrix are then
correlated to produce an n x n matrix. The columns of the new
matrix are then recorrelated, and so on, until these correlations
converge to +1 or -1 (usually within a few iterations). The
result is that people who are more or less structurally equivalent
appear to be perfectly positively correlated in the final correlation matrix. Note that:
   (1)   The initial input need not be binary matrices; any
         index will do, if it reflects the strength of the
         ties between people in the group.

   (2)   An iterated matrix may be produced from any ordinary
         correlation program that will take the kn x n input
         matrix as input.

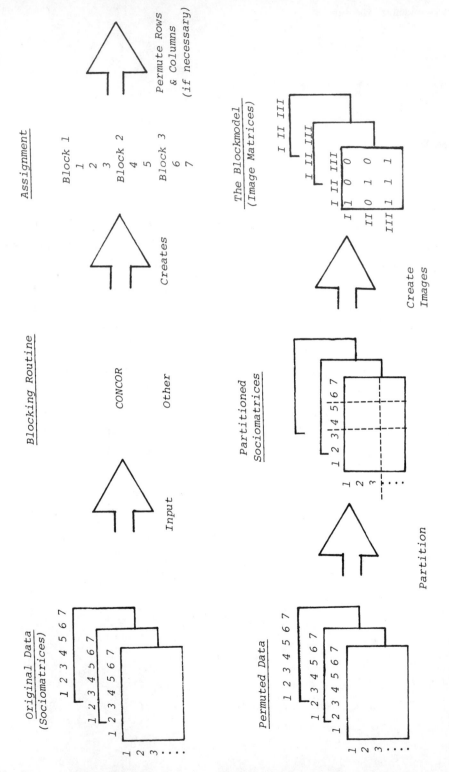

Fig. 5. The blocking process (see also Fig. 1).

CONCOR splits the group into two subgroups, having all plus correlations within and minus correlations between. The last operation is to permute rows and columns of the original n x n matrices. The new arrangement is the same for all matrices, of course. Structurally equivalent individuals now are blocked together along the rows (and columns) of the permuted matrix; this matrix now shows relationships between these first rough blocks, via submatrices filled with 1s and 0s (similar to the submatrices partitioned off in Figure 1). The correlating and splitting process is then continued within blocks until a useful solution is found.[6] The investigator hopes for the emergence of "intuitively sensible" blocks, but the blockmodel image that will have the most utility for a given study may not be obvious. Examples produced by CONCOR appear in White *et al.* (1976). Further description of the CONCOR algorithm is in Breiger, *et al.* (1975). Examples produced by a correlation program are in Mullins *et al.* (1977).

With inductive programs, density of ties must determine whether a 1 or a 0 is entered to "stand for" the relations of a submatrix (for example, in Figure 1, are the six 1s in the submatrix formed by the intersection of block I with itself sufficient to call this a 1 in the image matrix?). Sometimes it is suggested that a submatrix must include only 0s if it is to be assigned a 0; even a single 1 requires a 1 in the image matrix. More commonly (indeed, in most of the examples in White, *et al.* 1976), a higher cutoff density (proportion of 1s in the submatrix) is proposed. Mullins *et al.* (1977) assigned a 1 to all submatrices with a choice density above the mean for the whole matrix, and a 0 otherwise. Boorman and White (1976) show that radically different results do not occur unless the cutoff levels are also

[6]*This shows that if one uses a correlation program other than CONCOR, it will be necessary to write another program to perform the splitting.*

radically different. At this time, there is little reason to
pick one criterion over another *a priori*. Until the clear
superiority of one can be demonstrated, investigators should
choose 1-0 criteria to fit the needs of their studies. For
example, in research on communication, the existence of just one
tie in a submatrix may justify a 1 in the image matrix, because
we could say that there was an informational tie between positions.
In contrast, if only one person from a given block selects one
person from another block as friend, a 1 in the image matrix may
not be justified because the single friendship probably does not
mean that, in general, people in the one block tend to like
people in the other.

The CONCOR algorithm is not indispensible to blockmodeling.
Schwartz (1977) shows that mathematically the algorithm is
obscure, inefficient, and hard to interpret. White *et al.* (1976)
have shown that it works well, but it may not be the best method.
Any reasonable clustering method that takes into account all *k*
types of ties simultaneously is, in principle, acceptable. In
fact, it is reassuring that other quite different techniques (for
example, multidimensional scaling) produce results very similar to
CONCOR (White *et al.*, 1976, p. 737). See Bailey (1975) for a discussion of clustering methods.

The final set of blockmodel images may be defended on
substantive grounds even if they are not created by an algorithm
with well-known properties. For example, Laumann and Pappi (1976)
used their knowledge of a community in making an *a priori* choice
of occupations as blocks. Later they justified this choice with
data that demonstrate the internal coherence of occupational
groups.

The role structure is the Boolean matrix semigroup that is
generated by applying the compounding operation to the original
generators. Table 1 shows three image matrices (generators)
produced by CONCOR; they come from the same study of scientific

specialties. Algorithm GENSG takes as input the k generator
matrices and then creates a multiplication table for the role
structure. Figure 3a shows the multiplication table for the role
structure generated by the three image matrices of Table 1.[7]

The multiplication table for a role structure presents a
"picture" of the role structure. However, the role structure
may be quite large, and may contain many different matrices. The
16 generator matrices from Mullins *et al.* form a semigroup of
175 elements, clearly too many to discern much of a pattern.
Even the seven-element role structure shown in Figure 3 may be a
more detailed picture of the role structure than is desirable.
In general, roles structures must be simplified before we can
answer questions about them; if we think of the role structure as
a set of data about relations in a group, then this simplification
is a process of data reduction.

B. Analysis of Role Structures

A few simple properties of role structures may provide rough
indications of what the role structure "looks like." For example,
the size of a semigroup indicates general complexity (the seven
element semigroup shown in Figure 3 is relatively small, and therefore not very complex). Also the average "rank" of the elements
in the semigroup (i.e., the number of 1s in the matrix) can be
computed easily. If the elements in a system are mostly of high
rank, then the relations are not "restrictive"; that is, most

---

[7]*There are two ways to show multiplication tables. One is a
$K \times L$ array, with L the size of the semigroup; this procedure is
nonredundant. The second way is $L \times L$; this table is somewhat
more redundant but sometimes easier to read because it shows at
a glance the result of compounding any two words in the semigroup.*

blocks participate in most relationships (on the average, elements
of the scientific specialty role structure shown in Fig. 3 have
about 7 of 16 possible 1s, which is only moderately restrictive).
In contrast, if element ranks are generally low, then the lack of
pervasive relationships suggests a poorly integrated system. In
either case, extremely high or low numbers of 1s, with little
variation, would indicate the need for a different criterion for
assigning 1s. As with ordinary scaling procedures, there must be
enough variation to permit distinction among cases.

Other analytic devices allow us to say more about even large
and complicated role structures.

1. Inclusion. In Figure 6 we see that B is included in C, because C has all the ties that B has, plus (in this case) one more.
In contrast, even though it has fewer ties than D, B cannot be
included in D because B has a tie (at entry [1,2]) that D does
not have. It is not necessary for any pair of elements of R to

	I	II	III	IV
I	1	1	0	0
II	1	0	0	0
III	0	0	0	0
IV	0	0	0	0

is included in

	I	II	III	IV
I	1	1	0	0
II	1	1	0	0
III	0	0	0	0
IV	0	0	0	0

Know well (B)   *Coauthor (C)*

	I	II	III	IV
I	1	1	0	0
II	1	0	0	0
III	0	0	0	0
IV	0	0	0	0

is not included in

	I	II	III	IV
I	1	0	0	0
II	1	1	1	1
III	1	0	0	0
IV	1	0	0	0

Know well (B)   *Student of (D)*

*Fig. 6. Examples of inclusion (B ⊂ C) and noninclusion (B ⊄ D)
(Mullins et al., 1977).*

be comparable via inclusion. For example, we saw that B is not
included in D, but neither (obviously) is D included in B.

From the elements of R we can construct an "inclusion lattice."
This structure is not a lattice in the strict mathematical sense
(Birkoff, 1967); it is only a picture of the partially ordered set
of elements of R, with inclusion as the ordering relation. Figure
7 shows the inclusion lattice for the scientific specialty example
mentioned earlier.

The lattice can provide information that aids the search for
an overall structure of relations in the group being studied
(Mullins, 1977). For example, longer chains suggest a single principle of social organization. Blocks are systematically discarded
as one proceeds down the inclusion chain. Several unconnected
chains in the same lattice suggest that different principles probably control different types of relations. Length of jumps between elements in a chain (e.g., from rank 16 to rank 8) shows
if there is an overall organizing principle for participation in
various relationships; then larger numbers of words would appear
at levels represented by the deletion of entire rows or columns

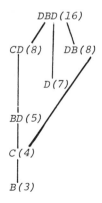

Fig. 7. Inclusion lattice for scientific specialty example
(see Fig. 3 for role structure). Parenthesized numbers are ranks
of the different elements.

from elements higher in the lattice. In Figure 7 the level that
contains eight 1s has the most elements, which suggests that two
entire rows or columns have been removed. This pattern is consistent with the hypothesis that all blocks unanimously fail to
include a given group or groups (in our example, groups III and
IV) in a more restrictive relationship. In contrast, if the lattice has about the same number of elements in each successively
smaller level (with fewer 1s), then blocks probably are making
their own decisions about relations without concern for consensus
with members of other blocks.

     It may also be useful to check the position of all generators
and compounding patterns of single generators. For example, if
most of the compounds of a given generator are close together,
then there may be a sense in which that type of tie is "conditioning" some other relations. Thus any compound that involves
colleague relations may have a pattern similar to that of col-
leagueship. Also, the location of generators *vis a vis* each other
and other words can give the investigator a general idea of how
similar different types of relations are (e.g., notice that in
Figure 7, "know well" B, and "coauthor" C are close in the lattice; they are also both quite restrictive and show a similar
pattern of relationships between blocks). Sometimes it is useful
to simplify the initial stages of lattice analysis by looking at
word lengths of less than or equal to two elements. It is intuitively plausible that longer chains will, in general, be interpretable as more obscure indirect relationships, and therefore
will be less useful to the analysis. Such a procedure would
therefore seem to be a sensible place to start, especially if the
role structure semigroup is quite large.

     Gross indicators of the sort discussed thus far usually re-
quire a deeper look into the actual nature of the ties and compounds involved. Thus even in a lattice that appears to be
highly interconnected, the connections between hierarchical in-

clusion chains may not be interesting, i.e., the structure may
be more unidimensionally ordered than it appears. If a generator
appears with most of its compounds, this fact only indicates that
something may be going on: exactly what depends on an analysis
that uses the substantive interpretation of the specific relations. In short, analysis of the inclusion lattice is basically a *substantive* interpretation of interesting structure.
The above-noted suggestions only help the investigator to notice
potentially interesting facets of the structure.

2. *Formal Simplification through Homomorphism.* We have discussed using the lattice to help make substantive observations
about particular structural properties of a role structure.
Boorman and White (1976) used it to help make more formal simplifications, which are based on the notion of inclusion. Inclusion can permit inferences about a role structure. For example, in the role structure shown in Figure 3, BC = C, which is
to say that BC ⊂ C and C ⊂ BC (according to the definition of the
equality of two sets). BC ⊂ C means that if block i has at least
one block h that it "knows well," and in turn tends to coauthor
with block j, then block i tends to coauthor with block j too.
Conversely, since C ⊂ BC, if block i coauthors with block j, then i
has at least one position h that it "knows well" whose members
also coauthor with j. Boorman and White suggest that this kind
of information (which may be gleaned from the inclusion lattice)
is often of considerable interest in and of itself. Indeed, various possibilities exist: we might hypothesize that certain
characteristic inclusions result from certain properties of the
group under study, or that groups will differ with regard to
certain important types of inclusions, and so forth. In such
analyses there is vast potential that has scarcely been tapped.
Some kind of outside theoretical perspective may inform such
structural analysis; for example, one might draw on an exchange

theoretic framework to explain the kind of interblock relations represented by C ⊂ BC.

Boorman and White were seeking a more sweeping and self-consistent way to simplify entire role structures, however. They pointed out (Boorman and White, 1976, p. 1399) that analyzing interesting *parts* of role structures is difficult, since what is and is not interesting may not be obvious, and since much of the apparent information in a role structure multiplication table is actually not informative. Their objective was a technique that would reduce the number of elements in a role structure in such a way that the *essential* structural properties became apparent. Such a simplification would allow role structures to be compared to other role structures, or to certain "canonical" structures that are easily interpretable, and may be expected to arise frequently (called "target tables," and discussed further below).

What form might this simplification take? Previous discussion shows that inclusion relations are "close" to semigroup equations (like BC = C) in the sense that the latter implies mutual inclusion. On the other hand, if we actually had only one-way inclusion, but the two semigroup elements only differed by one or two ties, we might be inclined to treat the two elements as equal for all intents and purposes. In essence, Boorman and White proposed that elements of R that are close to each other in the inclusion lattice (and therefore, possibly similar in patterns of 1s and 0s) ought to be studied to determine whether they were different forms of the same thing, and could therefore be reduced to the stronger of the two. Alternatively, the two elements may be treated as essentially equal due to some theoretical criterion. This equating procedure is more likely to apply to equations that involve both compounds and generators, while the "similar pattern" criterion usually will apply to similar generators or very simple relations. Closeness in the inclusion lattice is a device for singling out potential equations, but it seems to us that a theoretical criterion, where available, is preferable. Availability will depend on the particular application.

Imposing equations on R is, essentially, a process of simplification. In equating elements of R, we decide to treat them as the same element, and thus, reduce the number of elements we have to deal with.

If we now add one additional restriction, we have Boorman and White's idea of the proper type of simplification. Consider B and C, two elements of the role structure R shown in Fig. 3, and create a new simplified semigroup R' in which B and C are equated (call this new composite element "equivalence class" C_1, which now represents B and C). It is reasonable to expect C_1 to form compounds in R' in a manner consistent with the way in which B and C formed compounds in R. As a simple case (Fig. 8) suppose that in R, B*D creates a certain compound. Then if B and C are to have the same characteristics in R', C*D must create the same compound as B*D in R'. Unfortunately, as Figure 3 shows, B*B = BD, while C*D = CD, and in R, BD ≠ CD. But the problem is solved by letting BD = CD = C_2, a second equivalence class, in R'. In this way Boorman and White's criterion is satisfied: we will have two equivalence classes, and the criterion simply requires that elements of C_1, when compounded, create elements in C_2. Formally Boorman and White require that simplifications of R be homomorphic images of R. Observe that the homomorphism criterion essentially requires a certain type of consistency between more and less simple versions of R. As the last example shows, imposing an equation to simplify R will, generally, logically imply that certain other equations must hold. In the case presented, letting B = C logically implied that in R', BD would also have to equal CD. This followed from the two equations (B*D = BD and C*D = CD) and the homomorphism requirement. Notice that in this case BD = CD is the *only* other equation implied, so that the complete, simplified multiplication table for R' may be easily derived. This is shown

John M. Light and Nicholas C. Mullins

		C_I		C_2				
		B	C	BD	CD	D	DB	DBD (U)
C_1	(B	C	C	CD	CD	BD	C	CD
	(C	C	C	CD	CD	CD	C	CD
C_2	(BD	C	C	CD	CD	BD	C	CD
	(CD	C	C	CD	CD	CD	C	CD
	D	DB	DB	U	U	D	DB	U
	DB	DB	DB	U	U	U	DB	U
	DBD (U)	DB	DB	U	U	U	DB	U

(a)

x	C_1	C_2	D	DB	DBD (U)
C_1	C_1	C_2	C_2	C_1	C_2
C_2	C_1	C_2	C_2	C_1	C_2
D	DB	U	U	DB	U
DB	DB	U	U	DB	U
DBD (U)	DB	U	U	DB	U

(b)

Fig. 8. Homomorphic simplification of a role structure.
(a) Multiplication table for role structure R (From Fig. 3a)
permuted to put "equated" words together for a homomorphic simplification. R has seven elements. Note that after C_2 is defined, elements of C_1 are interchangeable in the sense that they
compound with other elements of R to form the same words or
classes (C_1,C_2) of words. (b) Multiplication table for role
structure R´, a homomorphic image of R. R´ has only five
elements.

in Figure 8b. In Figure 8a notice how the definition of C_1 and C_2 insures that the homomorphism criterion is met: for example, if any element of C_1 is compounded with any element of C_2, the result is an element of C_2. Thus in essence, in R', $C_1 * C_2 = C_2$, which is of course shown in Figure 8b.[8]

Usually there will be many homomorphic images of a given role structure. For example, we could always create tables of different sizes, and even within tables of a given size, there will be many ways in which elements can be equated and still be homomorphic images of the original R (Boorman and White, 1976, p. 1404). Thus even the homomorphism restriction does not automatically produce a "best" simplification of R, since there are many such simplifications.

There may be no best homomorphism. Indeed, the very point of a simplification is to ignore certain aspects of the original role structure in favor of others. However, there are a few guidelines:

(1) Impose equations, as we have been suggesting, on the basis of closeness of words in the role structure's inclusion lattice. This relatively mechanical procedure is designed only to aid the process of equating words for theoretical reasons (Boorman and White, 1976, p. 1408).

(2) Alternatively, concentrate not just on abstracting the salient feature of one particular role structure but

[8] *Actually, Boorman and White (1976, p. 1419) add one more restriction to these homomorphisms: that they be "generator-preserving." That is, for any generator g in R, homomorphic reduction mapping H must be such that $H(g) = g$ in R'. This additional restriction creates a serious problem in the concept of* joint *reductions, discussed below.*

also on comparing one role structure to another, or to
a "target" role structure. We now consider the latter
approach.

3. *Joint Reduction*. The "joint reduction" of two role structures is the largest multiplication table that is a homomorphic
image of both structures. Obviously, if the two structures are
identical, then either is the joint reduction. However, the
joint reduction may be vastly different from either of the
original tables. A computer program JNTHOM creates joint reductions. In a sense, the joint multiplication table represents the
structure that the two role structures have in common. This may
range from everything (if they are identical) to nothing (if the
joint reduction is degenerate).[9]

Joint reduction may be used on any two role structures that
have the same generators (or similar enough generators so that
generators in the two groups can be equated).[10] The data base may

[9]*This interpretation is claimed by Boorman and White (1976,
p. 1406). However, Bonacich (1978) has argued that since the
Boorman and White joint reduction has equations which are true in
either one of the original semigroups, and possibly even in
neither one alone, it really represents not their common structure so much as the union of their structure. Bonacich offers an
alternative which has a more natural interpretation as true common
structure. This is an important issue for future blockmodelers
to consider.*

[10]*In an earlier footnote we observed that Boorman and White
restrict their attention to generator-preserving (GP) homomorphisms. However, Bonacich (1978) has shown that the joint GP
reduction of two generator-identified semigroups may not exist!
This problem vanishes if the GP restriction is dropped. Thus the
wisdom of requiring GP homomorphisms is open to serious question.*

be two different groups of people, or it may be the same group
analyzed in slightly different ways. For example, Boorman and
White (1976, pp. 1426-1433) used JNTHOM to test the robustness of
various aspects of blocking (their evidence suggests that results
are not undesirably sensitive to choice of blocking criterion).

Reduction of role structures also may involve the hypothesized structures, or "target tables," mentioned earlier. These
are multiplication tables that are quite small and rather easily
interpretable. These tables have been extensively considered for
2×2 cases (Boorman and White, 1976, p. 1413), and somewhat less
considered for 3×3 cases (Boorman and White, 1976, pp. 1414-1415;
see also Schwartz, 1975). Tables exist that correspond to such
interesting structures as classical balance theory, weaker forms
of balance, special influence of particular generators at the
beginning or end of "words" in the semigroup, and the like. Such
structures are given a more thorough treatment by Boorman and
White (1976).

One may attempt to reduce a pair (or more) of role structures
to a given hypothesized (target) structure (to see if the two
share that type of structure) or simply try to reduce a single
table to the target structure. In all cases, the hypothesized
structure is the goal of the reduction. To say that it is possible to reduce a role structure to a particular target table
amounts to saying that the result of a joint reduction will be
the target table.

Finally, it is possible to measure the "distance" between
two role structures by using the joint reduction. Boorman and
White (1976, p. 1422) defined distance in terms of the amount
of simplification needed to create a joint reduction from two role
structures. Distance is directly useful in determining the relative similarity of different pairs of role structures; in addition, one may use dimensional analysis (for example, multidimensional scaling) to place the different role structures

in some appropriate Euclidian space. This approach may be
especially useful for uncovering latent structure in role structures.

IV. CRITIQUE AND COMMENT ON ANALYSIS TECHNIQUES

This section offers suggestions for the analysis of role
structures. The suggestions are informed ones; all are based on
experience with analysis of actual groups (see the applications
mentioned on the first page of this chapter). However, their
usefulness will vary with the specific application.

Because role structures are somewhat unfamiliar and often complex objects, virtually any technique that shows pattern in a
role structure, however tentatively, seems worthy of attention.
We have metnioned a set of somewhat *ad hoc* procedures of this
sort: size of the role structure, "rank" of elements, examination of the inclusion lattice, and so forth. We have noted that
such procedures are neither necessary nor sufficient for dis-
covering interesting patterns in a role structure--they are
merely indications of *possible* interesting patterns. On the other
hand, such procedures have been profitably employed by Mullins
(1977) for the study of scientific specialties, and some of the
examples in Boorman and White (1976) are also suggestive. In
most cases, these more informal techniques seem to be a sensible
first step in analyzing a role structure. Afterwards, creation
of homomorphic images is the strategy suggested. But we note
that even homomorphic simplification of a role structure is in a
sense a hypothesis (Levine and Mullins, 1978); it may turn out
that other simplifications give better results. However, examples
appearing in Boorman and White (1976) indicate that is is useful.

It is also worthwhile to try to discover abstract and general
features of various types of role structures. Target tables offer
one such approach. Boorman and White (1976) present examples

where some of these characteristic structures emerge; and in time, investigators may find themselves able to compare important aspects of group structure in terms of various target tables. Multidimensional scaling of different role structures, based on their "algebraic distance," is another way in which general features of latent structure might be recognized. Groups which are structurally similar in significant ways should tend to cluster in such analyses (Boorman and White, 1976, p. 1427).

V. EXTENSIONS

A. *Blockmodeling on Groups Other than People*

Blockmodeling can analyze structures composed of basic units other than people. For example, we might divide a large urban area into census tracts, and define relations between them in terms of economic interrelations (e.g., people who live in tract *i* and work in tract *j*) or social relations (people in tract *i* who have friends in tract *j*), and the like (Hecht, 1978). A blockmodel analysis of such data would yield something formally identical to a role structure, although the similarity to the structuralist notion of role would no longer be directly applicable. This suggests that one could not, to use this example, examine the structure of intertract relations as if the basic units were people. It may be that a completely different set of organizing principles would apply; however, surely this would be an interesting question for such a study.

B. *Large Datasets*

In principle, there is no reason why blockmodeling could not be done on a group consisting of a very large number of people (or other basic units), perhaps millions of them. At present, the basic problem is practical: Computers cannot perform any kind of blocking on a group of more than about a hundred.

One alternative approach to this problem would be to select "blocks" on the basis of some preexisting criteria [as Laumann and Pappi (1976) did in their study of community decision making], and justify the choice on the basis of other data. The analysis then proceeds by establishing ties between these blocks (Laumann and Pappi did this by survey, to estimate what proportion of members of one occupational group chose members of another as, for example, friends), and then generating the semigroup in the usual way.

Another possibility is to make use of network sampling methods (Granovetter, 1976), and estimate the composition of blocks in the population under study. Boorman and White (1976) offer evidence that blockmodel analysis is quite robust, so that sampling fluctuations might not distort the actual picture of the role structure. On the other hand, methods for network sampling are at present not well developed, and some innovative work in sampling theory might be necessary before this option is realistic.

A third possibility is architectural. Persons in small groups are analyzed and the roles are determined. Using this information, samples of role participants are collected and blocks of roles are created. The roles created by this process are aggregates of roles and may relate to organizational or community structure.

VI. CONCLUSION

Our intent in this chapter has been to give the reader a sense of what blockmodeling is, what it can be used for, and how it is actually carried out. We reiterate that the original papers by White and his associates (particularly Boorman and White, 1976) have many more examples and detailed discussions; we have emphasized the overall organization of the technique, and have focused on issues that were perhaps unclear in these original papers.

We believe that blockmodeling can be naturally integrated with existing sociological theory in several ways. First, even if we are eventually able to model social structures with generative models (Levine and Mullins, 1978), questions still exist about *why* certain rules of role organization hold, and probably will have to be answered in nonblockmodel language. Also, predicting when certain types of structures will arise seems to lead naturally to incorporating other existing theory. Candidates for use in such endeavors include exchange theory, symbolic interaction, attribution, cognitive consistency/balance, and probably many others. The point is this: Blockmodeling gives (1) a language with which to describe social structure, and (2) some techniques for abstracting the most important aspects of that structure. It can produce a new theory about structural relations, because for the first time, one is able to capture empirically all of the relational information implied by generator relations. Further, it permits modeling at the structural level, in which the investigator gives rules whereby the role structure can be generated. However, structural analysis has been guided fruitfully in the past by at least some of the abovementioned theoretical perspectives, and there is no reason why they cannot be drawn upon to aid blockmodel analysis. In fact, it is highly desirable to see how much of group structure (as displayed in a role structure) we can explain with existing theory.

ACKNOWLEDGMENTS

We wish to thank Carolyn Mullins for editorial work and Jamesina Edwards, Peggy Clarke, and Carol Schmiedeskamp for typing.

APPENDIX

Glossary of Terms

Block: A set of structurally equivalent persons (or other units).

Block matrix: *See* image matrix.

Blockmodel: The set of *m*-square matrices; one for each relation being modeled.

Blocking: The procedure for finding or trying to verify a partition of the original group of persons into structurally equivalent subgroups (blocks).

Boolean matrix multiplication: If A and B are two *m* × *m* binary matrices, then the (i,j)th entry of the project AB is 1 if and only if the inner product of the *i*th row of A and the *j*th column of B is not zero.

Compounding: *See* concatenation.

Concatenation: A procedure that demonstrates a link from one person or block to another through a third person or block. Boolean matrix multiplication operationalizes this procedure.

Degenerate reductions: Simple role tables derived from homomorphic simplification of larger role tables that are uninformative (for example, if all the elements of the reduction are the same, one cannot discern any interesting structural information).

Distance: The sum of entropy measures between two role structures and their joint reduction [discussed at greater length by Boorman and White (1976, p. 1422)]. Basically, the more either role structure has been simplified to produce the joint reduction, the larger the entropy measure between that role structure and the joint reduction.

Element: A member of a role structure, represented by a unique *m* × *m* binary matrix. Elements are either generators or compounds of generators. *See* word.

Equation: A statement of the form $W_1 = W_2$, where W_1 and W_2 are
   elements of a role structure; it indicates that either the
   matrices for W_1 and W_2 are identical, or they are similar
   enough to warrant equating them theoretically. Equations
   lead to a simplification of role structures by creating
   equivalence classes of elements.

Equivalence class: A set of equated words in a role structure.
   Within the role structure they are expected to compound in the
   same way. This assumption is formalized in the notion of
   homomorphism.

Generator: The image matrix for one type of relation.

Homomorphic image: *See* homomorphism.

Homomorphic reduction: *See* homomorphism.

Homomorphism: A simplification of a role structure that preserves
   the compounding operation.

Image matrix: A square binary matrix of order m, where m is the
   number of blocks.

Inclusion: An image A is included in an image B if all of the
   ties in A are also in B.

Inclusion lattice: A summary of inclusions in a semigroup.

Joint homomorphism: The homomorphism between a revised reduced
   role structure and the full role structures for two (or more)
   groups.

Lattice: *See* inclusion lattice.

Matrix: *See* submatrix, image matrix, sociomatrix.

Multiplication table: The summary of products generated by the
   semigroup. It may either be g (the number of generators) by
   u (the number of elements), or u by u (a redundant but convenient form).

Rank: The number of 1s in a matrix of the role structure.

Reduced table: The multiplication table associated with a
   homomorphic reduction of a role structure.

Relation: A type of connection between two people (or other
   basic units).

Role structure: *See* semigroup.

Semigroup: The set of all unique *m*-square binary matrices that
   can be created by compounding a given set of generators to
   any length of word.

Sociomatrix (for relation R): A square binary matrix of order *n*
   (*n* = number of people or other basic units) with a 1 in the
   (*i,j*)th position of person *i* has relation R with person *j*, and
   0 otherwise. These matrices may also contain weights of relations, with a range from 0 (no relation) to 1 (full relation).

Structural equivalence: Two people (or other basic units) are
   structurally equivalent if they tend to have the same pattern
   of relations with all other people.

Submatrix: The intersection of two structurally equivalent subgroups (blocks) obtained by rearranging the rows and columns
   of all sociomatrices to place structurally equivalent persons
   together along rows and columns. Each submatrix is assigned a
   1 or a 0 image in the image matrix.

Target table: A simple multiplication table that can be easily
   interpreted as a structural property of a group.

Tie: A type of connection between blocks.

Unique matrix: A binary matrix with a pattern that (1) is not
   repeated elsewhere in the semigroup or (2) is the first of a
   series of repeated matrices.

Word: A generator or any compounding of generators. Note that
   every word is associated with an *m*-square binary matrix
   representation (not necessarily a unique matrix, however).

REFERENCES

Arabie, P., Boorman, S. & Levitt, P. Constructing blockmodels:
   How and why. *Journal of Mathematical Psychology*, 1978, *17*, 1,
   21-63.

Bailey, K. Cluster analysis. In D. Heise (Ed.), *Sociological Methodology 1975*. San Francisco: Jossey-Bass, 1975, 59-128.

Birkhoff, B. *Lattice Theory* (rev. ed). Providence, Rhode Island: American Mathematical Society, 1967.

Bonacich, P. The algebra of blockmodeling, unpublished manuscript, 1978.

Boorman, S., and White, H. Social structure from multiple networks. II. Role structures. *American Journal of Sociology, 81*, 6, 1384-1446.

Breiger, R. Career attributes and network structure: A blockmodel study of a biomedical research specialty. *American Sociological Review*, 1976, *41*, 1, 117-135.

Breiger, R., Boorman, S., Arabie, P. An algorithm for clustering relational data with applications to social network analysis and comparison with multidimensional scaling. *Journal of Mathematical Psychology*, 1975, *12*, 328-383.

Coleman, J. *The adolescent society*. Glencoe, Illinois: The Free Press, 1961.

Granovetter, M. Network sampling: Some first steps. *American Journal of Sociology*, 1976, *81*, 6, 1287-1303.

Groeneveld, L. Bureaucracy and the organization of science: A structural analysis of the national science foundation. Unpublished Ph.D. Dissertation, Indiana University, 1975.

Hecht, P. The social structure of urban space. Unpublished Ph.D., Dissertation, Indiana University, 1978.

Heil, G., and White, H. An algorithm for finding simultaneous homomorphic correspondences between graphs and their image graphs. *Behavioral Science*, 1976, *21*, 26-45.

Katz, E. On the matrix analysis of sociometric data. *Sociometry*, 1947, *10*, 233-241.

Laumann, E., and Pappi, F. *Networks of collective action*. New York: Academic Press, 1976.

Levine, J., Mullins, N. Structuralist analysis of social data. *Connections*, 1978, *1*, 3, 16-22.

Mullins, N. The role structure of scientific specialties. Un-
    published Manuscript, 1977.

Mullins, N., Hargens, L., Hecht, P., & Kick, E. The group struc-
    ture of cocitation clusters: A comparative study. *American
    Sociological Review,* 1942, *42,* 4, 552-562.

Schwartz, J., A computation of 3-block, 3-role structures. Un-
    published manuscript, 1975.

Schwartz, J. An examination of CONCOR and related methods for
    blocking sociometric data. In D. Heise (Ed.), *Sociological
    Methodology 1977.* San Francisco: Jossey-Bass, 1977, 255-282.

White, H. *An anatomy of kinship.* Englewood Cliffs, New Jersey:
    Prentice-Hall, 1963.

White, H., Boorman, S. & Breiger, R. Social structure from
    multiple networks. I. Blockmodels of roles and positions.
    American Journal of Sociology, 1976, *81,* 4, 730-780.

CHAPTER 7

SOME PROBLEMS RELATING TO RANDOMLY
CONSTRUCTED BIASED NETWORKS

Anatol Rapoport[1]

Randomly constructed graphs viewed as models of some biological or social systems are rich sources of challenging mathematical problems. The problems, in turn, suggest some interesting theoretical conceptualizations of the systems examined.

I. A CONTAGION PROCESS MODEL

To start with perhaps an earliest example of such a model,
consider the following contagion process. There is a large population of *n* elements, constituting the *points* of a directed graph.
Each element can be in either of two states, "infected" or "un-
infected." Once infected, an element remains in that state. The
contagion process starts with one randomly selected element becoming infected. That element then makes a fixed number *a* of

[1]*Present address: 38 Wynchwood Park, Toronto, Ontario
M6G 2V6, Canada.*

contacts, that is, it sends arcs to a of the n elements in the
population. Each of the n elements is randomly contacted by a
single arc with the same probability. A target of a contact becomes infected and, in turn, makes a random contacts. If a target is already infected, its state does not change. The process
continues through the successive "removes" from the originally
infected element. Eventually the process must terminate because
if on a given remove the newly contacted elements are all already
infected, no further contacts will be made (since only a *newly*
infected element makes further contacts). The process can be
interpreted as an epidemic, a spread of a piece of information
or attitude or behavior pattern through a population by contact,
or the like, under the drastically simplified assumption that a
fixed number of contacts, a, is allotted to each individual. This
assumption can be somewhat relaxed in the sense that the parameter
a can be taken to be the average number of contacts per individual. Many of the interesting results remain the same in this
somewhat generalized model.

The   following questions now suggest themselves.

1.   When the process has run to completion, what is the probability that an arbitrarily selected individual has been infected (informed, etc.)? Equivalently, what is the expected
fraction of the population that is ever contacted?

2.   At each remove or upon completion (i.e., after an
infinite number of removes), what is the probability that a
given fraction of individuals have been contacted? In particular,
what is the probability that upon completion every one has been
contacted?

3.   What is the probability that a given individual has been
contacted after a given number of removes?

I will present a solution of the first problem and will then go on to some modifications of the model in the direction of somewhat greater realism.

Let $P(0)$ $(=1/n)$ be the portion of the population initially infected, $P(t)$ the expected fraction of the population contacted for the first time on the tth remove, and $X(t)$ the expected fraction infected by the tth remove, so that

$$X(t) = \sum_{j=0}^{t} P(j) \tag{1}$$

Consider the probability (strictly speaking the expectation of the probability) that an arbitrary element is infected on the $(t+1)$th remove. This event is the intersection of two independent events, namely, (1) that the element had not been infected on any remove prior to $t+1$ and (2) that it is contacted on the $(t + 1)$th remove. Hence,

$$P(t + 1) = [1 - X(t)] [1 - (1 - 1/n)^{anP(t)}]. \tag{2}$$

The first factor of the right side of Eq. (2) is the probability of the first event; the second factor is the probability of the second event. Specifically $(1 - 1/n)$ is the probability that an element is *not* the target of a particular arc, which can reach any of n elements with equal probability. Further, since $P(t)$ is the fraction of the population making contacts on the $(t + 1)$th remove, $nP(t)$ is the expected number of these elements, and $anP(t)$ is the expected number of contacts made by them. Thus, $(1-1/n)^{anPn(t)}$ is the expected probability that an element is not a target of any of the arcs of the tth remove, and the complementary probability is that of being the target of at least one.

We can now approximate $(1 - 1/n)^{anP(t)}$ by $\exp\{-aP(t)\}$. Using Eq. (1) and expanding, we obtain

$$P(t + 1) = [1- \sum_{j=0}^{t} P(t)][1-\exp\{-a(X(t)-X(t-1))\}] \tag{3}$$

$$\sum_{j=0}^{t+1} P(j) = X(t+1) = 1-\exp\{-a[X(t)-X(t-1)]\}\ [1-X(t)]$$

$$[1-X(t+1)][\exp\{aX(t)\}] = [1-X(t)][\exp\{aX(t-1)\}]$$

$$[1-X(t)]\ \exp\{aX(t-1)\} = \text{constant.}$$

We set $X(-1)=0$, reflecting none contacted before the start of the process.

Since $X(0) = 1/n \simeq 0$ for very large n, the constant must be 1.

Let $\gamma = \underset{t\to\infty}{\text{Lim}}[X(t)]$, that is, γ is the fraction of the population that is ever infected. Then

$$1-\gamma = e^{-a\gamma} \text{ or } \gamma = 1-e^{-a\gamma}\ , \tag{4}$$

which defines γ as the solution of a transcendental equation. Actually there are two solutions, since $\gamma \equiv 0$ satisfies Eq. (4) as well as the nontrivial solution, which approaches $-\infty$ as a tends to 0 and $+1$ as a tends to ∞. The physicially meaningful solution is a combination of the two. Namely for $a \leq 1$, $\gamma = 0$; for $a > 1$, γ increases monotonically, approaching 1 as a becomes infinitely large. We can interpret nonintegral values of a as the average number of contacts made by an infected element. The interpretation of Eq. (4) then is as follows.

1. If $a < 1$, the total expected fraction of infected elements will be negligible (for very large n).

2. If $a > 1$, the total fraction is nonzero.

To get an idea of the relation between a and γ, we see that γ is very nearly .8 for $a = 2$. That is to say, if in a very large population each infected element contacts two others at random, we can expect that ultimately about 80% of the population will be infected. If $a = 3$, $\gamma \simeq .94$, etc.

The model could be a reasonable representation of a general contagion process as in an epidemic or in the spread of information except for a very serious shortcoming: All of the targets of any contact are assumed to be equiprobable. This assumption precludes the notion of distance between pairs of elements. If the elements are people, distance is, of course, an important factor in the probability of contact. Moreover, the distance relevant to a contagion model is not necessarily a geographical distance but might be a social distance, which has a geographical component among other components.

We know very little about the topological properties of this vaguely conceived social distance. For instance, we cannot be sure whether the usual properties of geographical distance apply to social distance. Suppose we know that element A is in some sense close to element B, and B is close to C. Can we assume that this implies that A is relatively close to C? If we define a function $d(x,y)$ on pairs of points in our set to represent a "distance" and some way of estimating each distance empirically, can we be sure that the function has the properties of a metric, for example, that $d(x,z) \leq d(x,y) + d(y,z)$? And if this triangle inequality is satisfied, can we say anything about the dimensionality of the "social space"?

Useful models of contagion should include the topological and/or metric properties of the space in which the elements are imbedded, to effectively represent the probabilities of contacts. We must at least assume that contacts between elements close together (in terms of the distance function imposed on the space)

are more probable than those between elements far apart, contrary
to our previous assumption of equiprobable contacts.

On the other hand, introducing distance functions into the
contagion model complicates its analysis very much, so I will
abandon the purely analytic approach of model building and settle
for a more empirical approach, using the simple contagion model
as a base line for comparison. Systematic deviations of data
from the consequences of this model can give rise to interesting
conjectures about the effects of structure on the contagion process.

II. AN EMPIRICAL EXAMPLE

I will now present an example of such an approach. Several
years ago my colleagues and I performed the following experiment
(Rapoport and Horvath, 1961). Our populations were the students
of two junior high schools in Ann Arbor each containing about
1000 students. Each student was asked to name six others in the
same school in the order of the strength of the friendship relation, that is, "My best friend in this school is (name)"; "My
second best friend in this school is (name)" etc. It was important to have each student who was named as a friend name friends
in turn, so we had to follow up the session with another in order
to catch the students who were absent in the first session. In
this way the missing data were reduced to a very small fraction of
the students, and could be counted as errors.

A stack of cards, each identified by a number assigned to the
student with six other numbers as "targets" ranked in the order of
degree of friendship, constituted our raw data. From these data
directed graphs could be constructed, each with outdegree from
1 to 6. We actually worked with graphs with outdegree 2; that is,
with two arcs issuing from each point.

One set of such graphs was constructed as follows. Starting
with an arbitrary student, we traced first and second friends,

then traced the students whom these named as first or second
friends, and so on until the process terminated. We noted $X(t)$
associated with this tracing. We then repeated the process using
different "starters." From several such replications we constructed $X(t)$ as the average of the values obtained in this class
of tracings.

Similar plots were then obtained by using descending pairs of
friends (second and third, etc.) named in the tracing procedure,
producing five plots in all.

If the friends had been named randomly, the plots could be
represented by $X(t)$ given implicitly by the difference equation

$$1 - X(t) = \exp\{-aX(t - 1)\}$$

with the asymptotic value $X(\infty) = .8$. We can be sure, however,
that the naming of friends is not a random process. In particular,
although we do not know in detail the topological or metric structure of the "social space" in which the junior high school students are points, we can reasonably suppose that friends of
friends are likely to be friends and that the friendship relation
is "probabilistically symmetric." That is to say, if A names B
as a best friend, it is fairly likely that B will name A as a
best friend. This likelihood is not consistent with a completely
randomized model where B names A as best friend with probability
$1/n$ whether or not A has named B. Further, if A names B and C
as best and second best friends, respectively, the likelihood
that B and C will name each other is thereby enhanced, which is
also not the case in the completely randomized model.

Although we do not know enough about the network represented
by our sociogram to calculate the associated conditional probabilities of being named, we can propose a reasonable qualitative
model. The friendship relation introduces at least two kinds of
bias   into the process of constructing the sociogram by tracing

contacts (naming friends): the reciprocity bias, where in being
named as a friend enhances the likelihood of naming the namer; the
sibling bias, wherein if A names B and C, then B and C are likely
to name each other. (If naming is analogous to descent, then B
and C, being direct descendants of A are "siblings.") These
biases probably carry over the succeeding "generations," perhaps
attenuated.

Both the reciprocity bias and the sibling bias should "slow
down" the growth of $X(t)$ as a function of t and should depress
the asymptote. This is because the biases tend to "cluster"
the points and so reduce the numbers of "fresh" contacts. In the
extreme case, reciprocal and sibling naming are made with cer-
tainty. Then, starting with A we get B and C as the first two
contacts. But B would name A (because of reciprocity) and C (as
sibling); and C would name A and B. Thus, the tracing would be
ended on the second remove and would reach only three individuals.

Now we come to the qualitative test of our model of bias. We
would expect that the effect of bias in "slowing down" $X(t)$ and
of depressing the asymptote would be the greater the "tighter"
the bias associated with the friendship relation. The relation
"best friend" should be the tightest; "second best friend" the
next tightest, etc. We would expect, therefore, that the plot
of $X(t)$ traced through the first and second friends would be
below that traced through the second and third friends, and so
on. This is exactly what was found. Moreover, the plot of the
theoretical function $X(t)$ derived from the completely randomized
model was above all the others, although the plot traced through
the fifth and sixth friends was already close to it.

The characteristics of the $X(t)$ curve, such as the rate of
change of its slope, the position of the inflection point, if

any, the asymptote approached, etc. constitute mathematically
descriptive features of a network of relations with some sort
of distance bias imposed on the probabilities of connections.
Another feature is represented by the function $\gamma(a)$, the asymptotic fraction of the population reached as a function of the
average number of contacts per individual. In a completely
randomized net, $\gamma(a)$ rises rapidly to its asymptotic value of 1
(recall $\gamma(3) = .94$). In a population with distance bias, the
shape of $\gamma(a)$ must be different. Note also that $\gamma(\infty) = 1$ only if
the graph representing the network of relations is almost connected. If it is not almost connected, $\gamma(\infty)$ will be less than 1,
and its value will, in general, depend on the element taken as
the "starter" in the tracing. In fact, averaged over all
starters, we shall have for large a $\gamma(\infty) = \sum_{i=1}^{m} k_i^2/n^2$, if the graph
has m components with k_i elements in the ith component.

From the discussion, one would be tempted to draw the following conclusion: The "tighter" the population, the slower the
spread of something by contagion and the smaller the final fraction infected. Nevertheless, this conclusion is not warranted
without reservations. We have seen that for $a = 2$, the final
fraction of infected in a completely unstructured population (with
random contacts) is .8. Let the population now be "completely
structured" as follows: The individuals are arranged in a linear
array with each individual, and upon becoming infected each individual makes contact with his two immediate neighbors. Except
in the very beginning of the process, one of these has clearly
already been infected, since it is from this individual that the
newly infected individual has been infected. But the other

immediate neighbor must be a new contact. Thus, the infection
proceeds along the array until every one is infected, so that
$\gamma(\infty) = 1 > .8$, contrary to our conjecture that "structuring"
tends to depress the asymptotic fraction of the infected.

Thus, we see that the role of structuring as an inhibitory
or contributory factor in the contagian process is not clear cut.
The class of structures which insures a pandemic, a process where
everyone ultimately becomes infected, remains to be defined.

III. CONNECTIVITY IN RANDOM GRAPHS

In an attempt to gain some insight into this problem, we turn
toward some mathematical questions relating to the structure of
randomly constructed graphs. A whole class of these questions was
posed and answered by the two Hungarian mathematicians Erdös and
Rényi. Consider a typical one.

Given n points, consequently $\binom{n}{2}$ pairs of points, suppose k
of these $\binom{n}{2}$ pairs are selected at random to serve as edges of a
linear (nondirected) graph. What is the probability that this
graph is connected?

The probability is to be understood in the following way.
There are $\binom{\binom{n}{2}}{k}$ different labeled graphs with n points and k
edges. Of these c are connected. Hence, the probability that
an arbitrarily selected graph from this set is connected is
$c\binom{\binom{n}{2}}{k}^{-1}$. The problem is solved when c is computed.

Erdös and Rényi were interested in the asymptotic value of
this probability as both k and n become infinitely large. This
value depends on the ratio of k to the following "critical"
function of n:

$$f(n) = \frac{1}{2}n \cdot \log_e n + an + 0(n) \ .$$

As k and n become infinitely large, this ratio becomes infinite. In other words if $f(n)=0(k)$, the probability of connectedness approaches unity. If the ratio tends to zero (in other words, if $k = 0[f(n)]$), the probability of connectedness approaches zero. If the ratio remains finite, then the probability of connectedness approaches $\exp\{-e^{-2a}\}$.

IV. ORDER FROM CHAOS

The probability that a randomly constructed graph is connected has a bearing on sociological applications. If the points of the graph represent people or communication centers and the edges represent channels of communication, then information originating at some point and transmitted through the channels can spread to all the points only if the graph is connected. Analogously, if the points are organisms and the edges represent the possibility of matings between organisms, then a gene can spread to the entire population only if the graph is connected.

Models of random processes thus permit the conceptualization of regularity as an emergent property of chaos. Between the poles of complete randomness and complete order or determinism there is a continuum representable by bias parameters. As these parameters become large and represent "tight" couplings, progressively more ordered structures emerge. A sequence of points on a line at exponentially distributed intervals can be affected by a repulsive force tending to pull points apart. As this force becomes larger the frequency distribution of intervals becomes progressively sharper, until in the limit the points are equally spaced, and the frequency distribution of intervals is concentrated at a single point. We now have "complete order" from complete randomness. Of sociological interest is the notion that the process of evolution can be pictured as one in which certain bias parameters are "selected for" in such a way that the evolving system

progresses toward a structural order. To the extent that the
evolutionary process can be formulated in terms of randomness,
biases, emergent structures, and viability, it can in principle
be modeled mathematically.

V.   THE USEFULNESS OF RANDOM GRAPH MODELS: MORE EXAMPLES

    Mathematical modeling is a vehicle for absolutely rigorous
reasoning and therein lies its advantage. A disadvantage of
mathematical modeling is that it necessitates drastic paring
down of the details of the phenomena modeled. Outside the realm
of physical phenomena, these simplifications and abstractions can
impair or altogether destroy the model's pragmatic relevance. Because of its abstractness, a model may not lead to testable predictions in specific contexts, but it may generate new concepts
or sharpen established ones and so contribute to clearer formulations of problems or theories.
    It is in this spirit that the theory of randomly constructed
graphs should be approached. They are models of evolving structures determined by biases built into the probabilities governing
the construction. The conceptual payoff of these theories is in
the interpretations of the terms used in the models. For example,
let the points of a graph represent the elements (neurons) of
some idealized nervous system; the arcs or edges synaptic connections between the elements. A "bias" can be interpreted as
the probability of connection as a function of "distance," defined
in terms of geographic proximity or, perhaps, biochemical affinity
between pairs of neurons. Structure has, of course, a multitude
of meanings. To fix ideas, some concrete aspect of structure must
be selected as the focus of attention. A simple aspect of this
sort is the probability of connectedness. "Viability" might then
be defined as the probability that a random graph is connected.

In another context, let the points be individuals of a
species, the edges matings, the bias differential probabilities
of matings between individuals of, say, different phenotypes,
structure again the connectedness of the graph in the sense of
the existence of paths for the transmission of genes, or, perhaps, the speed with which a new gene can spread throughout the
population. In this case, the connection between connectedness
and the viability of the species *as a single species* is clear.
If the graph is not connected, the species will ultimately split
into two or more species.

Now a mathematical problem naturally presents itself. Given
a randomly connected graph with so many points and so many arcs
or edges, what is the relation between certain biases imposed on
the probabilities of establishing connections and the probability
that the resulting graph is connected? We already have examined
some empirical evidence suggesting that distance bias *reduces*
the probability of connectedness and have given an example where
such a bias increases this probability. Thus, the question of
when distance bias reduces the probability of connectedness and
when it increases it remains open.

Let us now formulate the problem in another way. Suppose boys
name only boys as friends and girls name only girls. Clearly,
this bias would preclude the formation of a connected graph altogether, since there would be no path from a boy to a girl or
vice versa. On the other hand, suppose boys named only girls
and girls named only boys. Certainly a connected graph would be
a possibility but would not be guaranteed any more than if
namings were random. The question arises whether strictly heterosexual naming would increase or decrease the probability of connectedness compared with random naming. In terms of contagion,
the question might be whether, all other things being equal, a
venereal or nonvenereal disease is more likely to result in
pandemic. More generally, suppose just two probabilities in

selecting the target operated, one associated with homosexual
naming, one with heterosexual. What ratio of these probabilities
would yield the largest probability of connectedness? Note that
the ratios 1 : 1, 1 : 0, and 0 : 1 represent random, homosexual,
and heterosexual naming, respectively.

The same problem may have some theoretical relevance in
another context. During the 1930s when mathematical theories of
population genetics were being developed, there ensued a lengthy
dispute between two outstanding representatives of that field,
Sir Ronald Fisher of England and Sewell Wright of the United
States. The issue was the question of mating patterns that insure
the optimum adaptibility of a species to a changing environment.
Such adaptibility, one might surmise, depends in part on the
efficiency with which a new gene, conducive to survival in a
changed environment, spreads through the population comprising
the species. One may further assume that this efficiency is
related to the "degree of connectivity" of the graph representing
the mating pattern. There are, to be sure, different ways of
defining "degree of connectivity," but these need not concern us
here.

Fisher argued that a completely random mating pattern, where
each individual of the opposite sex has the same probability of
being chosen, is the optimal pattern. Wright argued that other
patterns might be more efficient, in particular, one where the
population is partitioned into several subpopulations or subspecies so that the probability of mating *within* a subspecies is
considerably larger than that of mating across subspecies.
Clearly, the latter probability should not be zero, because this
would separate the subspecies genetically.

Now interpreting viability of the species in terms of the connectedness established by the mating pattern, we are faced with
the same mathematical problem: that of finding an optimal bias
among a class of biases imposed on within-species and across-
species matings.

Some years ago Hua Sung Na and I (Na and Rapoport, 1967) and later a student of mine (Perkins, 1970) attacked a very special case of this problem, where a randomly constructed graph has n points and $n - 1$ edges. For large values of n, the solutions are assumed identical with those of the case with n points and n edges. The biological interpretation is that a member of the species mates on the average once, and if the conjecture is correct, the model applies to that situation. The reason for assuming $n - 1$ rather than n edges is that a graph with n points and $n - 1$ edges is connected if and only if it is a tree (i.e., has no cycles). Techniques for enumerating trees are well known and provide the solutions of the problems posed.

The actual problem undertaken was the following. Let the n points be partitioned into two classes with n_1 and n_2 points, respectively, and let the $n - 1$ edges be all interlinks, that is, all between points of different subsets but otherwise chosen at random. What is the ratio $n_1 : n_2$ that yields the largest probability of connectedness? In biological terms, if the two subsets represent the sexes and the edges matings, what sex ratio results in the largest probability of connectedness? The answer, which was derived from symmetry considerations, is equipartition, and this was proved mathematically.

In addition, the probability of connectedness is larger by a factor that ranges from 1 to 2, approaching 2, as n becomes infinite, in a graph with all interlinks (with $n_1 = n_2$) than in a completely randomly constructed graph. Moreover, assuming k equal subsets, this factor, enhancing the probability of connectedness by confining all contacts to "exogamous ones" tends to

$$\left(\frac{k}{k-1}\right)^{k-1}\left[\exp\left\{\frac{k}{k-1} - 2\right\}\right]$$

as n approaches infinity.

Starting from this result, Perkins attacked a more general problem. Suppose now there are two equal subsets, so that $n_1 = n_2 = n/2$. Again $n-1$ edges are allotted of which ℓ_i are to be intralinks, that is, between points of the same subset and $\ell_0 = n - 1 - \ell_i$ interlinks between members of different subsets. What ratio of $\ell_0 : \ell_1$ yields the largest probability of connectedness? Let $P(r)$ be the probability of connectedness for very large n, where $r = \ell_i - (n-1)$. Clearly, $P(1) = 0$, since if all of the links are intralinks, the graph must be disconnected. Perkins proved that for very large n, $P(r)$ attains its maximal value at

$$r = (5 + \sqrt{5})/8 = .9045 \quad .$$

That is to say, to maximize the probability of connectedness (to make a tree) in the case of two equal subsets, let about 90% of the edges be intralinks, connecting points within the same class.

Perkins obtained also a generalization for k equal subsets with equal numbers of intralinks and interlinks. In that case the maximizing fraction of intralinks turns out to be

$$\frac{k + 3}{4k} + \frac{(k - 1)\sqrt{5}}{4k} \quad .$$

We see that the range of this maximizing fraction of intralinks is not large. As k increases, this fraction decreases slowly to the limit of about .809 as k becomes very large.

The very special assumptions of this model (e.g., that the graph is connected if and only if it is a tree) should be kept in mind. They restrict severely the range of applicability of the model. In fact, I cannot think of any noncontrived situations to which it could apply. Much more suggestive would be results analogous to Perkins' where the number of edges of a graph would be an independent variable. If analogous results could be derived in the more general situation, this might shed some light on the dispute in population genetic mentioned earlier. For analogous results would to a certain extent support Wright's position against Fisher's: A more efficient way of insuring the spread of new genes through a population would be shown to be that of dividing the species into subspecies with predominant intraspecies mating but with occasional interspecies mating, using the optimal ratio. Furthermore, interesting analogies suggest themselves, for instance, in the context of optimal communication patterns, etc.

I cannot emphasize too strongly that the focus in these models is primarily mathematical rather than biological or social. The starting point is not a biological or social situation but rather a mathematical problem, which, to be sure, is often inspired by some idealization of a biological or social situation. It is, however, essentially, mathematical questions rather than questions related to the underlying situation that guide the development of the model. The end product is not a substantive biological or social theory but rather a deeper understanding of the structural problem that may be involved in the construction of such a theory. To answer questions directed related to some situation of a genuine social or biological situation, one would be better advised to undertake computer simulations rather than approach the problem analytically. The latter approach all too often gets entangled in insuperable difficulties right from the start. The value of the analytic approach (where it can be applied) is that it generates ideas and concepts that may considerably enrich our formulation of the substantive situation and inspire effective simulation techniques to deal with it.

REFERENCES

Erdös, P., & Rényi, A.   On the evolution of random graphs
    *Publications of the Mathematical Institute of the Hungarian
    Academy of Sciences,* 1960, *5*, 17-61.
Na, H.S. & Rapoport, A.   A formula for the probability of obtain-
    ing a tree from a graph constructed randomly except for an
    "exogamous bias".   *Annuals of Mathematical Statistics,* 1967,
    38, 226-241.
Perkins, L. Unpublished thesis.   University of Michigan, 1970.
Rapoport, A., & Horvath, W.J.   A study of a large sociogram.
    Behavioral Science, 1961, *6*, 279-291.

CHAPTER 8

NETWORK ANALYSIS OF THE DIFFUSION OF INNOVATIONS[1]

Everett M. Rogers

Institute for Communication Research

Stanford University

Stanford, California

I. INTRODUCTION

In this chapter I argue that network analysis has unique advantages for the study of the diffusion of innovations, and I will illustrate certain of these with data from a study of the diffusion of family planning innovations among village women in Korea. My position is that most previous diffusion research, using the individual as the unit of analysis, contains a psycho-

[1]*This paper was prepared with the collaboration of Sea-Baick Lee, William S. Puppa, Brenda A. Doe, Muhiuddin Haider, and Gummadi Appa Rao of the University of Michigan; and Hyung Jong Park and Kyung-Kyoon Chung of the School of Public Health, Seoul National University. It also profits from the related research of D. Lawrence Kincaid of the East-West Communication Institute, and James A. Danowski of the Annenberg School of Communications, University of Southern California. Our collaborative research on mothers' clubs and communication networks in the diffusion of family planning innovations in Korea villages has appeared previously as Park et al. (1974), Rogers and Kincaid (in press), Rogers (1976), Kincaid et al. (1975), and Danowski (1976).*

logical bias that prevents complete understanding of the relational nature of interpersonal diffusion. Network analysis provides
a means to expand our understanding by putting social structure
back into diffusion research.

II. THE CLASSICAL DIFFUSION MODEL

A. *Elements and Origins*

   The four main elements in any diffusion event are (1) an
innovation, an idea perceived as new by the potential adopting
unit, (2) which is *communicated* through *channels*, (3) over *time*,
(4) among members of a *social system*. Because of the processual,
over-time interactive nature of diffusion, one might expect to
see studies of the social networks through which innovations
spread. However, in the diffusion literature, such network analysis is rare. The reason can be traced, I believe, to the historical origins of diffusion research and to the fact that diffusion
researchers are an invisible college structured around a revolutionary paradigm.
   The origins of research on the diffusion of innovations appear in writings of the German/Austrian and the British diffusion
anthropologists, who claimed that all changes in a society result
from the introduction of innovations from other societies, and
in the work of the French sociologist Gabriel Tarde (1903), who
introduced the *S*-shaped diffusion curve and the role of opinion
leaders. However, the revolutionary paradigm for diffusion stems
from the research of two North American sociologists, Bryce Ryan
and Neal Gross, on the diffusion of hybrid seed corn among Iowa
farmers.
   Ryan and Gross (1943) gathered their data by personal interviews with all the Iowa farmers in two communities. The rate of
adoption of the agricultural innovation followed an *S*-shaped,
cumulative normal curve. They argued that the first farmers to
adopt (the innovators) differed from later adopters in their

greater cosmopoliteness and higher socioeconomic status. One of
the deficiencies of this study was its lack of attention to opinion
leadership patterns in the interpersonal diffusion of the innovation within the two Iowa communities. Indeed, sociometric data
would have been easy to gather since all the farmers in the two
communities were interviewed (Katz, 1960).[2]

Research on the diffusion of innovations has, since Ryan and
Gross (1943), followed the rise-and-fall stages of a "revolutionary paradigm" leading to development of an invisible college
rather closely, although the final stage of demise has not yet
set in (Crane, 1972). The hybrid corn study set forth a new
approach to the study of communication and human behavior change,
that was soon followed up by an increasing number of scholars.
Within 10 years (by 1952), over 100 diffusion researches were
completed; during the next decade (by 1962), another 450; and by
the end of 1974, another 1200. Today, there are over 2700 publications about the diffusion of innovations (Rogers and Thomas,
1975). Thus, the amount of scientific activity spent in investigating the diffusion of innovations increased at an exponential
rate (doubling almost every 2 years) since the revolutionary
paradigm appeared 32 years ago, as Kuhn's (1962) theory of the
growth of science would predict.

*The consequent standardization of research approaches around
the classical diffusion model has greatly limited the contribution of diffusion research to furthering the scientific understanding of human behavior change.* The Ryan and Gross (1943)
study was so influential in affecting later studies on diffusion
that Crane's (1972, p. 74) analysis (of rural sociologists investigating diffusion) found the hybrid corn study was responsible

[2]*Such census-type sampling designs, in which a sample of intact groups like communities are selected, have not been especially
common in diffusion research since the Ryan and Gross (1943) study,
as diffusion researchers have mainly pursued the objective of
generalizability of results from random samples of individuals.*

for 15 of the 18 most widely used "innovations" (defined as the
first use of a dependent or independent variable in a research
publication in the diffusion field), and accounted for 21% of the
total 201 innovations! "A significant proportion of the innovative work in the area had already been done by the time the field
began to acquire a significant number of new members (Crane, 1972,
p. 67)."

III. PSYCHOLOGICAL BIAS[3]

The psychological bias in diffusion research stems (1) from
its overwhelming focus on the individual as the unit of analysis,
and (2) from the researchers' acceptance of social problems defined in terms of "person-blame." As a result, the transactional
and relational nature of human communication involved in the diffusion process has tended to be overlooked.

A. *The Individual as the Unit of Analysis*

The overwhelming focus on the *individual* as the unit of analysis in diffusion research (while largely ignoring the importance
of communication *relationships* between sources and receivers) is
often due to the assumption that if the individual is the unit
of response, he must consequently be the unit of analysis (Coleman,
1958).   This monadic view of human behavior determined that
"The kinds of substantive problems on which such research focuses
tended to be problems of 'aggregate psychology', that is, within
individual problems and never problems concerned with relations
between people (Coleman, 1958)." The use of survey methods in
diffusion research "de-structured" such human behavior: "Using
random sampling of individuals, the survey is a sociological
meat-grinder, tearing the individual from his social context and
guaranteeing that nobody in the study interacts with anyone else

[3]*This section of the present chapter borrows directly from
Rogers (1976).*

in it. It is a little like a biologist putting his experimental animals through a hamburger machine and looking at every hundredth cell through a microscope; anatomy and physiology get lost; structure and function disappear and one is left with cell biology (Barton, 1968)."

Only recently and rarely in diffusion research has focus shifted to the dyad, clique, network, or system of individuals and to the communication relationships between individuals. Gradually, we are beginning to move out of the upper left-hand corner of Table I, where almost all past diffusion research is concentrated.[4] Encouraging attempts to overcome the psychological bias in communication research are provided by the co-orientation model, by relational analysis,[5] by network analysis, and by the general systems approach (Rogers and Agarwala-Rogers, 1976).

These conceptual/methodological approaches suggest that even when the individual is the unit of response, the communication relationship (even though *it* can't "speak") can be the unit of analysis via some type of sociometric measurement. Sampling and data-analysis procedures for relational analysis are being worked out, but we still lack relational concepts, and theories linking these concepts.

[4]*A somewhat parallel criticism, and a plea for communication network analysis, has been made by Sheingold (1973) for the field of voting research.*

[5]Relational analysis *is a research approach in which the unit of analysis is a relationship between two or more individuals (Rogers and Bhowmik, 1971).*

TABLE I. *Illustrative Types of Diffusion Research Categorized on the Basis of the Unit at Which the Dependent and Independent Variables Are Measured*

Unit at which the dependent variable is measured	Unit at which the independent variable(s) is measured	
	1. Individual	2. Interpersonal relationship (dyad, clique, system)
1. Individual	Individual characteristics correlated with individual innovativeness;[a] an example (among hundreds) is Ryan and Gross (1943).	System effects[b] on individual innovativeness; examples are Davis (1968) and Saxena (1968).
2. Interpersonal relationship (dyad, clique, system)	Practically unknown, but a possible example might be to explain the system rate of adoption of an innovation with an independent variable like whether the system's top leader is innovative.	Network analysis to explain the rate of adoption of an innovation; an example is Rogers et al. (1975a).

[a] Innovativeness is the degree to which a unit (usually an individual) is relatively earlier to adopt new ideas than other units in a system.

[b] System effects are the influences of the structure and/or composition of a system on the behavior of the members of the system.

B.   Person-Blame

A second reason for the psychological bias in diffusion research is the acceptance of a *person-blame causal-attribution*
definition of the social problems that are investigated.
Individual-blame is the tendency to hold an individual responsible
or his problems, rather than society. Obviously, what is done
about a social problem, including research, depends upon how it
is defined.

Diffusion research was originally guilty in following an
individual-blame approach: "We note an assumption in diffusion
writings that the rate of adoption should be speeded up, that the
innovation should be adopted by receivers, etc. (this is also a
consequence of a pro-innovation bias in diffusion research).
Seldom is it implied in diffusion documents that the source or
the channels may be at fault for not providing more adequate
information, for promoting inadequate or inappropriate innovations, etc. (Rogers with Shoemaker, 1971, p. 79)."

The Ryan/Gross investigation was sponsored by the Iowa Agricultural Experiment Station and the Iowa Agricultural Extension
Service at Iowa State University, the major R&D agency and the
main change agency for hybrid seed, respectively. So it is not
surprising that Ryan and Gross accepted a person-blame viewpoint
of the diffusion problem they investigated; the researchers
assumed that the Iowa farmers *should* adopt the obviously advan-
tageous agricultural innovation.

IV.   RESTORING SOCIAL STRUCTURE TO DIFFUSION RESEARCH

The refocusing of diffusion researches had to wait until
later investigations, especially the drug study among medical
doctors by Coleman *et al.* (1966). Then it became a common procedure for diffusion scholars to ask their respondents socio-

metric questions of the general form: "From whom in this system
did you obtain information that led you to adopt this innovation?"
The sociometric dyad represented by each answer to this question
then became the unit of analysis.

A. Opinion Leadership

Relational data obtained from sociometric questions were
utilized to provide deeper insight into the role of opinion leaders in the two-step flow of communication, a conceptualization
that was originated prior to most diffusion research by
Lazarsfeld et al. (1944). The two-step flow hypothesis turned
out mainly to be an oversimplification (as the flow of communication may have any number of steps) later research showed, but the
concept of opinion leadership[6] has much theoretical and practical
utility. Diffusion researches were able to advance understand-
ings of opinion leadership because of their unique capacity to
focus on the flow of innovations, new messages (to the receivers)
that seemed to leave deeper (and hence more recallable) scratches
on men's minds. The tracer quality of an innovation's diffusion
pathways aids the investigation of the flow of communication
messages, and especially the role of certain individuals like
opinion leaders in this flow.

B. Communication Structure

Network analysis is a method for identifying the communication structure in a system. With it, sociometric data about
communication flows or patterns are analyzed by using interpersonal relationships as the units of analysis. This tool promises

[6]Opinion leadership was usually measured as the number of
sociometric choices received by an individual; thus it is measured in relational terms but reduced to an individual characteristic of the respondent by using the individual as the unit of
analysis.

to capitalize on the unique ability of diffusion inquiry to re-
construct specific message flows in a system, and then to over-
lay the social structure of the system on these flows. The innovation's diffusion brings life to the otherwise static nature of
the structural variables; network analysis permits understanding
the social structure as it channels the process of diffusion.[7]

The essence of the diffusion of an innovation is the human
interaction through which one individual communicates a new idea
to one or more other individuals. Any given individual in a system is likely to contact certain other individuals, and to ignore
many others. As these interpersonal communication flows become
patterned over time, a communication structure emerges and is
predictive of behavior. Basically, communication network analysis
describes these linkages in an interpersonal communication
structure.

The first, and very partial, attempts toward network analysis
of the diffusion process simply identified opinion leaders in a
system and determined that their mass media and interpersonal
communication behavior was different from that of their followers.
This approach was only a slight extension of the usual monadic
analysis in the direction of a more relational type of analysis.

Next, diffusion scholars began to plot sequential-over-time
sociograms of the diffusion of an innovation among the members of
a system. Tentative steps were taken toward using communication
relationships (such as sociometric dyads) as the units of analysis. This advance allowed the data-analysis of a "who-to-whom"
communication matrix, and facilitated inquiry into the identification (1) of cliques within the total system and how such structural sub-groupings affected the diffusion of an innovation, and

[7]*About the only other place in communication research where
network analysis has been used to restore social structure to the
communication process is in several recent investigations of organizational communication (Rogers and Agarwala-Rogers, 1976).*

(2) of specialized communication roles such as liaisons,[8] bridges,[9] and isolates. Now it was possible to identify and investigate the communication structure of a system.

Further, the measurement of various structural indexes (like communication integration, connectedness,[10] and system openness[11]) for individuals, cliques, or entire systems (like villages or organizations) now became possible, and could be related to the rate of diffusion or adoption occurring in these systems. General propositions began to emerge from such network analysis, for example, that a system's rate of adoption is positively related to (1) connectedness, and (2) to system openness.[12]

These network analyses necessitated a new kind of sampling, as well as a shift to relational units of analysis. Instead of random samples of scattered individuals in a large population, the network studies depended on gathering data from *all* of the eligible respondents in a system (like a village, for instance) or a sample of such systems (Table II). *Usually the sample designs for network analysis, as compared to monadic analysis, meant less emphasis on the ability to generalize the research*

[8]*Defined as an individual who links two or more cliques in a system, but who is not a member of any clique.*

[9]*Defined as an individual who links two or more cliques in a system from his position as a member of one of the cliques.*

[10]*Defined as the degree to which the units in a system are interconnected through communication linkages.*

[11]*Defined as the degree to which the units in a system exchange information across the system boundary with its environment.*

[12]*Illustrative of such network analyses are Yadav (1967), Guimarães (1972), Shoemaker (1971), Allen (1970), and Rogers and Kincaid (in press).*

TABLE II. *Comparison of Monadic and Relational Analysis in Research on the Diffusion of Innovations*

Characteristics of the research approach	Type of diffusion research approach	
	Monadic analysis	Relational analysis
1. Unit of analysis	The individual.	The communication relationship between two (or more) individuals.
2. Most frequent sample design	Random samples of scattered individuals in a large population (in order to maximize the generalizability of the research results).	Complete census of all eligible respondents in a system (like a village), or a sample of such intact systems.
3. Types of data	Personal and social characteristics of individuals, and their communication behavior.	Same as for monadic analysis, plus some sociometric data about communication relationships.
4. Types of data-analysis methods	Correlational analysis of cross-sectional survey data.	Various types of network analysis of cross-sectional survey data.
5. Main purpose of the research	To determine the variables (usually characteristics of individuals) related to innovativeness.	To determine how social structural variables affect diffusion flows in a system.

results, which was traded off for a greater focus on understand-
ing the role of social structures on diffusion flows. If such
research were to study social structure, it had to sample intact
social structures, or at least the relevant parts of them.

V. NETWORK ANALYSIS OF FAMILY PLANNING DIFFUSION IN KOREA

A. *Data and Method*

The potential usefulness of network analysis of diffusion can
be illustrated by examining some data gathered via personal interviews with all the 1003 married women of child-bearing age living
in a sample of 24 Korean villages (Park *et al.*, 1974). For the
sake of simplification, we deal here with a comparison of two of
these 24 villages, each of which has 39 respondents. Village A
has a relatively successful family planning program with 57% of
the eligible couples currently using a family planning method,
while Village B has only 26% practicing. Both villages had been
about equally exposed over 10 years to a standardized national
family planning program that sought to diffuse such methods as
the IUD, oral contraceptives, and sterilization.

During the personal interviews, the respondents were asked
several sociometric questions, including: "With whom in this
village have you discussed family planning ideas most frequently?"
These data were subjected to a four-phase cross-sectional network
analysis developed by Richards (1971).

Symmetrized communication data for the 39 respondents in each
village were arranged in the usual sociometric who-to-whom matrix. The respondents in the choice matrix were subsequently rearranged into cliques on the basis of similarity of interaction

pattern.[13] Ordering on this basis is accomplished simply by computing the mean of the identification numbers of the individuals
with whom a respondent interacts and rearranging matrix entries
using mean scores to order them. The process is iterative (see
Richards, 1971, for details) and was terminated when fewer than
10 percent of the respondent's positions changed.[14] Using these
reorganized data, a sociogram can be constructed (Figures 1 and
2). The sociogram presents (in an easily appreciated form) the
main features of the communication structure: (1) *cliques,*
(2) *liaisons,* who link two or more cliques but are not members of
them, (3) *bridges,* who belong to one clique but communicate with
individuals in another clique,[15] and (4) *isolates,* individuals
who do not communicate with anyone. We have identified the members of the family planning mothers' club[16] and the club leader
in each of the village sociograms, so as to allow contrasting the
formal relationships (membership and leadership) of the mothers'
club with the informal communication structure of family planning

[13]*In most previous attempts at clique identification, the criterion for grouping was to position individuals together if they
interacted with each other, rather than on the basis of the similarity of the units with whom they interacted. An exception is
Brum and Brundage (1950) and Alba (1975).*

[14]*We used hand methods, but a computer program has been developed by William D. Richards of the Department of Communication
Studies, Simon Fraser University, and is operational at Michigan
State University and at seven other universities. It has been
utilized with our data (by Danowski, 1976).*

[15]*An illustration is respondent #16 in Figure 2.*

[16]*Mothers clubs are local organizations of village women which
strive to promote family planning diffusion, adoption, and continuation and to provide a wide range of educational activities.
The 26,000 mothers' clubs in Korea are organized to link the informal cliques in villages and to mobilize them to diffuse family
planning ideas.*

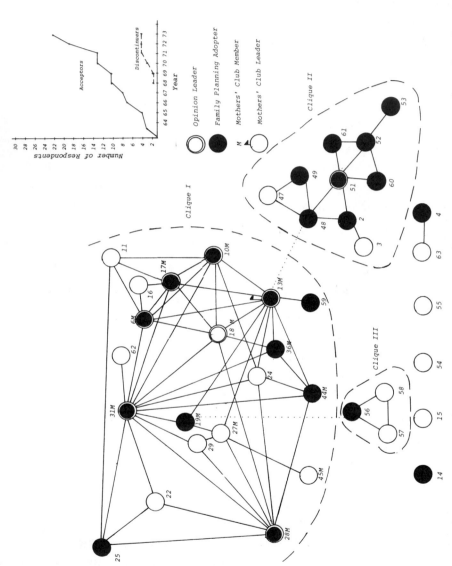

Fig. 1. Sociogram of the Interpersonal Communication Relationships about Family Planning in Village A.

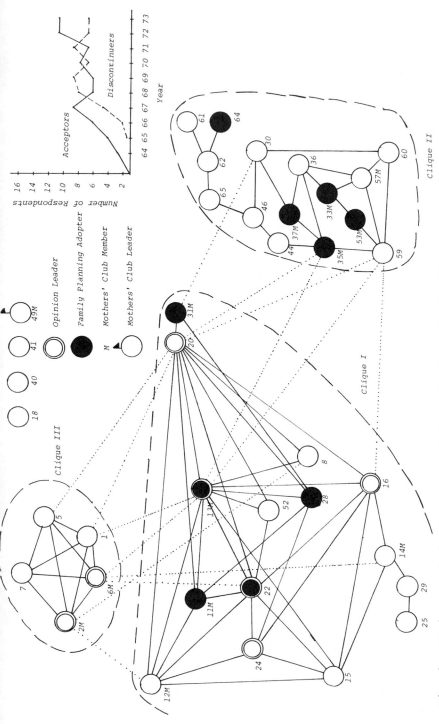

Fig. 2. Sociogram of the Interpersonal Communication Relationships about Family Planning in Village B.

diffusion.[17]

In addition to clique identification, Richards's (1971) network analysis routine computes various indexes of communication structure at the individual, clique, or system level, such as: connectedness, integration, diversity, and openness.

B. *Findings from Network Analysis in Korea*

Here we focus mainly on four sets of findings from our network analysis of family planning diffusion in the two Korean villages: (1) network variables, (2) personal communication networks, (3) "the strength of weak ties," and (4) differences in communication networks on the basis of the relative tabooness of the topics discussed.

1. *Network Variables and the Relative Success of Diffusion Activities.* Network variables explain why Village A has a more successful family planning program than does Village B.[18]

a. *In Village A, there is a higher degree of overlap of the informal clique structure with the mothers' club membership, than in Village B.*

b. *There is greater involvement of pro-family planning opinion leaders in the mothers' club in Village A than in Village B.*

[17]*We also identify the informal opinion leaders on the sociograms (Figures 1 and 2). These opinion leaders are those individuals sociometrically nominated by at least 10% of the other respondents in a village.*

[18]*Such nonnetwork explanations for the relatively greater success of family planning diffusion activities in Village A as (1) home visiting by family planning field workers, and (2) group meetings about family planning, are actually more frequently reported by respondents in Village B(Rogers, 1976). However, mass media exposure to family planning messages is somewhat greater in Village A than in Village B.*

   c. *The mothers' club leader in Village A is more centrally*
located in the communication network than is the case in Village
B.

The data in Figures 1 and 2 were gathered in our 1973 survey.
When we returned to these two villages in 1975, the mothers' club
in Village B had officially disbanded due to its inept leadership,
financial difficulties, and interclique rivalries within the
mothers' club caused by insufficient overlap with the informal
communication structure of the village.

   2. Personal Communication Networks. A *personal communication*
network is comprised of the interconnected individuals who are
linked by patterned communication flows to any given individual
Laumann, 1973, p. 7). For the purposes of our present analysis,
we find it convenient to anchor a network on an individual, rather
than a clique (Mitchell, 1969, p. 14). Each individual maintains
a small communication environment, a personal network of other
individuals with whom he/she consistently interacts about a given
topic.[19]

Our respondents' personal networks explain their decisions to
adopt (and/or discontinue) the innovation of family planning.
Figure 3 presents an illustration of how an increasing percentage
of Respondent #31's (in Village A) personal network adopted family
planning from 1969 to when she herself adopted in 1972. We found
that an individual is likely to adopt family planning if a larger
proportion of her personal network consists of individuals who
have adopted previously.

---

[19]*In the present section, the individual respondent is still*
the unit of analysis, but the independent variable of personal
network behavior is measured *as a relational variable, although*
the dependent variable of innovativeness is not.

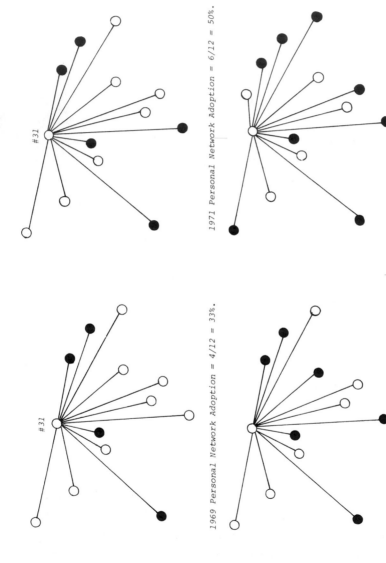

1971 Personal Network Adoption = 6/12 = 50%.

1972 Personal Network Adoption = 8/13 = 62%.

1969 Personal Network Adoption = 4/12 = 33%.

1970 Personal Network Adoption = 6/12 = 50%.

Fig. 3. An Illustration of Respondent #31's Adoption of Family Planning as the Percentage of Adoption Increased in Her Personal Communication Network from 1969 to 1972.

3. *The Strength of Weak Ties.* Out of the network analyses of interpersonal diffusion has grown a research issue called "the strength of weak ties" (Liu and Duff, 1972; Granovetter, 1973).[20] The general proposition underlying this research is: *The informational strength of dyadic communication relationships is inversely related to the degree of homophily (and the strenght of the attraction) between the source and the receiver.* In other words, an innovation is diffused to a larger number of individuals and transverses a greater social distance when passed through weak ties rather than strong (Granovetter, 1973).

Each individual's personal communication network, as previously discussed, consists of friends and acquaintances who are usually (1) highly homophilous (or similar) with the individual, and with each other, and (2) friends of each other, thus constituting an "interlocking network" (Rogers, 1973; Laumann, 1973). This homophily and close attraction facilitates effective communication, but it acts as a barrier to prevent new ideas from entering the network. There is not much innovative potential in an interlocking network; some heterophilous (dissimilar) ties in the network are needed to give it more openness. These "weak ties" enable innovations to flow from clique to clique via liaisons and bridges. Paradoxically, there is a cohesive power to the weak ties within the total network.

We analyzed the sociometric data from our two Korean villages to test the "strength of weak ties" hypothesis in their family planning communication networks. This analysis explored the strength of communication ties in five specific hypotheses, each derived from the original Granovetter statement, relating such

[20]*These two sets of authors independently discovered the diffusion strength of weak sociometric ties and published articles with identical titles but different approaches within a few months of each other in 1972-1973.*

variables as linking ties, reciprocality,[21] homophily on mothers'
club membership and adoption of family planning, and differences
in planning knowledge between dyadic partners. The unit of analysis in all cases is the communication *relationship* between two
individuals about family planning. The strength of a sociometric
tie between two dyadic partners is measured by the number of communication contacts which they share (this is the same measure that
we described previously as the basis for computing proximity in
clique identification).[22] The major findings of this dyadic analysis are:

   a. Tie strength and reciprocal ties: Reciprocal ties are
stronger in both villages than nonreciprocal ties.

   b. Tie strength and linking ties: The number of ties linking
communication cliques is rather small, but, as hypothesized, they
are weaker than nonlinking ties in both villages. As hypothesized,
the linking relationships are weaker than ties within cliques.

   *c. Tie strength and communication between mothers' club mem-
bers and nonmembers:* We had expected stronger ties in more homophilous relationships, but did not find support for our hypothesis
in Village B although we did in Village A. Nevertheless, these
data are consistent with our earlier finding that mothers' club
membership conforms more closely to natural communication cliques
in Village A than in Village B.

[21]*Reciprocal ties are communication relationships in which the
partners both nominate each other; nonreciprocal ties are relationships in which only one partner has been nominated.*

[22]*Each respondent was limited to a maximum of five nominations
in responding to the sociometric question, so our range in tie
strength measures is restricted compared to what we could have
obtained by asking each respondent about the strength of his relationship with each other member in the system. However, the distortion introduced by this factor does not appear to be very severe.*

d. *Tie strength and communication between adopters and non-adopters of family planning.* Although our results are not completely consistent, again we determined that homophilous ties are generally stronger than heterophilous ties.

e. *Tie strength and family planning knowledge.* The women in our two Korean villages were each asked a set of 10 "how-to" knowledge questions about family planning.[23] The difference in the number of correct responses by dyadic partners was calculated for each family planning communication relationship. Contrary to our expectations, we found heterophily on family planning knowledge to be related to tie strength in Village B.

The important point here is that by converting the knowledge variable, measured for each individual respondent, into a dyadic variable, we were able to relate it to tie strength using the empirical measures of relational concepts provided by network analysis.

5. *Taboo Communication.* Diffusion networks undoubtedly differ from innovation to innovation, and from situation to situation. For example, diffusion networks for family planning may differ from networks for abortion. Taboo communication is "the category of message transfer in which the messages are perceived as extremely private and personal in nature because they deal with proscribed behaviour" (Rogers, 1973). We discuss degree of tabooness on the basis of three diffusion networks: friendship, family planning, and abortion. Abortion is considered to be highly taboo communication in Korean villages, where it was illegal until a few months prior to our 1973 survey.

In both villages the number of communication contacts decreased from friendship, to family planning, to abortion; not

[23]These questions asked how often it was necessary to take contraceptive pills, if men could use the IUD, etc.

surprisingly the number of contacts decreased from the least taboo to the most taboo topic. Communication networks are more restricted for more taboo topics. In fact, there is so little abortion communication that cliques cannot be identified in Village A
using abortion communication links.

Table III shows that tabooness is related to less connectedness and weaker tie strength in both villages. This is consistent
with our expectations.

VI.   IMPLICATIONS FOR FUTURE RESEARCH

The theme of this chapter is that various types of network
analysis offer potential for diffusion research to break out of
its past psychological bias, by stressing alternative uses of
interpersonal communication relationships as (1) units of analysis,
and/or (2) units of measurement. We sought to illustrate this
potential with examples from our network analysis of family planning diffusion in Korea.

In addition to our specific findings this work has produced
the following implications for future research on diffusion networks.

A.   In order to improve the ability of the communication structure
to predict diffusion and adoption, a *content analysis* of the communication messages that flow through interpersonal patterns is
needed. Appropriate research designs and measurement techniques
need to be developed in order to sample and analyze the content of

Table III. Differences in Communication Networks on the Basis of the Tabooness of the Topic

	Village A			Village B		
	Friendship communication	Family planning	Abortion	Friendship communication	Family planning	Abortion
1. Connectedness index for the village	.10	.09	.01	.13	.11	.05
2. Average connectedness index for cliques	.64	.52	—	.70	.50	.30
3. Average tie strength	2.9	2.9	1.0	3.3	3.2	1.6

these interpersonal messages.[24]

B. Network analysis should be incorporated in research on *system
effects* in the diffusion of innovations. *System effects* are the
influences of the structure and/or composition of a system on the
behavior of the members of the system. System effects have been
referred to as "compositional effects," "contextual effects," and
"structural effects" in past behavioral research; in all cases,
the general prediction is that an individual's behavior is influenced, in part, by the system of which he is a member.

C. Improvements are needed in *sociometric measurements* of communication flows. A multimeasurement approach to the communication
flow data would contribute to greater accuracy, especially if
some nonsociometric measures (like observation) were also included. At present, one of the main weaknesses of communication network analysis is its complete dependence on sociometric measurement.

D. *Over-time measures* at t_2, t_3, etc. need to be made in order
to contrast these data and results with the cross-sectional correlational analysis of one-shot survey data. Such over-time data
about sociometric communication relationships are almost entirely

[24] *As an example, Robert Gillespie has used a small number of
diary-keepers to record what they heard (and overheard) about
family planning during a communication campaign in Esfahan Province, Iran (Rogers and Agarwala-Rogers, 1976); then he was able
to content analyze their daily diaries. Another approach, based
on the perceptions of Indian farmers and of their change agents of
agricultural innovations, followed a survey design to study the
message contents in interpersonal networks (Fliegel et al., 1971).*

missing in past research on networks. Essentially, we need to determine the reliability of sociometric data and their generalizability across time periods, as well as how network structures
change over time.

Perhaps in closing we might stress the possibility of incorporating network analysis as one component in the typical survey
research on the diffusion of innovations. For instance, personal
communication networks can be measured in a random sample design,
by asking each respondent questions about his/her network partners
(Laumann, 1973). Or, with appropriate changes in the sample design, a sample of all the respondents in intact systems (like villages) can be selected; the loss in generalizability may often be
compensated for by the extra insight offered by the network analyses thus made possible.

The research strategy of including network analysis as at
least one component of survey researches on diffusion would allow
use of alternative units of analysis, and units of measurement,
other than just the individual. And thus the psychological bias
of diffusion research might begin to be overcome.

REFERENCES

Alba, Richard D., & Kadushin, Charles, The introduction of
    social circles: A new measure of social proximity in
    networks, *Sociological Methods and Research*, 1976, *5*,
    77-102.
Allen, Richard K. *A comparison of communication behaviors in
    innovative and noninnovative secondary schools*. Ph.D. Thesis,
    East Lansing, Michigan State University.
Barton, Allen. Bringing society back in: Survey research and
    macro-methodology. *American Behavioral Scientist*, 1968, *12*,
    1-9.

Bevin, Corlin O., Jr. & Brundage, Everett G. A method for analy-
    zing the sociomatrix. *Sociomet,* 1950, *13,* 141-145.

Coleman, James S. Relational analysis: A study of social organ-
    ization with survey methods. *Human Organization,* 1958, *17,*
    28-36.

Coleman, James S., *et al. Medical innovation: a Diffusion study.*
    New York: Bobbs-Merrill, 1966.

Crane, Diana. *Invisible colleges: Diffusion of knowledge in
    scientific communities.* Chicago: University of Chicago Press,
    1972.

Danowski, James A. Communication network analysis and social
    change: Group structure and family planning in two Korean
    villages. In Goodwin Chu *et al* (Eds.) *Communication and Group
    Transformation in Development,* Honolulu East-West Communica-
    tion Institute, Monograph 2, 1976.

Davis, Burl Edward. *System variables and agricultural innovative-
    ness in Eastern Nigeria.* Ph.D. Thesis, East Lansing, Michigan
    State University, 1968.

Granovetter, Mark S. The strength of weak ties. *American Journal
    of Sociology,* 1973, *78,* 1360-1380.

Guimarães, Lytton. *Communication integration in modern and tra-
    ditional social systems: a Comparative analysis across twenty
    communities of Minas Gerais.* Ph.D. Thesis, East Lansing,
    Michigan State University, 1972.

Katz, Elihu. Communication research and the image of society:
    Convergence of two traditions. *American Journal of Sociology,*
    1960, *65,* 435-440.

Kincaid, D. Lawrence, *et al. Mothers' clubs and family planning
    in rural Korea: The case of Oryu Li.* Honolulu: East-West
    Communication Institute, Case Study 2, 1975.

Kuhn, Thomas K. *The structure of scientific revolutions.*
    Chicago: University of Chicago Press, 1962.

Laumann, Edward O. *Bonds of pluralism: The form and substance of urban social networks*. New York: Wiley-Interscience, 1973.

Lazarsfeld, Paul F., *et al. The people's choice*. New York: Duell, Sloan, and Pearce, 1944.

Liu, William T., & Duff, Robert W. The strength in weak ties. *Public Opinion Quarterly*, 1972, *36*, 361-366.

Mitchell, J. Clyde. The concept and use of social networks. In J. Clyde Mitchell (Ed.), *Social networks in urban situations*. Manchester, England: Manchester University Press, 1969.

Park, Hyung Jong, *et al. Mothers' clubs and family planning in Korea*. Seoul National University, School of Public Health, 1974.

Richards, William D. An improved conceptually based method for analysis of communication network structures of large complex organizations. Paper presented at the International Communication Association, Phoenix, 1971.

Rogers, Everett M. *Communication strategies for family planning*. New York: Free Press, 1973.

Rogers, Everett, M. Where are we in understanding the diffusion of innovations? In Wilbur Schramm and Daniel Lerner (Eds.), *Communication and change: The last ten years -- and the next*, Honolulu, University Press of Hawaii, 1976.

Rogers, Everett M., & Agarwala-Rogers, Rekha. *Communication in organizations*. New York: Free Press, 1976a.

Rogers, Everett, M., & Agarwala-Rogers, Rekha, *Evaluation research on family planning communication*, Paris, UNESCO, Technical Report 1976b.

Rogers, Everett M., & Bhowmik, Dilip K. Homophily-heterophily: Relational concepts for communication research. *Public Opinion Quarterly*, 1971, *34*, 523-528.

Rogers, Everett M., and Thomas, Patricia C. *Bibliography on the diffusion of innovations*. Ann Arbor: University of Michigan, Department of Population Planning, Mimeo Report, 1975.

Rogers, Everett M., & Kincaid, B. Laurence. *Communication network:*
    Toward a new paradigm for research, New York Free Press,
    (in press).

Rogers, Everett M. with Shoemaker, F. Floyd. *Communication of*
    innovations: A cross-cultural approach. New York: Free
    Press, 1971.

Ryan, Bryce, & Gross, Neal C. The diffusion of hybrid seed corn
    in two Iowa communities. *Rural Sociology,* 1943, *8,* 15-24.

Saxena, Anant P. *System effects on innovativeness among Indian*
    farmers. Ph.D. Thesis, East Lansing, Michigan State Univer-
    sity, 1968.

Sheingold, Carl A. Social networks and voting: The resurrection
    of a research agenda. *American Sociological Review,* 1973, *38,*
    712-720.

Shoemaker, F. Floyd. *System variables and educational innovative-*
    ness in Thai government secondary schools. Ph.D. Thesis, East
    Lansing, Michigan State University, 1971.

Tarde, Gabriel. *The laws of imitation,* trans. by Elsie Clews
    Parsons. New York: Holt, 1903.

Yadav, Dharam P. *Communication structure and innovation diffusion*
    in two Indian villages. Ph.D. Thesis, East Lansing, Michigan
    State University, 1967.

CHAPTER 9

DETERMINISTIC MODELS OF SOCIAL NETWORKS[1]

H. Russell Bernard

Department of Sociology and Anthropology

West Virginia University

Morgantown, West Virginia

Peter D. Killworth

Department of Applied Mathematics

University of Cambridge

Cambridge, England

I. INTRODUCTION

In this chapter we review some current mathematical models of social networks and examine the type and range of assumptions used in building these models. Also considered is the possibility for and the requirements of a social physics (which we assume to be the first goal of mathematical modeling). Models and modeling, together with the accompanying rationale, is in-and-of itself a little understood technique, despite the spasmodic exhortation in the literature to use models as one of a range of tools.

[1]*This work was supported under Office of Naval Research Contract #N0014-75-C-0441. Code 452. This chapter is a revision of report BK-111-75. We are indebted to Jack Hunter and Robert Abelson for extremely helpful criticism. The opinions expressed in this chapter are those of the authors and do not necessarily reflect the position of the supporting agency.*

II. WHY MODELS?

As a physicist/anthropologist team we perceive the dual needs
of precision and compromise required to model the complexities of
reality. It is in the spirit of this dual perception that we
offer the following preliminary comments on the reasons for modeling social networks.

In physics, models are built to isolate and understand at
most a few discrete phenomena, for example, what creates the Gulf
Stream? or, what causes a tornado? The advantage of studying such
phenomena is that over the centuries a great deal of complex but
logical physics (i.e., laws) have been deduced that simultaneously
describe and predict things that do or will actually happen. This
physics also tells us that many things affect any single phenomenon. Thus, the physical universe, contrary to the assumptions
of many behavioral scientists, is probably just as complicated as
the social universe; the dynamics of a "black hole" in a galaxy
are inherently no less complex than the relations of people in a
network. In modeling physical phenomena, however, our historical
perspective enables us to decide which phenomena to include in a
model, and which to reject, even though we know they are all important and contributory. This allows three important luxuries:

(1) Some elements may be rejected on grounds of time or space
scales: For example, the last Ice Age (and the next one) has little effect on the dynamics of surface waves, but must be considered
if the long-range movement of human populations is being discussed.

(2) Concentration may be focused on some small area, that is,
reasonably simple models of small phenomena may be produced.

(3) Complex numerical models of large, complex things, may
also be generated.

Three points must be made however to distinguish this last
luxury from what is currently available to social scientists:

(a) Macromodels can reproduce as many phenomena as computer
limitations allow. However, these phenomena are not parameterized
in any way; their physical basis is included explicitly.

(b) Much of the output of macromodels in physics remains in-
comprehensible. In this case one must decide whether the output
is merely a numerical artifact or an increment in our knowledge
about the phenomenon under study.

(c) Much of the physics in large (or small) models is sur-
prising--even counterintuitive. For example, it is not obvious
that a body moving in the northern hemisphere experiences a force,
proportional to its speed, at 90° to the right of its velocity.
The force is very weak but of great importance to all geophysical
phenomena, from the rotation of bathtub drain whirlpools, to the
movement of whole oceans. It requires a staggering amount of
observation to discover the force, describe it, and, finally, to
understand it. In fact, it was discovered theoretically *before*
it was ever observed.

In terms of social network models, these facts indicate that
there are two main approaches to modeling. The first is to produce rather simple-minded models which are particularly useful
where accurate measurement is lacking. The second is to declare
that everything is too complex to model simply, which leads either
to grandiose models whose basis is dubious (unspecified black
boxes connected by ill-defined arrows), or to giving up. Land
(1971) has made an excellent case that neither of these should
occur if we are to achieve the physics of behavior. This is a
long, slow business, however, as witness the work in psychophysics
by Stevens and his colleagues (1957, 1959, 1975) and the attempts
by Hamblin (1974) and others to formulate some principles of
social attitudes.

III.   WHY IS THERE NO SOCIAL PHYSICS?

Indeed, why *is* there no social physics? The "scientific
method" requires the following:

I.   Accurate measuring devices and a knowledge of precision
of the measuring devices used.

II.   Ability to make repeated experiments under varied conditions.

III.   Ability to test predictions based on observations and
hypotheses.[2]

The problems with II and III are well known. Even under the
"white-room" conditions of small-groups research, there is no way
to control the parameters. Furthermore, in sociometry repeated
experiments are generally avoided because sociometric parameters
are probably time-dependent. Network analysis fares poorly on
predictions, also. In the social sciences (with no pre-existing
laws) our theories proceed from data or intuition to a set of
probabilistic statements. Unlike theories in the physical sciences, however (which *do* start out with laws), these theories
yield only *more* probabilities.[3]

[2]*Some people note that prior to all the above lies a reasonable set of well defined things to study, but not to the exclusion of everything else. In the social sciences there is a well-
known penchant for naming things, on the assumption that if you
can name, you understand it. Recall Leach's exhortation (1961)
that naming the "class of blue butterflies" tells us nothing
about the structure of lepidoptera.*

[3]*In the physical sciences, hard numbers (e.g., the energy
levels in the hydrogen atom) can be found as eigenvalues of a differential equation--this despite the fact that the formulation of
the problem is totally probabilistic.*

This leaves the most basic problem I. We have no accurate measuring devices for what we believe to be the important parameters in social networks. This puts us somewhere in the pre-Archimedes era of science. We do, indeed, have reasonably good devices for obtaining background data such as SES, propinquity, attitudes, etc. All these must be included in any fully explanatory model of any subfield of human behavior. Apparently, the "basic" parameters to be measured include the varieties of affective and effective relations (trust, communication, love, etc.).

Consider effective relations, normally the province of anthropologists (e.g., Barnes, 1969, Mitchell, 1973). Effective interaction is usually measured by asking members of a network to make their best guess about their relationships within the network. Assuming veridicality, what results is a cognitive map of informants' relations to and/or from the members of the network. This says nothing about whether the relations inhere--short, of course, of straight observation. In any reasonably large network, of course, one can only observe a tiny fraction of the relations. Repeated questioning can check informant reliability, assuming that the network is steady but will not establish the accuracy of the data.

Traditionally in science, this difficulty is circumvented by measuring something related to the quantity to be measured. Thus, what people say is tacitly assumed to be correlated to what they do. The accuracy of this instrument, however, remains unchecked. Accepting this Holland and Leinhardt (1973) have attempted to assess the effects of certain forms of measurement error on the results of theoretical predictions. They found that with the proper form of statistical data analysis, some effects of error are filtered, allowing some weak signals to become readable. We (Bernard and Killworth, 1973) showed that the "catij" manipulations also filter out selected forms of error. However, both of these approaches pessimistically assume that the instrument

will always be faulty. We are currently trying to examine this
problem somewhat more formally by using a variety of naturally
occurring unobtrusive observers from within the network itself.

We (Killworth and Bernard, 1976b) took cognitive and behavioral data from a group of deaf persons who regularly communicate
via teletype (TTY). Each person ranked the others (there were a
total of 31 persons in the group) in order of "perceived communication" on TTY. They were asked to make no distinction between
length, importance, or frequency of contact.

The group members then logged their *actual* communications,
over a three-week period, measured by lines of TTY output.[4] This
enabled a variety of comparisons to be made between cognitive and
actual communications. We found a significant tendency for more
frequent communications to occur between an informant and someone
he or she ranked low (i.e., high communication) than someone
ranked high (i.e., low communication). However, rankings beyond
8 fared no better than chance. This is, of course, not a very
stringent criterion on which to base conclusions about accuracy.

We increased the stringency by examining how many people
needed to be ranked in order to account for a given percentage
of an informant's actual communication, with a given degree of
reliability. One can account for small percentages (e.g., less
than 30%) of total communication with a small number of rankings
(typically the first 7 for 90% reliability). However, if 70% of
the total communication is to be accounted for, with 95% reliability, a stunning 24 people (out of the 30) need to be ranked.
This raises the possibility that the data gathering procedure may

[4]*This simplistic approach to "measuring communication" is
essentially a first approximation. Experiments are in progress
to test the efficacy of other measures of communication, and its
multidimensional nature.*

be meaningless; ranking 24 out of 30, is almost the equivalent of declaring that everybody talks to everybody (which is, of course, untrue).

A second approach was to define suitable "scores" of accuracy for each informant. The simplest such score was a correlation between ranking of and communication with each person. These correlations, although significant, accounted for very little variance. So, the relationship between ranks and communication was, again, weak.

The most stringent criterion of all is to ask "if i ranked j nth, how close to nth did j actually come?" This enables scores to be devised based on a requirement of perfect accuracy or on a leeway of ± 1, ± 2, etc. Unfortunately, the only significant success rate (based on a crude null hypothesis of 1/31 of ranking anyone correctly) was for the first-ranked person. Even then, he was only communicated with first, second, third, or fourth most frequently (i.e., leeway = ± 3) half of the time.

We examined the effects of several of the system parameters (e.g., number of people chosen to be ranked, total communication with the group, total TTY communication with the world at large, the split into calls to and from others, etc.). Some of these parameters divided the group into two or three sections between which there were significant differences according to some of the criteria just given. However, there was *no* overall systematic effect of any parameter we examined.

The data were also examined for structure by the methods of Holland and Leinhardt (1975). Although interpretation of the results must involve caution (their method essentially involves the examination of many data sets), one striking fact emerges. Of the great variety of potential structures searched for, none appeared significantly more or less often than chance in the communication that *actually* occurred. But various structures

(e.g., transitivity) occurred significantly more or less often
than chance in the *reported* communication. This suggests that it
may be only cognitive behavior that possesses regularities; actual
behavior may be quite disordered.

The measurement of affect presents even greater difficulty.
For a psychophysiological state such as attitudes, we *might* be
able to establish reliable metrics. However, this research is in
its infancy. The evidence on galvanic skin response and cardiac
functions is equivocal (Rescorla and Solomon, 1967). Dobbs (1975)
indicates that fidgeting and body temperature are poor metrics
for attitudes, but that eye contact and voice tremor are likely
prospects for unobtrusive measures. Even if such measures are
defined, we are still left with the well-known problem of using
attitude measurement as a proxy for behavior. Fishbein noted in
1967 that "traditional measures of attitude (i.e., toward a given
object, person, or class of people) are *not* likely to be related
to behavior in any consistent fashion" (italics in the original).
In the most recent review of the issue (McGuire, 1975) the situation has not changed:

> ...an intimidating amount of research has been done on
> attitudes. This preoccupation with attitudes is puzzling since
> in practice the payoff usually depends on a person's gross be-
> havior rather than her or his felt attitudes. We cannot es-
> cape the puzzle by supposing that attitudes are closely related
> convenient surrogates of the behaviors of ultimate interest
> since we all know that, far from there being a strong rela-
> tionship, we shall have to struggle bravely in this paper to
> maintain that there is any relationship at all. [p. 17]

So, in measuring affective links in a network (i.e., asking
people who they like, trust, prefer to work with, etc.) we must

accept verbal representations of cognition about some psychophysiological condition, and then measure the condition through the
proxy of behavioral interaction--quite a leap. At best, one is
only measuring the relationship between verbalizations *about*
affect and some defined behavior or set of behaviors.

The result of this lack of practical data gathering techniques has been infrequent calls for examinations of the relationship between cognitive and behavioral systems (Kogan and
Tagiuri, 1958); and assumptions by most researchers that cognition (about affect, at that) is a valid proxy for behavior. Indeed, the enthusiasm of sociometricians for this assumption is
well known: "the sociometric test is a direct measure of a specific type of behavior" (Lorber, 1969; p. 243). Unfortunately,
the accuracy of the measure continues to be faulty: We have not
even established the error bounds on our measurements.

Twenty-five years ago, Tagiuri, Blake, and Bruner (1953) made
a rare examination of the accuracy of cognition about affective
relations in terms of other people's cognition. Within this admittedly tautological framework, they found that informants'
guesses about what others would say they felt were more accurate
than chance, but they failed to give any measure of how accurate
that was. There is, after all, a quite natural tendency to
avoid validating a technique (i.e., affective sociometry) that is
possibly incapable of being validated.

IV.   WHAT MODELS ARE THERE?

The ground rules for models that are normally quoted (e.g.,
Land, 1971) include the following:

(a) Definitions alone do not make a model. We thus re-
gretfully omit the pioneering work of Bavelas (1949) and all
similar set theoretic formalizations.

(b) A flow chart littered with undefined processes is
not a model. Of course, this does not reduce the need for
pseudomodels as conceptual aids.

(c) A set of statements about which one says, "This can
give us predictions about X" is not a model unless it does.

In addition to these rules there is also a stricture that the
fewer parameters in a model, the more useful and the more appealing is that model. If it is possible to predict a measurable
quantity that is independent of all parameters, this provides a
greater test of a model's power than if all quantities were functions of, say, three adjustable parameters.

These rules leave us with two kinds of models to review in
the area of social networks: those in which information propa-
gates through and is modified by a known network, and those in
which the relations within the network are predicted as a function of time. Hitherto, the feedback between these two subsets
of models appears to have been neglected (with the exception of
Rainio, 1966). Ultimately, more powerful models must include the
interaction of both.

Models of information diffusion have been developed by Rapoport (1953) and his associates, Coleman, Katz, and Menzel (1957).
Reviews of these have appeared in Kemeny and Snell (1962), Bartholomew (1967), and Coleman (1964). Therefore, we will restrict
our attention to models of change in social networks.

We are aware at this writing of five such models: Simon
(1952) (S); Rainio (1966) (R); Sorensen and Hallinan (1974) (SH);
Hunter (1974) (H); and Killworth and Bernard (1976a) (KB). In
addition to these there are several more models on attitude
change, reinforcement theory, information processing and cognitive dissonance all due to Hunter (1975a, b, and this volume) and
an early model of attitude change by Abelson and Berstein (1963)
(AB). Hunter's models are all designed with a similar background,

but with differing dynamics. We shall treat all these together
within H, with any exceptions noted when necessary. Abelson and
Bernstein's epic computer model defies all our rules about model-
building parsimony, which probably makes it more likely to be
relevant to real life! The difficulty with such feedback control models, as experienced frequently in economic macromodels,
is in the unpleasant mathematics involved in examining the nonlinear dependence of model output on input parameters. Considered
as a *simulation*, however, little or no mathematics is involved.

There are also three well-known pseudomodels (balance, transitivity, and positive balance) and at least two attempts to set up
the conditions for stochastic modeling (Mayhew and Gray, 1972;
Katz and Proctor, 1959).[5] The models of R and SH are stochastic;
those of S, H, AB, and KB are dynamic.

If we are ever to establish any social physics, some measures
of agreement on primitive assumptions will be necessary. We have
culled from the five models mentioned sixteen basic assumptions
which are common to some or all. These are given simply in Table
I. We have divided the assumptions into two main areas: setting
up (7 assumptions) and driving forces (9 assumptions) that we
shall discuss in turn.

[5] *We have used the term pseudomodel to denote models which do
not specify how processes occur. This does not negate the value
of such models. The neglect of process specification, however,
leads to problems. For example, Hallinan and McFarland (1974)
show that attempts to increase transitivity can lead to greater
intransitivity. Thus, a pseudomodel that claims "there is a
pressure towards transitivity" tells us nothing about what will
happen to a given group of people. This accounts for our narrow
focus on deterministic models.*

TABLE I. Assumptions in Five Social Network Models

	Assumptions					
Set up	AB	H	KB	R	S	SH
1. Closedness	no	yes	yes	yes	no	yes
2. Veridicality	yes	yes	yes	yes	yes	yes
3. Dyadic relations	yes	yes	yes	yes	?	yes
4. "Stability"	no	no	no	yes	no	yes
5. Limited conversation content	no?	no	no	no	no	no
6. Existence of measurement error	ignored	ignored	ignored	dealt with	ignored	ignored
7. Infinite information propagation speed	no	yes	yes	no	yes	no?
Driving force of change						
1. Contact	yes	yes	yes	yes	yes	yes
2. Reinforcement	yes	yes	yes	yes	yes	yes
3. Cognitive dissonance	yes	no	yes	yes	yes	yes
4. Feedback of affect on effect	no	yes?	yes	yes	yes	no
5. Feedback of effect on affect	yes	yes	yes	yes	yes	no
6. Pressure to mutuality	?	yes (prediction)	no	yes	?	yes
7. Change possible due to dyadic force	yes	yes	no	yes	?	no
8. Change possible due to presence of third party	no	yes	yes	no	?	yes
9. Effects of individual personalities	yes	no	yes	no	no	no

   The first of the assumptions is that of group closure. This
assumption is patently the widest departure from reality of all:
There are no naturally occurring physically closed groups. The
notion that outside influences play no part in the relationships
between group members is plainly absurd. Yet, all of the models
except S and AB make this assumption, either explicitly, (H, KB,
R), or implicitly (SH). Is this assumption adequate? If not,
how can we improve it? One (unproductive) way is to generate a
handful of parameters which hopefully describe external influences. This has a tendency to produce least-squares-type of fits
to data--normally a technique of last resort. S's model does away
with least-squares by treating the entire group as the unit of
analysis; thus external influences become a single function of
time. Only AB treats certain external affects explicitly. One
constructive way to deal with external influences might be to
analyze the goals of the various group members (if measurable)
and the effects of these goals on their behavior. For example,
if it turns out that the assumption "everyone wants to be loved
as much as possible" is true, then modeling is possible. However,
the *best* alternative is to investigate whether outside parameters
or goals are relevant anyway. If not, they should be eliminated.

   The second assumption is that of veridicality, although this
is only implicit in SH. Rainio allows either of two contradictory
opinions to be held by the same person with varying probabilities.
Yet we know that people lie, presumably to achieve personal ends.
This also may or may not be relevant; if it is, Hunter (this
volume) has suggested how lying could be included.

   Third, all the models except S's assume that relationships
(even contact) are dyadic. (This is, of course, partly for
mathematical convenience.) We cannot assess the relevance of
multiple contacts in group behavior. S avoids the problem by
not specifying details of relationships between persons.

The fourth assumption, "stability" (an ill-defined concept), is a necessary criterion for any stochastic model (R, SH), but irrelevant to dynamic models (H, AB, KB, S). Steadiness, however, is achieved in four of the six models: in a finite time (H) or an infinite time (KB, R, SH). The last two are steady only probabilistically, of course. The general behavior of AB's model for an extended time is unknown. H's model can "explode." It seems important that four quite distinct models should achieve steady states in distinct ways. Is this a function of the assumptions which went into the models, or a reflection of the real world? We would opt for the latter, since the assumptions are so varied.

The fifth assumption, a plus for five of the models (by our standards of parsimony), is that conversation content is unrestricted, hence removing a potential source of parameters. Conversation is restricted in AB, but can easily be allowed to cover all subjects. However, the existence of measurement error, the sixth assumption, is of even more concern. This has been examined by Holland and Leinhardt (1973), Hallinan (1972), and Killworth (1974). In no case is the treatment satisfactory since none of the authors had suspected that informants were capable of the gross inaccuracy we (Killworth and Bernard, 1976b) have discovered, and because each treatment assumed rather simplified forms of error for the purpose of analysis. The models handle measurement differently: SH recognize the difficulty quite explicitly and just as explicitly ignore it; KB mention it in passing and cavalierly fail to deal with it; AB and H ignore it from scratch. S also ignores it, since measurement of all quantities is ignored; White (1970) suggests how some of the quantities used in S could be measured, but does not discuss the errors involved. R, however, actually runs his model against real data, a feat of temerity yet unequalled by the other models.

Of course, his results are disastrous, a fact which probably
accounts for the timidity of later models. We should point out,
however, that our own results (KB, 1976b) show that bad fits of
data to models may be the fault of the data.

Finally, the models vary in their treatment of information
propagation. (More formally, this is within the domain of the
diffusion models.) AB and R are the only models that explicitly
allow for a finite speed of information propagation. The concept is ignored in SH, although a finite speed would not be dis-
allowed. H, KB, and S all have information propagating infinitely
quickly, mainly for convenience. Redefinition can be made in
terms of finite time steps, but yet another ratio of time scales,
this time depending on spatial allocation also, is required to
include the concept. Propinquity may indeed be important in the
development of social relations, but it is not obvious how to include it in most formal models.

The second area of assumptions concerns potential driving
forces. The first of these is the importance of contact for
change in relationships, assumed explicitly in all models. This
seems to be the least implausible of the assumptions. Second,
all the models at least imply the importance of positive reinforcement on the path of relationships; indeed, this is the
driving mechanism in one of Hunter's models. Such a driving
force seems plausible, but we have no way to judge its relevance.

The models begin to diverge on the issue of cognitive dissonance. AB, KB, R, S, SH all use the concept, while H uses a
different force completely. (He assumes that the rate of change
of an affective feeling about a person is proportional to the
information one has about that person.) Bem's work (1967, 1968)
should make us cautious about relying too heavily on cognitive
dissonance as a primitive force of behavior. There is also some
definitional problem regarding dissonance. The literature on
dissonance seems generally to reserve the term for complex

situations in which individuals' attitudes are not congruent with
reality. If one believes two lines to be of the same length, and
everyone else in the experiment says they are not of the same
length, dissonance is produced.

In KB's model, the notion of dissonance is used in a way which
may be interpreted as "imbalance." That model assumes a "primitive force" that drives people to act consistently with their perception of how others in a group feel or act; or, alternatively,
to accept a certain amount of "dissonance" (i.e., noncongruence)
between their own attitudes and behaviors versus their perception
of the attitudes and behaviors of others. It also assumes that
different people have different tolerances for this dissonance.
When this problem of noncongruence is stated in terms of triadic
relations, a primitive force towards *balance* seems to be in order.
Even when the problem is stated in terms of walks through a digraph, "balance" rather than "dissonance" seems to be preferred.
In our view, for the purposes of modeling network relations, the
force towards balance and the force towards reduction of dissonance (presumed to exist in the individual's head) are the same.
Dissonance large enough to be observed can be measured. The
feeling of imbalance (regarding one or a few triads) is more difficult to isolate and measure. We assume, however, that a dynamic
model must begin at some time and describe how things move through
time. Thus, we assume a force toward balance is equivalent to a
force toward consonance or congruence. The measurable effect of
dissonance we take as the consequence of imbalance.[6]

Further distinctions in the models may be made if we consider the feedback between effect and affect. A feedback of

[6]*This explanation of our use of the word "dissonance" has
benefited heavily from discussions with Robert Abelson and Jack
Hunter. They patiently pointed out that we do not derive our
use of the term from classical dissonance theory.*

affect on effect is retained explicitly by KB, R, and S, partially treated by H in an Appendix, and rejected by SH and AB. The feedback of effect on affect is retained by AB, KB, R, and S, and again rejected by SH. The uniform rejection by SH of feedback is the natural outcome of reliance upon a Markov process. The feedbacks in the other models are handled in various ways. H's assumption is of the crudest kind: The existence of contact allows the information in his model to flow. R adjusts the probabilities of contact and opinion simultaneously, following each contact. These adjustments are symmetrical.

By contrast AB and KB do not presuppose symmetry to be a necessary component of change in dyadic relations. Thus, they assume that i can desire a stronger contact with j independent of j's feelings.

This brings us to the sixth assumption in this set, that of pressure towards mutuality. H's model *predicts* (rather than assumes) eventual mutuality; SH and R assume it. AB's and KB's models appear to be the only nonmutual models extant, since mutuality is irrelevant to S.

The seventh and eighth assumptions define an environment within which changes of relations are possible. Again, these assumptions are irrelevant to S, who deals with the group rather than individuals. Of the models only H's allows change to derive directly from dyadic relations, *as well as* from multiple relations. The KB and SH models require a third party for change to occur to either partner of a dyad; this was a deliberate decision in KB but was forced by the formalism in SH. Of the models, only AB's and R's reject changes due directly to a third party.

Finally, the effects of individual personalities on the course of relations is given short shrift--even by KB, the only model that includes them (AB partially allows for individual affects). One may legitimately enquire whether this assumption is relevant to

modeling of networks at this stage. After all, we have consistently demanded a *reduction* in parameters, if their removal does
not alter the qualitative predictions of a model. Is it legitimate to dole out a parameter to every member of a group, while
rejecting all forms of external influence? Although KB's model
happens to require these parameters in order to function, this
does not imply that they are fundamental.

V.   CONCLUSION

To model the ecosystem of a semienclosed bay which is
bedevilled by typhoons at rather random intervals and yet neglect the typhoons is worthless--one would do better modeling
the typhoons. The fact that we can say this indicates our knowledge of the importance of typhoons (i.e., we understand some
of the physics). Further, the failure of the ecosystem model
does not mean that it was a failure as a *general* model. Furthermore, how can we judge the model if we neither understand all of
the physics nor have any means of making accurate measurements?

Thus, models can only be useful aids to research if they proceed simultaneously with the development of better research tools.
Our work indicates that devices currently used for gathering network data may be inadequate. Theories based upon data with unknown (but large) error bounds are likely to appear incorrect
regardless of their actual validity.

REFERENCES

Abelson, R. P., & Bernstein, A. A computer simulation model of
     community referendum controversies. *Public Opinion Quarterly,*
     1963, *27*, 93-122.
Barnes, J. A. Networks and political process. In J. C. Mitchel
     (Ed.), *Social Networks in Urban Situations*. Manchester: Man-
     chester University Press, 1969.

Bartholomew, D. J. *Stochastic models for social processes*. New York: Wiley-Interscience, 1967.

Bavelas, A. A mathematical model for group structures. *Applied Anthropology,* 1948, *7*, 16-30.

Bem, D. J. Self-perception: An alternative interpretation of cognitive dissonance. *Psychology Review,* 1967, *74*, 183-200.

Bem, D. J. Dissonance reduction in the behaviorist. In R. Abelson, E. Aaronson, Wm. McGuire, T. Newcomb, M. Rosenberg, and P. Tannenbaum (Eds.), *Theories of cognitive consistency*. Chicago: Rand-McNally, 1968.

Bernard, H. Russell, & Killworth, Peter D. On the social structure of an ocean-going research vessel and other important things. *Social Science Research,* 1973, *2*, 145-84.

Bernard, H. Russell, & Killworth, Peter D. Informant accuracy in social network data II. *Human Communications Research,* 1977.

Coleman, J. *Introduction to mathematical sociology*. Glencoe: Free Press, 1964.

Coleman, James, Katz, Elihu, & Menzel, Herbert. The diffusion of an innovation among physicians. *Sociometry,* 1957, *20*, 253-70.

Dobbs, James. Physiological and physical activity measures of attitudes. In H. W. Sinaiko and L. A. Broedling (Eds.), *Perspectives on attitude assessment*. Washington: Smithsonian Institution, Manpower Research and Advisory Services, 1975.

Fishbein, Martin. *Readings in attitude theory and measurement*. New York: Wiley, 1967.

Hallinan, Maureen. Comment on Holland and Leinhardt. *American Journal of Sociology,* 1972, *72*, 1201-5.

Hallinan, Maureen, & McFarland, David D. Higher order stability conditions in mathematical models sociometric or cognitive structure. Mimeo, University of Wisconsin, Dept. of Sociology, 1974.

Hamblin, Robert L. Social attitudes: Magnitude measurement and theory. In H. M. Blalock, Jr. (Ed.), *Measurement in the social sciences*. Chicago: Aldine Publishing Co., 1974.

Hunter, John E. Dynamic sociometry. *Journal of Mathematical Sociology*, 1974.

Hunter, John E. Mathematical models of the development of sentiment in small groups based on dissonance theory. Unpublished manuscript presented to the conference Advanced Research Symposium on Social Networks, of the Mathematical Social Science Board, National Science Foundation, Hanover, New Hampshire, 1975. (a)

Hunter, John E. The development of sentiment in small groups: Three mathematical models derived from information processing theories of attitude change. Unpublished manuscript presented to the conference Advanced Research Symposium on Social Networks, of the Mathematical Social Science Board, National Science Foundation. Hanover, New Hampshire, 1975. (b)

Katz, Leo, & Proctor, Charles H. The concepts of configurations of interpersonal relations in a group as a time dependent stochastic process. *Psychometrika*, 1959, *24(4)*, 317-27.

Kemeny, John C., & Snell, J. L. *Mathematical models in the social sciences*. Boston: Ginn and Co., 1962.

Killworth, Peter D. Intransitivity in the structure of small closed groups. *Social Science Research*, 1974, *3*, 1-23.

Killworth, Peter D., & Bernard, H. R. A model of human group dynamics. *Social Science Research*, 1976, *5*,173-224. (a)

Killworth, Peter D., & Bernard, H. R. Informant accuracy in social network data. *Human Organization*, 1976, *35(3)*, 269-286. (b)

Kogan, Nathan, & Tagiu, Reanto. Interpersonal preference and cognitive organization. *Journal of Abnormal and Social Psychology*, 1958, *56*, 113-16.

Land, Kenneth. Formal theory. In Herbert Costner (Ed.), *Sociological methodology*. Washington: Jossey-Bass, Inc. 1971.

Leach, Edmund R. *Rethinking anthropology*. London: University of London Press, 1961.

Lorber, Neil. The reliability of validity of sociometric measures. *American Sociologist,* 1969, *4*, 243-4.

McGuire, Wm. The concepts of attitudes and their relationships to behaviors. In H. W. Sinaiko and L. A. Broedling (Eds.), *Perspectives on attitude assessment*. Washington: Smithsonian Institution, Manpower Research and Advisory Services, 1975.

Mayhew, Bruce H., & Gray, Louis N. Growth and decay of structure in interaction. *Comparative Group Studies*. 1972, May, 131-60.

Mitchell, J. C. Network norms and institutions. In J. Boissevian and J. C. Mitchell (Eds.), *Network analysis: Studies in human interaction*. The Hague: Mouton, 1973.

Rainio, K. A study of sociometric group structure: An application of a stochastic theory of social interaction. In J. Berger, M. Zelditch Jr., and B. Anderson (Eds.), *Sociological theories in progress*. Boston: Houghton Mifflin, 1966.

Rappaport, Anatol. Spread of information through a population with sociostructural bias: I Assumption of transitivity. *Bulletin of Mathematics and Biophysics,* 1953, *15,* 523-33.

Rescorla, Robert A., & Solomon, Rochard, L. Two-processes learning theory: Relationships between pavlovian conditioning and instrumental learning. *Psychological Review,* 1967, *74(3),* 151-82.

Rosenberg, Seymour. Mathematical models of social behavior. In G. Lindzey and E. Aaronson (Eds.), *The handbook of social psychology*. London: Addison-Wesley Publishing Co., 1968.

Simon, Herbert A. A formal theory of interaction in social groups. *American Sociological Review,* 1952, *17,* 202-11.

Sorensen, A. B., & Hallinan, Maureen T. A stochastic model for change in group structure. Working paper 74-9, Center for Demography and Ecology, University of Wisconsin, 1974.

Stevens, S. S.   On the psychophysical law. *Psychological Review,*
      1957, *64*, 153-81.

Stevens, S. S., Tactile variation: Dynamics of sensory intensity.
      Journal of Experimental Psychology, 1959, *57*, 210-18.

Stevens, S. S. *Psychophysics*. New York: Wiley-Interscience,
      1975.

Tagiuri, Tenato, lake, R. R., & Bruner, Jerome S.   Some deter-
      minants of the perception of positive and negative feelings
      in others. *Journal of Abnormal and Social Psychology,*1953,
      48, 585-92.

White, H.   Simon out of Homans by Coleman. *American Journal of*
      Sociology, 1970, *75*, 852-62.

CHAPTER 10

INDEPENDENT GENERALIZATIONS OF BALANCE

Claude Flament

Laboratorire de Psychologie Sociale

Universite de Provence

Aix-en-Provence, France

I. INTRODUCTION

"Now that it is recognized that balance is a specific instance of clusterability, it is evident that two separate questions should be distinguished: what conditions bring about a
tendency toward clustering? And what determines the number of
clusters that will be formed? [Cartwright and Harary, 1979]."

During the last years, a part of the formal and experimental
work in our laboratory was devoted to trying to answer questions
similar to those of Cartwright and Harary in the field of the
representation of social structures, an area that lies within
cognitive social psychology.

Cartwright and Harary suggest that there exist two "successive" phenomena: first, a tendency toward clustering and second, after this first tendency is achieved, an eventual tendency toward balance. Formally, this leads to three classes of signed graphs:

(a)   those that are balanced;

(b)   those that are clustered but not balanced;

(c)   those that are neither.

This approach is enforced by the tendency of many to focus on triads (e.g., Davis, 1979). The eight classical triads fit the classification just listed exactly:

(a')   (+++), (+--), (-+-), (--+);

(b')   (---);

(c')   (++-), (+-+), (-++).

But it is possible to have a different approach to the problem by considering two *independent* phenomena: one, relative to the transitivity of positive relations (which leads to clusterability); and another, relative to the idea of *parsimony* in the division of the set of points by the structure of the negative relations. Thus, Flament (1968) proposed a set of two axioms in such a way that:

(i)   the two axioms are independent;

(ii)   one of the axioms is the clusterability axiom;

(iii) the axioms together are equivalent to the balance axiom.

The difficulty with (iii) is not to formulate an axiom to add to the clusterability axiom, but, rather, to choose, from among several possibilities, the best one for the analysis of social networks. Before we try to do this, it is convenient to

formulate balance problems in terms of *cocycles* of a signed
graph (Flament, 1970).

II. COCYCLES AND BALANCE

Let $S = (X, N, P)$ be a signed graph with a set X of points,
a set N of negative edges, and a set P of positive edges. We
assume further that S is connected and that $N \cap P = \phi$ (i.e., that
no edge is both positive and negative). Note, however, that we
do not assume that every pair of points is connected by an edge.
Let $U = N \cup P$ be the set of all edges, either positive or negative.

Balance Axiom: *The number of negative edges in any cycle
is always even.*

Clusterability Axiom: *The number of negative edges in any
cycle is never equal to one.*

For completeness we state the

Balance Theorem: (Cartwright and Harary, 1956) *The Balance
Axiom holds for* S *if and only if* X *can be partitioned into at
most two subsets such that all positive edges connect points in
the same subset and all negative edges connect points in different subsets,*

and the

Clusterability Theorem: (Davis, 1967) *The Clusterability
Axiom holds for* S *if and only if* X *can be partitioned into subsets such that all positive edges connect points in the same
subset and all negative edges connect points in different subsets.*

If A is a subset of X, let $W(A)$ be the subset of U consisting of the edges with exactly *one* extremity in A. By definition, $W(A)$ is the cocycle defined by A, or the *boundary* of A (Cartwright and Harary, 1976). It is easy to show that

$$W(A) = W(X - A),$$

and

$$W(X) = W(\emptyset) = \emptyset$$

(and if the graph is connected, there is no other null cocycle).

The next result will be used several times in the remainder of this chapter.

Theorem 1: A subset W *of* U *is a cocycle if and only if for every cycle* C *the cardinality of* C $\cap$ W *is even.*

The proof of Theorem 1 may be found in Rosenstiehl (1967).

From Theorem 1 and the Balance Theorem we immediately have the following result.

Theorem 2: A signed graph S *is balanced if and only if* N *is a cocycle of* S.

By definition, an *elementary cocycle* is a cocycle W that contains *no* other cocycle (except $\emptyset$).

We propose the following definition.

Definition: A signed graph S *is strictly balanced if and only if* N *is an elementary cocycle of* S.

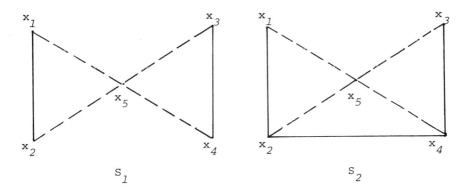

$$S_1 \qquad\qquad S_2$$

Fig. 1. S_1 is balanced but not strictly balanced. S_2 is strictly balanced.

In Figure 1, both graphs are balanced because $N = W(\{x_5\})$. The graph S_1 is *not* strictly balanced because the cocycle $W(\{x_1, x_2\})$ is contained in N. The graph S_2 is strictly balanced by inspection.

The next two results relate strict balance to other concepts.

Theorem 3: A balanced graph S has a unique clustering if and only if it is strictly balanced.

Theorem 4: If S is strictly balanced with N = W(A) then A or (X - A) is a component of the subgraph (X, P) (i.e., is a positive component).

From this last property, we see that our set of two independent axioms can be constituted by the *Clusterability Axiom* and the

Parsimony axiom: (X, P) has no more than two components.

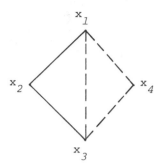

Fig. 2.   A graph with two positive components that is not
clusterable.

The Axioms of Parsimony and of Clusterability are independent.   This is shown in Figure 2 where the graph has two positive
components ($\{x_1, x_2, x_3\}$) and $\{x_4\}$, but is not clusterable because of the negative edge connecting x_1 and x_3.

III.   SOME PSYCHOLOGICAL DATA

In this paper we are not interested in the psychological
validity of clusterability for the representation of social structures, but only in processes that might be responsible for re-
stricting structures to more parsimonious ones.

We work from a general hypothesis (i.e., Easterbrook, 1959;
Janis, 1969):

(a)   in *normal* situations, individuals have a (more or less)
      complex view of the world;
(b)   in *stressful* situations, individuals have a tendency to
      have a *dichotomous* view of the world.

Then we hypothesize that stressed individuals will prefer
structures with two positive components (i.e., balanced struc-

tures if clusterability is present). This psychological hypothesis has applications to other fields. For example, Harary (1961) has shown the balance of intercountry relations during an international crisis.

A first experiment (Rossignol and Flament, 1975) used the classical eight three-point structures. The results were:

(a) in normal situations, individuals preferred clusterable structures, but were indifferent to the number of positive components;

(b) in stressful situations, individuals always preferred clusterable structures (but slightly less strongly than in normal situations), and clearly preferred structures with two positive components.

So our hypothesis has some support, but three-point structures are not rich enough to study our problem in detail. A second experiment (Rossignol and Pichevin, 1975) was performed with five-point structures; individuals were asked to produce structures, with three rules:

(a) the structure had to be complete,

(b) the relations had to be reciprocal, and

(c) the structure had to contain at least one negative relation.

The analysis of the data, in terms of the above hypothesis, is distressful (Table I): There was no difference between stressful and normal situations ; there were very few structures with more than two positive components, and about half of the structures had only one positive component! (Note that it was impossible to have clusterable structures with exactly one positive component because each structure had to contain at least one negative edge.)

TABLE I: *Percentage of produced structures*

	Number of positive components		
	1	*2*	*3*
Clusterable structures		38% (balanced structures)	2%
Other Structures	49%	10%	1%

But consider the two examples in Figure 3 of unique positive components. We have the "feeling" that (X, P_1) is "nearer" to a structure with two "blocs" than (X, P_2).

To formalize this "feeling," we have to solve a problem of the *minimal decomposition* of a graph. After some trials, we decide to consider, for each graph (X, P), the number θ, (defined in Berge, 1970, Chap. 16) as the minimum number of *complete* subgraphs that cover X. For the examples of Figure 3, we have

$$\theta(X, P_1) = 2, \quad \text{with } \{x_1\} \text{ and } \{x_2, x_3, x_4, x_5\},$$

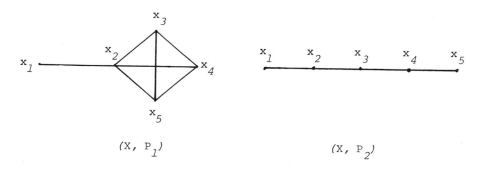

(X, P_1) (X, P_2)

Fig. 3.   Two single component graphs with different values of θ.

TABLE II: Percentage of produced structures

θ(X, P)	2	3	1	Total
Normal Situation	49%	34%	17%	100%
Stressful Situation	70%	27%	3%	100%

and

$$\theta(X, P_2) = 3, \quad \text{with } \{x_1, x_2\}, \{x_3\}, \text{ and } \{x_4, x_5\}.$$

(Note that (X, P_2) accepts three decompositions into three complete subgraphs.) With this new formulation, the data confirm our hypothesis (Table II), when the number of positive components is replaced by θ.

Note that, in this experiment, $\theta > 1$, because each structure contained at least one negative edge and hence (X, P) could never be the complete graph on five points.

IV. NEW AXIOMS

Our results lead us toward a decomposition of the balance axiom that is more sophisticated than the one we started with.

One possibility is related to the *coloring* approach to clusterability and balance (Cartwright and Harary, 1968). If $\bar{G}$ is the complementary graph of a graph G, then $\theta(G) = \chi(\bar{G})$, where $\chi(\bar{G})$ is the chromatic number of $\bar{G}$. In the conditions of our experiment, we have $(\bar{X}, \bar{P}) = (X, N)$, because each structure is complete. Then a generalization to incomplete structures can be obtained by replacing $\theta(X, P)$ by $\chi(X, N)$ and asking for χ to be less than or equal to 2. Another possibility is to continue in terms of *cocycle,* as we did for the balance axiom. This is the course we shall follow here. In terms of cocycles we may state two new axioms.

Clusterability* Axiom: N *is equal to the union of some* cocycles of S.

Parsimony* Axiom: N *is contained in an elementary cocycle of* S.

First, we show that the two notions of clusterability are equivalent.

Theorem 5: The Clusterability Axiom and the Clusterability* Axiom are equivalent.

Proof: If S is clusterable then consider the cocycles defined by the positive components of S. Clearly, N is the union of these cocycles. Now suppose S is Clusterable* so that $N = \bigcup_i W_i$. Let C be a cycle and suppose C contains a negative edge, u. Then u belongs to a cocycle $W_i \subseteq N$. By Theorem 1, $C \cap W_i$ has at least two elements so that C has at least two negative edges. Hence, S is clusterable. *QED*

Next, we show the relationship between Clusterability, Parsimony*, and Strict Balance.

THEOREM 6: S is strictly balanced if and only if both the Clusterability Axiom and the Parsimony* Axiom hold.

Proof: If $N = \emptyset$ the proposition is trivially true, so suppose that $N \neq \emptyset$. If S is strictly balanced then by definition N is an elementary cocycle, and obviously both the Clusterability* and Parsimony* Axioms hold so there is nothing to prove.

Now suppose that S is Clusterable*. Since $N \neq \emptyset$ there is a nonempty cocycle $W_1 \subseteq N$. By the Parsimony* Axiom there is an *elementary* cocycle W_2 such that $N \subseteq W_2$. Hence, $W_1 \subseteq W_2$. Since W_2 is elementary we must have $W_1 = W_2 = N$, and therefore S is strictly balanced. *QED*

Theorem 6 shows that Parsimony* is a stronger condition than Parsimony because strict balance is stronger than balance. The first definitions of balance and clusterability were given in terms of cycles and not of cocycles. However, strict balance is not easily defined with cocycles, using the notion of an elementary cocycle. Hence, it would appear natural to try to weaken the Parsimony* Axiom by the following one.

Weak Parsimony Axiom:* N *is contained in a cocycle of* S.

We may characterize the Weak Parsimony* Axiom in terms of cycles as follows.

Theorem 7: The Weak Parsimony Axiom holds if and only if every cycle of* S *contains either an even number of negative edges or has no positive edges.*

Proof: We may suppose that $N \neq \emptyset$. So first suppose that $N \subseteq W = $ a cocycle. Let C be a cycle without any positive edges, then $C \subseteq N \subseteq W$; so that $C \cap W = C$. By Theorem 1, C has an even number of elements. This shows the first half of the implication. Now suppose that the conclusion of the theorem holds. The subgraph (X, N) has no cycles with an odd number of edges. Hence

(X,N) is bicolorable so that X may be partitioned into two color sets, X_1 and X_2, and $W(X_1) = W(X_2)$. Therefore, $N \subseteq W(X_1)$. QED

Observe that a signed graph that is clusterable and weakly parsimonious* is not necessarily balanced. This is shown in Figure 4.

The graph in Figure 4 has three clusters ($\{x_1, x_2\}$, $\{x_3, x_4\}$, $\{x_5, x_6\}$); N is included in the cocycle $W(\{x_1, x_3, x_4\})$ [which is not elementary, because it includes $W(\{x_3, x_4\})$]; but the graph is not balanced (because it has a cycle with three negative edges).

A useful fact for many applications, is that, in a *complete* graph, all cocycles are elementary.

V.   COMING BACK TO THE DATA

Table III presents the data of the experiment on the representation of social structures, and shows that the concept of parsimony in a good formalization of our psychological hypothesis. The structures produced by stressed individuals are more parsimonious than those produced in normal situation.

It seems that parismonious structures are important in some types of social networks, in sociology (Granovetter, 1976), and in ethnology (White, 1976). Thus, it will be useful to continue the study of signed graph and cocycles and their relationship to clusterability and balance.

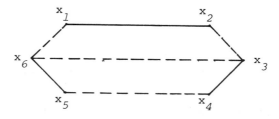

Fig. 4. A graph that is clusterable, weakly parsimonious, but not balanced.

TABLE III. *Percentage of produced structures*

Clusterability	Yes		No		Total	
Parsimony	yes	no	yes	no	cluster-ability	parsi-mony
	(balance)					
Normal situation	27%	25%	22%	26%	52%	49%
Stressful situation	38%	2%	32%	28%	40%	7.0%
Possible structures	2%	5%	18%	75%	7%	20%

REFERENCES

Berge, C. *Graphes et hypergraphes,* Paris: Dunod, 1970.

Cartwright, D., & Harary, F. On the coloring of signed graphs. *Elemente der Mathematik,* 1968, *23/4,* 85-89.

Cartwright, D., & Harary, F. Structural balance: A generalization of Heider's theory. *Psychological Review,* 1956, *63,* 277-293.

Cartwright, D., & Harary, F. Balance and clusterability: An overview. This volume, 1979.

Davis, J.A. Clustering and structural balance in graphs. *Human Relations,* 1967, *20,* 181-187.

Davis, J.A. The Davis-Holland-Leinhardt studies: An overview. This volume , 1979.

Easterbrook, J.A. The effect of emotion on cue utilization and the organization of behavior. *Psychological Review,* 1959, *66,* 183-201.

Flament, C. Structural balance theories: *in Algebraic models in psychology.* University of Leiden (mimeographed), 1968.

Flament, C. L'équilibre d'un graphe: Quelques résultats algébriques. *Mathématiques et Sciences Humaines,* 1970, *8,* 5-10.

Granovetter, M. Discussion, presented at the Advanced Research
    Symposium on Social Networks, Hanover, New Hampshire,
    September, 1975.

Harary, F. A mathematical analysis of the situation in the
    Middle East in 1956. *Journal of Conflict Resolution,* 1961,
    5, 167-178.

Janis, I.L. *Stress and frustration.* New York: Harcourt, 1969.

Rosenstiehl, P., L'arbre minimum d'ungraph. in P. Rosenstiehl
    (Ed.), *Theorie des Graphes,* Paris, Dunod, 1967, 357-368.

Rossignol, C., & Flament, C. Decomposition de l'equilibre
    structural. *Annee Psychologigue,* 1975, *75,* 417-425.

Rossignol, C., & Pichevin, M.F. Representation du groupe,
    structure de sujet et equilibre structural, *Bulletin de
    Psychologic,*(In Press).

White, D.R. Communicative avoidance in social networks.
    Presented at the Advanced Research Symposium on Social
    Networks. Hanover, New Hampshire, September, 1975.

CHAPTER 11

STRUCTURAL CONTROL MODELS FOR GROUP PROCESSES

Patrick Doreian

Department of Sociology

and

Program in Environmental Systems Engineering

University of Pittsburgh

Pittsburgh, Pennsylvania

I. INTRODUCTION

In this chapter I am concerned with examining approaches to the study of human groups that explicitly consider changes over time. When such changes are considered, two broad concerns seem manifest in the literature. First, there is the concern to predict, model, and understand the (changes of the) distribution of some attribute or variable across the members making up the group: Examples of this are the distribution of attitudes (Abelson, 1964), the distribution of commitments (Ford, 1974), and the distribution of statuses (Taylor, 1969). Second, there is a concern for understanding the structural configuration of the relations among the group members. There is a vast literature on the structure of groups, but it appears that very little of it deals explicitly with structural dynamics.[1]

[1] *Hunter (1974) appears to have constructed the first model in this domain. This has been followed by one constructed by Killworth and Bernard (1975).*

When the focus is changes in attributes, the structure of the
group is regarded as being important, but, in general, the two
broad concerns have been dealt with separately. At first sight,
an appealing objective would be to model the two types of concerns
simultaneously. However, the difficulties are immense and the
magnitude of these difficulties may well provide a sufficient
account of why the two types of processes are modeled separately.
Things become even more difficult if we decide to estimate the
models we build.

With these comments in mind, I have two primary objectives:

(1) the presentation of the perspective of structural control
within which it is possible to naturally construct differential-
equation models of group processes, and

(2) the presentation of a strategy for estimating these differential equations.

II. STRUCTURAL CONTROL[2]

A convenient, and conventional, approach to any subject of
inquiry is to define the units of analysis. For modeling group
processes the individuals making up the group generally constitute the units of analysis, although other definitions are plausible. Having defined the units of analysis, it is possible to
define the relations among them that are of interest. These can
be defined either in terms of a concrete group and its "obvious"
behaviors or in terms of more abstract, analytic features. The
set of units and the (relevant) relations defined over them constitute the group structure. Thus defined, group structure can be
simple or complex depending upon how many relations are defined

[2]*This section draws upon, and elaborates, a previous discussion of structural control (see Doreian and Hummon, 1976).*

and how they stand in relation to each other. Further elaborations could be introduced if distributed characteristics, for
example, age, sex, ethnicity, competence, etc., were also explicitly considered. Structures can be changed or maintained
through time, and the means whereby this occurs can be regarded
as process. The concern with constructing dynamic models is with
understanding those processes that generate structures and changes
of structure.

The analysis could proceed in the straightforward sociometric
sense by focusing upon concrete actors and concrete relations, or
it could proceed by defining structure in terms of normatively defined (interrelated) statuses where the structure persists even
though there is a flow of concrete actors through the structure.[3]
For presentational purposes, I shall use the imagery of the first
approach, although I suspect that the formal procedures that I
outline can accommodate both.

When control is operative, some comparison is being made. The
very idea of control implies that some objective is being sought.
This objective defines, in some way, the desired state of the
system and the comparison is made between that desired state and
the actual, or realized, state. If there is a discrepancy, some
corrective measure needs to be taken and if there is no discrepancy, the system is assumed to be operating properly. Of
course, there can be differing degrees of tolerance for the dis-
crepancies detected in the comparison operation. Very often the
control relationship is defined for an operating system and a
controlling system external to it. Input to the controlling

---

[3]*Either approach might be more fruitfully persued if structurally equivalent positions are collapsed. This would provide
an abstraction from concrete relations in the first case (White
et al., 1976), and in either case provides a different locus
for examining group structures and processes.*

system is made up of the specification of the objective and the
output from the operating system. The comparison operation is
made in the controlling system and, as a result, some input is
made to the operating system. A production system is an obvious
example and the operation of law-enforcement institutions is
another.

A further distinction can be made between open-loop control
and closed-loop control (Melsa and Schultz, 1969). If neither
the output (of the operating system) nor any other system variable
has an effect upon movement toward or away from the desired state,
then the control can be described as open-loop. An example of
this is some preset device that cannot respond to the current
state of the system. A closed-loop control system is one in
which the output, as well as other system variables, affect how
the control of the system operates. The utilization of output,
via some comparison operation to control the process, constitutes
a use of feedback. Ashby (1952) makes a distinction between a
loosely connected system and a richly connected system. In a
richly connected system, changes at any one place in the system
have ramifications throughout the system and do so relatively
quickly.

Social groups would appear to be richly connected rather than
loosely connected. Further, they also are subject to closed-
loop control rather than open-loop control. The members of the
group constantly receive input from elsewhere in the group,
utilize that input, and transmit output to the group.

The imagery of the foregoing discussion used a controller
external to the system being controlled. For human groups, it
appears reasonable to assume that control is located within the
group itself. That is, the locus of control will be found among
the relations defined over the members of the group. For example,
the actual configuration of sentiment can be viewed as constraining the distribution of sentiment by any one member of the group,

or a normatively defined status structure as constraining the behaviors of the group members toward each other, or the existence of normative standards and sanctions as constraining the behaviors of individual members. Hence the idea of structural control for group processes.[4]

Let X* denote the specification of the required value of some variable(s). In the context of social groups, X* could be some normative standard for behavior or attitude (in the group) or it could be the desired, or even required, value for some relationship. In the former case, any specific model deals with attributes or characteristics distributed across the group members, and in the latter case, it deals with the actual relationship. Any reasonable number of variables may be considered simultaneously, so X* can be treated as a vector of control values. Corresponding to X* is the actual value, X, for the system being considered. The discrepancy between the two is (X* - X). This discrepancy is then treated as an input that somehow translates into a controlling instruction for change. The basic, structural control relationship is given by (for each X_i in X)

$$\Delta X_i = c_i \Delta t (X_i{}^* - X_i) \tag{1}$$

where ΔX_i is the incremental change in X_i in an increment of time

---

[4] *This is not to say that the structure is the same as the group. Also, there may be cases where attempts are made to exert control over a group by some other system or supersystem. This would entail further complexity in that a hierarchical control model would have to be formulated. However, unless the control from outside the group operates on each individual member separately, the way control works within the group would still have to be considered.*

Δt due to the discrepancy $(X_i^* - X_i)$.[5] The parameter c_i represents a sensitivity parameter that indicates the responsiveness
of X_i to system control. Each X_i helps define the state space,
and in locating control within the group's (system's) structural
configuration, it is possible to define

$$X_i^* = f_i(\{X_j\})_{j \neq i} \tag{2}$$

Substituting Eq. (2) into Eq. (1) and taking the limit we have

$$\dot{X}_i = c_i\{f_i(\{X_j\})_{j \neq i} - X_i\}, \tag{3}$$

which represents a differential equation model for X_i. A similar
equation can be established for the other variables and together
the equations form a system of equations that describe the process. This rests upon an assumption that we can adequately specify the functional form of Eq. (2). The following section provides specifications that lead to linear differential equations
and also provides a more concrete discussion of structural control
as it applies to social groups.

[5] *X* may or may not be fixed. If X* is a fixed value, then
the process operates so as to target on the fixed values specified by X*. However, if Eq. (2) specified X* in terms of X,
then the controlling variables are themselves changing through
time and the structural control mechanisms lead the system to
the moving target, X*. The latter is the more interesting and
realistic case. Finally, if X* = X at any point of time, then
the control input indicates no change is necessary and, in effect,
equilibrium has been reached. Whether this equilibrium is stable
or unstable is another issue that can be explored if the form
and parameterization of the model are known.*

III. SOME STRUCTURAL CONTROL MODELS

The first model considered here is one that focuses upon attitudes and behaviors in a small group. Heise (1973) formulated a model of group processes where attitudes and behaviors were considered. His approach leads to a system of simultaneous equations (in the econometric sense) that were estimated by two-stage least-squares procedures. In form and estimation details, the models proposed here are quite different from those suggested by Heise but the conceptual base is similar. Heise treats a norm concerned with specific behaviors as the average of all behaviors in the group that then acts so as to control the behaviors of individuals in the group. This notion can be readily included in the structural control framework through considering deviance as the discrepancy between the behavior norm and the behavior displayed in the group.

Let B and A be generic symbols for behavior and attitude, respectively. I assume that both behavior and attitude can be measured on some continuous scale. In taking the norm regarding behavior as the average of exhibited behaviors, it is reasonable to assume that different individuals will contribute differently to the setting of the norm. Individuals with greater status, popularity, persuasiveness, or whatever, will have more important or salient contributions. Put differently, the norm regarding behavior is a weighted sum of exhibited behaviors where, for the moment, the weights are unknown. For individual i, we have the norm regarding behavior, B_i^*, as

$$B_i^* = \sum_{\substack{k=1 \\ k \neq i}}^{n} b_{ik} B_k + b_i \qquad (4)$$

Here, the b_{ik} are the differential weights and b_i the mean effect due to a surrounding environment. The structural control equation will be

$$\Delta B_i = c_i \Delta t (B_i{}^* - B_i)$$

or

$$\frac{\Delta B_i}{\Delta t} = c_i \left(\sum_{k=1}^{n} b_{ik} B_i + b_i \right)$$

where $b_{ii} = -1$. Treating the equations for each individual simultaneously and taking the limit we have

$$\dot{B} = GB + h \qquad\qquad (5)$$

where $\dot{B} = [\dot{B}_1, \dot{B}_2, \ldots, \dot{B}_n]'$, $B = [B_1, B_2, \ldots, B_n]'$,

$$G = [g_{ij}] \quad \text{with } g_{ij} = -c_i, \quad i = j$$

$$= c_i b_{ij} \text{ otherwise}$$

and h is a column vector whose elements are $(c_i b_i)$.

The norm regarding behavior for individual i is defined as the weighted sum of all other behaviors in the group for two reasons. First, it makes sense that the norms an individual perceives are generated by the others around him/her. And, second, to include B_i in Eq. (4) defining the norms leads to a model where the sensitivity parameter, c_i, cannot be estimated. Part of the intuition behind this model is that individuals in the group may have differing perceptions of what the group norm (with respect to some behavior) actually is. If the norm was truly public and common to all, then $B_i{}^* = B_j{}^*$ for all i, j. Further, different individuals can have different sensitivities to control by the group through its norms. The higher the value

of the sensitivity parameter, c, the quicker the response of the
individual to a discrepancy between behavior norms and actual behavior, or the quicker the response to perceived deviance. The
parameter c could be taken as a measure of the commitment in that
the higher the value of c the less committed a group member is to
her/his behavior or position. In previous uses of structural control (Doreian and Hummon, 1976), the parameter c was taken to be
positive. Thus, if $B^* > B$, then the structural control mechanism
operates so as to pull B up toward B^* and, similarly, if $B^* < B$,
then the mechanism operates so as to lower B toward B^*. In the
context of small groups, however, it seems reasonable to allow c
to take negative values. An individual with behavior (or attitude) discrepant with the norm concerning that behavior (or attitude) is, by definition, deviant but an individual with a negative c is deviant in a different sense: the group control does
not constrain the individual toward the group norm. This could
be regarded as an instance of psychological reactance (Brehm,
1972).

Such a model is strictly behavioral or strictly attitudinal,
but it is possible to ask whether behavior and attitude should
both be included. The attitude/behavior relation is regarded as
problematic (see for example, Wicker, 1969), although the precise
nature of what the problem is needs to be carefully stated (Alwin,
1973). When attitudes are incorporated, Eq. (4) can be modified
to

$$B_i^* = b_i + \sum_{\substack{k=1 \\ k \neq i}}^{n} b_{ik} B_k + \sum_{k=1}^{n} a_{ik} A_k \tag{6}$$

This equation specifies that the norm regarding behavior (for
individual i) is a weighted sum of all individuals' behaviors and
a weighted sum of all attitudes concerning the behvaior in the
group (including his/her own). In the same way, it is possible

to specify an attitude norm that indicates what an individual's attitude ought to be with regard to some behavior of relevance to the group:

$$A_i^* = a_i + \sum_{\substack{k=1}}^{n} d_{ik} B_k + \sum_{\substack{k=1 \\ k \neq i}}^{n} e_{ik} A_k \tag{7}$$

This equation states that the attitude norm is a weighted sum of all behaviors and a weighted sum of all attitudes of others in the group. The structural control equations for individual i are

$$\Delta B_i = c_{i1} \{ \sum_{k \neq i} b_{ik} B_k + \sum_k a_{ik} A_k + b_i - B_i \} \Delta t$$

$$\tag{8}$$

$$\Delta A_i = c_{i2} \{ \sum_k d_{ik} B_k + \sum_{k \neq i} e_{ik} A_k + a_i - A_i \} \Delta t$$

Each indidivual is now characterized by two sensitivity parameters, one parameterizing control with respect to behavior and one parameterizing control with respect to attitude.

When the equations for all individuals are considered simultaneously and the limit is taken, then

$$\dot{X} = GX + h \tag{9}$$

is the dynamic model where

$$\dot{X} = [\dot{B}_1, \dot{B}_2, \ldots, \dot{B}_n, \dot{A}_1, \dot{A}_2, \ldots, \dot{A}_n]',$$

$$X = [B_1, B_2, \ldots, B_n, A_1, A_2, \ldots, A_n]',$$

$$h = [c_{11} b_1, c_{21} b_2, \ldots, c_{n1} b_n, c_{12}, a_1, \ldots, c_{n2}, a_n]'$$

and G is a partitioned matrix $\begin{bmatrix} G_{11} & G_{12} \\ C_{21} & G_{22} \end{bmatrix}$

The elements of G_{11} are given by $g_{ij} = -c_{i1} \qquad i = j$

$$= c_{ij} b_{ij} \qquad \text{otherwise.}$$

The elements of G_{12} are given by $g_{ij} = c_{i1} a_{ij}$. The elements G_{21} are given by $g_{ij} = c_{i2} d_{ij}$. Finally, the elements of G_{22} are given by

$$g_{ij} = -c_{i2} \qquad i = j$$

$$= c_{i2} e_{ij} \qquad \text{otherwise.}$$

The models that have been discussed thus far are all closed-group models where there are no exogeneous inputs. To incorporate such inputs the equation giving the control variables, X*, can be specified as

$$B_i^* = b_i + \sum_{\substack{k=1 \\ k \neq i}}^{n} b_{ik} B_k + \sum_{j=1} r_{ij} Z_j \qquad (10a)$$

for the strictly behavioral model, and

$$B_i^* = b_i + \sum_{\substack{k=1 \\ k \neq i}}^{n} b_{ik} B_k + \sum_{i=1}^{n} a_{ik} A_k + \sum_{j=1}^{m} r_{ij} Z_{ij} \qquad (10b)$$

$$A_i^* = a_i + \sum_{k=1}^{n} d_{ik} B_k + \sum_{\substack{k=1 \\ k \neq i}}^{n} e_{ik} A_k + \sum_{j=1}^{m} s_{ij} Z_j$$

for the model dealing with both attitudes and behaviors where the

Z_j represent m exogenous input variables. Applying structural
control as before and taking the limit gives, in obvious notation,

$$\dot{X}(t) = GX(t) + HZ(t) \tag{11}$$

where the (old) vector h is incorporated into H by defining an
appropriate column of ones.

Equation (11) is a fairly general process model that captures,
albeit in a complex way, the following intuitions (in addition to
those already mentioned). Each individual's behavior is determined by (i) her/his own attitude, (ii) the attitude of others in
the group, (iii) the behavior of group members, and (iv) exogenous factors. Each individual's attitude toward some relevant behavior is determined by (i) the attitude of the other members of
the group, (ii) his/her own (through the specification of the
structural control mechanism), (iii) the behavior of others,
and (iv) exogenous factors. Deviance, by definition, is the
discrepancy between the actual behavior and/or attitude, and
those that are required. Group norms are determined by (i)
individuals' behaviors, (ii) individuals' attitudes, and (iii)
exogenous factors that can be construed as inputs from the surrounding culture within which the group is embedded.

Equation (11) may represent quite a wide class of models when
the definitions of the variables of interest are changed. For
example, Abelson's (1964) model of attitude change, as extended
by Taylor (1968), to incorporate sources of information external
to the group can be put in this form (with certain constraints on
the parameters) as can Ford's (1974) differential-equation model
of commitment. If this is correct, and we can estimate the
model's parameters, then the models that can be expressed in
terms of Eq. (11) have a fairly wide relevance. The question is:
Can we estimate the parameters of Eq. (11)?

IV. AN ESTIMATION PROCEDURE

An estimation procedure for Eq. (11) has already been constructed and fruitfully applied. (See Doreian and Hummon (1976,
Chaps. 4 and 5)). Doreian and Hummon applied their procedure in
a quite different context, so in part, this is an exercise in
technology transfer.

The starting point for the procedure is an assumption that
the exogenous variables and the endogenous variables can be frequently and regularly monitored. The solution equation for (11)
yields values for each of the endogenous variables at each point
in time given the values of the exogenous variables but does not
immediately permit an estimation of the parameters in (11). If
some unit of time, say T, is adopted and observations on the variables are made at successive intervals of length T, then it is
possible to establish

$$X(\overline{n+1}\ T) = e^{GT}X(nT) + G^{-1}[e^{GT} - I]H\ Z(nT) \tag{12}$$

This equation is the basic estimating equation employed by Doreian
and Hummon, where nT and $(n+1)T$ represent successive sampling
points.

The observations are spaced regularly in time so, without loss
of generality, T can be taken to be unity. The matrices e^{G} and
$G^{-1}[e^{G}-I]H$ can be estimated and estimates of G and H can be obtained from these estimates. See Doreian and Hummon (1976).

This estimation procedure has not yet been applied to networks. So the model remains a proposed model. Were it estimated, and the matrix G known, then it would be possible to perform the usual analyses of stability and equilibrium. The
through-time trajectories of attitude and/or behavior could be
plotted by using the solution form for the model. Because the
behavioral standards are constructed from the realized behavior

and attitude in the group, it would be possible to construct the
through-time trajectories of the (perceived) behavioral standards. The construction of, and analysis of, these trajectories
would be of interest in their own right. In essence, an implicit
model of the dynamics of the normative structure has been constructed as X^* is a linear transformation of X. This relation is,
in matrix form, given by

$$X^* = SX \qquad\qquad\qquad\qquad\qquad (13)$$

where S is a $(n \times n)$ matrix when attitudes or behaviors are
modeled separately. If attitudes and behaviors are modeled together then S is a $(2n \times 2n)$ matrix. In the former case, S is a
$(n \times n)$ matrix with zeroes on the main diagonal. It is akin to a
sociomatrix. Indeed, it could be taken to be a form of the
sociomatrix where the (valued) entries of each row represent the
relative importance of every other individual to the norms as
perceived by an individual in the group.

V.   THE GROUP SOCIOMATRIX

Equations (4), (6), and (7) are all statements utilizing a
sociomatrix in an implied fashion. The argument in the previous
section suggests a method of estimating a particular sociomatrix
S. At first sight, this is a backward way of proceeding, but it
may have certain uses. What is being proposed is that certain
exhibited behaviors (or attitudes) can be regularly monitored.
A specific process mechanism is also being proposed that posits
how the changes in the monitored phenomena are generated through
the social structure of the group. From the two, it is possible
to infer measurements of the relations, of a particular type to
be sure, in the social group. To the extent that it is easier
to measure the behavior and/or attitude than it is to measure the
relations is a real gain.

We could go further. Suppose we had a long time series of
measurements of attitudes or behaviors of the members of the
group. Imagine a "window" placed over the first t rows of a
data matrix having these attitudes or behaviors in columns ordered
by time. Estimates of G and H could be made using the first t
observations. Then move the window down one row, so that the
first observation is removed through the top of the window and
the $(t+1)$st observation is brought in through the bottom of the
window. G and H could then be obtained for this set of observations. The "sliding window" procedure was suggested by
Smoker (1967) and can provide, in this context, a sequence of
estimated sociomatrices. This sounds very nice. However,
through-time data (of any reasonable duration) of this sort are
extremely rare--in fact, it is so rare, I know of none. Yet in
order to empirically examine models of changes of group structure,
such as those proposed by Hunter (1974) or Killworth and Bernard
(1975), such data are necessary. The coupling of a model, such
as the one proposed here, with the sliding window technique,
might provide the required data. In an admittedly two-stage way,
it may also conjoin the two modeling concerns that I discussed
earlier.[6]

Such a model and estimating procedure are profligate in the
number of parameters to be estimated. Restrictions will, pro-

---

[6]*Even if the basic idea is feasible, there are still considerable difficulties: (i) the sliding-window procedure assumes
that there may be changes of the structure underlying the process
and attempts to detect it, yet, the model assumed that the structure is fixed, (ii) adding and deleting rows from a matrix pose
statistical problems due to updating (Beckman and Trussell, 1975),
and (iii) the matrices are obtained from complex nonlinear transformation of the empirical estimates of d^G and $D = G^{-1}(e^G - I)H$.*

bably have to be placed on G with the ultimate restriction that G
is fixed and known. The sociomatrix, as used here, will also be
fixed and known. Even with G fixed it is possible to estimate the
model from time series data, only interest would then focus on
the exogenous input, which can include demographic or background
variables. Interest focuses upon estimating H, and it appears
that this can be done directly after an appropriate transformation of X. Rewriting Eq. (12) gives

$$(e^G - I)^{-1} G[X(\overline{n+1T}) - e^G X(nT)] = X^+(nT) = H\,Z(nT) \qquad (14)$$

If OLS is appropriate $X^+(nT)$ can be regressed on $Z(nT)$ to estimate H. Elsewise a more complex procedure could be employed.

Suppose only cross-sectional data are available. In such a
situation a structural control model can still be constructed,
only its estimation assumes an equilibrium and makes no attempt
to estimate a sociomatrix. As before, the basic structural control equation is, in matrix form,

$$\Delta X = c\,\Delta t(X^* - X) \qquad (15)$$

and we can specify

$$X^* = kS\,X + Z\beta \qquad (16)$$

where S is a sociomatrix for the group, and Z represents the
exogenous inputs. β is a vector of parameters to be estimated
and k is a parameter to be estimated. In this case, the (socio)-
matrix S is known and does not have to be estimated. The matrix
of contact rates or some transformation of it, given by Abelson
(1964), would provide an example of such a matrix. By applying
structural control and taking the limit, the following equation
is obtained

$$\dot{X}(t) = c(I - kS)\ X(t) + Z(t)\beta \tag{17}$$

If data at only one point in time are available, then it is necessary to assume that equilibrium holds. Setting $\dot{X} = 0$, and rearranging gives

$$X = kS\ X + Z\beta \tag{18}$$

as an estimating equation. A procedure for estimating this is given in Doreian and Hummon (1976, Chap. 7). A more complete discussion, also using maximum likelihood procedures, is given by Ord (1975).

VI. CHANGES OF STRUCTURE

Thus far, attention has focused upon changes of some attribute(s) but structural control can also be used to model changes of structure, although the estimation problems for the resulting models are likely to be even more acute. The major modifications lie in specifying how the control variable, X^*, is defined and what the structural control equation is. Let x_{ij} be the sentiment of individual i toward individual j, then x_{ij}^* is defined in terms of the structural configuration in which i and j are located. Suppose that, from a balance-theory perspective, there are mechanisms of consistency governing the network. Then x_{ij}^* can be defined in terms of interactions between i and some other individual k, where information concerning j is exchanged, and also in terms of interaction between i and j where information about k is exchanged (or, indeed, about any other object of relevance).

Let the two be considered as separate mechanisms. Then, in the case of the former, x_{ij}^* could be taken to the x_{kj}. It seems reasonable that the effect of the discrepancy between x_{ij}^* and

x_{ij} is also contingent upon the relation between i and k: namely, x_{ik}, and that both the magnitude and sign of x_{ik} are relevant. The structural control equation can then be specified as

$$\Delta_k x_{ij} = c_i\ \Delta t\ x_{ik}(x_{ij}^* - x_{ij}) \tag{19}$$

$$= c_i\ \Delta t\ x_{ik}(x_{kj} - x_{ij})$$

where the subscript, k, for the increment of change in x_{ij} denotes that the increment pertains to an interaction with k.   Incorporating a variable like x_{ik} represents another form of structural control, but it is one that is disaggregated in terms of dyads in the group.   For an interaction between i and j, the structural-control equation can be specified as

$$\Delta x_{ij(k)} = c_i\ \Delta t\ x_{ij}(x_{jk} - x_{ik}) \tag{20}$$

The subscript k, in parentheses indicates that k is the object of the exchange of information between i and j.   The form of this equation differs in another way from those discussed earlier.   The discrepancy component does not involve the entity upon which the control mechanism operates; namely, x_{ij}.   The discrepancy is defined in terms of the difference between i and j with respect to some other individual in the group k.   This discrepancy is specified multiplicatively so as to operate in an inflating or diminishing way upon x_{ij}.[7]   If the mechanisms operate simultaneously, the limits are taken and if it is possible to sum over all other ks in the network, then

[7]*As such, it well may be yet another qualitatively different mechanism of structural control.*

$$\frac{dx_{ij}}{dt} = c_i \; [\Sigma' \; x_{ik}x_{kj} - \Sigma' \; x_{ik} \; x_{ij} + \Sigma' \; x_{ij}x_{jk}$$

$$- \; \Sigma' \; x_{ij}x_{ik}]$$

(21)

where Σ' denotes a summation over k with $k \neq i, j$. In terms of the network, the summations deal with, respectively, the implicitly triadic configurations of $i{\to}k{\to}j$, $j{\leftarrow}i{\to}k$, $i{\to}j{\to}k$ and $k{\leftarrow}i{\to}j$.

In terms of the dynamics of the group, this may or may not be feasible. Certainly it is in contrast to Hunter (1974) who considered $i{\to}k{\to}j$ and $i{\leftarrow}k{\to}j$ under the rubric of influence, and $i{\to}k{\leftarrow}j$ and $i{\leftarrow}k{\leftarrow}j$ under the rubric of congruence. However, the basic difference is that Hunter's model is not one of structural control. In effect, Killworth and Bernard (1975) note this. They define dissonance to be the driving force in changes of relations. Focusing only upon $i{\to}k{\to}j$ (and, as they observe, the other three semipaths of Hunter's model can be included) they define the dissonance as perceived by i to be $s_i x_{ik}(x_{kj} - x_{ij})$ where s_i is a sensitivity factor.

VII. CONCLUSION

I have advocated a general perspective; namely, structural control for conceptualizing and organizing models of changes within human groups. I have also indicated how some of these models may be estimated. There are, however, a variety of further agenda items that need to be pursued. Structural control is but one conceptualization of what the term control means for social systems. It seems necessary to explore the way in which these different conceptualizations can be brought together within a single framework. In terms of estimation, it would appear that the full estimation approach suggested in this paper can only apply to very small groups or to dyads embedded in a group where the remainder of the group could be viewed as the sources of exogenous input. However, it does merit exploration and will be pursued. For larger groups and more restricted data bases, the alternate estimation procedures seem very reasonable. However, these issues can be judged only in the light of empirical reality and the theoretical concerns of those investigators studying dynamics within human groups.

ACKNOWLEDGMENTS

I wish to thank Thomas J. Fararo, Omar K. Moore, David Ford, Norman P. Hummon, and Klaus Teuter for providing me with helpful criticism and for being generous with their time.

REFERENCES

Abelson, R.P. Mathematical models of the distribution of Attitudes under controversy. In N. Frederiksen and H. Gulliksen (Eds.), *Contributions to mathematical psychology,* New York: Holt, Rinehart, & Win, 1964.

Alwin, D.F. Making inferences from attiude-behavior correlations. *Sociometry,* 1973, *36,* 253-278.

Ashby, W.R. *Design for a brain.* London: Chapman & Hall, 1952.

Beckman, R.J. & Trussell, H.J. The distribution of an arbitrary studentized residual and the effects of updating in multiple regression. *Journal of the American Statistical Association,* 1974, *69,* 199-201.

Brehm, J.W. Responses to loss of freedom: *A theory of psychological reactance.* Morristown, New Jersey: General Learning Press, Module 4032v00, 1972.

Doreian, P., & Hummon, N.P. *Modeling social processes.* Amsterdam and New York: Elsevier, 1976.

Ford, D.A. Commitment: A mathematical model. *Quality and Quantity,* 1973, *7,* 1-40.

Heise, David R. Group dynamics and attitude-behavior correlations. Department of Sociology, University of North Carolina (Chapel Hill), 1974.

Hummon, N.P., Doreian, P., & Teuter, K. A structural control model of organizational change. *American Sociological Review,* 1975, *40,* No. 6, 813-824.

Hunter, J. Dynamic sociometry. Presented at the Conference on Mathematical Models of Social Networks, MSSB, Cheat Lake, West Virginia, 1974.

Killworth, P., & Bernard H.R. A model of human group dynamics. ONR Code 452. Contract #N00014-73-A-0417-0001. (unpublished).

Melsa, J.F., & Schultz, D.G. *Linear control systems.* New York: McGraw-Hill, 1969.

Ord, K. Estimation methods for models of spatial interaction. *Journal of the American Statistical Association,* 1975, *70,* 120-126.

Smoker, P. A time-series analysis of Sino-Indian relations. *Journal of Conflict Resolution,* 1969, *13,* No. 2, 172-191.

Taylor, M. Influence structures. *Sociometry,* 1969, *32,* 490-502.

Taylor, M. Towards a mathematical theory of influence and attitude change. *Human Relations,* 1968, *21,* 121-139.

Wicker, A.W. Attitudes versus actions: The relationship of verbal and overt behavioral responses to attitude objectives. *Journal of Social Issues,* 1969, *25,* 41-78.

White, H.C., Boorman, S.A. & Breiger, R.L. Social structure from multiple networks: Part I, Block models of roles and positions. *American Journal of Sociology,* 1976, *81,* 730-780.

CHAPTER 12

TOWARD A GENERAL FRAMEWORK FOR DYNAMIC THEORIES OF
SENTIMENT IN SMALL GROUPS
DERIVED FROM THEORIES OF ATTITUDE CHANGE

John E. Hunter

Department of Psychology
Michigan State University
East Lansing, Michigan

I.   THE STRUCTURE OF GROUP SENTIMENTS

For years, documentation on the structure of sentiment in
small groups was limited, specifying only that certain groups would
be stable while certain others would not. Little was said, however, about how the unstable groups would change. A break in this
pattern was made by a mathematical model presented by Hunter
(1970, 1978), which has been modified by Killworth and Bernard
(1976).

Hunter assumed that in a purely social group the main topic
of conversation would be the members of the group. Thus, he
structured his model around dyadic interactions in which two members of the group discussed some third member. He then noted that
while one person is listening to the other, two processes take
place inside the listener: (1) the listener is influenced by what
the speaker has to say and hence changes his sentiment about the
third party being discussed, and (2) the listener reacts positively or negatively to what the speaker has to say and judges

their views to be compatible or not, and hence changes his sentiment toward the speaker. The two processes of influence and
compatibility can be identified with changes in the listener's
attitudes toward the object as well as the source of the message
that the listener was receiving.

An analysis of attitude change in the "passive communication
context" was offered by Hunter and Cohen (1972). They considered
a situation in which a receiver is presented with a message about
some object from a source who is not physically present. They
noted that the message carries information about two things: the
object of the message and the source of the message. Thus, they
assumed that there might be change in two attitudes: the subject's
attitude toward the object of the message (which has always been
called "attitude change") and the subject's attitude toward the
source (which they dubbed "source change"). This assumption was
reinforced by theories like congruity theory (Osgood and Tannenbaum, 1955) and dissonance theory (Festinger, 1957; Aronson,
Turner, and Carlsmith, 1963) which assert that the amount of attitude change and the amount of source change are nonindependent
and are, in fact, negatively correlated such that one will "com-
pensate" for the other. The attitude change theory adopted by
Hunter actually consisted of a version of balance theory derived
from Heider (1946), Newcomb (1953), Cartwright and Harary (1956),
and Abelson and Rosenberg (1958).

This synthesization of the analysis of attitude change
theories carried out by Hunter and Cohen (1972) combined with the
general theory of interpersonal sentiment presented by Hunter
(1978) provide a general framework within which any theory of
attitude change can be converted into a theory of sociometric
structure in small groups.

A. Attitude Change

Hunter and Cohen (1972) noted that in the passive communication paradigm there are three key variables: (1) the receiver's
attitude toward the object of the message, denoted as *a*, (2) the
receiver's attitude toward the source of the message, denoted *s*,
and (3) the message itself, which they assumed could be scaled on
the same continuum and then given the value *m*. Since their message value *m* is the "objective" or scaled value of the message,
the perceived value of the message was not viewed as a "critical"
variable. But indeed most theories that assert the distortion
of the message by an intervening process ultimately assert that
the perceived value is a function of the actual value, the subject's attitude toward the object (i.e., bias), and the subject's
attitude toward the source (i.e., expectations). That is, if *p*
is the perceived value of the message, then most theories assert
that

$$p = f(a, s, m).$$

The value *p* can therefore be eliminated from the list of independent variables.

Hunter and Cohen also make one subtle assumption, which
actually follows from their assertion that *a*, *s*, *m* could all be
measured on the same continuum: the underlying dimension must
be affect. Such dimensions as expertise or subjective probability
are linked to one variable or another of the basic three and are
not universally applicable. Thus, Hunter and Cohen specifically
limit the usefulness of their analysis to affect and warned that
their theories might not generalize to such situations as judging
the guilt or innocence of a person on trial. For our purposes,
this limitation to affect is not a liability, but an asset. Affect is what interpersonal sentiment is all about.

In passive communication, the message is given and hence there
is no equation necessary for the change in the variable m. Thus,
in that context, each theory of attitude change should ultimately
reduce to two equations: one for attitude change and one for
source change. That is, in the passive communication context,
Hunter and Cohen reduced each theory to two mathematical equations of the form:

$$\Delta a = f(a,\ s,\ m) \tag{1}$$

$$\Delta s = g(a,\ s,\ m) \tag{2}$$

B. Dynamic Sociometry

In developing his general model of change in sociometric relations, Hunter (1978) assumed that all sociometric change took
place during dyadic interactions in which two persons talk to
each other about each other or about some third party in the same
group. To do so, Hunter had to assume that interpersonal feelings
are not directly determined according to the role structure of the
group; this assumption will also be adopted here. Furthermore, if
attitudes toward objects outside the group (such as the war in
Vietnam) are not to be a source of interpersonal feeling, then
the group must either have norms against such topics of conversation (as in the bridge club rule, "no religion or politics") or
must be relatively uninterested in such things (as among the hab-
itues of certain lower class bars). Thus, Hunter's restriction
of the "change agents" to those that operate when the group members talk to each other about each other is not a theoretically
empty assumption but is a restriction in the range of all models
similar to the form developed subsequently.

Hunter defined four sets of variables. First he assessed the
contact among the group members by specifying:

c_{ijk} = the amount of time person i spends talking to person j about person k.

Second he defined two sets of sentiments: actual and perceived sentiments, which he assumed were bipolar quantities and could range from $-\infty$ (infinite hate) to $+\infty$ (infinite love):

x_{ij} = how person i feels about person j .

p_{ij} = how person i thinks that person j feels about him.

Third he defined a set of message variables

s_{ijk} = what person i says to person j about person k.

Suppose now that person k is talking to person i about person j. Then the listener is person i, the source is person k, and the object of the message is person j. The listener's attitude toward the object is x_{ij}, the listener's attitude toward the source is x_{ik}, and the message value is s_{kij}. Thus, according to the analysis of Hunter and Cohen (1972), the change in senti-ment during that interaction should be attitude change Δx_{ij} and source change Δx_{ik}:

$$\Delta x_{ij} = f(x_{ij}, x_{ik}, s_{kij}) \tag{3}$$

$$\Delta x_{ik} = g(x_{ij}, x_{ik}, s_{kij}) \tag{4}$$

where f and g are the attitude and source change equations of a given attitude change theory. For example Hunter's version of balance theory was

$$\Delta x_{ij} = \alpha\, x_{ik}\, s_{kij} \tag{5}$$

$$\Delta x_{ik} = \beta\, x_{ij}\, s_{kij} \tag{6}$$

However, Hunter did not stop there. Instead he noted that a
person has two links with any other person: how he feels toward
the other and how he thinks the other feels toward him. While k
is talking to i, person i can either be thinking about how he
feels about the source or about how (he thinks) the source feels
about him. If he is reacting in terms of his feeling toward the
source, then the relevant equation is (3) or (5). But if he is
reacting in terms of how (he thinks) the source feels about him,
then the relevant equation is

$$\Delta x_{ij} = f(x_{ij}, p_{ik}, s_{kij}) \tag{7}$$

or, for Hunter's balance theory,

$$\Delta x_{ij} = \alpha p_{ik} s_{kij} \tag{8}$$

In similar fashion, the listener also has two links to the *object*
of the message: how he feels toward the subject of conversation
and how (he thinks) the object of the message feels about him. If
he is reacting in terms of how he feels about the object in
assessing the compatibility of the source, then the relevant
equation is (4) or (6). But if the listener is reacting to how
(he thinks) the third party feels about him, then the relevant
equation for compatibility or source change would be

$$\Delta x_{ik} = g(p_{ij}, x_{ik}, s_{kij}) \tag{9}$$

or Hunter's equation

$$\Delta x_{ik} = \beta p_{ij} s_{kij} \tag{10}$$

Actually Hunter put these together into one equation

$$\Delta x_{ij} = \alpha f(x_{ij}, x_{ik}, s_{kij}) + \gamma \quad f(x_{ij}, p_{ik}, s_{kij}) \tag{11}$$

$$\Delta x_{ik} = \beta g(x_{ij}, x_{ik}, s_{kij}) + \delta \quad g(p_{ij}, x_{ik}, s_{kij}) \tag{12}$$

where the difference between the parameters α and γ represents the differential in time spent thinking in terms of his reaction to the source and (his perception of) how the source feels about him. The difference between the parameters β and δ similarly reflects the difference in the amount of time spent thinking in terms of how he feels about the object and the time spent thinking about (his perception of) how the object feels about him.

Do these perceptions matter? White (1961) has argued that these perceptions are ephemeral and highly inaccurate, in which case the parameters γ and δ would be 0. However, his finding that only one in four "choices" were reciprocated was based on data that has two problems: First, he used an extremely restrictive sociometric criterion ("Would you single out...? Who is the individual...?") that guaranteed that multiple choices in fact would show up as a high rate of apparently unreciprocated choices in his observations. Second, his measure of "dislike" was uncomfortable interaction. But the executives in his study were chosen because they engaged in a large number of policy conflicts. And since some men find conflict challenging while others find it painful, the uncomfortable associations reported by his executives would not be a reflection of dislike per se and would not be expected to be reciprocated.

Hunter assumed that the change induced in any one interaction would be very small. If this is true, then it is possible to aggregate the change in several interactions without taking account of the specific order of those interactions. Rather the change in each interaction can simply be added to the change produced by the others. This then produces Hunter's aggregate change formula:

$$\Delta x_{ij} = \alpha \ \sum_{k}' \ c_{ikj} x_{ik} s_{kij} + \gamma \ \sum_{k}' \ c_{ikj} p_{ik} s_{kij}$$

$$+ \ \beta \ \sum_{k}' \ c_{ijk} x_{ik} s_{jik} + \delta \ \sum_{k}' \ c_{ijk} p_{ik} s_{jik} \tag{13}$$

where the prime on the summation symbol means that the subscript
k is not allowed to take on either the value i or the value j.
The excluded "diagonal" terms correspond to the effects of the
persons talking about each other per se and to the direct effects
of their actions toward one another and these effects may or may
not be deemed to be given by the attitude change functions f and
g of Eq. (1) and (2). In Hunter's balance theory scheme, a good
argument could be made for simply handling the direct effects of
interaction by extending the summation symbols to include the
"diagonal" terms, but this might not be the case in reinforcement
theory or information processing theory, etc. If not, then alternative equations would have to be built. The corresponding
general equation for the present chapter is

$$\Delta x_{ij} = \alpha \ \sum_{k}' \ c_{kij} \ f(x_{ij}, \ x_{ik}, \ s_{kij})$$

$$+ \ \gamma \ \sum_{k}' \ c_{kij} \ f(x_{ij}, \ p_{ik}, \ s_{kij})$$

$$+ \ \beta \ \sum_{k}' \ c_{jik} \ g(x_{ik}, \ x_{ij}, \ s_{jik}) \tag{14}$$

$$+ \ \delta \ \sum_{k}' \ c_{jik} \ g(p_{ik}, \ x_{ij}, \ s_{jik})$$

with unspecified equations for the "diagonal" terms.

Hunter treated the interaction variables c_{ijk} as being constant over time. This reflected his assumption that these numbers are largely determined by role relations, propinquity, and
other processes that are largely outside the scope of the model.
However he did warn that this overlooks the possibility that
people adapt to growing negative feelings by avoiding contact.

On the other hand, Killworth and Bernard (1976) attempt to deal
with both the change in interaction and the change in sentiment
in their model.

Hunter dealt with the message variables s_{kij} by assuming that
communication in the group was honest, that is, by assuming that
each person would say how he felt without consideration of its
effect on the listener. This assumption is written simply

$$s_{kij} = x_{kj}$$

However, he noted that he derived the assumption of veridicality from his assumption that the group be an informal social
group within which there is interaction among all members of the
group. As a result, a person is quite likely to get "caught" if
he tells different stories to different people and people are
quite likely to (correctly) discount him if he perennially biases
his messages away from his true feelings.

Hunter dealt with the perceptual variables p_{ik} by assuming
that they were perfectly accurate, that is, by using the assumption
that $p_{ij} = x_{ji}$. However, again he noted that this assumption is
only likely to be good in groups in which either there is a norm
for honesty or in which there is so much communication that things
said elsewhere "get back" to the person.

Other assumptions about messages and about perception are probably best made together, because the "rules" that operate in any
group are likely to be at least partly known to the members of
that group. Consider, for example, a group in which it is anathema
to say anything negative about someone else. Then one sort of distortion function would be

$$s_{kij} = x_{kj} + \mu$$

where µ is an upwards positive bias. However, if this is true
and if it is a norm in the group, then it is also likely to be
true that perception of the message will be "discounted" by a
function such as

$$\text{Perceived message} = s_{kij} - d$$

where d is the discount value. If $d = µ$, then the perceived message is

$$\text{Perceived message} = x_{kj} + µ - d = x_{kj}$$

If d is not equal to µ, then there would be a net bias one way or
the other in the group. This in turn would be crucial to the perceptions p_{ik}. If the discounting matches the bias, then the message that k gives to i about his feelings for i would be correctly perceived as $s_{kii} = x_{ki}$ and would match the reports from
others as well. Thus,

$$p_{ik} = \text{perceived } s_{kii} = x_{ki}$$

would be perfectly veridical.

A quite different bias is "saying what the other person wants
to hear." This is the sort of bias that might exist in a group in
which there is a high premium placed on short-term goodwill and
where there is no great cost to being found out as a manipulator.
That is, since this bias necessarily means giving different messages to different people, it becomes just a matter of time until
these disparate messages are compared and found to be false. How
might we model such a bias? Suppose we assume that the speaker
selects his message to be a weighted average between what he would
say if he were direct and honest and what he thinks the other
wants to hear, say

$$s_{kij} = \varepsilon \, x_{kj} + (1-\varepsilon) \, d_{ij}$$

where ε is the probability-like weight given to honesty and where d_{ij} is what k thinks the listener wants to hear. But what is d_{ij}? According to popular thought, the listener i would like to hear the speaker agree with him (though according to balance theory this would be true only if x_{ik} is positive), that is, $d_{ij} = x_{ij}$. But the speaker does not know x_{ij}; he knows only what person j *says*, therefore he can only set

$$d_{ij} = s_{ikj}$$

Thus, we have

$$s_{kij} = \varepsilon \, x_{kj} + (1-\varepsilon) \, s_{ikj} \qquad (15)$$

Similarly, person i is biased in the direction of what person k is saying:

$$s_{ikj} = \varepsilon \, x_{ij} + (1-\varepsilon) \, s_{kij} \qquad (16)$$

Together Eqs. (15) and (16) make up a pair of simultaneous equations for the content of a given exchange between person i and person k about person j. The solution for the two message values is

$$s_{kij} = \frac{1}{2-\varepsilon} \, x_{kj} + \frac{1-\varepsilon}{2-\varepsilon} \, x_{ij} \qquad (17)$$

$$s_{ikj} = \frac{1-\varepsilon}{2-\varepsilon} \, x_{kj} + \frac{1}{2-\varepsilon} \, x_{ij} \qquad (18)$$

Thus, we see that a bias in the direction of agreeableness requires that both sentiments be taken into account at the same

time. To the extent that honesty is small, then each message is
the average of the two sentiments and there would be little difference between them. To the extent that the call to honesty
is large, the two message values will tend to be verdical.

The preceding argument assumed that people lie to each other,
but accept what the other says in an uncritical way. This is very
unlikely. Suppose instead that the person discounts the message
in a manner suitable to the bias just described. Then the person
would increase the apparent discrepancy between his own position
and that of the message. That is, he would assume that the true
feelings of person k are

Perceived message = own position + ρ (message - own)

That is, person i would perceive person k as feeling

k's perceived feeling = $x_{ij} + \rho \ (s_{kij} - x_{ij})$

where $\rho > 1$ is a discrepancy inflating factor. In fact, if $\rho = 2 - \varepsilon$, then

$$\text{Perceived message} = (1 - \rho \ \frac{1}{2-\varepsilon}) x_{ij} + \rho \ \frac{1}{2-\varepsilon} x_{kj} \qquad (19)$$

would become

$$\text{Perceived message} = 0 \ x_{ij} + 1 \ x_{kj} = x_{kj}$$

That is, if $\rho = 2-\varepsilon$, then the perceived message would be k's true
feeling and the net effect of all the lying would be nil.

Actually there is one grave complicating factor that deserves
mention. If such distortion effects as the above exist, then they
probably exist in only part of the group. For example, the research done on the Machiavellianism scale (Christie and Geis,

1970) would suggest that there is a minority of persons who would lie on the one hand and discount on the other. Thus models of groups under pressure to lie to obtain material reward must take such individual differences into account.

C. *Social Structure*

From his theory of change in interpersonal relations, Hunter (1978) developed a theory of social structure. He noted first that structure is not likely to be found in the early phase of the development of a group, but only in the later phases. The simplifying effects of structure are not the direct product of interaction, but are the indirect effects of mutual influence that spreads information around and smooths differences within groups while sharpening differences between groups (at least according to balance theory). Thus, the theory of social structure that emerges from a dynamic theory of human interaction is the theory of the structure that develops in groups over an extended period. Mathematically this is called the "stability analysis" of a dynamic model.

There are three radically different types of dynamic models: these that predict that all the variables in the system will converge to some finite value; those that predict that some of the values diverge to plus or minus infinity, and those that predict that the ultimate behavior of the system is a cycle. The structural implications of a model are quite different in each case.

If the model predicts that the sentiments will all converge to some constant (as does information processing theory), then the structural predictions of the model can be found by solving the simultaneous equations

$$\Delta x_{ij} = 0$$

for all sociomatrices X that satisfy such equations. Every such
sociomatrix will be a social structure that would not change under
the assumptions of the given model. There are then procedures
available for assessing which of these structures are "stable"
and which are "unstable", where a "stable" matrix is one that
would survive small random shocks. That is, if a small perturbation is introduced into a stable limiting state, then that perturbation tends to vanish while the system goes back to the ini -
tial limiting state. But if the limiting state is unstable, then
a small perturbation causes the system to move to a different
limiting state that is stable.

However, for Hunter's balance model and for reinforcement
theory, the predicted sentiments simply become stronger and stronger over time and do not level off at any finite value. What is
the theory of social structure for such a sociomatrix? Hunter
presented a solution to this problem which he has subsequently
sharpened (Hunter, 1974). He stated that if some of the elements
of the matrix grow to infinity over time, then the critical question becomes: What are the relative sizes of the elements as they
become infinite? To find out, he "normalized" the sociomatrix
in various ways. The simplest method is to divide through the
matrix by the largest element at any given point in time. Thus,
the largest element in the normalized matrix is always 1 and every
other element can be compared to that. In most models, this normalized matrix would converge to a finite limit that Hunter called
an "invariant structure." For his model, Hunter (1974) showed
that the general procedure for finding "invariant structures" is
to solve the equation

$$\Delta X = \mu X \tag{20}$$

where μ is any multiplier and X is the sociomatrix. Eq. 20
would also yield limiting normalized matrices or "invariant struc-

tures" in other models that have matrices going to infinity. However, there are models in which there would be additional structures; for example, certain models constructed from reinforcement theory.

The third dynamic model, representing the cyclical behavior of systems is left untouched here. Although systems that converge to cycles are well known in physiology and electrical engineering, there is no attitude change theory that seems likely to produce such a result in its predictions for sociometry. The rather tricky mathematics of this third possibility continue to pose a challenge to sociometrists concerned with extrapolations from attitude change theories.

REFERENCES

Abelson, R. P., & Rosenberg, M. J. Symbolic psychologic: A model of attitudinal cognition. *Behavioral Science,* 1958, *3*, 1-13.

Aronson, E., Turner, J. A., & Carlsmith, J. M. Communicator credibility and communication discrepancy as determinants of opinion change. *Journal of Abnormal and Social Psychology,* 1963, *67*, 31-36.

Cartwright, D., & Harary, F. Structural balance: A generalization of Heider's theory. *Psychological Review,* 1961, *63*, 277-293.

Christie, R., Geis, F., et al. *Studies in Machiavellianism.* New York: Academic Press, 1970.

Cohen, S. H. Models of attitude change in the passive communication paradigm: Information processing, social judgment, dissonance, balance, and congruity. Unpublished doctoral dissertation, Michigan State University, 1971.

Festinger, L. *A theory of cognitive dissonance.* New York: Harper and Row, 1957.

Heider, F.   Attitudes and cognitive organization. *Journal of Psychology,* 1946, *21,* 107-112.

Hunter, J. E.   Dynamic sociometry. *Journal of Mathematical Sociology,* 1978, *6,* 87-138.

Hunter, J. E., & Cohen, S. H.   Mathematical models of attitude change in the passive communication context. Unpublished mimeo, Michigan State University, 1972.

Hunter, J. E.   Dynamic sociometry. Paper presented at the MSSB conference. Mathematical techniques in social network analysis, Morgantown, West Virginia, 1974.

Hunter, J. E.   Some notes on asymmetric sociomatrices. Unpublished manuscript, Michigan State University, 1974.

Killworth, P. D., & Bernard, H. R.   A model of human group dynamics. *Social Science Research,* 1975, *5,* 173-224.

Newcommb, T. M.   An approach to the study of communication acts. *Psychological Review,* 1953, *60,* 393-404.

Osgood, C. E., & Tannenbaum, P. H.   The principle of congruity in the prediction of attitude change. *Psychological Review,* 1955, *62,* 42-55.

White, H.   Management conflict and sociometric structure. *American Journal of Sociology,* 1961, *68,* 185-199.

CHAPTER 13

SOCIAL CLUSTERS AND OPINION CLUSTERS

Robert P. Abelson

Department of Psychology

Yale University

New Haven, Connecticut

I. INTRODUCTION

Some years ago (Abelson, 1964) I published a mathematical
model that linked social network as independent variable with
attitude change as dependent variable. I want to take this
occasion to expand that analysis to elucidate an important, previously unnoticed property of clusterable networks.

My basic interest is in large social networks through which
influence on controversial topics is propagated, for example, a
local community facing an issue referendum, or a political election campaign (Abelson and Berstein, 1963). The mathematical
model, however, is capable of being applied to small groups as
well as large, and the consequences I will develop are of general
theoretical applicability beyond the few contexts I discuss.

The original model was concerned with the distribution in a
social group of opinion positions on a single issue, and how that
distribution would change dynamically under a process of repeated
mutual influence attempts by individuals in social contact.

In this chapter, I want to discuss the dynamics of distribution of *multiple* opinions in a social group. Of particular interest is what happens dynamically to the correlation between opinion positions on any pair of issues. Opinion correlations are important both politically and psychologically. While it would not be appropriate here to discuss at great length the reasons for this importance, a few comments are necessary to motivate the later developments.

Politically, opinion correlations are important when many different issues "line up," so that partisans on a particular side of issue *i* tend also to be consistently partisan on particular sides of issues *j, k,* etc. Such concurrent polarization allows interest blocs or political parties to coalesce on a platform of a large set of positions, with a minimum of intraparty divisiveness. Furthermore, if one bloc has a safe legislative voting majority in a two-bloc or two-party system with concurrent issue polarization, then the minority can never logroll with subblocs within the majority to win on any particular high priority issue. This frustrating fate is the lot of embittered ethnic minorities such as the French Canadians and the Catholic Northern Irish. Coleman (1957) and many others have therefore pointed out the important condition for political stability that issue positions to some extent "cross-cut" each other, that is, correlate loosely over interest blocs.

At the level of single individuals, issue correlations are interesting because consistent high correlations seem to indicate that people can organize issues together into meaningful clusters or ideologies, whereas consistent low correlations seem to indicate a disorganized and incoherent state of public opinion. Debate rages on the extent to which the general public is or is not ideological (Converse, 1964, 1975; Luttberg, 1968; Nie, 1974), and issue correlations enter this debate as evidence.

We will see later that the use of correlations to suggest coherent cognitive organization may be illusory. The problem is that issue positions can line up at a given point in history because they are jointly advocated by a popular figure or group without any uniquely compelling connection among the issues. Elite advocates may spell out connections, but the mass public may or may not absorb the connections as well as they absorb the positions. For example, opposition to the Equal Rights Amendment and opposition to the Panama Canal Treaty seem conceptually distant, but may in practice covary because of simultaneous opposition campaigns within overlapping groups.

We will approach this psychological question with a baseline model: We will assume that opinion changes on each given issue have no effect in changing opinions on any other issue. Opinion changes on multiple issues will be treated as parallel processes, all dependent on influence within the same social network. Our starting point is the original (Abelson, 1964) model, which is of the type labeled by Hunter and Cohen (1972) as an "information processing model."

II. THE MODEL

We assume a group of individuals "continuously" discussing issues of interest. The continuity of discussion is a covenient mathematical fiction. Each individual is assumed to be in pairwise contact with every other individual, and each such contact is characterized by a parameter y_{ij} representing the "rate of effective communicative influence" on individual i by individual j. Each individual has a position on a hypothetical opinion scale for each issue under discussion, the entry for individual i and issue m being denoted z_{im}.

These positions change as the result of persuasive discussion, in which each individual accommodates his position toward the

position of the other. We assume that person i's opinion on issue m changes proportionately to the difference between i's opinion and that of communicator j, weighted by the effective influence rate from j to i, and summed over j.

$$\dot{z}_{im} = \sum_j y_{ij}(z_{jm} - z_{im}) \tag{1}$$

Because in this simple model there is no persuasive effect
when $j = i$, one might as well take $y_{ii} = 0$, whereupon it is possible to rearrange terms into a single summation:

$$\dot{z}_{im} = \sum_j y^*_{ij} z_{jm}, \tag{2}$$

where

$$y^*_{ij} = \begin{cases} y_{ij} & \text{for } j \neq i \\ -\sum_k y_{ik} & \text{for } j \neq i \end{cases} \tag{3}$$

In matrix terms, we have

$$\dot{Z} = Y^* Z \tag{4}$$

where Z is the person by issue position matrix, and Y^* is the
matrix of effective communication rates with negative row sums in
its diagonals.

The solution to this linear differential equation system
arises naturally from the eigenvalue decomposition of Y^* (assumed
symmetrical so that we may more easily see what is going on):

$$Y^* = PDP', \tag{5}$$

where the columns of P are the eigenvectors ("factors") of Y^* and
D is a diagonal matrix of eigenvalues. The substitution

$$W = P'Z \tag{6}$$

then leads to the simple form

$$\dot{W} = P'\dot{Z} = P'PDP'Z = DW. \tag{7}$$

Considering one element at a time, what this says is:

$$\dot{w}_{km} = d_k w_{km} \tag{8}$$

with solution

$$w_{km} = (w_{km})_0 \, e^{d_k t} \tag{9}$$

where the rows k represent linear combinations of people ("factors"), the columns m represent issues, and w_{km} is the net position on issue m of the linear combination k of people. (The zero subscript indicates initial value.)

It can be shown from the form Y^* that none of the d_k can be positive. There is always a zero d associated with an eigenvector with all entries identical. This is an "aggregate factor" and from Eq. (9) it follows that the sum (or average) opinion on any issue stays constant [under process (1)]. All other factors are necessarily bipolar; that is, there are some positive and some negative coefficients (in each column of P), which is to say that they represent *cleavages*. If we use the term "cleaved opinion" to refer to the linear combination of opinion scores using coefficients from a given cleavage factor, then Eq. (9) says that for all factors with negative d_k, cleaved opinions on all issues decay to zero--that is, there is asymptotic consensus.

In the case of symmetric communication parameters Y^*, all factors in fact have negative d_k unless the communication network

is separated into disjoint subgroups with no interaction. (The
asymmetric case is more complicated. Aschinger (1974) has pointed
out a misstatement in my original analysis of the asymmetric case
(Abelson, 1964), but we will not pursue the details here). Thus,
in the usual case there is asymptotic consensus on all issues for
all cleavage factors. (If the network is disjoint, then the corresponding cleaved opinions remain constant rather than decaying
to zero.) Of course the d_k in general differ in magnitude, so
that some cleaved opinions decay much more slowly than others.
The most slowly decaying cleavages define the structural weaknesses in the effective communication network, under the model
(1). Factoring Y^* is thus one way to analyze network structure.

The most striking feature of model (1), though, is that it
predicts virtually inexorable consensus. For some issues, this
is implausible; there are several processes which can lead to
other results, including using the affective rather than effective
network (so that entries in Y^* can be negative and some roots
positive), or allowing changes in the effective network, or replacing the difference feature of Eq. (1). Bernard and Killworth (1975) consider certain combinations of these, and we will
take up yet another possibility later.

First, I want to develop a further set of consequences of the
simple model (1), having to do with the correlations between separate issue positions. Our model in general produces decay of all
opinion differences. We ask, however, how the correlations between issue positions change during the process. This is of
interest because if the general decay process were to be inter-
reputed by some exogenous influence, the issue coalignments or
constellations within the group might turn out to have been
jostled from the way they were initially. This would have further consequences for other dynamic network processes which might
begin after the interruption.

III. CORRELATIONS BETWEEN ISSUE POSITIONS

To explore the correlations between issue positions, assume the positions z_{im} on each issue to sum to zero. (This can be done without loss of generality.) Then the matrix of issue co-variance in an n-person group would be simply:

$$C = \frac{1}{n} Z'Z. \tag{10}$$

The rates of change of these covariances would then be:

$$\dot{C} = \frac{1}{n}(Z'\dot{Z} + \dot{Z}'Z) \tag{11}$$

Substituting from equations (4), (5), (6) this reduces to:

$$\dot{C} = \frac{2}{n} W'DW \tag{12}$$

Focusing on the single element c_{lm} representing the covariance between issues l and m, we have:

$$\dot{c}_{lm} = \frac{2}{n} \sum_k d_k w_{km} w_{kl} \tag{13}$$

Applying the solution (9) for the w's yields:

$$\dot{c}_{lm} = \frac{2}{n} \sum_k d_k \left(w_{km}\right)_0 \left(w_{kl}\right)_0 e^{2d_k t} \tag{14}$$

Simple integration of this equation yields the solution for the time course of c_{lm}.

$$c_{lm} = c_{lm_0} + \frac{1}{n} \sum_k \left(w_{km}\right)_0 \left(w_{kl}\right)_0 (e^{2d_k t} - 1) \tag{15}$$

This can be further simplified, because there is a relationship between the initial cleaved opinion scores on two issues and their initial covariance:

$$\left(c_{1m}\right)_0 = \frac{1}{n} \sum_k \left(w_{km}\right)_0 \left(w_{k1}\right)_0 \tag{16}$$

Thus

$$c_{1m} = \frac{1}{n} \sum_k \left(w_{km}\right)_0 \left(w_{k1}\right)_0 e^{2d_k t} \tag{17}$$

The aggregate factor (say, $k = 1$) makes no contribution to the summation, because the setting of mean opinion on each issue to zero forces $\left(w_m\right)_0 = \left(w_1\right)_0 = 0$. Each cleavage makes a contribution, however, to the extent that initial opinions on issues 1 and m line up coordinately across the cleavage. Thereby, the covariance between issues 1 and m is dominated by the initial cross-product of the corresponding cleaved opinions in the dominant cleavage factors, the more so as time goes on. (Of course all the covariances shrink to zero, but the contributions from the important cleavages shrink more slowly.)

Having the covariance formula, it is easy to write the correlation between issues 1 and m:

$$r_{1m} = c_{1m} / \sqrt{c_{11} c_{mm}}$$

$$= \frac{\sum_k \left(w_{km}\right)_0 \left(w_{k1}\right)_0 e^{2d_k t}}{\left(\left(\sum_k \left(w_{km}\right)_0^2 e^{2d_k t}\right)\left(\sum_k \left(w_{k1}\right)_0^2 e^{2d_k t}\right)\right)^{\frac{1}{2}}} \tag{18}$$

Two particular cases are interesting to consider; first, that there are two camps with heavy rate of contact within camps and very little contact between camps.

This case produces one zero root, one slightly negative root, and $(n - 2)$ highly negative roots. The slightly negative

root corresponding to the dominant cleavage we index as $k = 2$.
As t increases, the other factors contribute very little to the
summations and the correlation between issues l and m approaches:

$$r_{lm} \approx \left(w_{2m}\right)_0 \left(w_{2l}\right)_0 \; e^{2d_2 t} \Bigg/ \left(\left(w_{2m}\right)_0^2 \; e^{2d_2 t} \left(w_{2l}\right)_0^2 \; e^{2d_2 t}\right)^{\frac{1}{2}} \qquad (19)$$

$$= \left(w_{2m}\right)_0 \left(w_{2l}\right)_0 \Bigg/ \left|\left(w_{2m}\right)_0 \left(w_{2l}\right)_0\right| = \pm 1.$$

That is, (to a first approximation) *when there is one dominant
effective cleavage, and all opinions in the group change according to the model of equation (1), then all opinions within the
group soon correlate perfectly.* The direction of the perfect
correlation depends upon the initial direction of association
within the opposing camps. The only exception to this generalization comes from the issue(s) with zero initial cleaved opinion(s),
in other words, where neither camp has a net opinion one way or
the other. (In this subcase, the approximation leading to Eq.
(19) is inappropriate.)

This result seems quite commonsensical, albeit it is always
nice to find a mathematical model coordinate with common sense.
Figure 1 shows graphically the phenomenon of increasing correlation between two issues when there are two social clusters with
differing positions on both issues, but the issues initially correlate zero within the clusters. We assume model (1) with high
communicative rates within clusters but low rates between clusters (this is what is meant, of course, by a dominant cleavage).
The correlation increases because consensus is achieved on each
issue within each group faster than the two groups accommodate
to each other.

Next we consider a slightly more complex case. Suppose
there are two important cleavage factors rather than one, which

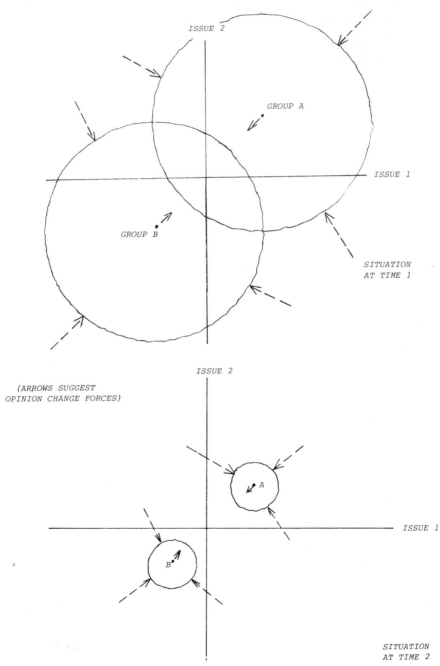

Fig. 1. Increased issue correlation through joint social
process.

might arise, for example, when there are three social camps
instead of two. Indexing these factors as $k = 2, 3$, assuming the
roots $d_2 = d_3$, (and dropping the initial value subscript from the
w's for brevity), we would have:

$$r_{1m} \approx \left(w_{2m}w_{21} + w_{3m}w_{31} \right) \Big/ \left(\left(w_{2m}^2 + w_{3m}^2 \right)\left(w_{21}^2 + w_{31}^2 \right) \right)^{\frac{1}{2}} \tag{20}$$

Recall that the w's by Eq. (6), are linear combinations of the
issue positions Z of individual members, with weights determined
by factoring the effective network Y^*. In the case of three
equally sized cliques or clusters, (denote a, b, c), let the
average opinions on issue m of the three clusters be denoted z_{am},
z_{bm}, z_{cm}. A straightforward derivation shows that equation (20)
can be rewritten in terms of these z averages as:

$$r_{1m} \sim \frac{\left(z_{am}z_{a1} + z_{bm}z_{b1} + z_{cm}z_{c1} \right)}{\left(\left(z_{am}^2 + z_{bm}^2 + z_{cm}^2 \right)\left(z_{a1}^2 + z_{b1}^2 + z_{c1}^2 \right) \right)^{\frac{1}{2}}} \tag{21}$$

The expression (21) is nothing more nor less than the correlation between issue positions 1 and m over the three clusters,
using cluster averages as points. With four equal clusters and
three equal roots, a comparable equation holds; with s equal clusters and $(s - 1)$ equal roots, the same idea is applicable. What
this says is that model (1) over time causes the correlation pattern between issue positions in the total group to regress to the
correlation pattern defined by the averages within the several
clusters. The issue variations within clusters soon cease to
matter. Issues which "line up" from cluster to cluster will line
up in the total group. Perhaps it is pretentious to say so, but
there is a principle here that is an aspect of a social physics:
Each social cluster can be represented by its centroid, which to
a first approximation captures the consequences pertaining to the

whole set of individuals. Thus, for example, ethnic or social
class communication clusters define the clustering of political
issues in the course of a political campaign or time of national
controversy. *Social clustering begets opinion clustering,* independent of whether the issues involved are conceptually related.

The preceding statement is of course a theoretical one, not
necessarily an empirical one. What is required theoretically is
that two or more issues are simultaneously "hot," with discussion
of them taking place via model (1) at equivalent rates in a communicative network cleaved into social clusters which *on the
average* on each issue are correspondingly pro or con, and correspondingly extreme. Within clusters, the issues may initially
have no correlation with each other. Although this set of conditions is multiply hypothetical, the reader may be able to think
of real contexts in which most of these conditions occurred or
were at least plausible. One such example concerns cold war issues and civil rights issues in the 1960s. In a large sample of
the mass public (Nie, 1974) the correlation between these two disparate issues was only .08 in 1956, but increased to .20 in 1964
and .27 in 1972. Nie (1974) argued that increased correlations
of this kind showed that the public was becoming more ideological.
But it is unclear to what extent the conceptual connections between the issues were well elaborated in the general public--both
issues could be seen as involving tolerance of the forces of
change in the world, but both could be seen in many other ways as
well. Rather, it may have been an instance of increased simultaneous discussion of both issues, invoking the parallel persuasive
process dynamic we have outlined. In fact, whenever issue correlations increase, it might suggest the operation of this dynamic.
Closer empirical examination of this kind would be useful.

IV.   EXTENSIONS AND QUALIFICATIONS

There is no reason why one or more of the "issues" under discussion could not be evaluations of individuals known to all members of the total group (e.g., Richard Nixon). In a local social context, it might be the case that everyone knew several individual members of each social cluster within the total group, and the goodness or badness of these persons became the issues under discussion. Coleman (1957), in his classic monograph on community controversies reported a common phenomenon of this kind. During the intense debate of a hot community issue (such as Communist teaching in the schools), one or more speakers would let fly a personal insult toward one or more members of the opposition, whereupon everyone would very soon become engaged in hotly debating the integrity and intelligence of everyone else, rather than the original content issue(s). The net result of such a free-for-all would be a deeply polarized community for months or years after the original issue had ceased to be important.

This phenomenon can be considered under the rubric of model (1), with the variable z_{im} taken to represent the sentiment of individual i toward individual m. Take these "target" individuals to be a subset of individuals in the group, one or more from each social cluster. Then the model of the previous section would imply that with equal-sized social clusters with high communication rates within cluster and low rates between clusters, *the correlation structure between sentiments toward individuals would approach the correlation structure defined by average sentiments within effective clusters*.

In the interesting case of just two communication clusters, correlations between sentiments would all approach either plus or minus one. If each cluster had, on the average, initially favorable sentiments toward its own members and initially unfavorable sentiments toward members of the other group (certainly a

plausible circumstance) the net tendency of the discussion process would be to pull every member of both clusters into line
with these initial sentiments. Thus, a balanced sentiment network would be produced. Under the appropriate circumstances, in
other words, model (1) predicts that the effective communication
network governs the affective network. One might say that *social
unit balance begets social sentiment balance*.

The strong theoretical statements in this paper depend, of
course, on the assumed form of the model. In particular, the
assumption that the effective communication rates y_{ij} are constant over the set of issues seems rather unrealistic in general.
This assumption becomes hidden when we talk about "the" social
network, begging the question whether the same network is used
for discussing different issues. It seems unlikely that communications about, say, the Kentucky Derby and about the world
hunger problem travel through the same networks. However, one
can plausibly suppose that bundles of issues of similar type
(foreign policy, local news, gossip about entertainment figues,
etc.) share approximately the same network. One can also picture
circumstances (e.g., crisis situations) in which particular networks are impressed upon a group for all the issues it might
discuss. Incidentally, if the rates of communicative influence
on different issues are not strictly the same but are proportional
(the same networks being involved, but some issues simply being
talked about more than others), then our conclusions hold to a
weakened extent. The circles in the right-hand panel of Figure 1
become ellipses, and the goodness of the approximations (19) and
(20) depends not only on the ratio of the eigenvalues for separate
cleavages, but also upon the ratio of communication rates for the
two issues. (More specifically, the approximations are good only
if the ratio of the dominant eigenvalue to the next eigenvalue is
distinctly bigger than the ratio of the rate of discussion of
the faster to the slower issue.)

Another feature of model (1) that raises questions is its proclivity for producing asymptotic issue consensus in the entire group. The eventual fate of the distribution in Figure 1 is a total concentration at the origin. While it is a compelling result of the model that opinion (or sentiment) structures echo communication structures, it is disturbing that the model makes the echoed structures grow fainter and fainter over time.

If there were process models which made opinion distributions expand instead of collapse, then these processes could be invoked to counteract the shrinkage inherent in the "information processing" model of Eq. (1). Indeed, there are such models, notably Hunter's (1974) model, which makes sentiments not only expand, but explode! The explosive ingredient in his mathematical formula is a multiplicative term between two sentiments on the right-hand side of an equation analogous to (1), without any difference term. Psychologically, Hunter's model presents a process of intensification of affect, a sort of social amplification or celebration which expands the extremity of evaluations of other individuals. It is a subjective, "warm" process in contrast to the objective, "cool" information-processing model.

Ideally, one would like a process model which neither went to zero nor to infinity, but played these two tendencies against each other to maintain a reasonable distribution on the opinion or sentiment variable. This is extremely difficult to do with models of the kind we are concerned with; the models are too sensitive. We can, however, suggest a modification of Eq. (1) which is more in line with psychological reality and does in one particular circumstance create a stable opinion distribution.

There is recent evidence that moderate opinions tend to become more extreme when like-minded individuals enter a group discussion (Myers and Lamm, 1976), or even when a lone individual is pressured into thinking hard about an issue--discussing it with himself, as it were (Tesser, 1978). The differential salience of arguments or considerations on a single side of the

issue seems to compel the feeling that one is even more pro (con)
than one had previously supposed before reviewing the details.
One rough way to capture this phenomenon is through Eq. (22):

$$\dot{z}_{im} = \sum_{j} y_{ij}\left(z_{jm} - z_{im}\right) + cz_{im} \tag{22}$$

This is identical to equation (1) except that a term has been
added on the right. This term says that above and beyond persuasive accommodation to the opinions of others, one's own
opinion tends to change toward greater extremity in its present
direction, proportional (by the positive factor, c) to its present
extremity.

Simplification of this equation yields an analog of matrix
Eq. (4):

$$\dot{Z} = (Y^* + cI)Z. \tag{23}$$

The effect of the extra term is very simple. The factoring of Y^*
into cleavage factors remains the same, but all eigenvalues are
increased by the constant, c. The solution of the system is thus:

$$w_{km} = \left(w_{km}\right)_0 e^{\left(c + d_k\right)t}, \tag{24}$$

where as before the rows k represent the cleavages derived by
factoring Y^*, the columns m represent issues, and w_{km} is the net
position on issue m for the cleavage k. As before, the root for
the aggregate first factor is zero, and all the other d's are
negative.

It follows from Eq. (24) that it is possible for a cleavage to
maintain itself. If $-c$ happens to equal some d_k, then the corresponding cleavage has its initial value throughtout. If we consider the case of essentially two communication clusters, so that
d_2 dominates the other roots, then if $c + d_2 = 0$, the two clusters maintain their separation on all issues, while all variations

within the two clusters damp out. That is, disagreement on all issues is increasingly confined to disagreements between the clusters, and these disagreements do not diminish. If $c + d_2 > 0$, then the disagreements increase rather than diminish, and move toward infinity. Thus, this model with the "warm" process term cz_{ij} permits an explosive result depending on the relative size of the constant c.

Tinkering with very idealized systems such as (1) or (22) is not likely to produce a fully realistic imitation of group process. Life is much too "lumpy" with discrete events that jostle social processes away from the smooth trajectories of deterministic models. However, these models can give us a good understanding of the qualitative features of different process dynsmics. A more realistic view of actual processes might involve a succession of phases in which a variety of cold and warm processes attach themselves for periods of time to different issues in different networks.

REFERENCES

Abelson, R. P. Mathematical models of the distribution of attitudes under controversy. In N. Frederiksen & H. Gulliksen (Eds.), *Contributions to mathematical psychology*. New York: Holt, Rinehart & Winston, 1964.

Abelson, R. P., & Berstein, A. A computer simulation model of community referendum controversies. *Public Opinion Quarterly,* 1963, *27*, 93-122.

Aschinger, G. Das dynamic social choice Modell: Ein dynamisches Modell der Gruppenentscheidung. *Schriftenreihe des Instituts fur betriebswirtschaftliche Forschung an der Universitat Zurich,* Vol. 14. Haupt:Berne, 1974.

Bernard, H. R., & Killworth, P. D. On the structure of affective
    and effective sociometric relations in a closed group over
    time. Technical Report #BK-107-75, Office of Naval Research,
    1975.

Coleman, J. S. *Community conflict*. New York: Free Press of
    Glencoe, 1957.

Converse, P. E. The nature of belief systems in mass publics.
    in D. E. Apter (Ed.), *Ideology and discontent*. New York:
    Free Press of Glencoe, 1964.

Converse, P. E. Public opinion and voting behavior. In F. I.
    Greenstein and N. W. Polsby (Eds.) *Handbook of political
    science, Vol. 4: Non-governmental politics,* Reading,
    Massachusetts, Addison-Wesley, 1975.

Hunter, J. E. Dynamic sociometry. Presented at the Mathematical
    Social Science Board Conference: Mathematical techniques in
    social network analysis, Morgantown, West Virginia, 1974.

Hunter, J. E., & Cohen, S. R. *Mathematical models of attitude
    change in the passive communication context*. Unpublished
    book. Michigan State University, 1972.

Luttberg, N. R. The structure of beliefs among leaders and the
    public. *Public Opinion Quarterly,* 1968, *32*, 398-409.

Myers, D. G., & Lamm, H. The group polarization phenomenon.
    Psychological Bulletin, 1976, *83*, 602-627.

Nie, N. H. Mass belief systems revisited: Political change and
    attitude structure. *Journal of Politics,* 1974, *36*, 540,591.

Tesser, A. Self-generated attitude change. In L. Berkowitz
    (Ed.), *Advances in experimental social psychology, Vol. 11.*
    New York: Academic Press, 1978.

CHAPTER 14

EQUILIBRATING PROCESSES IN SOCIAL NETWORKS:

A MODEL FOR CONCEPTUALIZATION AND ANALYSIS[1]

D. Garth Taylor[2]

James S. Coleman[3]

University of Chicago

National Opinion Research Center

Chicago, Illinois

I.   INTRODUCTION

The aim of this chapter is to apply a model of exchange and
purposive action (Coleman, 1975) to the sociometric choices of
students in high schools studied in *The Adolescent Society*
(Coleman, 1961). There are a few key concepts in the exchange
model that we must carefully operationalize before our questions
can be put to the data. Chief among these concepts are:
(1) power in a sociometric system; (2) exchange of resources or
interests in a sociometric system; and (3) the equilibrium state

[1]*This research was supported by National Science Foundation
Grant number SOC73-05504-801. We would like to thank Scott Feld
for being helpful and thinking about these problems with us, and
Sylvia Piechocka for assistance in manuscript preparation.*

[2]*Present address: Department of Political Science, University of Chicago, Chicago, Illinois.*

[3]*Present address: Department of Sociology, University of
Chicago, Chicago, Illinois.*

of resources in a sociometric system. First we will discuss
operationalization of interests in the sociometric system.
Although interest is based upon expressions of friendship, our
formulation goes beyond the usual matrix of ones or zeroes,
representing friendship or its absence. In the second section
we will discuss the method of calculating power in a sociometric
system from a matrix of interests based on sociometric choices.
Third we will discuss what we mean by equilibrium in a system
of sociometric choices and derive formulas for predicting sociometric choices and for determining which persons' choices are
dominant, in that they shape the future choices of others. These
formulas should be accurate to the extent that the system follows
the model of social power and exchange that we hypothesize. In
the fourth section we will develop an approach to sociometric
data using structural equation models. In the latter sections we
will test the predictions of our models against some of the
data available to us.

                              PART I

I.   WHAT DO PEOPLE CONTROL AND WHAT ARE THEY INTERESTED IN?

     We start with the assumption that people control themselves
and that they are interested in each other. Operationally, this
means that each person can be thought of in two separate roles
in a sociometric system: (1) as an object who is chosen by
other people as desirable to be with; and (2) as a subject who
desires to associate with other people. Our approach is to think
of person i giving attention to person j as an event. It should
not be too controversial to assume that actor j has control over
the event of giving attention to actor j. That is, if we were
to think of a matrix whose rows were the actors in the system
and whose columns were the events in the system (i.e., the
attention of each actor in the system), then the matrix that

showed what actors controlled what events would be an identity matrix. In this sense, each actor constitutes his own resource in the system.

It is a principle not foreign to sociological thinking that each actor will employ his resources to gain control over those events in which he is interested. In a sociometric system an actor is interested in the attention of certain other actors. This interest can be quantified in a number of ways. In the simplest application we take the sociometric matrix of actors as subjects (rows) by actors as objects (columns) and enter a 1.0 in the (i, j) cell if actor i expressed an interest in actor j, and a zero otherwise. If we do this, we assume that each actor spreads his interest evenly among those people whose attention he wants. It may be more appropriate to assume that within a set of people who are chosen by actor i there are some people whom i is very interested in and some people whom i is less interested in. That is, in many cases it may be appropriate to assume that i has ranked his choices. The data from the high schools that are available to us are of this nature. The sociometric question used was not perfect from our point of view, for it asked about association with another, rather than his interest in the attention of another. The actual question was "Who are the boys (girls) here at school that you go around with most often?" Association of i and j, unlike attention of i to j, is jointly controlled by both parties, and thus not as appropriate to our conceptual scheme as attention. However, we will proceed as if the data were fully appropriate, but regarding the substantive conclusions with some caution.

A way to operationalize this kind of preferential ordering is to assume that the ratio of interest between i's first and second choice is the same as the ratio of interest between the second and third choices, which is the same as the ratio between the third and fourth choices, and so on. That is, if x_{i1} is the proportion of i's interest that he has invested in his first choice then:

$$\frac{x_{i2}}{x_{i1}} = \frac{x_{i3}}{x_{i2}} = \cdots = \frac{x_{i(n)}}{x_{i(n-1)}} = s \tag{1}$$

where n equals the number of choices made by actor i.

If this ratio is 1.0, then we have the case alluded to above where actor i assigns his interest evenly over the choices he has made. We are interested in ratios between 0 and 1. If we impose the general condition that a person's interests in the other actors in the system sum to unity, then the interest in any specific actor is easy to derive once we specify the ratio between adjacent choices. If the n terms in a series which sums to unity satisfy condition (1), then the magnitude of the cth choice (x_{ic}, $c = 1, 2, 3, \ldots n$) is given by:

$$x_{ic} = \frac{(1 - s) * s^{(c - 1)}}{(1 - s^n)} \tag{2}$$

where:

x_{ic} = the magnitude of i's interest in his cth choice
($c = 1, 2, 3, \ldots n$),

n = the number of choices made by actor i, and

s = the ratio between the $(c + 1)$st and the cth choice.

This result holds because the sum over c of x_{ic} is the sum of a geometric series (Thomas, 1960). Table I shows the behavior of this equation for selected values of n and s. The way to read Table I is as follows: If a person made 5 choices and the ratio between adjacent choices was .6 (the magnitude of the second choice is .6 times the magnitude of the first choice), then the proportion of his interest which is invested in the first choice is .434. The proportion of his interest in the fifth choice is .056. The sum of his interest over the 5 choices he has made is 1.0. In our data each actor made between 1 and 10 choices.

Our method for assigning interest scores to these choices is:
(1) to assume that every actor had the same ration between adjacent choices; (2) count the number of choices made by any
actor; and (3) use Eq. (2) to assign an interest score to each
ranked choice made by the ith actor. Table I shows that the
closer the ratio between choices is to 1.0 the more evenly
spread is an actor's interest over the choices he has made. It
is an empirical question as to which is the correct choice of
the parameter s. For exploratory purposes we have replicated
our results for the following three values of s:

(1) We used $s = .99$ to approximate an even distribution
of attention over one's choices.
(2) We used $s = .80$ to approximate the condition where
there is some rank order in an actor's choices but not an
extreme amount.
(3) We used $s = .50$ to test the sensitivity of our results
to the assumption of extreme rank ordering of choices.

An additional modification is based on the recognition that
persons do not have zero interest in others they fail to name.
There is presumably some threshold such that, if interest is below it, the person will not be named. Thus, we assumed that some
proportion of each person's interest was not allocated to those
he named, but was distributed equally over all others in the
total group. We need, therefore, to make another assumption
about the properties of the sociometric matrix: This time the
assumption is the amount of a person's attention that is spread
over the other people in the system whom he did not choose, or,
conversely, the amount of attention an actor devotes to his
choices. We can experiment with different values for this
parameter: In this report we have run analyses using .5, .7,
and .95 for the proportion of a person's attention that is
allocated to his choices. Thus, each person has interest in
each other person in the system with a certain proportion of his

TABLE I. The Relation between Ranked Preferences and Interest Scores for Selected Values of the Ratio between Adjacent Choices and for Varying Numbers of Choices

Values for the ratio between adjacent interests

Number of choices	.4		.5		.6		.7		.8		.9	
	Choice #	Interest	Choice #	Interest	Choice #	Interest	Choice #	Interest	Choice #	Interest	Choice #	Interest
3	1	.641	1	.571	1	.510	1	.457	1	.410	1	.369
	2	.256	2	.286	2	.306	2	.320	2	.328	2	.332
	3	.103	3	.143	3	.184	3	.224	3	.262	3	.299
4	1	.616	1	.533	1	.460	1	.395	1	.339	1	.291
	2	.246	2	.267	2	.276	2	.276	2	.271	2	.262
	3	.099	3	.133	3	.165	3	.193	3	.217	3	.236
	4	.039	4	.067	4	.099	4	.135	4	.173	4	.212

5

Choice #	Interest	Choice #	Interest	Choice #	Interest	Choice #	Interest	Choice #	Interest	Choice #	Interest
1	.606	1	.516	1	.434	1	.361	1	.297	1	.244
2	.242	2	.253	2	.260	2	.252	2	.238	2	.220
3	.097	3	.129	3	.156	3	.177	3	.190	3	.198
4	.039	4	.065	4	.094	4	.124	4	.152	4	.178
5	.016	5	.032	5	.056	5	.087	5	.122	5	.160

6

Choice #	Interest	Choice #	Interest	Choice #	Interest	Choice #	Interest	Choice #	Interest	Choice #	Interest
1	.602	1	.508	1	.420	1	.340	1	.271	1	.213
2	.241	2	.254	2	.252	2	.238	2	.217	2	.192
3	.096	3	.127	3	.151	3	.167	3	.173	3	.173
4	.039	4	.063	4	.091	4	.117	4	.139	4	.156
5	.015	5	.032	5	.054	5	.082	5	.111	5	.140
6	.006	6	.016	6	.033	6	.057	6	.089	6	.126

interest distributed among named and the rest distributed equally among those he did not name. It would be easy to design questions that would get at the amount of variation in interest among each person's choices, but since we do not presently have this information, we will assume everyone is alike in the ratio of interest in adjacent choices and in his total interest in those named.

We obtain by this method a sociometric matrix of ranked choices, which has the following characteristics:

(1) The rows are actors as subjects, or choosers.

(2) The columns are actors as objects, people who have had interest expressed in them.

(3) The (i, j) cell is the proportion of actor i's interest in actor j.

(4) Each row sums to 1.0--there are zeros on the diagonal.

The values are obtained in two ways: (a) For those actors j named by actor i, the interest scores were obtained from Eq. (2), using for example, $s = .8$, and then scaling down x_{ic} by multiplying it by .8. (b) For those actor j not named by actor i, the interest is obtained by $(1 - a)/(n - m_i - 1)$, where n is the total number of persons in the group, m_i is the number chosen by actor i, a is the proportion of actor i's interest that he allocates to his choices, and therefore $(1 - a)$ is the proportion diffused among the rest of the actors in the system.

An example of a sociometric matrix of this type is shown in Table II. This is the interest matrix. We will use this along with the control matrix (the identity matrix, actor i's control of himself as his resource) to study other characteristics of the system. Specifically, we will solve for the power of each actor (the extent to which other (powerful) people are interested in what actor j controls), and we will attempt to predict actor i's choice of j based on whether or not j chose i and the

TABLE II. *Fall Sociometric Choices, Senior Girls, School #0 (95% of Interest Allocated to Chosen Actors; Ratio of Second to First Choice = .8; Each Entry Shows the First Two Decimal Places.)*

		Actor ID Number												
		83	84	85	87	89	90	91	93	94	95	96	97	98
	83	0	1	1	1	25	1	1	31	1	1	39	1	1
	84	1	0	95	1	1	1	1	1	1	1	1	1	1
	85	1	95	0	1	1	1	1	1	1	1	1	1	1
	87	1	1	1	0	1	53	42	1	1	1	1	1	1
	89	1	1	1	1	0	1	1	53	1	1	42	1	1
	90	1	1	1	42	1	0	53	1	1	1	1	1	1
ID#	91	1	1	1	42	1	53	0	1	1	1	1	1	1
	93	1	1	1	1	53	1	1	0	1	1	42	1	1
	94	1	1	1	1	1	1	1	1	0	31	1	39	25
	95	1	1	1	1	1	1	1	1	31	0	1	39	25
	96	1	1	1	1	31	1	1	39	1	1	0	1	25
	97	1	1	1	1	1	1	1	1	31	25	1	0	39
	98	1	1	1	1	1	1	1	1	31	25	1	39	0

relative power of the two actors. But this is getting ahead of the story. First we need to take a longer look at what we mean by power in a sociometric system.

PART II

I. POWER: WHO GETS WHOM

In order to determine who the powerful actors are in a sociometric system we have to make some assumptions about how the system operates. We have already suggested that person j is powerful if j has something that others want. We know what each person wants because we know his ranked interests. We know what j
has because we have assumed that the matrix that shows the events
controlled by each actor is an identity matrix. We assume that
people will employ or exchange their resources to gain control
over those events (people) that are of interest to them. That
is, people will allocate their attention to others in such a way
that they end up gaining the attention of those they are interested in.[4] Given this way of looking at things, a powerful
person is someone in whom a lot of people are interested, or
possibly someone in whom another powerful person is interested.

[4]*The model used here assumes that the resources controlled
by each actor are alienable and thus can be transferred from i
to j to k. A person's attention is not like this, and thus
strictly speaking, a model like this one assuming alienability
of resources (i.e., indirect exchanges) is not fully appropriate.
In substantive terms, it can be put this way: The model assumes
that the power j receives through the interest that i shows in
him can be used to gain the attention of k, in whom j is interested. This is not true for attention; however, such transfera-
bility is not completely absent either. The interest that i
shows in j does increase his general status in the group, which
can make him more attractive to k. It seems probable that a
model of partial, rather than full, alienability is appropriate
here.*

This is essentially how we calculate power in a sociometric system.[5] For each actor we calculate a value that is something like the amount of interest that people in the system have in that actor, weighted by the power of each of those people. To state it mathematically, the power of j, v_j, is equal to the sum of the interests of each actor i in j, times i's power:

$$v_j = \Sigma_i r_i x_{ij} \tag{3}$$

or, in matrix notation, where R is the power vector (whose elements sum to 1), and X is the interest matrix,

$$R = RX \tag{3'}$$

Equation (3) may be used to calculate the power of each actor, though in the subsequent exposition we will use a somewhat different approach.

We reason that if actor i has chosen actor j and j does not reciprocate, then j has in some sense "absorbed" a portion of i's resources in the system. This notion of a resource that is transferred between actors is essential to solving for the power of actors in the system. Powerful actors are those who have absorbed more than their "share" of the resources in the system.

What is an actor's rightful "share" of resources in the system? We should recall our interpretation of events. An event is association with a given actor. If there are 10 actors, then there are 10 events. Each actor is assumed to control the event of association with himself. This means that if there are 10 actors, each actor starts out owning 1/10 of the resources in

[5]*The substantive idea expressed here is not new. In 1953, Leo Katz developed a measure of sociometric status that depended not merely on the number of choices received, but on the number of choices made as well, each choice weighted by the status of others who chose him.*

the system. Powerful people are those who have absorbed a dis-
proportionate amount of the resources of other actors.

How are resources absorbed? We assume a process of social
interaction or social exchange with the following characteri-
istics:

(1) When the system begins each actor has an equal share of
the resources, that is, $1/n$.

(2) When actor i chooses j he "gives" j his resources in
proportion to the strength of his choice of j. That is,
looking at the matrix of Senior Girls' choices in Table II,
actor 83 starts with $(1/13)$ of the resources--about .077 of the
total. In making her choice of 89 she gives to actor 89, 25%
her resources. Similarly, she gives 31% of her resources to
actor 93.

(3) Interaction in our model consists of people continually
giving up and receiving resources: giving to people they are
interested in and taking from people who are interested in them.
It is helpful to think of stages. At stage 1 each actor gives
his resources to the actors he is interested in, according to
the entries in a matrix like Table II. At the end of this stage,
there is a new distribution of power or resources. At stage 2,
exactly the same process occurs, but with the new resources distribution. We will illustrate this when we examine the properties of the exchange more fully. We do not propose that social
interaction is described by this demarcation into stages, but
this is a useful heuristic device for seeing how a power distribution is arrived at.

(4) After a number of stages in systems of exchange like we
have just described there will be a tendency for the power vector
to not change between one cycle and the next. In applying this
methodology to a different example, Berger and Snell (1957) call
this stable power vector the equilibrium distribution of resources in the system.

With sociometric systems in which interests are expressed as
we described earlier, the vector of power (or states in Markov
terminology) will move toward a stable distribution because the
interest matrix (and the product of the interest and control
matrices) gives rise to what is known in the terminology of
Markov processes as an ergodic set (Kemeny and Snell, 1960,
1962). For our purposes the phrase "an ergodic set" means that
every actor is connected to every other actor either directly or
indirectly, that is, there are no isolated cliques, dyads, or
mutually exclusive subgroups within the system. This is a condition we imposed on the matrix of choices by assuming that a
certain proportion of each actor's interest was spread over all
the other actors in the system, although they may not have
occasioned enough interest to be chosen.

At the beginning of the process we just outlined, each member of the Girls' Senior Class has 1/13 of the power in the system (since there are 13 girls in the class). We will denote
the vector of power at time t as R_t. At the start of the process
($t = 0$) the power vector is:

$$R_0 = (1/13, 1/13, \ldots, 1/13)$$

After stage 1 of the process the power vector is generally different from R_0. If each girl allocates her resources to other girls
in proportion to the strength of her choice of them and receives
resources in a similar fashion, then the power vector after the
first period is:

$$R_1 = R_0 X \tag{4}$$

where R_1 is the power vector after the first period and X is the
matrix of interests (Table II). This result is shown in the
first row of Table III. Before the first cycle each girl had
.077 of the resources in the system. After the first cycle this
is no longer true. Some girls have .09 and .10 (one girl has
.01). This is because the resource allocation worked out so

TABLE III. Results from Vector Multiplication into the Girls' Sociometric Matrix in Table II

	Actor ID Number												
# of multiplications	83	84	85	87	89	90	91	93	94	95	96	97	98
v_1	1	8	8	7	9	9	8	10	8	7	10	9	9
v_2	1	8	8	7	9	8	8	9	8	7	8	9	10
. . .													
v_n	1	9	9	8	4	9	8	5	11	10	5	13	11

(v_n = the final power distribution. Each entry shows the first two decimal places.)

that each actor did not receive the same amount she gave. If we let the process go through one more stage, we obtain:

$$R_2 = R_1 X$$
$$= (R_0 X) X$$
$$= R_0 X^2 \tag{5}$$

This result is shown in the second row of Table II. The values are very similar to the values for R_1. This means that the process is already very near its equilibrium and the power vector R_2 can be described as very close to the equilibrium power distribution for the girls given the expressions of interest in the sociometric matrix. In general, we can solve for the power vector at any time t by using the following formula:

$$R_t = R_0 X^t \tag{6}$$

This should be clear from looking at Eq. (5). (Kemeny and Snell, 1960 prove it.)

We have defined equilibrium in this system in such a manner that the distribution of power among actors does not change from one stage to the next. If the system is at equilibrium at stage s, then:

$$R_s = R_s X$$

and

$$R_{s+1} = R_s$$

Another way of saying this is that the equilibrium power vector R_e is a vector such that:

$$R_e = R_e X \tag{7}$$

(Note that this is the same as Eq. (3')).

If X is, in Markov terminology, an ergodic set, then we can solve for R_e by methods which require inverting a function of the X matrix. These are described in Coleman (1973, p. 80).

Although by allocating some proportion of each person's interest
equally across those he did not choose, we have arbitrarily created an ergodic set from the group, it is useful to develop alternative methods for solving for the power of actors at equilibrium which do not assume full connectedness. This will require longer, iterative methods.

We noted in our discussion of Table III that the power vector for the senior girls did not change much between the first
and the second periods. This indicates how one may find the
power vector without inverting the matrix: We can keep multiplying the power vector at stage s into the choice matrix until
the vector does not change to the required degree of accuracy between stage s and stage $s + 1$. Or alternatively (using Eq. (6)),
we can raise the choice matrix to a very high power and then multiply it by the original vector twice. If the power vector after
the first and second multiplications were the same, then this is
the power vector for the equilibrium. This is the method used to
solve for the power vector at equilibrium presented in the last
row of Table III. The advantages of this method are that it
allows the researcher to: (1) calculate the power scores at
various stages in the approach to the equilibrium condition, and
(2) calculate power scores for matrices that are not ergodic
sets, thus allowing one to relax the assumption that some of a
person's interest is dispersed among actors who are not named.

PART III

I. MUTUALITY AND EQUILIBRIUM

In all that has transpired, we have merely defined a concept
of power (or equally reasonably, status) in a sociometric matrix.
Although we have written of this as the "equilibrium" power
distribution, it is a purely static concept, with the "stages"
introduced only as an expository aid. Now, however, we will

discuss a process that we do propose to be operative over time, not (necessarily) to change the power distribution, but rather to change the matrix of interests. The general idea, expressed in a loose way, is this: If i expresses interest in j, this is in effect a demand for attention from j, as well as attention directed toward j. If j also expresses interest in i, this attention supplies the demand expressed by i, and at the same time expresses a demand for attention from i, which in this case, i has given. There is, then, what might be thought of as an equilibrium between this pair of interests. But if j does not express an interest in i, then i's interest remains unfulfilled, while j looks elsewhere. Movement toward an equilibrium of interests is movement toward fulfillment of interests in the sense expressed above.

This may be made more precise by returning to the mathematics of the model. In the initial discussion we indicated that each person may be conceived at the outset to have full control over his own attention, but that he gives up that control in return for the attention of others he is interested in. It can be shown (see Coleman, 1973) that under reasonable assumptions this implies that the degree of control that an actor j will exercise over the attention of i at equilibrium will depend on his interest in i, x_{ji}, and the ratio of his power to i's power, in the following way:

$$c_{ij} = x_{ji} \frac{r_j}{r_i} . \tag{8}$$

Or to express it differently, i's power times the control of j over i, $r_i c_{ij}$, equals at equilibrium j's power times the interest of j in i.

But what, operationally, does the control of j over i, c_{ij}, consist of? It is the claim that j has on i's attention, or the interest of i in j. That is, the process that is being proposed is one in which i's initial interests in j, whatever they

start out to be, come to adjust to j's initial interests in i.
That is,

$$r_i x_{ij2} = r_j x_{ji1} \tag{9}$$

where x_{ji1} is j's initial interest. This means that the interests of one member of each pair are dominant and do not change,
while the interests of the other member adjust to those of the
first. It is perhaps easiest to imagine in a two-population
case, such as boys expressing interest in girls, and girls expressing interest in boys. After a process of adjustment, then,
if the interests of the boys are dominant, the girls will have
adjusted their interests to those of the boys, just as in Eq. (9)
actor i has adjusted his interests to those of actor j. If the
interests of the girls are dominant, then, after the adjustment
process, the boys' interests will adjust to those initially expressed by the girls.

The matter is similar in the one-population case. Here,
since the adjustment is proposed to take place within each pair,
the interests of one or the other member of the pair may be
dominant, with the other adjusting to his. If the members of
the pair may be distinguished in some criterion (e.g., the
older and younger, the smarter and less smart, the taller and
shorter, the more sociometrically powerful and the less sociometrically powerful), then the adjustment of interests may always
be on the part of one labeled member of the pair (e.g., always on
the part of the older, or always on the part of the younger).
Then we could say that the interests of the younger (or the older)
are dominant; that is, the one whose interests did not change to
come into conformity with the other. More generally, if there is
such an adjustment process, there will likely be some movement
from both sides of the pair, so that one can express a measure of
degree of dominance of the two members of a pair: the relative
degree of dominance of the older and the younger, the sociometrically more and less powerful, etc.

It is important to distinguish between, on the one hand, this process of adjustment of interests, which, we propose, does operate over time to move toward an equilibrium interest matrix, and, on the other hand, the concept of a power distribution, which depends upon the interest matrix at a single point in time. The stages and the concept of equilibrium discussed then were purely as aids in exposition. Now we turn our attention to a more detailed discussion of the equilibrium which would come about through the adjustment of sociometric interests; this entails a discussion of Eq. (9).

By examining Eq. (9) we can get some feel for what this equilibrium means. If both actors have equal power ($R_i = R_j$), they should show the same degree of interest in each other ($X_{ij} = X_{ji}$). Our equilibrium condition suggests that if actor i's choice of j was greater than j's choice of i, then one of the following should happen:

(1) i would reduce the strength of his choice of j;

(2) j would increase his choice of i; or,

(3) both actors would modify their choices so that the

following deviation is smaller at time two than at time one:

$$r_j * x_{ji} - r_i * x_{ij} \tag{10a}$$

since, from Eq. (9) this deviation equals zero when the equilibrium condition is met.

If human groups behave according to Eq. (9), then we can make some interesting statements about the effect of power on the level of interest actors show in each other. Figure 1, which is based on Eq. (9) shows the effect that different power distribution should have on the strength of mutual choices for two actors. The x-axis is labeled X_{ij}--this is the strength of actor i's choice of j: likewise the y-axis shows X_{ji}--the reciprocal choice. The lines in Figure 1 are similar to contours. They show the points on the graph that satisfy Eq. (9) for different

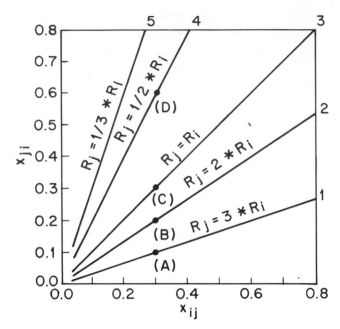

Fig. 1.   Graph showing the predicted level of j's choice of i, given i's choice of j and the ratio of power between the two actors.

distributions of power between the two actors. For example, line #1 shows the possible choices which will satisfy Eq. (9) if actor j is three times as powerful as actor i. The way to read Figure 1 is to:

(1) Locate the strength of i's choice of j on the x-axis. (As an example let us suppose x_{ij} = .3.)

(2) Find the contour line which describes the distribution of power between the two actors. (For this example let us say that j is three times as powerful as i; then the equilibrium conditions will lie on line #1.)

(3) Starting with the x_{ij} point on the x-axis, trace a line straight up to the appropriate contour line from step 2. (For our example this takes us to point (A).)

(4) From the point on the contour from step 3, trace a line directly across to the y-axis and find the predicted strength

of j's choice of i, given the power distribution specified and
the model in Eq. (9). (For our example, if x_{ij} = .3 and j is
three times more powerful than i, then x_{ji} should be .1 under
our model.)

If the power distribution had been different, then we would
have gotten different estimates for j's reciprocal choice of
i. For example, Figure 1 shows that if the actors have the same
power (line 3), then x_{ij} should equal x_{ji}, or if i chose j with a
strength of .3, he should get .3 of j's interest. This corresponds to point (C). Point (D) shows the case when j is half as
powerful as i. Thus, a .3 investment from i requires a .6 investment from j to satisfy the market conditions of Eq. (9). This
extended example should illustrate the nature of power in the
sociometric model we are developing: More powerful actors get a
higher "payoff" for interest they show in others. The payoff for
power is shown by the slopes of the lines in Figure 1. If i is
twice as powerful as j (line 4), then a .3 investment should get
a .6 return.

Each pair of actors is characterized by a line such as in
Figure 1 that would show the ratio of power for the two actors.
Our equilibrium model basically states that two actors will
start somewhere in the space of the graph in Figure 1 and move
toward the line that characterizes their equilibrium positions.
For example, at time one their choices can be described by the
(x_{ij}, x_{ji}) point on the graph.

The mutual choices for three hypothetical actors and the
lines that show the power ratios for each pair of actors are
shown in Figure 2a. The (ab) point shows that at time one
actor A gave actor B .2 of his interest and B chose A with a .8.
The line showing the equilibrium points (or the ratio of the
power of A to the power of B) is labeled Ra/Rb. Actor A is 2.6
times as powerful as actor B in this hypothetical system.

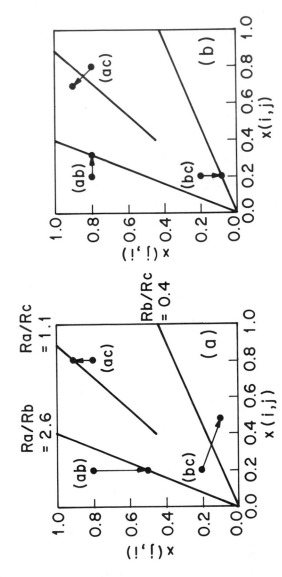

Fig. 2. Graphs showing two of the possible ways interests in the hypothetical three actor system could change over time. (The labeled points (a,b) (a,c) and (b,c) show interests at time 1, the arrowhead shows the mutual interests for that pair at time 2. Data for these graphs are in Table IV.)

We can measure the deviation of the entire system from equilibrium by summing Eq. (10a) over all pairs of actors:

$$\sqrt{\dfrac{\Sigma_{i \neq j}\ (r_j * x_{ji} - r_i * x_{ij})^2}{N}} \qquad (10b)$$

where N = the number of pairs of actors in the system. From our previous discussion it follows that this deviation is zero when the mutual choices of all pairs of actors fall on the line that describes the ratio of power between the actors in a graph such as Figure 1 or Figure 2. If this deviation is smaller at time two than at time one, it means that at time two the points in the graph of mutual choices are closer to the lines that show the ratio of power for each pair of actors. In other words, we could restate our notion of the equilibrium process in the following terms: The interests of each pair of actors will adjust so that the ratio of interests could be predicted from the ratio of power, or the points in a graph like Figure 2a will move closer to the lines that show the power ratios.

We emphasize once again that whether sociometric systems approach this kind of equilibrium is an empirical question that can be answered by calculating the average deviation in Eq. (10b) at various points in the life of the system.

In Figures 2a and 2b we have shown two ways the mutual interests among our three hypothetical actors could adjust so that the deviation at time two is smaller than at time one. The data for these graphs and the calculations that show that the deviations at time two are indeed less than at time one in each graph are included in Table IV. In these figures the point at the end of each arrow (vector) shows the (x_{ij}, x_{ji}) point at time two for each pair. It should be clear from Figures 2a and 2b

that there are an indefinite number of ways in which the system
could adjust to approach an equilibrium.

In Figure 2a the (*ab*) pair achieves equilibrium by actor *B*
lowering the level of his choice of actor *A* and *A* not changing
his interest at all. (The vector is vertical.) In this case we
can say that actor *A* dominated the move toward equilibrium since
actor *B*'s interests had to change to accommodate *A*. In Figure 2b
the opposite occurs. *B* dominates the change since it is *A*'s
interest which changes (the equilibrium line is approached, only
this time horizontally).

It would be an advance in the study of human groups to be
able to answer the question: What kind of people dominate the
changes in sociometric interest in a group over time. Is it the
smarter, the wealthier, the more popular, the more powerful person who determines the structure of interests in a group of actors? To study this question we need observations at two or more
points in time and we formulate a scale to rank the actors in
intelligence, wealth, power, or whatever it is we are interested
in studying. Since we already derived power scores for the actors in Figure 2, we will use power as the dimension and we will
show how to study the question of whether it is the more powerful actors who dominated the change in the structure of interests
in the group between time one and time two. The power of each
actor (*A, B,* and *C*) is given in Table IV. Also shown are the
interests for each actor at each time. The way to determine
whether it was the more powerful actors (or the less powerful
actors) who dominated the changes in interests between the two
points in time is to calculate the following measure of deviation for:

TABLE IV. Interest Matrices, Power Scores, and Deviations From Exchange Model Predictions for a Hypothetical System of Three Actors with Observations at Two Points in Time

Interests			Time 1	Pair	Deviation	Eq. (10a)
	A	B	C	ab	.44 * .2 - .17 * .8	
A		.2	.8	ac	.44 * .8 - .39 * .8	
B	.8		.2	ba	.17 * .8 - .44 * .2	
C	.8	.2		bc	.17 * .2 - .39 * .2	
				ca	.39 * .8 - .44 * .8	
				cb	.39 * .2 - .17 * .2	

Average absolute deviation from exchange model = .05

Time 2, for Figure 1

	A	B	C
A		.2	.8
B	.52		.48
C	.9	.1	

Average absolute deviation = .02

Time 2, for Figure 2

	A	B	C
A		.31	.69
B	.8		.2
C	.91	.09	

Average absolute deviation = .03

Power for each actor: A = .44   (calculated at time 1)
                         B = .17
                         C = .39

(1) pairs where actor i was less powerful than actor j; and

(2) pairs where actor i was more powerful than actor j.

The measure of deviation is:

$$\sqrt{\sum \frac{(r_j^{t1} * x_{ji}^{t2} - r_i^{t1} * x_{ij}^{t1})^2}{N_s}} \qquad (10c)$$

where N_s = the number of terms in the summation

$t1$ refers to the measure of interest (or power) at time one.

If the deviation for the first summation (i less powerful than j) is larger than the deviation for the second summation, then we conclude that the more powerful members are dominant, with their interests moving less toward the "weaker" members' interests than the "weaker" (less powerful) members' interests moving toward theirs. The calculations for our hypothetical data are carried out in detail in Table V.

We recall from Table IV that actor A was more powerful than actor C and both were more powerful than actor B. In discussing the trajectories in Figure 2a we noted that the directions of the vectors indicate that A dominated B's choice, A dominated C's choice, and the (bc) vector was ambiguous. Therefore, it is not surprising that the calculations in Table V show that in Figure 2a it is the more powerful actors who dominate the changes in interests. The calculations for figure 2b, where vectors indicate that B dominated A and C show that it is, indeed, the weaker member of the average pair who dominated the change in interests between time one and time two.

This test for who dominates the change in interests can be extended to any measure where actors are ranked. Therefore we could have summed the deviations in Eq. (10c) for pairs where actors were ranked on intelligence, wealth, attractiveness, etc.

TABLE V. Calculations for Studying the Predominance of the Less or the More Powerful Actors in the Changes in Interests for the Data in Figure 2a and Figure 2b

Data for Figure 2a

Pair	Calculation	Squared deviation	
		$R_i < R_j$	$R_i > R_j$
ab	.17 * .52 - .44 * .2	XXXXXXX	.000002
ac	.39 * .9 - .44 * .8	XXXXXXX	.000001
ba	.44 * .2 - .17 * .8	.018946	XXXXXXX
bc	.39 * .1 - .17 * .2	.000025	XXXXXXX
ca	.44 * .8 - .39 * .8	.001600	XXXXXXX
cb	.17 * .48 - .39 * .2	XXXXXXX	.000013
TOTAL		.020121 >	.000015

implies more powerful are more dominant

Data for Figure 2b

Pair	Squared deviation	
	$R_i < R_j$	$R_i > R_j$
ab	XXXXXXX	.002304
ac	XXXXXXX	.000084
ba	.000002	XXXXXXX
bc	.000001	XXXXXXX
ca	.000070	XXXXXXX
cb	XXXXXXX	.001936
TOTAL	.000073 <	.004324

implies the less powerful are more dominant

(Power and Interest Scores for These Calculations are in Table IV)

PART IV

I.   IDENTIFICATION OF A SIMULTANEOUS EQUATION MODEL
     FOR POWER AND SOCIOMETRIC CHOICE

So far we have presented measures that will allow us to make
certain global statements about the system under study: whether
the system tends to approach equilibrium or what kinds of actors
tend to dominate the adjustment of choices between different
times. We can obtain much insight into the structure of sociometric matrices by noting that Eq. (9) can be rewritten so that
actor i's choice of j is predicted from three measures: x_{ji}, r_j,
and r_i. Eq. (9) shows:

$$x_{ij} = \frac{r_j * x_{ji}}{r_i}$$

If we take logarithms of each side we obtain a linear equation
for predicting x_{ij} from the three quantities on the right:

$$\ln(x_{ij}) = \ln(x_{ji}) + \ln(r_j) - \ln(r_i) \tag{10d}$$

In other words, our equilibrium model predicts that the slope coefficients in Eq. (10d) are equal to plus or minus one. We can
test this. Generally, the additive model in Eq. (10d) suggests
that if we knew the variances and covariances of the four variables, then we could estimate the regression of the dependent
variable (the strength of i's choice of j) on the three independent variables. This would ignore the fact that x_{ij} and x_{ji} are
observed simultaneously. It is possible to estimate an even more
powerful regression model that estimates all the coefficients of
interest and preserves the reciprocal causality of the actors'
interests. In this model we have the power of each pair of
actors as exogenous variables with paths running into x_{ij} and

x_{ji}. The latter, dependent variables, form a loop, or a reciprocally causal block (Heise, 1975). The path diagram looks like
Figure 3.

We could calculate the goodness of fit of this model by calculating the usual measures of multiple correlation and variance
explained, although the nature of our data suggests that statements of significance are inappropriate since there are
$n * (n - 1)$ terms in each covariance although there are only
n actors in the system. Using the logic of stepwise regression
we could also measure the amount of variation that is "explained"
by each factor separately (r_i, r_j, and x_{ji}).

Our basic data consists of a variance-covariance matrix of
the following form:

	(1) $\ln(r_j)$	(2) $\ln(r_i)$	(3) $\ln(x_{ji})$	(4) $\ln(x_{ij})$
(1) $\ln(r_j)$	r_{jj}	r_{ij}	$r_j x_{ij}$	$r_j x_{ij}$
(2) $\ln(r_i)$		r_{ii}	$r_i x_{ji}$	$r_i x_{ij}$
(3) $\ln(x_{ji})$			$x_{ji} x_{ji}$	$x_{ji} x_{ij}$
(4) $\ln(x_{ij})$				$x_{ij} x_{ij}$

This is the variance-covariance matrix for the four variables
in our system. R_i is the power of actor i, r_j is the power of
actor j, x_{ji} is the strength of actor j's choice of actor i, and
x_{ij} is the strength of actor i's choice of actor j. To make
things easier in the notation that follows we have numbered each
of these variables so that r_j will be referred to as V_1.

There are some symmetries in this matrix. When we take the sum of squared deviations over subscripts i and j of the power of actor i, we get the same result as though we were estimating the variance of r_j instead. That is, in the previous matrix,

$$r_{ii} = r_{jj}$$

or, in the numbered notation:

$$V_{11} = V_{22}. \qquad\qquad (11a)$$

Other symmetries that we will take advantage of in estimating the model are:

$$x_{ji}x_{ji} = x_{ij}x_{ij} \quad\text{-or-}\quad V_{33} = V_{44} \qquad\qquad (11b)$$

$$r_j x_{ij} = r_i x_{ji} \quad\text{-or-}\quad V_{14} = V_{23} \qquad\qquad (11c)$$

$$r_j x_{ji} = r_i x_{ij} = 0 \quad\text{-or-}\quad V_{13} = V_{24} = 0 \qquad\qquad (11d)$$

We want to combine the pieces of information from the matrix above to estimate the coefficients of a model that claims that actor j's choice of actor i depends on three things: whether actor i chose actor j, the power of actor j, and the power of actor i. We will assume that at any time the power of each actor relative to the other is given, that is, r_i and r_j are exogenous variables. x_{ij} and x_{ji} are variables that occur simultaneously and that are assumed to influence each other. Therefore, they must be handled as reciprocally causal variables--a loop.

When we write the equations for the relations among these variables, we see that there are also some symmetries in the structural coefficients for the model. Since the choice of subscripts is arbitrary, we find, for instance, that the path from x_{ji} to x_{ij} has to be the same as the reverse path from x_{ij} to x_{ji}. This is elucidated in the flow graph for the system of equations relating these four variables.

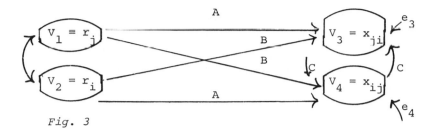

Fig. 3

Our flow graph says the following:

(1) For each pair of actors the power of each actor is taken as predetermined (exogenous). There is, however, a correlation between the power of actor i and the power of actor j that we will estimate directly from the zero order correlation between these variables. This arises because the total amount of power in the system sums to unity. If actor i has a lot of power, then actor j is likely to have less power than actor i. This holds for all i and j. This means that we expect to see a very small or possibly negligible correlation between V_1 and V_2 in the data.

(2) For any pair of actors, the strength of j's choice of i is determined by three factors in the model plus an error term. These three factors are the power of actor j (which is multiplied by coefficient A); the power of actor i (which is multiplied by coefficient B); and the strength of the reciprocal choice, x_{ij} (which is multiplied by coefficient C). This leads to the following equation for predicting the strength of actor j's choice of actor i:

$$V_3 = A * V_1 + B * V_2 + C * V_4 + e_3 \tag{12}$$

(3) Because the choice of subscripts i and j is arbitrary, the coefficients which predict i's choice of j are the same as in Eq. (12), except that the roles of R_i and R_j are reversed. This leads to the following equation for predicting actor i's choice of j:

$$V_4 = B * V_1 + A * V_2 + C * V_3 + e_4 \tag{13}$$

(4) Because each actor is in each position (X_{ji} and X_{ij}) with respect to each other actor in the system, the net covariation for the disturbance terms e_3 and e_4 is zero. Or, using standard notation for the algebra of expectations:

$$E(V_3, e_4) = E(V_4, e_3) = 0 \tag{14}$$

Although it would appear that there are too many arrows, it turns out that because of the symmetry of path coefficients in Eqs. (12) and (13) and the uncorrelated disturbances in Eq. (14), the model is just identified--we have three independent equations in three unknowns. (For a consideration of a similar model and its identification problems, see Duncan, 1975.) For each dependent variable there are three paths coming in--A, B, and C. For either dependent variable it is possible to use V_1 and V_2 as instruments. Because of condition 8, it is also possible to use V_3 as an instrument for V_4 and vice versa.

We will illustrate the use of these equations--we choose V_3 as the dependent variable for the equations V_1, V_2, and V_4 as the instrumental variables.

The structural model is expressed in Eqs. (11a-11d), (12), (13), and (14). For the estimation equations we start with Eq. (12) followed by the equations for the covariance using V_1, V_2, and V_4 as instruments.

$$V_3 = A * V_1 + B * V_2 + C * V_4 + e_3 \tag{12}$$

$$\sigma_{31} = A * \sigma_{11} + B * \sigma_{21} + C * \sigma_{41} \tag{15a}$$

$$\sigma_{32} = A * \sigma_{12} + B * \sigma_{22} + C * \sigma_{42} \tag{15b}$$

$$\sigma_{34} = A * \sigma_{14} + B * \sigma_{24} + C * \sigma_{44} \tag{15c}$$

We note that had we chosen V_4, as the dependent variable, then the second equation would have been:

$$\sigma_{42} = B * \sigma_{12} + A * \sigma_{22} + C * \sigma_{32} \tag{16}$$

which, after substituting for the identities in (11a-11d) is exactly the same as Eq. (15a). There are similar identities for the other two equations obtained using V_4 as dependent. The result in (15c) stems from Eq. (14) in the model. The zero covariance between V_4 and e_3 makes it possible to use the former as an instrument and thus achieve an identified model, since we do not have to include a term in (15c) for the covariation between V_4 and e_3.

After substituting results from the identities (11a-11d) and rearranging the symbols into a matrix formulation for the solution, we obtain:

$$
\begin{array}{ccc} & _3\,M\,_3 & \end{array}
\begin{bmatrix} \sigma_{11} & \sigma_{21} & \sigma_{41} \\ \sigma_{12} & \sigma_{22} & 0 \\ \sigma_{14} & 0 & \sigma_{44} \end{bmatrix}
\quad
\begin{array}{c} _3\,P\,_1 \\ \begin{Bmatrix} A \\ B \\ C \end{Bmatrix} \end{array}
=
\begin{array}{c} _3\,N\,_1 \\ \begin{Bmatrix} 0 \\ \sigma_{32} \\ \sigma_{34} \end{Bmatrix} \end{array}
\tag{17}
$$

Unfortunately we do not obtain simple expressions for the coefficients of matrix P in terms of the variances and covariances in matrices M and N. Therefore, the easiest procedure is to find a computer or an HP-65 and calculate the vector of path coefficients P as follows:

$$P = M^{-1}\,N \tag{18}$$

and this will give unbiased estimates for the structural parameters in the flow graph.

In applying this method to the data for a girls senior class, we started with the following variance-covariance matrix:

	(1) $\ln(_j)$	(2) $\ln(_i)$	(3) $\ln(_{ji})$	(4) $\ln(_{ij})$
(1) $\ln(_j)$	13.09	-1.09	0	5.87
(2) $\ln(_i)$		13.09	5.87	0
(3) $\ln(_{ji})$			123.60	107.33
(4) $\ln(_{ij})$				123.60

Plugging values from here into the matrix Eq. (17) we obtain

$$
\begin{bmatrix} 13.09 & -1.09 & 5.87 \\ -1.09 & 13.09 & 0 \\ 5.87 & 0 & 123.60 \end{bmatrix}
\begin{Bmatrix} A \\ B \\ C \end{Bmatrix}
=
\begin{Bmatrix} 0 \\ 5.87 \\ 107.33 \end{Bmatrix}
$$

$$
\qquad M \qquad\qquad P \quad = \quad N
$$

And therefore we obtain as our estimates of the coefficients:

$$A = -.362 \qquad\qquad B = .418 \qquad\qquad C = .885$$

We note from the covariance matrix that the correlation between r_i and r_j is -.08. This gives us the last number we need for the flow graph, the path between r_i and r_j. With these additions we can flesh out Figure 3 to obtain the flow graph for the relations between power and mutuality in predicting sociometric choices.

For this particular set of data it was the case that:

(1) An increment of 1 unit in an actor's power meant that any other actor's power was decremented by .08 units. This is the negative (and somewhat artifactual) correlation we expected to

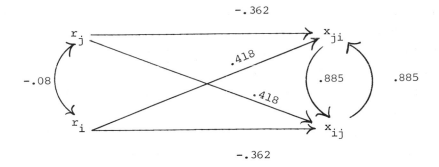

Fig. 4

see between the power of *i* and the power of *j*.

(2) An increment of 1 unit in an actor's power tended to depress his choice of any other given actor by .362 units.

(3) Conversely, an increment of 1 unit in an actor's power meant that the interest shown in him by any other randomly chosen actor tended to increase by about .418 units.

(4) Finally, an actor increasing his interest in another person by 1 unit was likely to receive a direct return on that investment in terms of a reciprocal choice of about .885 units.

Further insight into these equations can be gained by examining the reduced form of the equation for either x_{ij} or x_{ji} (the results for one are the same as for the other).

The reduced form for Eq. (12) (paths into V_3, or x_{ji}) is gained by writing out Eq. (12) and substituting Eq. (13) for the V_4 term. If we do this and take expected values of both sides of the equation, we obtain:

$$E(X_{ji}) = \frac{(A + CB) * E(r_j)}{(1 - c^2)} \quad \frac{(B + CA) * E(r_i)}{(1 - c^2)} \tag{19}$$

Numerically, the result is:

$$X_{ji} = .037 * (r_j) + .450 * (r_i) \tag{19'}$$

Basically, this operation determines the effect of a one unit change in the exogenous variables (r_i and r_j) on x_{ji}. It does this, taking account of the fact that a change in an exogenous variable has indirect as well as direct effects on the dependent variable (i.e., it takes account of the fact that r_j influences x_{ij} which exerts an influence on the dependent variable as well). We have in Eq. (19') the gross (as opposed to the net) influence of changes in power on interpersonal choice. In a different application, Duncan (1975) points out that this is the result that would be obtained if we regress x_{ji} on only the exogenous variables r_j and r_i.

Comparing this result with our interpretation of Figure 2, we can make the following observations:

If the power of actor j goes up by one unit, there is both an increase and a decrease in the strength of his choice of other actors. The decrease is shown by the direct path between r_j and x_{ji} (-.362). We interpret this to mean that as actor j's power in the system goes up, he has less time to devote to any specific other actor, hence the path is negative. There is also an indirect consequence of an increase in j's power. This is the path from r_j to x_{ij} and then through the loop of x_{ji}. This effect can be interpreted by saying that if actor j's power goes up, he is more likely to be chosen by actor i. The values on the loop show that there is a tendency toward reciprocity in this system so that i chooses j, then j will be more likely to choose i in return. Since the indirect path is positive, it means that if actor j's power goes up, there is an offsetting dynamic that will make him more likely to choose an arbitrary actor i. The relative magnitudes of the direct and the indirect paths are shown by the sign of the coefficient for r_j in the reduced form equation. Whether this path is positive or negative in a particular system, depends on the relative magnitudes of the various coefficients. In our example the reduced form coefficient is slightly positive (.037) and so we conclude that the indirect effect of an increase in actor j's power would offset the direct effect and tend to raise the strength of his choice of any actor i.

The second term of the reduced form equation shows the effect of a one unit increase in actor i's power on the strength of other people's choice of him. The coefficient is greater than one and even greater than the direct path between r_i and x_{ji}. This means that both the direct and indirect effects of an increase in actor i's power tend to operate to increase the strength of other people's choice of him.

Many fruitful properties of sociometric matrices can be examined via this structural equation approach. For instance, by examining the relative absolute magnitudes of the A and B coefficients in graphs like Figure 4, it is possible to address the question of whether choices tend to be made between actors of approximately equal power. If this is the case, then the absolute value of A will equal the absolute value of B. If there are measures on a system at several points in time, it is possible to incorporate dynamic aspects into the structural equation either through the use of time-lagged variables or by considering measures on the system at time one causally prior to measures at time two and writing equations for the flow graph which is shown in Figure 5, where the power and choices of each actor are superscripted to show the time at which they are measured. Such a system would derive measures for:

(1) the stability of power distributions over time;

(2) the stability of individual sociometric choices; and

(3) the effect of i's choice of j at time one on j's choice of i at time two (this gets at the move toward equilibrium that we discussed earlier--but this is for another chapter).

The R-squares for the structural models vary between .25 and .80, depending on the group being studied. Most of them are over .40 and the average over all classes and replications is .455. The R-squares did not vary systematically with the choice of

TABLE VI.   The Average Values for the Structural Parameters
             for Each Class by Sex Group at Each Point in Time

Sex	Class	Time	R^2	$R_j \rightarrow X_{ji}$	$R_i \rightarrow X_{ji}$	$X_{ij} \leftrightarrow X_{ji}$
Boys	Fresh	Fall	.234	-.150	.439	.385
		Spring	.247	-.194	.536	.411
	Soph	Fall	.432	-.237	.408	.619
		Spring	.404	-.244	.435	.603
	Jr	Fall	.339	-.284	.541	.605
		Spring	.196	-.116	.648	.219
	Sr	Fall	.329	-.277	.621	.520
		Spring	.212	-.168	.778	.270
Girls	Fresh	Fall	.365	-.183	.364	.559
		Spring	.429	-.284	.478	.629
	Soph	Fall	.540	-.290	.407	.730
		Spring	.525	-.280	.395	.730
	Jr	Fall	.635	-.227	.286	.803
		Spring	.474	-.226	.338	.688
	Sr	Fall	.797	-.337	.394	.877
		Spring	.738	-.362	.430	.870

(Values were averaged over the nine replications for the
parameter assumptions in the sociometric matrix; see text for
details.)

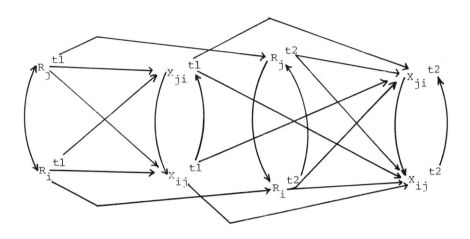

Fig.5. Some of the paths implied in extending the structural equation model to two points in time.

parameters for the ratio of interest or percentage of time
allocated to one's choices. The average R^2 for each class (averaged over the nine combinations of parameters) is reported in
the first column of Table VI. Although we have not conducted extensive tests, it appears that 50 to 80% of the variance is
accounted for by predicting x_{ij} from x_{ji}. The remaining 20 to
50% is accounted for, in about equal proportion, by the power of
actor i and the power of actor j.

It was almost always the case that the R^2 in the spring was
lower than the R^2 in the fall. The average drop in variance explained (over all groups and all replications) was .043 points.
Again, the magnitude of this drop was not different for different
choices of the parameters for the sociometric matrix.

A declining R^2 suggests that the group was closer to equilibrium at time one than at time two. We can analyze this move
from equilibrium by examining the changes in the structural coefficients.

If we were to draw a generic path diagram for all the groups
examined, we would draw the following:

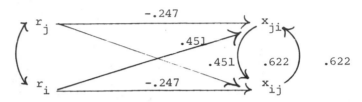

The coefficients on this diagram are the averages over all groups
and all replications. The strongest path is the prediction of
x_{ij} from x_{ji} (.622). This result, coupled with the high R^2, indicates that simple mutuality is an important element of the
matrices we are considering. Interestingly, the paths for r_i and
r_j into x_{ji} are not of the same absolute magnitude. This suggests
that the sociometric systems here do not operate exactly as we
hypothesized. Our theory was that the paths would have the same
absolute magnitude; what we find is that a one-unit increase in
the strength of actor i has a greater effect on actor j's choice
of him than can be simply offset by a one-unit increase in the
power of actor j--in terms of establishing the "market rate" of
exchange between the two actors. We suggested earlier that this
pattern for the coefficients indicates that there is a tendency
for people to form asymmetric relationships, choosing people more
powerful than themselves. The negative path from r_j to x_{ji} is
expected (although not quite as large), indicating that more
powerful people have less interest to allocate to any specific
other person.

The pattern of coefficients in each class/sex group is in most
cases the same as in the "generic" diagram. These coefficients
(averaged over the nine parameter replications) are presented in

Table VI. The coefficients in the structural models showed
a fairly reliable pattern of change between time one and time
two. Almost every group showed the following pattern:

(1) The r_j to x_{ji} path did not change.

(2) The loop coefficient (x_{ij} to x_{ji}) got smaller, by about
.043 units. Mutuality became slightly less important. This is
probably the reason for the decline in R^2 between the two times.

(3) The path from the power of actor i to actor j's choice
of actor i (x_{ji}) became larger by about .068 units. The asymmetry in coefficients alluded to above tended to increase over
time. The power of actors became a relatively more important
variable in the prediction of sociometric choices between the
two time periods.

PART V

I. THE SENSITIVITY OF THE RESULTS TO ASSUMPTIONS
ABOUT THE PARAMETERS IN THE SOCIOMETRIC MATRIX

We tried three different assumptions about the ratio of
interests (using .5, .8, and .99 as the ratio between adjacent
choices) and three different assumptions about the amount of
attention a person devotes to his chosen associates. (We have
results assuming a person devotes 50, 70, and 95% of his
time to his sociometric choices.) Thus, we have a 3 x 3 design
(or nine replications under different parameter assumptions for
each test we make).

We found that the structural coefficients were not entirely
insensitive to the choice of parameters for the sociometric matrix. The loop coefficient was not affected but the other two
coefficients were slightly affected, although not enough to offset the pattern observed in the previous paragraphs. The paths
from the power scores showed larger absolute magnitudes for

TABLE VII. Deviation from the Equilibrium Prediction and
            Changes in Deviations from Prediction between
            Time One and Time Two

		Average deviation from equilibrium, over all groups at both times		
		Ratio between adjacent choices		
		.5	.8	.99
Proportion	.5	.0041	.0027	.0032
of interest	.7	.0048	.0039	.0041
allocated to	.95	.0061	.0049	.0052
chosen actors				

		Average change in deviation from equilibrium = Time 2 average minus Time 1 average		
		Ratio between adjacent choices		
		.5	.8	.99
Proportion	.5	.0019	.0004	.0014
of interest	.7	.0017	.0011	.0011
allocated to	.95	.0023	.0013	.0013
chosen actors				

(Results are averaged over all classes for each replication.)

"flatter" distributions of interest and for lower proportions of interest allocated to the actors chosen. The differences here are not great; the magnitudes of the coefficients in the "generic" diagram did not fluctuate by more than about 11% in either direction.

The absolute measure of deviation from equilibrium, Eq. (10b) seemed to depend slightly on the parameter for the ratio between adjacent choices--"flatter" choices (parameter close to 1.0) showed smaller deviations. This is shown as the "column" effect in Table VII. It also appears that the lower the amount of interest allocated to the chosen actors, the lower the measure of deviation from equilibrium. This result indicates that we can arbitrarily improve the fit of the model by reducing the variability in the sociometric matrix. Indeed, if everyone chose everyone else evenly all power scores would be the same and the model would predict trivially but perfectly. We note, however, that within the range of our choices of parameters we are far from this trivial result and the coefficients seem relatively stable. Also shown in Table VII is the difference between the average deviation at time one and at time two for the 3 x 3 design. The change in deviation that is observed does not appear to depend very much on the parameter assumptions for the sociometric matrix.

The model we have developed seems to have enough stability and intuitive justification to make it a worthwhile approach to the study of networks of relations. The robustness of the coefficients to assumptions about the parameters governing the sociometric choices was something we had not anticipated but that is an encouraging result, permitting us to turn a greater proportion of our attention to replicating the results in this chapter with some of the other data sets available to us.

REFERENCES

Berger, Joseph, & Snell, J. L.   On the concept of equal exchange.
     Behavioral Science, 1957, *2* (2), 111-118.

Coleman, James S.   *The adolescent society.*   New York: Free Press,
     1961.

Coleman, James S.   Social action systems.   University of Chicago:
     Department of Sociology.   (Unpublished).

Coleman, James S.   *The mathematics of collective action.*
     Chicago: Aldine, 1973.

Duncan, O. D.   *Introduction to structural equation models.*   New
     York: Academic Press, 1975.

Feller, William.   *An introduction to probability theory and its
     applications* 3rd ed.).   (Chapters 15-16), 1968.

Heise, David.   *Causal analysis.*   New York: Wiley-Interscience,
     1975.

Katz, Leo.   A new status index derived from sociometric analysis.
     Psychometrika, 1953, *18,* 39-43.

Kemeney, John G., & Snell, J. L.   *Finite Markov chains.*
     Princeton: Van Nostrand, 1960.

Kemeney, John G., & Snell, J. L.   *Mathematical models in the
     social sciences.*   Waltham: Blaisdell, 1962.

Thomas, George B.   *Calculus and analytic geometry.*   Reading:
     Addison-Wesley, 1960.

CHAPTER 15

GRAPH SAMPLING COMPARED TO CONVENTIONAL SAMPLING

Charles H. Proctor

Department of Statistics

North Carolina State University

Raleigh, North Carolina

I. INTRODUCTION

It may be a little early to foresee that graph sampling, particularly social network sampling, will have a development at all
parallel to that of sampling in statistics, particularly social
survey sampling. The signs are that it has and will demonstrate
a similar progression. In particular, there are three phases in
the unfolding of social survey sampling that have parallel phases
in the development of social network sampling: the "random sample
from a hypothetically infinite population" phase (Yule and Kendall,
1968); the "analytical survey as distinguished from the enumerative" phase   (Deming, 1950); and the "highly controlled selection methods from a finite population drawn from a super population" phase (Cochran, 1963).

Within the field of statistics, the subfield of sampling can
be defined only in the broadest of terms. To declare a data
collection problem as a sampling problem reflects a concern over
the location of the measuring operations and the possibility that

some random device ought perhaps to be used to decide where to take them. To describe the data *analysis* problem as a sampling problem suggests that the data should or can be treated as if some random selection had been made. When the investigator controls the positioning of the observations, and this involves complicated considerations of relative costs and relative precision for estimating numerous parameters, then the full splendor of sampling technology and theory is displayed -- both in the design of the investigation as well as in the calculation of estimates.

Treating data that have already been collected as if they were produced by a random sampling scheme washes away much of the distinctive "sampling flavor" of the problem, but makes possible a fuller application of sample selection principles. Neyman's (1934) paper was a turning point for active intervention using random numbers in the selection of samples.

In this chapter I will trace, somewhat chronologically, work in graph sampling showing its development from the minimum essential techniques to the more elaborate. Discovered in the course of this study is the fact that theoretical developments in network sample design and estimation can quickly outrun applications.

II. NETWORK RANDOM SAMPLING

The earliest viewpoint that sociometric data is a sample from a hypothetically infinite population was postulated by Moreno and Jennings (1938), who acknowledge consultations with Lazarsfeld. The class of problems they considered can be characterized as problems in elementary probability, or counting problems, although their actual combinatorial complexity was not revealed until Katz and Powell (1954) furnished a general solution. It is remarkable the extent to which the Moreno/Jennings/Lazarsfeld (MJL) approach has retained its validity and appeal. They not only verified their formulas empirically against Monte Carlo or randomly simulated data, but the indices they chose for study are still important.

The probabilistic model has the ith person of n persons making d_i choices as an ordered (or unordered) equally likely sample from the other $n-1$ persons, and doing so independently of the choices of the others. The MJL paper used $d_i = d$ for all $i = 1, 2, \ldots, n$. Numerical indices of the whole choice pattern were then defined and their distributions worked out for this case of equally likely, independent (ELI) choosings. It is obvious that observed values of these indices that depart greatly from those predicted by ELI suggest that some other mechanism is responsible for the choice patterns. However, other such models have only recently emerged.

Shortly after MJL appeared, a paper by Bronfenbrenner (1938) was published, which had a curious effect on the field. It covered much the same ground as MJL, and took joint credit for establishing the viewpoint. It then extended their results, correctly in some cases, but incorrectly in some important cases, as evidenced here.

A focus on the "choices received" of one particular individual permits the use of the binomial expansion, $(d/n-1 + n-d-1/n-1)^{n-1}$, to express the distribution of probability over his choices received. This result was given in both papers and is correct, although it does not indicate whether the distribution of choice statuses in a group is unusual. The expected choices received per person can be obtained by multiplying the total possible number of persons, $n-1$, by the chance, $d/n-1$. A similar point of view permits one to compute (as MJL did) the expected number of mutual choices in a group as the total possible number $N(N-1)/2$, by the chance, $d^2/(n-1)^2$.[1]

Next the distribution for choices received was given on multiple criteria as a binomial. The sum of two binomial variables is again binomial if the probability of success is the same. The calculation of binomial probabilities is quite important here since the distribution seemed to have such wide applications in sociometry. The probability of interclass choice was also obtained, but the subsequent expression for the distribution of the number of isolates was given incorrectly and the mistake about mutuals was repeated.

These errors were pointed out by Criswell (1946) and Edwards (1948) along with Loomis and Pepinski (1948), and also by Katz (pp. 203-204 of Moreno, 1960). It was Katz who set the subject back on its feet by solving some of the outstanding problems in the most elegant ways. The distribution of the number of isolates was given first in its full detail and then in a more convenient approximate form (Katz, 1952).

While progress on the distribution of the number of mutuals has always been limited, Katz and Wilson (1956) discovered the variance of the number of mutuals, which then provides a way of judging statistical significance of observed number of mutuals. They also gave the full distribution for the case where each person makes only one choice.

A great deal of attention was expended on choice statuses or the numbers of choices received within a group. One attempt at

[1]This derivation seems to have prompted Bronfenbrenner to make the statement that the probabilities of various numbers of mutual choices in a group are "... again obtained by expansion of the binomial."

fitting a negative binomial distribution appeared to be strikingly successful, but Katz pointed out that neither the contagion nor the unequal propensity models could reflect the presumed dependence in sociometric choice. The negative binomial, however, seems a natural to try since people differ in their attracting power. In addition we know that the binomial distribution is appropriate for choices received in chance ballotting. The detailed results of the probability distribution over the choice status distribution was furnished by Katz and Powell (1957) as a distribution over an n-dimensional integer-valued lattice.

At first glance this solution resembles the concise statement of the problem rather than its solution. Using this method, the two vectors of choices received and of choices made are subjected to modifications by operators, which reduces certain entries, and the numerous modified vectors are then each converted to a count by a bipartitional function. The counts are subsequently added or subtracted. Such a process could be done conveniently by computer for moderate sized groups. It would then be possible to obtain, for example, the probability that the highest chosen individual should receive $n-1$ or $n-2$ or...or as few as d choices. Equally evident would be the probability that the highest chosen person receives choices from 50% or more of the group members or that the two highest chosen do, or three do, etc. It would also be possible to work out the distribution of various indices of concentration of choices received.

It seems to me that there are very good reasons (in addition to improved computing facilities) for extending this work on distributions of indices of group structure from chance balloting. Some of the distributions have already been worked out, and this suggests that further results may not be too difficult. What we're talking about here is essentially the requirement that each person make a fixed number of choices to different other persons.

Although a variable number of choices seems more realistic (and the Katz/Powell solution admits variable numbers of outgoing choices), it may also reflect tendencies toward loquaciousness rather than interpersonal climate. Boastful or hopeful respondents may give as many names as well as the truly expansive ones, while the loners, as well as the gregarious but reserved, may give relatively few names.

From the other side, the results on the distribution of isolates and of mutuals are so convenient when all persons make an equal number of choices that one is tempted to judge observed values of isolates and mutuals relative to the distribution obtained by assuming that everyone makes the average number of outgoing choices even though, in fact, the numbers differ from person to person.

After stating clearly the null distribution and finding indices of interesting departures from it, a logical next development is to furnish alternative distributions. In the equal probability selection of persons chosen, one could propose some unequal probabilities such as draw probabilities in pps sampling theory. Aside from the awkward feature of a person not being able to choose himself, the observed relative numbers of choices received would estimate so-called inclusion probabilities while, the draw probabilities could be computed from these in the usual laborious manner. Such estimates of underlying probabilities are, however, little more than monotonic transformations of the choice statuses with a bit more spread.

The other departure from the null distribution involves interdependence of the choices of one person with others. Fararo and Sunshine (1964) model choice dependencies, while Rapoport and Horvath (1961) bring in a parameter to reflect a tendency for chains of choices to close back on themselves. A most interesting approach was offered by Holland and Leinhardt (1970) whereby the quotas of types of pair relationships were fixed, but their

locations were determined by an equal probability mechanism. It
is a little early for me to see how these findings will fit in
with older work and so I'll change topics after a few final
observations.

One has to do with the influence on this sociometric probability theory of development in general probability theory on
inclusion/exclusion rules and the use of generating functions
begun by Frechet (1940, 1943) and reinforced by Feller (1950).
It was very satisfying to see these basic results applied with
such success in Katz's work. It may be worthwhile to distinguish
in a practical sense the counting series of Harary (1967), for
example, that furnish the numbers of nonisomorphic graph structures of various kinds, and the probability generating functions
that furnish the chances with which each of these types may
arise.

Another observation has to do with the metatheoretical status
of sociometric choice data at that time. I now find myself taking
issue with the second part of a statement by Moreno himself although the viewpoint is powerfully compelling: "Sociometric
structures, like musical notation, are languages, symbolic
references not the process itself. They are analogous to the
frames of time and space in the sense of Kant. The conceptual
mind uses them to align the phenomena." Whereas the collection
of ordered pairs does furnish a "frame in the sense of Kant" the
sociometric choices themselves are a phenomena of a more concrete
nature. They were actually taken as *the* phenomena to be explained, and this viewpoint became very quickly widely understood.
The paper by Daisy Starkey Edwards (1948) on the Frame of
Reference Problem summarizes this early viewpoint.

Handled in this fashion, sociometric data play a role
similar to that of univariate data in challenging probabilists
and statisticians to furnish models of their distributions. Although univariate distribution theory can be as complex

and demanding a topic as any, in statistical theory, it is usually
of more limited application in the sciences since the crucial
questions in practice concern relationships among variables.
Thus, we will now turn to this problem of studying relationships
among variables that include some sociometric choice data. With
profoundest apologies to a large body of workers in social psychology and other fields, I am not going to try to review empirical studies that have related such variables, but rather I'm just
going to review some of my own ideas.

III.   FROM ENUMERATIVE TO ANALYTIC SURVEYS OF NETWORKS

The second topic concerns the logical or metatheoretical
status of interpersonal data. Early consideration of this subject
was furnished by Coleman (1958-1959) and later by Stephan (1969).
Another article and application is by E. O. Laumann, L. M. Ver-
bugge, and F. U. Pappi (1974). Despite the remarkable current
popularity of path analysis, or perhaps because of it, I feel that
a regression analysis viewpoint is more comprehensive than path
analysis when dealing with interrelationships among variables.
But in order to apply the techniques of regression analysis requires attention to what is to serve as the unit of analysis, and
what are the variables, what are their causal statuses (dependent
Ys, independent Xs, or control Zs), what are their randomness
statuses (fixed or random), and what are their measurement levels
(numerical or qualitative). These are the kinds of questions I
would like to put, very briefly, concerning interpersonal data.
The first issue is the unit of analysis.

A familiar situation is the presence of social groups in a
survey as households, classrooms or neighborhood clusters. Each
member of the group stands in a special relationship to his fellow
members that is different from his outgroup relationships. This
situation is often handled by treating the groups as blocks would

be dealt with in experimental design and each member becomes a
unit of analysis. That is, one expects the members of a group to
resemble one another more than nonmembers. The effect is taken to
be random (sometimes this is deliberately made more realistic by
using random numbers to select a cluster sample) and usually it
represents a source of influence that can be taken as separate
from that of the independent variables of interest. In regression
computations one uses dummy variables in place of groups and labels
them control or Z variables.

When one is interested in the effect of groups, the choice
of analysis depends greatly on whether the groups in the survey
represent a sample of a greater population or the entire range
of interest. The groups, in other words, can be random or fixed.
If they are taken as random, then attention shifts to estimating
the component of variance for groups. If fixed, the same dummy
variables are used, but now labeled as Xs. Looking upon group
membership itself as the dependent variable, Y, is a less common
approach, although studies of the sizes of conversational or
casual walking groups take such a viewpoint. Techniques of multivariate analysis such as discriminant functions and multivariate
classification have also been used when the variable of interest
is categorical or group membership.

Partitioning a larger population into groups is the same as
defining an equals relation and is thus a special case of network.
If our interest is (as in fact it is) in more general networks then
what methods of analysis are available? As with groups we should
distinguish the case when the relationships of the network are a
Z, an X or a Y variable, when it is random or fixed, etc.

The first and perhaps the most difficult task is to settle on
a unit of analysis other than the person or individual case. The
units may be taken to be unordered pairs, ordered pairs, or triples (unordered, partially, or well-ordered), quadruples, etc.
The only case I've handled (Proctor, 1969) or seen handled
(Laumann *et al.*, 1974) so far has been that of pairs. In the

full case of ordered pairs there are $n(n-1)$ units of analysis
that are available to be used, each carrying the value of the
variable that describes the relationship. To represent the
point data any functions of two arguments (the first and second
point values) can be employed, although the mean and the signed
difference are likely to be the most useful ones.

When the point data are taken as independent and the pair
data as dependent it becomes more reasonable to use a simple
regression model for including a stochastic aspect in the model.
Each ordered pair is then taken to have whatever point data are
found, and the nature of the relationship is subsequently decided
by a random event. These events become the objective of the
study. If the nature of the relationship is measured along a
continuum as numerical observations, then a multiple regression
of $Y_{(ij)}$ on $X_{1(ij)}$ and $X_{2(ij)}$, where X_1 is the mean and X_2 the
signed difference can be calculated.

An example of such an analysis was done by Eun Sul Lee in
his Ph.D. thesis (1970) at North Carolina State University. The
relationship variable was taken as a departure in expected value'
of the flow of chemists from one university to another, from
Baccalaureate to Doctorate, while the point data were entered as
signed differences in (1) latitude and longitude of the university,
in (2) a prestige score, and in (3) a salary level score. Since
there were 86 universities there were 7310 ordered pairs in the
regression. Historical changes in the flow pattern are shown by
the data, which were split into two groups: cases with BS before
1950 (old cohort) and 1950 or after (new cohort). The results
looked like:

Analysis of 7310 ordered pairs of t values

Institutions	Old Cohort	New Cohort	Total
North/South distance	-1.6	-.2	-.9
East/West distance	-3.1**	-.5	-1.7
Prestige difference	-1.3	-.4	-2.2*
Compensation difference	1.8	1.7	4.6***
R^2 =	.012	.002	.004

The three "significances" indicate that movements are generally (in both cohorts) greater from lower to higher prestige, and from higher to lower levels of compensation, while the old cohort shows a West to East preference that does not exist for the more recent group.

Residuals from the regressions were examined for normality of distribution and the kurtosis was found to be positive; for heteroscedasticity, which was found to be minor; and for dependence, which was found to be strong when present. The dependence is that between two overlapping ordered pairs. Dr. Lee's conclusions were that "Leptokurtosis has a conservative effect on F ratios, the variance heterogeneity does not seem to be to extreme, and the non-zero correlations of errors affects only...2.3 percent of the cases..." That correlation, however, was estimated at .998 by the following argument:

When $i \neq i'$ and $j \neq j'$ then define σ_e^2 as $V(e_{ij} - e_{i'j'}) = 2\sigma_e^2$, where e_{ij} and $e_{i'j'}$ are residuals of the ordered pairs (i,j) and (i',j'). However, we define ρ as in:

$$V(e_{ij} - e_{ij'}) = V(e_{ij} - e_{i'j}) = 2\sigma_e^2(1-\rho).$$

The observed variances of nonoverlapping pairs and of over-lapped pairs were calculated as $s^2_{xc} = 586.07$ and $s^2_{lap} = 1.26$, respectively from which $\hat{\rho} = .998$ was calculated as $1 - \hat{\rho} = 1.26/586.07$.

The fit in terms of R^2 values must be judged as meager and so it may be argued that only the large size of 7310 observations saves significances for some of the regression coefficients. My viewpoint is that in the case of flow between each ordered pair, a model granting a separate error term to each ordered pair is realistic and therefore so is $n = 7310$ and the related significances.

When, however, the point data are taken as dependent and the pair data as independent, the situation changes. All interpoint distances derived from point data fit, by definition, an under-lying one-dimensional pattern perfectly. The fit of pair data, as interpoint distances, to a one-dimensional pattern is still in question, as is the correlation between this pattern and that of the point data.

The latter question can be handled by returning to a point-by-point regression; conventional tests of significance, using the number of points as sample size, should be appropriate. Point data on the ordered pair data can be regressed with $n(n-1)$ units of analysis and then corrected for the degrees of freedom and standard errors (Proctor, 1969). This involves multiplying t-values (F-values) from the pair regression analysis with $n(n-1)$ cases by (the square of) $\sqrt{(n-r)/[n(n-1)-r]}$ where r is the number of independent variables plus one for the constant in the multiple regression. Degrees of freedom should be $n-r$ rather than $n(n-1)-r$. When unordered point data are in the role of dependent variable then the number of observations is effectively $n(n-1)/2$ and so t values must be divided by $\sqrt{2}$, F values by 2, and error degrees of freedom set to $n(n-1)/2-r$ rather than $n(n-1)-r$.

IV. ELABORATIONS OF NETWORK SAMPLE DESIGN

The third and final viewpoint concerns sampling of a population graph. In many respects the problems here are the same as in any sampling procedure. The variable of interest is the nature of the relationship, while the elements of the frame are ordered pairs of points, *n*-tuples, etc. Obtaining lists of the points, locating and measuring the relationship, estimating population parameters, calculating standard errors are all operations very much parallel to their counterparts in point sampling.

Whereas the problems in general may be similar their more specific statement and solution can be quite unique. There is no doubt that clustering, stratification, multistage selections, two-step or two-phase designs, and many other features will come to have their counterparts in graph sampling and very much remains to be done along these lines. Much as I would like to speculate as to how these features might be incorporated, it would be more useful if I simply report on what steps have actually been taken by myself and two others.

As for my work (1967) on estimating the density of linkages using the subgraph over a simple random set of *n* points from the *N* it followed the usual pattern found in Cochran's (1963) sampling textbook. He describes a sample selection scheme giving an estimator, finding its bias and variance, and finally giving an estimator of variance. (Most of the results were given earlier by Hayashi and are presented clearly by Ove Frank, 1971.) I was able to interest two students to carry this work somewhat further. Al Sheardon (1970) investigated the effect of various changes in the nature of the population graph on the variance of the linkages density estimator. Prachoom Suwattee obtained the usual series of results for clustered, multistage, and unequal probabilities sampling schemes. Sheardon also obtained higher moments of the linkage density estimator, although he used the rather cumbersome notation in Bloemena's (1964) monograph.

The interesting feature of Sheardon's approach was the use of
a superpopulation or of various superpopulations that allow for
comparisons of variance and therefore lead to recommendations for
or against the use of the estimator. The superpopulations were
constructed by designating two subpopulations of points within
which and between which differences in density of links appear
or from which and to which such differences were to be found.

When a high density of within-linkages is assumed, the population graphs will show cliques, while if the between-linkages are
numerous the graphs will appear to be stringy. Likewise when the
outgoing linkages are supposed very likely then the structure
will appear to be of radiating stars, whereas when the incoming
linkages are frequent the population will exhibit some absorbing
stars. The limitation to only two subpopulations or factions were
perhaps unfortunate. The findings were that any unbalance from
equal propensities of between and within or from and to result in
increased variance in the estimate of linkage density overall.

In some field work done in a small town (Proctor, 1966), the
sample selection methods used were designed to attain lower
variances of estimation than the point SRS method. This technique consisted of subsampling households from an area sample so
as to control the proportion of pairs of households within the
same block relative to that of pairs from nonneighboring households. The reduction in variance expected from this method was
worked out by Prachoom Suwattee (1970).

Suwattee also employed a superpopulation model with two parameters: p_1 for a chance of a within-cluster link appearing; and
p_2 for the chance of between-cluster links. The number of clusters was denoted by N, their size by M, the cluster sample size
by n, and the size of subsampling within each cluster by m.
For equal number of sampled nodes he showed that a cluster sample

design is more efficient than a SRA of nM nodes if $p_1 \geq Cp_2$ where C is a constant determined by N, M, and n. Unfortunately the constant may become quite large, so that it is generally necessary to use the full expressions for variances with the particular values of p_1, p_2, N, M, and n that are of interest.

Similarly, in deciding to subsample clusters, Suwattee showed with a numerical example that when within-cluster enumeration costs are sufficiently small relative to between-cluster costs then subsampling ceases to be superior. For fixed ratio of these costs the relative efficiency of subsampling was seen to depend inversely on the ratio $p_1(1-p_1)/p_2(1-p_2)$. The ratio reflects within-cluster heterogeneity relative to between-cluster heterogeneity of linkages. When it rises it should be met by increased effort expended within clusters, within in turn suggests foregoing the subsampling.

V. SUMMARY AND CONCLUSIONS

Developments parallel to those in conventional sampling have taken place in graph sampling. Random sampling from a hypothetically infinite population of graphs can be distinguished from simple random sampling from a finite graph just as the binomial distribution is distinguished from the hypergeometric. A shift of emphasis from enumerative to analytical surveys can be noted in the graph sampling field as well as in the social survey field. The general principle of attacking high variance by spending more of the survey budget can be applied in the graph sampling business just as in sample surveys whenever the variance and cost relationships become known.

A capability for mounting a systematic attack on problems of survey design in graph sampling to discover the key variance and cost relationships depends a great deal on having firmly in mind

a clear characterization of the survey objectives. What are the
parameters to be estimated? Is it a linkage density or other
graph moment? Is it a measure of association between or among
point and pair data? Is it, rather, a parameter of the stochastic process that is being held responsible for the sociometric choice configuration or network?

REFERENCES

Bloemena, A. R. *Sampling from a graph,* Mathematisch Centrum
     Amsterdam, 1964.

Cochran, W. G. *Sampling techniques,* 2nd ed., Wiley, New York,
     1963.

Coleman, J. S. Relational analysis: The study of social or-
     ganizations with survey methods, *Human Organization,* 1958-59,
     17, 28-36.

Criswell, J. H. Foundations of sociometric measurement, *Sociome-
     try,* 1946, *9,* 7-13.

Deming, W. E. *Some theory of sampling,* Wiley, New York, Chapter
     7, 1950.

Edwards, D. S. The constant frame of reference problem in soci-
     ometry, *Sociometry,* 1948, *11,* 372-379.

Fararo, T. J., & Sunshine, M. H. *A study of a biased friendship
     net,* Youth Development Center, Syracuse University, Syracuse
     University Press, New York, 1964.

Feller, W. *An introduction to probability theory and its appli-
     cations,* Wiley, New York, 1950.

Frank, Ove, *Statistical inference in graphs,* FOA Repro, Stockholm,
     1971.

Frechet, M. *Les probabilités associées à un systèm de'événements
     compatibles et dépendents, actualites scientifiques et
     industrielles,* 1943.

Frechet, M. *Les probabilités associées a un system de'événements compatibles et dépendants, actualites scientifiques et indus-trielles*, 1940.

Harary, F., & Beineke, I., (Eds.), *A seminar on graph theory*, Holt, Rinehart and Winston, New York. 1967, Applications of Polya's Theorem to Permutation Groups.

Hayashi, Chikio, Note on sampling from a sociometric pattern, *Annals of the Institute of Statistical Mathematics*, 1958, *9*, 49-52.

Holland, P. W., & Leinhardt, S. A method for detecting structure in sociometric data, *American Journal of Sociology*, 1970, *76*, 492-513.

Katz, L. The distribution of the number of isolates in a social group, *Annals of Mathematical Statistics*, 1952, *23*, 271-276.

Katz, L., & Powell, J. H. Probability distributions of random variables associated with a structure of the sample space of sociometric investigations, *Annals of the Mathematical Statistics*, 1957, *28*, 442-448.

Katz, L, & Wilson, T. R. The variance of the number of mutual choices in sociometry, *Psychometrika*, 1956, *21*, 299-304.

Laumann, E. O., Verbrugge, L. M., & Pappi, F. U. A causal modeling approach to the study of a community elite's influence structure, *American Sociological Review*, 1974, *39*, 162-174.

Lee, E. S. Aspects of institutional mobility pattern of chemists in higher education, Mimeo. Series No. 676, Institute of Statistics, North Carolina State University, Raleigh, North Carolina, 1970.

Loomis, C. P., & Pepinsky, H. B. Sociometry, 1937-1947: Theory and methods, *Sociometry*, 1948, *11*, 262-286.

Moreno, J. L., & Jennings, H. Statistics of social configurations, *Sociometry*, 1938, *1*, 342-374.

Neyman, J.   On the two different aspects of the representative
    method: The method of stratified sampling and the method
    of purposive selection, *Journal of Royal Statistical Society,*
    1934, *97,* 558-606.

Proctor, C. H.   Analyzing prior data and point data on social
    relationships, attitudes and background characteristics of
    Costa Rican Census Bureau employees, *Proceedings of the Social
    Statistics Section, American Statistical Association,* 1969,
    457-465.

Proctor, C. H.   Two measurement and sampling methods for studying
    social networks, Mimeo.   Institute of Statistics Project
    Report, North Carolina State University, Raleigh, North
    Carolina, 1966.

Proctor, C. H.   The variance of an estimate of linkage density
    from a simple random sample of graph nodes, *Proceedings of
    the Social Statistics Section, American Statistical Association,* 1967, 457-465.

Rapoport, A., & Horvath, W. J.   A study of a large sociogram,
    Behavioral Science, 1961, *6,* 279-291.

Sheardon, A. W.   Sampling directed graphs, Unpublished Ph.D.
    Thesis, Department of Statistics, North Carolina State
    University, Raleigh, North Carolina, 1970.

Stephan, F. F.   Three extensions of sample survey technique:
    Hybrid, nexus, and graduated sampling, in N. L. Johnson and
    Harry Smith, Ed., *New Developments in Survey Sampling,* Wiley,
    New York, 1969, 81-104.

Suwattee, P., Some estimators, variances and variance
    estimators for point-cluster sampling of digraphs, Mimeo.
    Series No. 721, Institute of Statistics, North Carolina
    State University, 1970.

Yule, G. U., & Kendall, M. G.   *An introduction to the theory of
    statistics,* 14th ed., Hafner, New York, 1968, 367.

CHAPTER 16

ESTIMATION OF POPULATION TOTALS

BY USE OF SNOWBALL SAMPLES

Ove Frank

Department of Statistics

University of Lund

Lund, Sweden

I. INTRODUCTION

We shall consider a population as a valued graph with unknown
node values and known or unknown adjacencies. The node value may
be an attributive property which has nothing to do with the graph
structure, for example, the size or type of the node, but may
also depend on the graph, for example, the degree of the node or
the number of mutual arcs incident to the node. If the node
values are real numbers, that is, values on a quantitative variable or a numerically coded qualitative variable, it may make
sense to consider the population total, that is, the sum of the
node values. In particular the population totals may represent
various frequencies in the graph, for example, the total arc
frequency, the total number of mutual arcs, or the total number
of isolated nodes.

The problem of estimating the node value total from sample
data has been considered in the literature under various degrees
of generality and various assumptions concerning the sampling
procedure. Proctor (1966, 1967) considered estimation of the

total arc frequency in a simple undirected graph by using a subgraph induced by a simple random node sample. The same problem
in a simple directed graph was treated by Sherdon (1970). Proctor and Suwattee (1970) considered the generalization to node
cluster sampling designs. Frank (1969, 1971, 1977b) introduced
node and arc values and estimated node and arc value totals by
use of node sampling with or without replacement, Bernoulli-
sampling of nodes or arcs and some more general sampling designs.
Capobianco (1970) and Tapiero, Capobianco and Lewin (1975) used
samples of node pairs and observations of arc occurrences in
the sampled node pairs. Capobianco also considered star samples,
that is samples of nodes together with their incident arcs and
adjacent nodes. The graph sampling designs of Frank and the
star samples of Capobianco involve the idea of joining incident
arcs or adjacent nodes to an initial node sample. This procedure was called snowball sampling by Goodman (1961), who used
it to estimate the total frequency of mutual arcs in a special
kind of regular graph with one out-arc from each node. Goodman
also generalized his results to other graph parameters in regular
graphs defined by constant out-degrees.

The purpose of this chapter is to describe some snowball
sampling procedures and show how some standard methods of survey
sampling apply if sufficient information is available about the
graph. We also make some comparisons between linear unbiased
estimators based on snowball samples. In the next section the
needed notation will be introduced. Section III gives some
preliminaries on estimation of totals. Section IV gives some
general results pertaining to snowball sampling. Section V considers some snowball sampling procedures involving contact processes. Finally, Section VI gives some concluding remarks.

II.   NOTATION

Consider a finite population V of N units labeled by the integers $1,\ldots,N$.   A binary relation between the units is given as a graph with adjacency matrix $\underline{x}$; the matrix element x_{ij} is 1 or 0 according to whether node i has an arc to node j or not. It is convenient to define $x_{ii} = 1$ for all $i \in V$, and this will be tacitly assumed in what follows.   The set of nodes which have an arc from node i is denoted A_i, and the set of nodes which have an arc to node j is denoted B_j.   The sets A_i and B_j are said to be *adjacent after* i and *before* j, respectively.   We will also denote the unions of adjacent sets by

$$A(I) = \bigcup_{i \in I} A_i \quad \text{and} \quad B(J) = \bigcup_{j \in J} B_j$$

for subsets I and J of V.

A *probability sampling design* of a node sample S is a non-negative function $p(I)$ which states the probability of selecting the set I as the sample, that is,

$$P(S = I) = p(I) \geq 0, \quad \sum_{I \subseteq V} p(I) = 1.$$

The *probability of inclusion* in the sample of all units in a subset $I \subseteq V$ is denoted by

$$\pi(I) = P(I \subseteq S),$$

and the *probability of exclusion* from the sample of all units in a subset $I \subseteq V$ is denoted by

$$\bar{\pi}(I) = P(I \subseteq \bar{S}),$$

where $\bar{S}$ denotes the complementary set of S.   If I contains only one or two nodes we will also denote the inclusion and exclusion probabilities by π_i, π_{ij}, $\bar{\pi}_i$, $\bar{\pi}_{ij}$, where, in particular, $\pi_{ii}=\pi_i$ and $\bar{\pi}_{ii}=\bar{\pi}_i$.

By the principle of inclusion and exclusion we obtain the well-known identities

$$\bar{\pi}_j = 1 - \pi_j \, ,$$

$$\bar{\pi}_{ij} = 1 - \pi_i - \pi_j + \pi_{ij} \, ,$$

and generally

$$\bar{\pi}(J) = \sum_{I \subseteq J} (-1)^{|I|} \pi(I)$$

where $|I|$ denotes the number of units in the set I, and the sum ranges over all the $2^{|J|}$ subsets of J. Analogous identities are valid with π and $\bar{\pi}$ interchanged.

By introducing the stochastic indicator variables

$$S_j = \begin{cases} 1 \text{ if } j \in S \, , \\ \\ 0 \text{ otherwise} \, , \end{cases}$$

it is possible to interpret the inclusion and exclusion probabilities as the expected values

$$\pi(J) = E \prod_{j \in J} S_j \, , \quad \bar{\pi}(J) = E \prod_{j \in J} (1-S_j) \, .$$

III.   ESTIMATION OF NODE VALUE TOTALS

Consider a numerical attribute y defined in the node set V. Let y_i be the value of y for node $i \in V$. We will be interested in estimating the total

$$T = \sum_{i \in V} y_i$$

of the population by using the observed values of y in a sampled subset S of the population. The subset S is selected according to a probability sampling design which may depend on the graph. The graph may be known or unknown, and if it is unknown it is assumed that the survey provides information not only about y-values but also about the adjacency properties in the graph.

An unbiased estimator of the total T is given by the Horvitz-Thompson estimator

$$\hat{T} = \sum_{i \in S} y_i/\pi_i \ ,$$

provided the inclusion probabilities π_i are known or observable for $i \in S$ and positive for $i \in V$. If the inclusion probabilities are unknown, but can be estimated from the sample, we may modify $\hat{T}$ by replacing π_i with its estimator $\hat{\pi}_i$. The modified $\hat{T}$ is generally not unbiased, and its properties have to be investigated before it can be assured that it is useful as an estimator of T. We will illustrate this type of modification in Section V.

The variance of T is equal to

$$\sigma^2 = \text{Var } \hat{T} = \sum_{i \in V} \sum_{j \in V} y_i y_j (\pi_{ij} - \pi_i \pi_j)/\pi_i \pi_j \ .$$

The Horvitz-Thompson variance estimator is

$$\hat{\sigma}^2_{HT} = \sum_{i \in S} \sum_{j \in S} y_i y_j (\pi_{ij} - \pi_i \pi_j)/\pi_{ij} \pi_i \pi_j \ ,$$

and the Sen-Yates-Grundy variance estimator is

$$\hat{\sigma}^2_{SYG} = \sum_{i \in S} \sum_{j \in S} (y_i/\pi_i - y_j/\pi_j)^2 (\pi_i \pi_j - \pi_{ij})/2\pi_{ij} \ ,$$

provided all π_{ij} are positive and known or observable. $\hat{\sigma}^2_{HT}$ is always unbiased and $\hat{\sigma}^2_{SYG}$ is unbiased if the sample size is non-random.

Consider a general linear unbiased estimator of T, say

$$\phi = \sum_{i \in V} a_i y_i \ ,$$

where the coefficients a_i depend on the sample S and the graph adjacencies, but not on the node values. The observability and unbiasedness of ϕ require that $a_i = S_i a_i$ and $E a_i = 1$ for all $i \in V$. If the covariances of the coefficients are denoted by $\mathrm{Cov}(a_i, a_j) = \alpha_{ij}$, then the variance of ϕ becomes

$$\mathrm{Var}\ \phi = \sum_{i \in V} \sum_{i \in V} \alpha_{ij} y_i y_j \ .$$

Let ψ be another general linear unbiased estimator of T with coefficients b_i and coefficient covariances β_{ij}. For later reference we now state without proofs two simple lemmas concerning the coefficients and the variance properties of the estimators. We will say that ϕ is *at least as good as* ψ if $\mathrm{Var}\ \phi \leq \mathrm{Var}\ \psi$ for all $y_1, \ldots, y_N$.

Lemma 3.1 ϕ *cannot be at least as good as* ψ *if there is an* $i \in V$ *with* $\alpha_{ii} > \beta_{ii}$.

Lemma 3.2 *Neither* ϕ *nor* ψ *can be at least as good as the other if there is an* $(i,j) \in V^2$ *with*

$$(\alpha_{ii} - \beta_{ii})(\alpha_{jj} - \beta_{jj}) < (\alpha_{ij} - \beta_{ij})^2 \ .$$

IV. SNOWBALL SAMPLING

Consider the snowball sampling procedure of successively enlarging a node sample by joining adjacent nodes. The final snowball sample consists of the initial sample together with a number of adjacent stages; an s-stage snowball sample comprises the
nodes which can be reached in a path of at most s arcs from some
initial sample node. If $S^{(0)}$ denotes the initial node sample a
one-stage snowball sample is $S^{(1)} = A(S^{(0)})$, a two-stage snowball
sample is $S^{(2)} = A(S^{(1)})$ and so on. We obtain a non-decreasing
sequence of snowball samples

$$S^{(0)} \subseteq S^{(1)} \subseteq S^{(2)} \subseteq \cdots \;.$$

The stages of a snowball sample are defined as the successively
joined parts. The initial stage $S^{(0)}$ is joined with the first
stage $S^{(0)} \cap S^{(1)}$, the second stage $S^{(1)} \cap S^{(2)}$, and so on. Consequently an s-stage snowball sample is composed of the initial
stage and s further stages all of which are disjoint. As is
well-known from graph theory, this stage-partition of the snowball sample can be found by examining the Boolean powers of the
adjacency matrix.

We shall consider a snowball sample $S = A(S')$ and relate its
sampling design to the design of the preceding sample S'. In
particular, S can be a one-stage snowball sample and S' an
initial sample selected according to an arbitrary probability
sampling design. Since $P(S' \subseteq S) = 1$, the sampling design of S
is a simple example of an *extension* of the sampling design of
S' in the terminology of Lanke (1975), and it follows from his
Theorems 3.5 and 3.10 that the inclusion probabilities of S and
S' satisfy $\pi(I) \geq \pi'(I)$ for all $I \subseteq V$. The following Theorem
4.2 gives the exact relationship between the two sampling
designs. First we need a lemma.

Lemma 4.1 Let I and J be arbitrary subsets of V. *Then* $A(I) \subseteq \bar{J}$
if and only if $B(J) \subseteq \bar{I}$.

Proof. The equivalence between $A(I) \subseteq \bar{J}$ and $B(J) \subseteq \bar{I}$ is a consequence of the equivalence between $j \notin A(I)$ and $B_j \subseteq \bar{I}$ for every
$j \in J$. Now these equivalences follow by noticing that $j \notin A(I)$
implies that $j \notin A_i$ for all $i \in I$, that is, $i \in \bar{B}_j$ for all $i \in I$, and
thus $I \subseteq \bar{B}_j$, i.e., $B_j \subseteq \bar{I}$.

Theorem 4.2 If S = A(S') *the exclusion probabilities of* S *and* S'
satisfy $\bar{\pi}(J) = \bar{\pi}'(B(J))$ *for all* $J \subseteq V$. *In particular* $\bar{\pi}_i = \bar{\pi}'(B_i)$
and $\bar{\pi}_{ij} = \bar{\pi}'(B_i \cup B_j)$.

Proof. The exclusion probability $\bar{\pi}(J)$ of S can be written

$$\bar{\pi}(J) = P(J \subseteq \bar{S}) = P(A(S') \subseteq \bar{J}),$$

and by application of Lemma 4.1 it follows that

$$\bar{\pi}(J) = P(B(J) \subseteq \overline{S'}) = \bar{\pi}'(B(J)).$$

Corrollary 4.3 If S = A(S') *the inclusion probabilities of* S *are
given by*

$$\pi(J) = \sum_{I \subseteq J} (-1)^{|I|} \bar{\pi}'(B(I))$$

for all $J \subseteq V$. *In particular* $\pi_i = 1 - \bar{\pi}'(B_i)$ *and* $\pi_{ij} = 1 - \bar{\pi}'(B_i) - \bar{\pi}'(B_j) + \bar{\pi}'(B_i \cup B_j)$.

Proof. The result follows immediately by expressing the inclusion
probabilities of S in terms of the exclusion probabilities of
S which are given according to Theorem 4.2.

    We see from Corollary 4.3 that all π_i are positive if and
only if for each node $j \in V$ there is at least one node i

belonging to B_j which has $\pi_i' > 0$. Moreover, in that case the Horvitz-Thompson estimator $\hat{T}$ based on S can be used if the sets B_j are observed for $j \in S$.

If the initial sample S' is selected according to a *Bernoulli-sampling design* defined by independently giving each node a certain probability of inclusion in the sample, then the initial inclusion and exclusion probabilities of the subset I are given by

$$\pi'(I) = p(I) = \begin{cases} \prod\limits_{i \in I} p_i & \text{if } I \text{ is non-empty,} \\ 1 & \text{otherwise ,} \end{cases}$$

$$\bar{\pi}'(I) = q(I) = \begin{cases} \prod\limits_{i \in I} q_i & \text{if } I \text{ is non-empty,} \\ 1 & \text{otherwise ,} \end{cases}$$

where p_i and q_i are the probabilities of including and excluding node i in the initial sample. It follows from Corollary 4.3 that

$$\pi_j = 1 - q(B_j) ,$$

$$\pi_{ij} = 1 - q(B_i) - q(B_j) + q(B_i \cup B_j) .$$

If $0 < p_i < 1$ for all i, and if B_i is observed for all $i \in S$, then we see that the Horvitz-Thompson estimator can be applied. By noticing the relationship

$$q(I \cup J) = q(I) q(J) / q(I \cap J)$$

for subsets I and J of V it follows that

$$\pi_{ij} = \pi_i \pi_j [1 + f(B_i \cap B_j) / f(B_i) f(B_j)]$$

where

$$f(I) = [1 - q(I)]/q(I)$$

for $I \subseteq V$. The last representation of π_{ij} is convenient for calculating the variance, σ^2, and the variance estimators, $\hat{\sigma}^2_{HT}$ and
$\hat{\sigma}^2_{SYG}$, given in the preceding section.

If the initial sampling design is further simplified so that
$p_i = p$ for all i and $0 < p = 1 - q < 1$ it follows that $p(I) = p^{|I|}$
and $q(I) = q^{|I|}$ depend only on the size $|I|$ of the subset I.
This *constant-probability Bernoulli-sampling design* implies that

$$\pi_j = 1 - q^{x_{\cdot j}},$$

and consequently the Horvitz-Thompson estimator $\hat{T}$ merely requires
that the sizes $x_{\cdot j}$ of B_j are observed for $j \in S$. Moreover,

$$\pi_{ij} = 1 - q^{x_{\cdot i}} - q^{x_{\cdot j}} + q^{x_{\cdot i} + x_{\cdot j} - (\underline{x'x})_{ij}},$$

where

$$(\underline{x'x})_{ij} = \sum_{k=1}^{N} x_{ki}\, x_{kj}$$

is the size of $B_i \cap B_j$. If we introduce the function

$$f(u) = (1 - q^u)/q^u$$

for $u \geq 0$, we obtain that

$$\pi_{ij} = \pi_i \pi_j [1 + f((\underline{x'x})_{ij})/f(x_{\cdot i}) f(x_{\cdot j})].$$

We can sum up our findings in the following theorem.

Theorem 4.4 If a Bernoulli-sampling design is used for S' the single and double inclusion probabilities of $S = A(S')$ are given by $\pi_j = 1 - q(B_j)$ and $\pi_{ij} = 1 - q(B_i) - q(B_j) + q(B_j \cup B_j) = \pi_i \pi_j [1 - f(B_i \cap B_j)/ f(B_i) f(B_j)]$ where $f(I) = [1 - q(I)]/q(I)$ for $I \subseteq V$. In particular, the constant-probability Bernoulli-sampling design implies that $q(I) = q^{|I|}$, and π_{ij} depends on $x_{\cdot i}$, $x_{\cdot j}$ and $(\underline{x}'\underline{x})_{ij}$.

Let us now compare the Horvitz-Thompson estimators based on S' and $A(S')$ in the case of a constant-probability Bernoulli-sampling design for S'. We will apply Lemma 3.1 and its notations with

$$\phi = \sum_{i \in S} y_i/\pi_i' \quad \text{and} \quad \psi = \sum_{i \in S} y_i/\pi_i.$$

Now $\alpha_{ii} = q/p$ and $\beta_{ii} = q^{x_{\cdot i}}/(1-q^{x_{\cdot i}})$ and consequently ϕ cannot be at least as good as ψ if there is an i with $x_{\cdot i} > 1$. This condition is obviously satisfied if S is a strict extension of S', i.e. if $x_{\cdot i} > 1$ for at least one i. In this case there exists an unbiased estimator based on S which is at least as good as ϕ, namely $E(\phi|S)$. That this estimator is unbiased and at least as good as ϕ is immediately obvious since $E(E(\phi|S)) = E(\phi) = T$ and $Var\ E(\phi|S) < Var\ \phi$. That

$$E(\phi|S) = \sum_{i=1}^{N} (y_i/\pi_i') E(S_i'|S_1,\ldots,S_N)$$

only depends on those y observed in the sample follows from $S' \subset S$ since $S_i' = S_i S_i'$ and consequently,

$$E(S_i'|S_1,\ldots,S_N) = S_i\ E(S_i'|S_1,\ldots,S_N).$$

It seems difficult to obtain an explicit expression for the dependence of $E(\phi|S)$ on the adjacency matrix $\underline{x}$. However, it is

easy to show that $E(S_i'|S_i) = S_i \pi_i'/\pi_i$, and ψ may thus be con-
sidered as an approximation to $E(\phi|S)$ obtained by replacing
$E(S_i'|S_1,\dots,S_N)$ with $E(S_i'|S_i)$. It may be asked wether ψ is at
least as good as ϕ if S is a strict extension of S'. The following theorem shows that this need not be the case.

*Theorem 4.5 Let ϕ and ψ be the Horvitz-Thompson estimators based
on S' and S = A(S'), where S' has a p-probability Bernoulli-
sampling design with $0 < p < 1$. Then neither ϕ nor ψ is at least
as good as the other if $x_{j\cdot} > x_{\cdot j} = 1$ for some j.*

Proof. We will show that the condition $x_{j\cdot} > x_{\cdot j} = 1$ for some j
implies the condition in Lemma 3.2 from which the theorem
follows. Now

$$\alpha_{ij} = (\pi_{ij}' - \pi_i'\pi_j')/\pi_i'\pi_j' = \begin{cases} q/p & \text{if } i=j, \\ 0 & \text{otherwise,} \end{cases}$$

and according to Theorem 4.4

$$\beta_{ij} = f((\underline{x}'\underline{x})_{ij})/f(x_{\cdot i})f(x_{\cdot j}),$$

where $f(u) = (1-q^u)/q^u$ for $u \geq 0$. Choose (i,j) such that $i \neq j$,
$x_{ji} = x_{\cdot j} = 1$. It follows that $(\underline{x}'\underline{x})_{ij} = 1$ and

$$(\alpha_{ij} - \beta_{ij})^2 - (\alpha_{ii} - \beta_{ii})(\alpha_{jj} - \beta_{jj}) = 1/f(x_{\cdot i})^2 > 0$$

which is the condition in Lemma 3.2.

The rest of this section reports some results concerning a
class of linear unbiased estimators of T. Consider a snowball
sample $S = A(S')$ and its last stage $S'' = \overline{S'} \cap S$. A linear unbiased
estimator of T is defined by

$$\phi = \sum_{j=1}^{N} y_j(\theta_j' S_j'/\pi_j' + \theta_j'' S_j''/\pi_j'')$$

where $0 \leq \theta'_j \leq 1$, $0 \leq \theta''_j \leq 1$, $\theta'_j + \theta''_j = 1$ for all j, and $\theta'_j = 1$ if $\pi''_j = 0$. The θ's may depend on the adjacencies but not on the sample, S. The inclusion probabilities of S'' can be given in terms of exclusion probabilities of S' as

$$\pi''_j = \pi_j - \pi'_j = \bar{\pi}'_j - \bar{\pi}'(B_j).$$

It follows that ϕ differs from the Horvitz-Thompson estimator based on S' if and only if the sampling designs of S and S' differ and $\theta'_j < 1$ for at least one j. If $\theta'_j = \pi'_j/\pi_j$ for all j the estimator ϕ becomes equal to the Horvitz-Thompson estimator based on S. The class of estimators ϕ might be of no interest if the Horvitz-Thompson estimator based on S was at least as good as every member ϕ. That this is not the case, and that consequently an interest in the class of estimators ϕ is motivated, is shown by the following theorem.

Theorem 4.6 If there exist two different nodes i and $j \in A_i$ which satisfy $\pi'_i > \bar{\pi}'(B_i)$ and $\bar{\pi}'(B_j) > \bar{\pi}'(B_i \cup B_j)$ then the Horvitz-Thompson estimator based on S is not at least as good as every member of the class of estimators ϕ.

Proof. We intend to use Lemma 3.2 and we write

$$Var\ \phi = \sum_{i=1}^{N} \sum_{j=1}^{N} \alpha_{ij} y_i y_j \text{ and } Var\ \psi = \sum_{i=1}^{N} \sum_{j=1}^{N} \beta_{ij} y_i y_j$$

where ψ is the Horvitz-Thompson estimator based on S. Now, according to the assumptions, i can be chosen so that $\pi''_i > 0$ but $\pi''_j \geq 0$. If $\pi''_j > 0$ it follows after some calculations that

$$\alpha_{ij} = \theta'_i \theta'_j \pi'_{ij}/\pi'_i \pi'_j + \theta'_i \theta''_j \pi''_{ij}{}'/\pi'_i \pi''_j + \theta''_i \theta'_j \pi''_{ji}{}'/\pi''_i \pi'_j + \theta''_i \theta''_j \pi''_{ij}/\pi''_i \pi''_j - 1$$

where $\pi''_{ij}{}' = ES'_i S''_j$. If $\pi''_j = 0$ we obtain

$$\alpha_{ij} = \theta'_i \pi'_{ij}/\pi'_i \pi'_j + \theta''_i \pi''_{ji}{}'/\pi''_i \pi'_j - 1.$$

We also have

$$\beta_{ij} = \pi_{ij}/\pi_i\pi_j - 1 = (\pi'_{ij} + \pi''_{ij} + \pi''_{ji} + \pi''_{ij})/\pi_i\pi_j - 1,$$

and thus

$$\alpha_{ij} - \beta_{ij} = \pi'_{ij}(\theta'_i\theta'_j/\pi'_i\pi'_j - 1/\pi_i\pi_j) + \pi''_{ji}(\theta''_i\theta'_j/\pi''_i\pi'_j - 1/\pi_i\pi_j)$$

$$+ \pi''_{ij}(\theta'_i\theta''_j/\pi'_i\pi''_j - 1/\pi_i\pi_j) + \pi''_{ij}(\theta''_i\theta''_j/\pi''_i\pi''_j - 1/\pi_i\pi_j),$$

where the last two terms are omitted if $\pi''_j = 0$. For arbitrary i it follows that

$$\alpha_{ii} - \beta_{ii} = \begin{cases} \pi_i(\theta'_i - \pi'_i/\pi_i)^2/\pi'_i\pi''_i & \text{if } \pi''_i > 0, \\ (\theta'_i - \pi'_i/\pi_i)(\theta'_i/\pi'_i + 1/\pi_i) & \text{if } \pi''_i = 0. \end{cases}$$

Let us now choose two fixed nodes i and j satisfying the assumptions of the theorem and put $\theta'_i \neq \pi'_i/\pi_i$ and $\theta'_j = \pi'_j/\pi_j$ (which is possible since $\pi''_i > 0$). It follows that $\alpha_{ii} - \beta_{ii} > 0$ and $\alpha_{jj} - \beta_{jj} = 0$. Moreover it follows after some calculations that

$$\alpha_{ij} - \beta_{ij} = (\theta'_i - \pi'_i/\pi_i)[\bar{\pi}'(B_j) - \bar{\pi}'(B_i \cup B_j)]/\pi''_i\pi_j$$

and according to the assumptions this quantity is different from zero. Consequently

$$(\alpha_{ij} - \beta_{ij})^2 - (\alpha_{ii} - \beta_{ii})(\alpha_{jj} - \beta_{jj}) > 0,$$

and the theorem follows by using Lemma 3.2.

If we choose S as an s-stage snowball sample where the initial stage is a constant-probability Bernoulli-sample the conditions of the above theorem can be given in terms of properties of the adjacency matrix $\underline{x}$. Let us define the Boolean powers $\underline{x}^{(s)}$ as $\underline{x}^{(1)} = \underline{x}$ and

$$x_{ij}^{(s)} = \max_{k} x_{ik}^{(s-1)} x_{kj}$$

for all (i,j) and $s=2,3,\ldots$. The column sums of the Boolean power matrix $\underline{x}^{(s)}$ are denoted by $x_{\cdot j}^{(s)}$. Now, S' is an $(s-1)$-stage snowball sample and $\bar{\pi}_i'$ is equal to q raised to $x_{\cdot i}^{(s-1)}$, $\bar{\pi}'(B_i)$ is equal to q raised to $x_{\cdot i}^{(s)}$ and $\bar{\pi}'(B_i \cup B_j)$ is equal to q raised to

$$x_{\cdot i}^{(s)} + x_{\cdot j}^{(s)} - \sum_{k=1}^{N} x_{ki}^{(s)} x_{kj}^{(s)}$$

The existance of a pair (i,j) with $i \neq j$ which satisfies

$$x_{ij} = 1, \; x_{\cdot i}^{(s-1)} < x_{\cdot i}^{(s)}, \; \sum_{k=1}^{N} x_{ki}^{(s)} x_{kj}^{(s)} < x_{\cdot i}^{(s)}$$

thus implies that some unbiased linear estimator ϕ has, for some choice of node values, a smaller variance than the Horvitz-Thompson estimator. Using graph concepts this condition means that for some pair of distinct nodes i and j there is an arc from i to j, there is a node at distance s before i, and there is a node at distance not larger than s before i but larger than s before j. In particular, for one-stage snowball sample the condition becomes that there exist three distinct nodes i, j, k with arcs from k to i and from i to j but no arc from k to j, that is, $x_{ki} x_{ij} (1-x_{kj}) = 1$. A comparison between that condition and the corresponding condition in Theorem 4.5 shows that neither implies the other, that is, the one-stage case in Theorem 4.6 cannot be proved by using Theorem 4.5 and the particular ϕ used there.

V. CONTACT PROCESSES

Assume that the adjacencies represent contacts which take place occasionally in an irregular manner which can be described by a random process, that is, the adjacency matrix $\underline{x}(t)$ is a multidimensional stochastic process varying with time, t. We shall only consider the simple model where at each fixed time point t, $x_{ii}(t) = 1$ for all i, and $x_{ij}(t) = x_{ji}(t)$ are independent Bernoulli-variables for $i < j$. Consequently we have $\binom{N}{2}$ independent stochastic processes $x_{ij}(t)$ for $i < j$. Each such process will be assumed stationary with contact intensity $Ex_{ij}(t) = \lambda_{ij}$. It will be convenient to define $\lambda_{ii} = 1$ and $\lambda_{ij} = \lambda_{ji}$ for all i and j. The contact intensities λ_{ij} may depend on the node values y_i and y_j, which are assumed not to change with time.

To illustrate the model we may think of a population of N individuals of which T have a certain characteristic ($y=1$), and $N-T$ do not have that characteristic ($y=0$). The contact intensity is λ between 1-individuals, λ' between 0- and 1-individuals and λ'' between 0-individuals. The $\binom{N}{2}$ independent contact processes are of three kinds: $\binom{T}{2}$ are identically distributed with contact intensity λ, $T(N-T)$ are identically distributed with contact intensity λ' and $\binom{N-T}{2}$ are identically distributed with contact intensity λ''.

Consider now the choice of a final sample S for the node data survey. An individual i is selected from the population according to an initial probability sampling design. When, at time t, he is asked to report his y-value all the persons $j \in A_i(t)$ who happen to have contact with him on that particular occasion t are also asked to report their y-values. Several individuals may be selected at the same time, and the same individual may be selected at several distinct time points. An individual who is selected again even though he has already been interviewed previously may now have other contacts which have not been previously asked about their y-values. In order to specify the final sample S, for which the y-values are observed, we will specify an initial sampling process and the way in which it is combined with the contact processes.

Consider a sequence of samples $S'(t)$ selected at different time points t. Each person $i \in S'(t)$ is asked to report his y-value, and all the persons j who happen to have contact with at least one person in $S'(t)$ on that particular occasion t are also asked to report their y-values. Data are thus observed at time t for the individuals in

$$S(t) = \bigcup_{i \in S'(t)} A_i(t)$$

During a specified period of time the data are observed for the individuals in

$$S = \bigcup_t S(t)$$

where the range of t is understood to be a finite set of time points. We will here adopt a simple sampling process where the occurring time points t are sufficiently separated to justify an assumption of stochastically independent adjacency matrices $\underline{x}(t)$. Another assumption which may seem more realistic in certain cases is to use contact processes of Markovian type, but we will not consider such models here. It should be noticed that the assumption of stochastically independent adjacency matrices, $\underline{x}(t)$, does not imply that the samples, $S(t)$, are necessarily independent. The sequence of initial samples, $S'(t)$, generally affects the sequence of samples, $S(t)$.

We will consider two different choices of sample sequences, $S'(t)$, namely:

1) a *panel sample* $S'(t) = S'$ selected according to a specified probability sampling design and remaining the same during the whole period of time,

and

2)   a sequence of samples $S'(t)$ which are independently selected
     at the various time points t according to a common probability
     sampling design.

The first choice results in dependent and the second in independent samples, $S(t)$. In both cases the initial sampling design
will be specified by the inclusion probabilities, $\pi'(I)$, for
$I \subseteq V$.

In the first case the final sample, S, consists of the individuals who on at least one occasion have had contact with at
least one panel individual. If we set

$$A_i = \bigcup_t A_i(t) \text{ and } x_{ij} = \max_t x_{ij}(t)$$

it is possible to obtain the representation $S = A(S')$ and thus
use the results of the preceding section. In the second case
similar representations are possible for each $S(t)$, and the
results of the preceding section are again applicable since the
$S(t)$ are independent.

The following theorems give the single and double unit inclusion probabilities of the final sample, S, in terms of the
sampling design of the initial samples and the intensities of the
contact processes. The general results are illustrated by two
different kinds of initial sampling design: *a Bernoulli-
sampling design* specified by

$$\pi'(I) = \prod_{i \in I} p_i \quad \text{for non-empty } I \subseteq V$$

where $0 < p_i = 1 - q_i < 1$ for all i, and *a single unit sampling
design* specified by

$$\pi'(I) = \begin{cases} p_i & \text{if } I = \{i\} \text{ for all } i \in V, \\ 0 & \text{if } |I| > 1, \end{cases}$$

where $0 < p_i < 1$ for all i and $\sum_i p_i = 1$. Of particular interest is the constant-probability Bernoulli-sampling design, which is normally a good approximation to simple random sampling. The single unit sampling design is of interest if the interviewing procedure is performed at different occasions for all the initially sampled individuals. In that case a sequence of n independent samples, $S'(t)$, constitutes a simple random sample of n units drawn with replacement.

Theorem 5.1 When the final sample S *is obtained from a panel sample* S' *and its contacts on* n *different occasions the single and double inclusion probabilities of* S *are given by*

$$\pi_j = 1 - E \prod_{i=1}^{N} [1 - S_i'(1 - (1 - \lambda_{ij})^n)] ,$$

$$\pi_{ij} = \pi_i + \pi_j - 1 + E \prod_{k=1}^{N} [1 - S_k'(1 - (1 - \lambda_{ki})^n (1 - \lambda_{kj})^n)] .$$

In particular a Bernoulli-sampling design for the panel sample implies that

$$\pi_j = 1 - \prod_{i=1}^{N} [q_i + p_i(1 - \lambda_{ij})^n] ,$$

$$\pi_{ij} = \pi_i + \pi_j - 1 + \prod_{k=1}^{N} [q_k + p_k(1 - \lambda_{ki})^n (1 - \lambda_{kj})^n] ,$$

and a single unit sampling design for the panel sample implies that

$$\pi_j = 1 - \sum_{i=1}^{N} p_i (1-\lambda_{ij})^n \quad,$$

$$\pi_{ij} = 1 - \sum_{k=1}^{N} p_k [(1-\lambda_{ki})^n + (1-\lambda_{kj})^n - (1-\lambda_{ki})^n (1-\lambda_{kj})^n] \quad.$$

Proof. By applying Corollary 4.3 we obtain

$$\pi_j = 1 - E \, \bar{\pi}'(B_j) = 1 - E \prod_{i \in B_j} (1-S_i')$$

$$= 1 - E \prod_{i=1}^{N} (1-S_i' x_{ij}) = 1 - E \prod_{i=1}^{N} (1-S_i' E \, x_{ij}) \quad,$$

where

$$E \, x_{ij} = E \max_{t} x_{ij}(t) = 1 - (1-\lambda_{ij})^n$$

if there are n distinct time points, t. Moreover for $i \neq j$

$$\pi_{ij} = 1 - E \, \bar{\pi}'(B_i) - E \, \bar{\pi}'(B_j) + E \, \bar{\pi}'(B_i \cup B_j)$$

and

$$E \, \bar{\pi}'(B_i \cup B_j) = E \prod_{k \in B_i \cup B_j} (1-S_k') =$$

$$= E \prod_{k=1}^{N} [1-S_k'(x_{ki} + x_{kj} - x_{ki} x_{kj})].$$

Considering the factors for k=i and k=j and remembering that $x_{ii} = 1$ for all i, it follows that the last expectation can be written

$$E \prod_{k=1}^{N} [1-S'_k E(x_{ki} + x_{kj} - x_{ki}x_{kj})]$$

$$= E \prod_{k=1}^{N} [1-S'_k (1-(1-\lambda_{ki})^n (1-\lambda_{kj})^n)]$$

from which the general result follows. The particular results
are obtained by straightforward calculations.

*Theorem 5.2 When the final sample S is obtained from independent
identically distributed initial samples and their contacts on n
different occasions, the single and double inclusion probabilities
of S are given by*

$$\pi_j = 1 - [E \prod_{i=1}^{N} (1-S'_i \lambda_{ij})]^n \quad ,$$

$$\pi_{ij} = \pi_i + \pi_j - 1 + [E \prod_{k=1}^{N} (1-S'_k (\lambda_{ki}+\lambda_{kj}-\lambda_{ki}\lambda_{kj}))]^n$$

*In particular a Bernoulli-sampling design for the initial samples
implies that*

$$\pi_j = 1 - \prod_{i=1}^{N} (1-p_i \lambda_{ij})^n \quad ,$$

$$\pi_{ij} = \pi_i + \pi_j - 1 + \prod_{k=1}^{N} [1-p_k (\lambda_{ki}+\lambda_{kj}-\lambda_{ki}\lambda_{kj})]^n \quad ,$$

*and a single unit sampling design for the initial samples im-
plies that*

$$\pi_j = 1 - (1 - \sum_{i=1}^{N} p_i \lambda_{ij})^n \quad ,$$

$$\pi_{ij} = \pi_i + \pi_j - 1 + [1 - \sum_{k=1}^{N} p_k (\lambda_{ki} + \lambda_{kj} - \lambda_{ki}\lambda_{kj})]^n \quad ,$$

Proof. Since the $S(t)$ are independent it follows that

$$\bar{\pi}_j = \prod_t \bar{\pi}_j(t) \text{ and } \bar{\pi}_{ij} = \prod_t \bar{\pi}_{ij}(t)$$

where $\bar{\pi}_j(t)$ and $\bar{\pi}_{ij}(t)$ denote the exclusion probabilities for $S(t)$. Applying Theorem 4.2 and Corollary 4.3 yields

$$\pi_j = 1 - \prod_t E\,\bar{\pi}'(B_j(t)) = 1 - \prod_t E \prod_{i=1}^{N} (1 - S'_i\,\lambda_{ij}(t))$$

$$= 1 - [E \prod_{i=1}^{N} (1 - S'_i\lambda_{ij})]^n \quad ,$$

$$\pi_{ij} = \pi_i + \pi_j - 1 + \prod_t E\,\bar{\pi}'(B_i(t) \cup B_j(t)) =$$

$$= \pi_i + \pi_j - 1 + \prod_t E \prod_{k=1}^{N} [1 - S'_k E(x_{ki}(t) + x_{kj}(t) - x_{ki}(t)x_{kj}(t))]$$

$$= \pi_i + \pi_j - 1 + [E \prod_{k=1}^{N} (1 - S'_k(\lambda_{ki} + \lambda_{kj} - \lambda_{ki}\lambda_{kj}))]^n \quad .$$

Routine calculations establish the formula for the two particular sampling designs.

Let us now consider a binary variable y, and the case with contact intensities λ, λ', λ'' mentioned in the beginning of this section. Let us further assume that a constant-probability Bernoulli-sampling design or single unit sampling design is used

for the initial sample. Substitution in the formulas above
yields

$$\pi_j = 1 - q[q+p(1-\lambda')^n]^{N-T} [q+p(1-\lambda)^n]^{T-1}$$

if y_j = 1 and if a Bernoulli-sampling design with constant probability p is used for the panel. Moreover

$$\pi_j = 1 - [(N-T)(1-\lambda')^n - (T-1)(1-\lambda)^n]/N$$

if y_j = 1 and a simple random sample single unit panel is used.
In the case of independent identically distributed initial samples the inclusion probabilities become

$$\pi_j = 1 - [q(1-p\lambda')^{N-T} (1-p\lambda)^{T-1}]^n$$

and

$$\pi_j = 1 - [N-1-(N-T)\lambda' - (T-1)\lambda]^n/N^n$$

for the two initial sampling designs, provided y_j = 1. Consequently we have found in all the four cases that π_j is some
function of T, say $\pi_j = g(T)$ if y_j = 1. It further follows that

$$\hat{T} = \sum_{j \in S} y_j/g(T) \ ,$$

is observable only if $\lambda = \lambda'$ and the common value of the contact
intensity is known. However, since $\hat{T}$ is unbiased a sequence of
estimators may be defined recursively by

$$\phi_k = \sum_{j \in S} y_j/g(\phi_{k-1})$$

for $k = 1, 2,..$ with $\phi_0 = 1$. While we have not made a thorough study of the convergence conditions and the bias and variance properties of such estimators, the following analysis will illustrate the kinds of result which are possible.

Let us denote the sample total by t sc that $E\ t = T\ g(T)$ and $\phi_k = t/g(\phi_{k-1})$. If we assume that the function $f(T) = T\ g(T)$ is monotone and denote the inverse function by ϕ, we have that $T = \phi(Et)$. Moreover, if the sequence of estimators ϕ_k converges, it converges to $\phi(t)$. Since $ET = f(T)$ and $Var\ t = \sigma^2 f(T)^2/T^2$, we can consider approximating $\phi(t)$ by the second degree Taylor expansion (assuming the existance of the needed derivatives and quotients):

$$T + [t-f(T)]\phi'(f(T)) + [t-f(T)]^2\ \phi''(f(T))/2$$

where

$$\phi'(f(T)) = 1/f'(T) \quad \text{and} \quad \phi''(f(T)) = -\ f''(T)/f'(T)^3\ .$$

Taking expectations we obtain the following approximation to $E\phi(t)$:

$$T - \sigma^2 f''(T)f(T)^2/2T^2 f'(T)^3\ .$$

A sufficient condition for convergence of ϕ_k is that the function $h(T) = t/g(T)$ is decreasing and has a derivative satisfying $|h'(T)| \leq c$ for some constant $c < 1$. To see this we use $\phi_k = h(\phi_{k-1})$ to obtain

$$\phi_{k+1} - \phi_k = (\phi_k - \phi_{k-1})h'(T_k)$$

where T_k lies between ϕ_{k-1} and ϕ_k. Since $h'(T_k) < 0$ the sequence $\phi_{k+1} - \phi_k$ is of alternating signs. Moreover,

$$\left| \phi_{k+1} - \phi_k \right| \le c \left| \phi_k - \phi_{k-1} \right| \le c^k \left| \phi_1 - \phi_0 \right| ,$$

and convergence follows. It follows from

$$\left| h'(T) \right| = t \, g'(T)/g(T)^2 \le N \, g'(T)/g(1)^2$$

that a sufficient condition for convergence is

$$g'(T) < g(1)^2/N$$

for $T \le N$.

Let us apply the above reasoning to the case of n independent constant-probability Bernoulli-samples. We have

$$g(T) = 1 - a \, b^T$$

where

$$a = [q(1-p\lambda')^N/(1-p\lambda)]^n ,$$

$$b = [(1-p\lambda)/(1-p\lambda')]^n .$$

Obviously $0 \le a < 1$ and, if we assume $\lambda' < \lambda$, $0 \le b < 1$. It therefore follows that $g(T)$ is increasing and $h(T)$ decreasing. Furthermore

$$h'(T) = atb^T \, \log b/(1-ab^T)^2 ,$$

and by using $\log(1/b) \le (1-b)/b$ and $tb^T/(1-ab^T)^2 \le Nb(1-ab)^2$ it follows that

$$\left| h'(T) \right| \le a(1-b)N/(1-ab)^2 \le aN/(1-ab).$$

The upper bound is less than 1 if and only if

$$N[q(1-p\lambda')^N/(1-p\lambda)]^n + q^n < 1. \tag{1}$$

We note that the left-hand side decreases to 0 when n increases.
For $n = 1$ the condition becomes

$$N(1-p)(1-p\lambda')^N - p(1-p\lambda) < 0 \tag{2}$$

which is obviously satisfied if p is sufficiently close to 1.
Thus we have proved the following result.

*Theorem 5.3 If the final sample is obtained from independent
p-probability Bernoulli-samples and their contacts on   different
occasions, then the sequence of estimators ϕ_k converges for
arbitrary values of N, p, λ and $\lambda'(\lambda' < \lambda)$ if n is sufficiently
large. It is sufficient to choose n such that (1) is satisfied.
For arbitrary values of N, n, λ and λ' ($\lambda' < \lambda$) the sequence
ϕ_k converges if p satisfies (2).*

VI. SOME REMARKS

   Graph models can be used for describing and analyzing individual contacts or relationships, communication chains, transportation networks, organizational structures, et cetera. The
data provided by various kinds of sample surveys may concern the
nodes, arcs, paths or any other parts of the graph. The present
chapter has been confined to snowball sample surveys in a graph
with a numerical variable defined on the node set. More general
valued graphs are obtained if there is a numerical variable y
defined for the pairs of nodes. We may, for instance, think of
a value y_{ij} as some measure of similarity between i and j, some
measure of distance, capacity or strength of a connection from i
to j, some intensity of contacts from i to j, et cetera. Frank

(1969, 1971, 1977a,b,c) has considered the problem of estimating a total

$$T = \sum_{i=1}^{N} \sum_{j=1}^{N} y_{ij}$$

by the use of y-observations obtained from various kinds of sampling procedures. The sampling distributions of induced sub-graph counts have been considered by Holland and Leinhardt (1975), Wasserman (1977) and Frank (1978c) and been applied to various estimation problems by Frank (1977b, 1978a,c) and Frank and Karlsson (1978). Other statistical inference problems in graphs and further references can be found in Capobianco (1972, 1974) and Frank (1975, 1977b, 1978b).

REFERENCES

Capobianco, M. F. Statistical inference in finite populations having structure. *Transactions of the New York Academy of Sciences,* 1970, *32,* 401-413.

Capobianco, M. F. Estimating the connectivity of a graph. In Y Alavi, D. R. Lick, A. T. White (Eds.), *Graph Theory and Applications,* Springer-Verlag, Berlin, 1972.

Capobianco, M. F. Recent progress in stagraphics. *Annals of the New York Academy of Sciences,* 1974, *231,* 139-141.

Frank, O. Structure inference and stochastic graphs. *FOA Reports* 1969, *3,* 1-8.

Frank, O. *Statistical inference in graphs*. Swedish Research Institute of National Defence, Stockholm, 1971.

Frank, O. Sampling population graphs. Paper presented at the meeting of the International Association of Survey Statisticians in Warzaw, September 2-9, 1975.

Frank, O. Estimation of graph totals. *Scandinavian Journal of Statistics,* 1977a, *4,* 81-89.

Frank, O.   Survey sampling in graphs, *Journal of Statistical Planning and Inference,* 1977b, 235-264.

Frank, O.   A note on Bernoulli sampling in graphs and Horvitz-Thompson estimation. *Scandinavian Journal of Statistics,* 1977c, *4,* 178-180.

Frank, O.   Sampling and estimation in large social networks. *Social Networks,* 1978a, *1,* 91-101.

Frank, O.   Estimation of the number of connected components in a graph by using a sampled subgraph. *Scandinavian Journal of Statistics,* 1978b, *5,* 177-188.

Frank, O.   Moment properties of subgraph counts in stochastic graphs, *Annals of the New York Academy of Sciences,* 1978c.

Frank, O., & Karlsson, G.   Inferences concerning interpersonal choices given anonymously, University of Lund: Department of Statistics, 1978.

Goodman, L. A.   Snowball sampling. *Annals of Mathematical Statistics,* 1961, *32,* 148-170.

Holland, P., & Leinhardt, S.   Local structure in social networks. *Sociological Methodology 1976,* Davis Heise, (Ed.), Jossey-Bass, San Francisco, 1975.

Lanke, J.   *Some contributions to the theory of survey sampling.* University of Lund, Sweden, 1975.

Proctor, C. H.   Two measurement and sampling methods for studying social networks, North Carolina State University at Raleigh: Department of Statistics, 1966.

Proctor, C. H.   The variance of an estimate of linkage density from a simple random sample of graph nodes. *Proceedings of the Social Statistics Section of the American Statistical Association,* 1967, 342-343.

Proctor, C. H., & Suwattee, P.   Some estimators, variances and variance estimators for point-cluster sampling of digraphs. North Carolina State University at Raleigh: Department of Statistics, 1970.

Sherdon, A. W. Sampling directed graphs, North Carolina State
    University at Raleigh: Department of Statistics, 1970.

Tapiero, C. S., Capobianco, M. F., & Lewin, A. Y. Structural
    inference in organizations, *Journal of Mathematical Soci-
    ology,* 1975, *4,* 121-130.

Wasserman, S. Random directed graph distributions and the triad
    census in social networks. *Journal of Mathematical Sociology,*
    1977, *5,* 61-86.

CHAPTER 17

A STUDY OF INTERLOCKING DIRECTORATES:

VITAL CONCEPTS OF ORGANIZATION

Joel H. Levine

Department of Sociology

Dartmouth College

Hanover, New Hampshire

William S. Roy[1]

Norris Cotton Cancer Center

Dartmouth College

Hanover, New Hampshire

I. INTRODUCTION

This is a study of interlocks. The major business corporations of the U.S. are linked together into cliques and subgroups
and into informal (or at least not-formally-recognized) organizations by means of interlocking directorates. For example, Equitable Life is "interlocked" with Chemical Bank by virtue of their
four common directors. For this real-world of at least putative-

[1]*Present address: Atex, Inc., Bedford, Massachusetts.*

ly significant corporations and individuals, the abstract problems are the familiar problems of structural research. We know
the pairwise links in this network but what we need to know, or
need to have, is a way of treating its global properties. We
need to know what these properties are, and we need to know how
these global properties define and effect the separate positions
of each of the members and subsets of the group.

We will begin our discussion with a brief overview of the
data on interlocks, presenting interlock data that were previously unavailable. These data are in conflict with many of the conceptual reflexes current in elite theory, and we will use the
data as a starting point from which to discuss these concepts.
We will suggest that conventional concepts--both in elite theory
and in organization theory--are counterproductive to useful research. Current structural research seems to be leading to
fundamental changes in the conventional view of these data, and
thus it poses a dilemma: From within the structuralist perspective one sees problems for which we have few methods and solutions. Yet from within this perspective there is no road block
to conventional assumptions. We will close our chapter by presenting a device that reifies elements of the structural perspective and that offers the possibility of tractable analyses
of realistically large, real-world networks.

II. OVERVIEW OF THE DATA

Our data for this analysis is an archive of interlock
data for 797 prominent corporations as they were linked during
1970-1971. The corporations include the 500 "largest" industrials, 50 commercial banks, 50 insurance companies, 50 retailers,
50 transportation companies, 50 utilities, and 47 miscellaneous
corporations that were the *Fortune* 800 for that year. The

interlock archive, which is itself an important achievement, was
compiled by two sociologists, Schwartz and Mariolis at SUNY Stony
Brook.

The archive they have established (known as BARON in its public form at Dartmouth) is important because in its absence the
study of these networks has been either blocked or badly misdi-
rected. With few exceptions (see Warner, 1967) previous researchers have limited themselves to a curious form of pseudo-
explanation and to what was only a fragment of the relevant data.
It was considered important, and perhaps sufficient, to "explain"
Richard Nixon and Lyndon Johnson by noting that their "ties"
joined them to the South and the West, to the newer aerospace and
arms industries, ties that were in contrast to "liberal Eastern
establishment" ties of a Kennedy or a Rockefeller. Such styles
of "explanation" were peculiar in that they swapped regression
for explanation: one "explained" *A* by linking it to *B* and
assumed that the well-known attributes and interests of *B* eliminated the need for further explanation. Moreover, such explanations plucked facts from their context without reference to
other links that may have existed, or to the normal run of data
from which selected facts had been produced.

At Dartmouth we have built a data management system that
begins to make subsets of these interlock data as accessible as
are the "cross-tabs" of conventional analysis. It is now possible to ask narrow questions like "what are the interlocks of
IT&T," and it is equally possible to ask unasked questions about
these directors and corporations as a whole. As we now begin
to answer these general questions, the answers begin to threaten
the very context within which the narrower questions and the
"explanations" by regression seemed to make sense. In this
chapter we will begin with some simple facts and proceed to the
facts that pose this threat.

As usual, the simplest questions concern the marginals of
the data. For example, what is the size of a typical board of
directors? A typical board might be a closet-sized group of two
or three members or it might be the size of a legislative as-
sembly (i.e., large, and therefore probably formalized, and probably differentiated into subgroups). Assembling the data, we
find that among all types of boards, a typical board of directors has 10 to 15 members: the median is 13. A typical board
is a seminar-sized group that can meet face-to-face in a "board
room." The boards range in size from 3 directors to 47; an un-
usually large board (one in the upper 5% of the distribution)
is a board of 24 or more members.

Thus, the population of 8623 directors are coalesced into 797
"small groups." A similar question is, what are the memberships
of a typical director? A typical director might belong to one
and only one board or he might be a link "incarnate," representing broad conjunctions that weave together the corporate economy. From the data on 8623 directors, a typical director (and
five-sixths of *all* dreictors) belongs to exactly one of these
boards. Only one out of 6 directors is an interlocker. However,
the distribution of memberships is highly skewed. While 82% sit
on one and only one board, 18% (1562) sit on two or more boards;
and only 20 directors (2%) reach 7 or more boards. The maximum,
achieved by one director in these data, is 11.

The surprising and, we think, unsettling overview emerges
when we inquire further into the relations among these boards.
For example, is interlocking among the leading corporations a
rare event or a common one? From the data we find that interlocking is quite common. The median number of links to other
corporations is eight. Thus, is it important or noteworthy that
DuPont, for example, is linked to 8 other corporations? The
answer is no. Eight interlocks make DuPont just a run-of-the-
mill corporation with respect to interlocks. In fact the

unusual corporation is one that is *not* interlocked to others.
Only 62 corporations have no links within the 797, while 5%
have 28 or more.

The histogram of interlocks per corporation is rather plain
and smooth, suggesting that it is essentially one population with
no sharp division between corporations that link and corporations
that do not.

The next question we have asked is, what are the sizes of the
connected networks within this overall network of 797? That is,
as the networks spin-out from one or another corporation, what
are the sizes of the groups they ultimately reach? Are we
dealing with sets of 10 to 15 corporations, or is the typical
corporation an isolate? From the data we count 62 "isolates."
There are four dyadic nets of exactly 2 corporations; there is
one triadic net of exactly 3 corporations; and then there is a
complete discontinuity in the distribution of sizes of these
sets. The next set contains all of the remaining 724 corporations and a similar proportion of all directors. Henceforth
we may dispense with the plural term "networks" in referring to
these data. The data, including most of the well-known "names,"
are essentially one connected net.

Continuing with the data, and given this one large network,
how long are the paths within it? The connectivity of the net
may extend to 724 corporations but still there is considerable
leeway for the lengths of paths within it. The paths could vary
between length 1 and length 723, counting a corp-person-corp
path as length one. The data show that the actual lengths are
at the low end of what is possible. The median path length is
3, which means that more than half (actually 62%) of all possible pairs (among the 724) are connected in paths of length 3
or less.

Thus, for a quick summary of the network of prominent corporations and of directors, one should note that the network is large only in terms of the absolute number of corporations and directors involved. The typical board of directors is a small group. The typical path length between groups and directors is short. The network of corporations and directors appears to be as intricately and tightly tied together as is a small community with its multiplicity of cross-cutting ties. This characteristic of the data is already a threat to those who would couch the study of these data in terms of narrow questions about corporations and events, for what is an outstanding corporation when the median-sized corporation has eight links?

The more serious challenge posed by these data appears when we inquire further into the texture and robustness of this network. The typical path is, as we have noted, short, but short path length is consistent with several possible patterns of organization. The organization could be tree-like, with short paths directed through common "superiors." Or, without invoking hierarchical concepts, the organization could be star-like with nodes linked to central nodes which are themselves linked to central nodes. In either case, the organization would have critical nodes, persons, or corporations upon whom the global connectivity and global shortness of paths would depend.

Alternatively, there may be no such critical nodes. The corporations and their directors could be woven together seamlessly and redundantly with no point being critical to the whole. The question we raise here is, is there an elite? That is, is there a minimal-sized subset whose absence would disrupt the comprehensive, short-linked phenomenon we have observed—and upon whom the phenomenon may be said to depend?

Having raised the question, we will have to equivocate in our answer because it is hard to define an efficient search for such a group. In rough terms, however, we may attempt to establish some reasonable bounds on the possible answer. For example, what if the banks and all their directors were withdrawn from the network? Other analyses of these data show that the banks have the largest boards and that the directors of these banks are the heavily linked directors. Do they contain within themselves an "elite"? Does the connected, redundant, short-linked phenomenon we have observed disintegrate if these corporations and directors are simultaneously removed?

Understanding that we are taking a first cut at the question, the answer is no. The largest connected component is 724 with the banks and 621 without them, down 103, 48 of which we have removed in the course of answering the question. Where several points among the 724 could reach the whole in 5 steps or less *with* the banks, several points can reach the whole 621 in 6 steps without them.

This search would have been interesting because--had it worked--we would have localized a potential elite within an interpretable subset of the data (among the banks and their directors), but the test failed.

Our second test was less delicate. One of us was determined to divide this network by brute force if necessary, and to divide it even if interpretability were a casualty of the technique. Hence we attacked the links crudely by simply counting links-- and removing the most-linked corporation and all its directors. The first removed was Equitable Life with 63 links, but only one of these 63 was thereby isolate cut from the core. The rest had "alternative" connections. Then the necessary link-statistics were recomputed for this latered net; the corporations were reranked, and again the most-linked corporation and all its directors were removed.

One of us expected this procedure to divide the network. This rather brute force division would have had little importance--had it worked--because of the non-substantive strategy

of simply removing great numbers of links. However, it would
have provided a starting point for more delicate procedures.
Yet 9 such removals left the core at 710 (down 14) and 21 such
removals (as far as we have proceeded) left the core at 681.
This too failed to break the network.

The large-graph, short-linked phenomenon we have observed
does not break up under this massive destruction of its parts.
Removing the likes of Bankamerica and Chase Manhattan does not
have an effect like breaking off the limbs of a tree. (On the
average, each node removed took only one other node from the
central net.) The network does not have such a tree-like or-
ganization(or, at least, we have not found its "trunk").

While analyzing this social net, analyzing it in the literal
sense of taking out its parts, one is reminded of physiological
psychology experiments dating back to the late 1920s and 1930s.
Some psychologists expected that specific brain functions would
be localized in specific tissues of the brain. The locales were
not known, but it seemed reasonable to search them out by surgical destruction of tissue. Instead it turned out (in Lashley's
experiments) that many functions and even much learned information could not be localized or, if destroyed, its functions
could be recovered--in time--from other areas of the brain. Re-
calling these surgical experiments, and drawing an analogy to the
simulated destruction of these real-world data, one is forced
to consider that elite networks, so-called, are a parallel phenomenon.

This destructive data analysis we have described is important because the existence of a critical set is presumed by many
studies of elites, and that presumption appears to be wrong.[2]

[2]*The destructive analysis was suggested by Bernard Segal,
while the possible analogy between this phenomenon and Lashley's
results (see review in Wolman, 1960, Chapter 3) was suggested by
John Lanzetta.*

Many studies of groups and establishments, of clubs and meeting
places, of key individuals and critical episodes, presume that
such foci are of critical importance or else why direct our attention toward them (and not toward characteristics of the whole
from which these are drawn).

This new data would seem to be an elite theorist's or a
"power researcher's" dream. Through our data management we can
ask for an instantly obtained set of affiliations spinning-out
from Exxon or from First National Boston or from the target of
one's choice; yet the answers mock such questions. Why?

III. VITALIST CONCEPTS

The problem lies in the implicit model used in trying to
understand organizations in general and "power structures" in particular. The conventional sociologist's world is populated by
actors who have attributes such as wealth and status. Not with-
standing the nineteenth century injunctions to study social facts
and social forces *sui generis*, it is people whom we interview (or
corporations on whom we obtain records), people who have opinions
and whose attributes we correlate and whose actions we predict.
Following this conventional mold, "power structure" research
isolates actors (corporeal or corporate) and highlights their
wealth or assets, their biographies or corporate histories, and
their clubs or interest groups. The temptation to think of the
social world as a world of actors is all the more tempting when
one is studying an "elite." In the nineteenth century equivalent
of the Schwartz and Mariolis data (being prepared and analyzed
by Brian Kingsbury at Dartmouth), one finds historical names like
"Morgan," "Rockefeller," "Scott," "Harriman," and "Stanford." It
is difficult *not* to give credence to the basic importance of such
actors; yet the contemporary data deny it. The contemporary data
appear to be robust under wholesale destruction of their separate
parts. The obvious importance of any one path or corporate or

personal linkage is no longer obvious, and the conventional
thinking that causes us to look at them in the first place is
under attack.

What is this conventional thinking? In *The Power Elite*,
C. Wright Mills states that, "they (the elite) are not made by
their jobs...they do not merely 'meet the demands of the day and
hour'; in some part they create these demands and cause others to
meet them (1956, p. 3)."

This viewpoint is not at all confined to the literature on
elites. In mainline organization theory such classics as
Barnard's *Functions of the Executive* partake of the same point of
view. Barnard's executive is an actor possessing free will and
the power to control the forces that will motivate and command
others; he himself does not seem to be part of the organization.
Barnard's executive is a benign demigod while Mill's elite have
more feisty personalities, but the assumptions are the same.

In the conventional view, prime-moving forces reside in these
individuals who determine and direct the forces of the ordinary
world. This model lends color to elite theory for it studies only
the most extraordinary persons and events. Yet the same assumption vitiates our ability to obtain results. How does one study
a primary force, which is exempt from rules governing ordinary
forces? How does one construct laws for behavior that is not
governed by laws of behavior? How does one know the unknowable?

Strangely, conventional elite theory and organization theory
actually try to answer these seemingly rhetorical questions. It
attempts to know the unknowable by transforming research into
espionage. Interlock data, ownership data, and observable records
are rejected because they do not contain the "essence" of what
"really" went on at the board meeting, or at the bar, or on the
golf course, or of what was said. Therefore, the research becomes tales of the great and mighty, suitably interpreted by the
researcher of his or her informant or by the great and mighty

themselves. Somehow "informants" are blessed with the ability to detect what is not directly observable. Informants, or the subjects themselves, report to us, and thus we know the directions and conflicts among the vital forces that lurk behind major events.

This research strategy is nonsense. Clearly the gross facts of economic or social determination in the United States cannot reside in events that are too subtle to be observed without the interpretation of informants. One cannot claim to be dealing with the forces that shape the lives of millions, that shape the "values" of society, and that mold the broadscale deployment of resources, and still claim that the proper arena for theory and explanation is an arena of events too subtle to be observed. Either the key terms and key concepts of social organization and elite theory have observable, clear consequences as patterns in data or else, in a scientific sense, they do not exist.

One could respond to this need for observables and to the "anomalies" we have found in these data by extending the data base. One researcher is now attempting to cope with the frustrations of the Schwartz and Mariolis data by coding power as a variable and adding it in to the data. Having failed to discover patterns that fit a model of simple, localizable power, he is now precoding the power of bank *A* over industrial *B* so that he can be sure to "discover" it the next time around.

This is a sophisticated response to the difficulties, as power and dominance will now appear as a machine-readable cipher in a data bank. However, it is really an attempt to rescue and to hang scientific trappings onto a model that violates the canons of science.

The persistent attempt to find extraordinary causal forces and to localize them in isolated circles or individuals is essentially social vitalism, more akin to medieval biology than to

research. It is as useful to tell me that "power" is localized
in the *X* club of New York or the *Y* club of Philadelphia as it is
to tell me that my soul resides in my pineal gland; the premise
is false. This analogy between the now-quaint concepts of medieval biology and current concepts of elites and organizations is
more than a shallow analogy; in some sense, the problems faced by
these two fields are the same. The underlying question of organization theory, the underlying problem that one wishes to address with the aid of interlock data is: What *is* organization?
What is this thing called "organization" that seems to settle over
individuals and acquire a life of its own? How is it that organizations appear to develop purpose that cannot be ascribed to
each of the individual participants?

Biologists after Aristotle faced a similar question. They
asked, what is life? What is it that overtakes ordinary matter
and causes it to be organized? What causes it to acquire "purpose" and what causes life to evade--as was once thought--the laws
that should apply to the separate elements of which it is composed? Organization theory may well adopt a biological metaphor.

An extended passage from Bertrand Russell's monograph on
Power (1938) is a clear statement of this position. This phi-
lospher's statement differs from a sociologist's statement only
in its embarrassing lack of quantification. In a chapter titled
"The Biology of Organizations," Russell wrote:

We come now to...the study of the organizations through which
power is exercised, considered first as organisms with a life
of their own...The subject..., namely the biology of organizations, depends upon the fact that an organization is also
an organism, with a life of its own, and a tendency to
growth and decay.

Thus Russell chose the biological model and stated some of his
reasons. He continues:

An organization is a set of people who are combined in virtue of activities directed to common ends...The purpose...may
be explicit or unexpressed, conscious or unconscious; it may
be military or political, economic or religious, educational
or athletic, and so on. Every organization, whatever its
character and whatever its purpose, involves some redistri-
bution of power...Owing to the love of power which is to be
expected in those who acquire governmental posts, every organization will, in the absence of any counteracting force,
tend to grow both in size and in density of power...growth
in size is only stopped either by the pressure of other
organizations, or by the organization in question becoming
world-wide; and the growth in density is only stopped where
love of personal independence becomes overwhelmingly strong.
(1938, Chap. 11).

This is pure social vitalism. Vitalism was Aristotle's solution to the problem of life: He simply invoked an unseen force
that was able to come upon ordinary matter from the outside--like
the breath of a God outside nature--and exempt it from the ordinary laws.

Conventional elite studies and organization theory adopt the
same appeal to unseen forces when they begin by exempting key
actors and executives from the play of ordinary forces. Note,
with Russell, that we are to study "organization through which
power is exercised." Thus, power is awarded an independent
existence. Note that organizations redistribute power, suggesting
that power has an original "state of nature" as well as an independent existence.

Russell tells us that an "organization is a set of people who
are combined in virtue of activity directed to common ends, and
he hedges by stating that the common ends may be either explicit
or unexpressed, which is to say that no purpose is present whether

we observe it or not. He explains growth by a "love of power,"
decay by a "love of liberty" and competition by the collision of
vital forces.

   This glamorous insistence on the free will and individualized
separate importance of key individuals is the kind of solution
that crippled biology: It kept researchers from looking for a
structured circulatory system until Harvey, and it kept them from
looking for an observable nervous system until Helmholtz. After
all, there was no need for profane observables (in fact, it was
argued that the *observables* did not exist) when the intentions of
the vital force could be invoked.

   Vitalistic research into elites and power looks for key units
characterized by attributes and interest, the essence of which is
supposed to remove any need for further explanation, but vital
concepts of organization should be as unnecessary in elite and
organization studies as they are in biology. Let us look at the
facts we have to work with. Interlock data are surely not "all
one could ask for" in the study of elites and of the social organization of economic power. But the difficulties encountered
in the use of these data are intrinsic to the study of social
networks "in vivo" and, thus, need to be dealt with. Even
in the structure of the database, the interlock data defy conventional methods. The new Schwartz and Mariolis data base describes 797 corporations and 8623 people. If this were a standard database, we could ask: What is the unit of analysis? What
is the sample? How many variables were measured on each unit of
analysis and were the measures valid? But the standard questions
and the standard paradigm that they presume do not readily fit.
Neither the corporations nor the persons can be isolated as the
unit of analysis, and there are no variables in the common sense.
The data have a basic symmetry that does not have a parallel in
conventional "subject by variable" data arrays. Persons are links

among corporations; corporations are links among persons; neither is subordinate to the other. A board of directors is the set of persons who constitute it; and a person is the boards on which he sits. The interlock data per se are silent on the difference between persons and corporations. One solution (Breiger, 1975) is to straddle the problem by making both choices. Interlock data are silent and provide no precoding of direction. If one thinks that person P functions as an intermediary *from* A directed *toward* B (and not vice versa), then the point needs to be argued analytically and not by precoding that A is more powerful. Interlock data also provide no precoding of strength: A person either belongs to a board or does not. Any imputation of strength must be inferred and justified by the analyst: it cannot be evaded by reference to informants. The reality described by the data knows no natural boundary. This is not a 5-person, or 20-person, or 200-person group. The data describe 797 corporations and 8623 people, most of whom form a single net that has no obvious boundary (except as imposed by these data). These are the problems that one buys with structural analysis of real-world data. Interlock data offer no empirical distinction between "nonlinks" that are data and "nonlinks" that are missing data. Among the 7 major U.S. oil corporations, for example, there are no directorate interlocks (1970 data). Are the links suppressed (because of antitrust law); are the links nonexistent; are there missing data? We submit that these difficulties are intrinsic to elite and power structure research. They will not be solved by deferring them until larger and more subtle data archives become available, nor can we retreat to the more glamorous studies of powerful persons and interests. The unavoidable problem lies in the fact that conventional methods have become inadequate as a framework within which to study organization, while adequate new concepts have yet to emerge.

IV.   THE WHOLE AND THE PARTS: AN ANALYTICAL ENGINE FOR NETWORKS

Our overview discloses a well-linked phenomenon in which
interlocks draw most of the persons and corporations into a
single net, an overview in which linking is a common event and in
which the paths are short and repetitive so as to diminish the
global importance of any critical subset. Faced with this overview, we have then commented on the framework that would have led
one to expect otherwise, commenting on vitalistic assumptions
that try to localize key units whose attributes give force to
(and "explain") the whole. We find these conventional assumptions are a poor fit. Even such apparently atheoretical questions as "What is your unit of analysis?" and "What are the
variables that describe it?" are difficult to match up against
the phenomenon.

We would *like* to close our chapter by supplying the requi-
site new and sufficient framework for all further research. However, failing that, we will present a physical model that is at
once a physical demonstration of network attributes and also an
analytical engine for working out their implications. The device
is above all pedagogically sound: It clearly demonstrates how
one can proceed without atomizing a phenomenon into units and
variables; and it demonstrates quite naturally how global properties can define the separate positions of subsets of the
group.

In its physical form, the device is a rectangle featuring
two horizontal bars and two supporting members. A collection of
"hooks" represents corporate and personal nodes in the network
(two sets of paper clips will suffice), one set being supported
by each of the bars. Finally, the device is completed by a set
of flexible bands that join the appropriate hooks and physically
represent the inclusion between persons and boards.

The model does not subordinate persons to corporations; there is no obvious "unit of analysis" and there are no conventional variables, demonstrating that a model can function without them. It turns the absence of "strengths" to computational advantage, it achieves some robustness to the distinction between nonreported and nonexistent links, and it appears to accept very large sets of data. (When analyzing a thousand or more points, it becomes impractical to deal with large multiplication tables as in the early White and Lorrain models (1971) or inventories of all three-point subsets as in the Davis, Leinhardt, Holland techniques (see review by Davis in this proceedings); and one cannot even perform the matrix inversion algorithms of factor analytical or smallest space techniques.)

The dynamic of the apparatus lies in the relation between the bands and the positions of the points. The local tensions exerted by the bands convert the individual links into a global configuration.

Figure 1 is a small set of data including the first 5 *Fortune* industrials, 2 of the first 3 banks (the first bank, Bankamerica, is not connected to this subset), and the 10 directors who sit on 2 or more of these 7 boards. In Figure 2, Frame 0, the same data are "physically" represented on the model. In this computer simulation of the device, the "corporations" are at the top and the "directors" are at the bottom. The tangle of lines between them represents the rubber band membership ties (for example, persons 5 and 10 are members of board 4). In Frame 1 the machine has been allowed to move; each corporation and each person has been moved as dictated by local tensions to which it is individually subject. (After each round of changes the coordinates have been rescaled to have zero mean and unit variance.) In Frame 1 some signs of a pattern begin to emerge.

BARON	1 GEN. MOTOR	2 STAND. OIL	3 FORD MOTOR	4 GEN. ELECT	5 INT. BUSIN	6 FIRST NAT.	7 CHASE MANH
1 CONNOR JOHN T	X					X	
2 HOUGHTON AMORY JR					X	X	
3 JAMIESON J K		X				X	
4 KAPPEL FREDERICK R		X				X	
5 LAZARUS RALPH				X		X	
6 LEARSON T VINCE		X			X		
7 MORTIMER CHARLES G			X			X	
8 OELMAN ROBERT S			X			X	
9 WILLIAMS ALBERT L	X				X	X	
10 WRISTON WALTER B				X		X	

Fig. 1. *Person by corporation links for 7 corporations and 10 persons.*

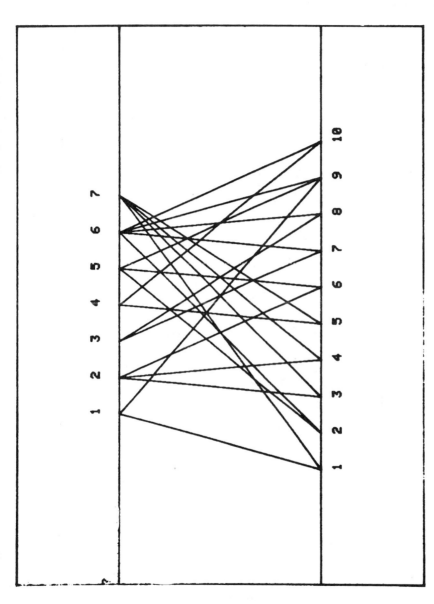

Fig. 2. Frame 0. Starting configuration for 7 corporations, 10 persons, and 21 links as presented in Fig. 1.

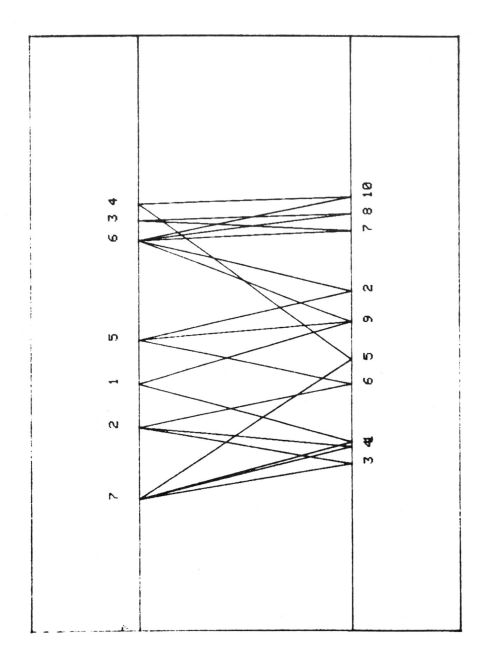

Fig. 2. Frame 1.

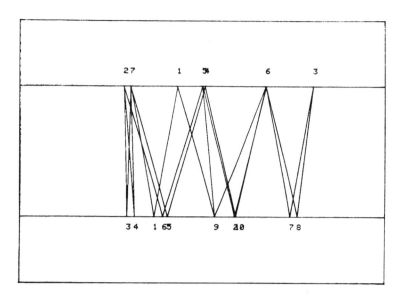

Fig. 2. Frame 5.

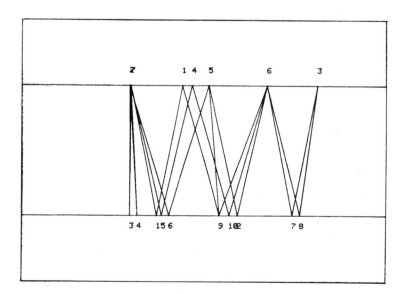

Fig. 2. Frame 15.

As we continue the process the patterns take form, organizing the corporations and persons together as dictated by their ties. By the fifth frame the ties look more organized than in Frame 1. They are more nearly vertical and there are relatively few that span any considerable horizontal distance. By Frame 5 both directors and corporations are beginning to differentiate into neighborhoods, and we have terminated the process arbitrarily at the fifteenths frame. Inspecting the fifteenth frame, we now know that in global terms Standard of New Jersey is more like Chase Manhattan than like IBM, and structurally Jamieson is more like Kappel than like Lazarus or Connor. Chase and Standard are indicated to be equivalent in this solution, while GM, GE, and IBM are on the paths between Chase/Standard and First National City. The arrangement is surprisingly orderly in the sense of being chain-like with no links unduly stretched from one distant point to another.

Even this small network partakes of some of the characteristics of the full data. The graph of this solution, shown in Figure 3, is surprisingly devoid of critical points, much like the robust whole we examined earlier. There is no one link whose absence would globally disrupt the pattern of even this small network. There is only one single-point whose absence would sever the net (First National City); there are 2 sets of two that could do it (Chase/Standard and Mortimer/Oelman) and 3 sets of three whose removal would disrupt the connectivity.

Figure 4 is a more extended example based on 7 oil companies, plus the 19 companies that are linked to 2 or more of the 7, plus the 49 directors who are linked to 2 or more of these 29 companies. Figure 5, Frame 0 is the start. By Frame 5, 2 corporations have clearly separated from the rest; the number of links is high, but the pattern distinguishes them (Texaco and Freeport Sulphur). In Frame 40 a second small group is becoming differentiated from the main group and is moving toward the already differentiated 2.

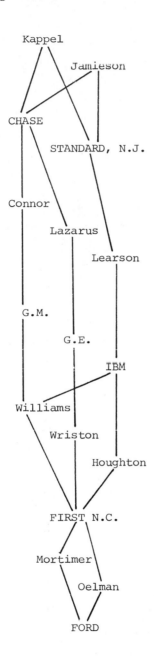

Fig. 3. Labeled graph of Figure 2, Frame 15.

BARON	1	2	3	4	5	6	7	8	9	10	11	12	13	14	15	16	17	18	19	20	21	22	23	24	25	26
1 APPLEY LAWRENCE A												X			λ											
2 BALDWIN E COLIN											X	X														X
3 BARKER ROBINSON F													X												X	
4 BEEGHLY CHARLES M					X								X												X	
5 BLACKIE WILLIAM								X	X									X								
6 BOYER WILLIS B												X													X	
7 BROCKETT ERNEST I							λ																	λ		
8 BURKE ARLEIGH					X													X				X				
9 CONNOR JOHN T	X									X													X			
10 COOK CHAUNCEY W										X												X				
11 DAVIES PAUL L SR		λ						X																		
12 DENTON FRANK R						λ								X										X		
13 DORSEY B R						λ		X																		
14 FRANKLIN W H		λ							X																	
15 FUNSTON G KEITH			X									X												X		X
16 GLENNAN T KEITH											λ	X														
17 GWINN WILLIAM P								X											λ							
18 HARPER JOHN D JR																								λ		X
19 HARRIS HENRY U P J					X																		X			
20 HOUGHTON AMORY JR		X																			λ					
21 HUMPHREY GILBERT				λ														λ							λ	
22 JAMIESON J K	X																		X							
23 JENKINS GEORGE P																		λ								λ
24 KAPPEL FREDERICK		λ							λ													X				λ
25 KIRK GRAYSON L			λ	X																						
26 LAPHAM LEWIS A				X										λ												
27 LEARSON T VINCE	X		λ															X					X			
28 LONG AUGUSTUS C				X																X			X			
29 LUCKS ROY G						λ											X									
30 MARTING WALTER A																				λ					λ	
31 MAYER JOHN F	X										λ													λ		
32 MCLAUGHLIN W EARL I	X																									X
33 MELLON RICHARD K	X					λ					λ												λ			
34 MOORE WILLIAM H		X																X								
35 MORSE ROBERT W													X		X											X
36 MORTIMER CHARLES			X								X										λ					
37 NEWMAN J WILSO						λ																	X			
38 NICKERSON ALBERT			X																							λ
39 PATTON THOMAS F											X															λ
40 PEARSON NATHAN W					λ				X							X	X	X								
41 PEET E CHEST						λ						λ														
42 RAMBIN J HO JR				X															X							
43 SHEPARD HORACE A												X		X												
44 SPAHR CHARLES E											X	λ													λ	
45 TULLIS RICHARD B													X												λ	
46 WILLIAMS ALBERT II	X		X	X								X										X				
47 WILLIAMS LANGBOUR				X																		X				
48 WRIGHT JOHN DAVII												X													λ	
49 WYCKOFF GEORGE W																		X						X		

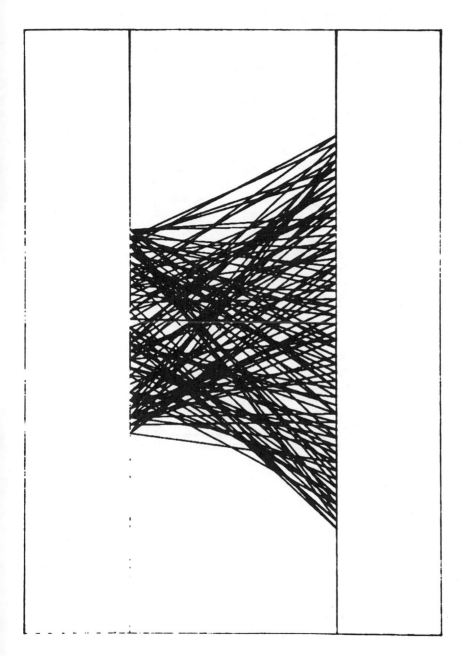

Fig. 5. Frame 0. Starting configuration for 49 persons, 26 corporations, and 124 links as presented in Fig. 4.

← *Fig. 4. Extended example: person by corporation links for 49 persons and 26 corporations including 7 oil companies.*

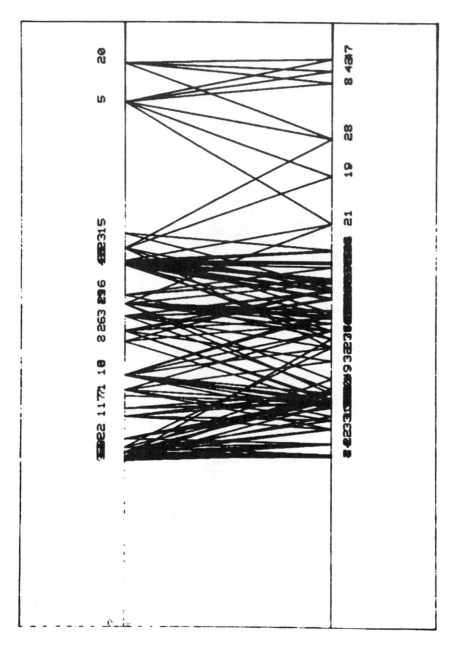

Fig. 5. Frame 5.

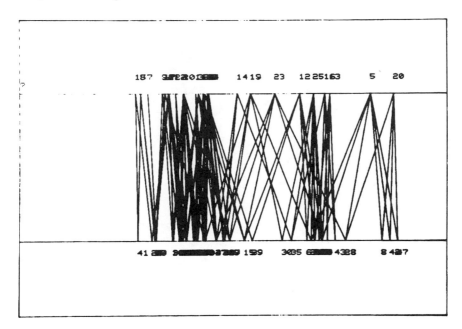

Fig. 5. Frame 40.

(The process was terminated at 320, which was indistinguishable
from 160.) In this limited example, the network, while still
highly connected, begins to show internal structure: differ-
entiating a Cleveland/mid-South group (Standard of Ohio, Texaco)
from the remainder (particularly Gulf, Standard of New Jersey,
and Mobil), and leaving a "thin" bridging network between them
including Chemical Bank (N.Y.), Hanna Mining (Cleveland), PPG
Industries (Pittsburgh), G. Keith Funston (Connecticut), and
Thomas F. Patton (Ohio).

The device is somewhat robust under the distinction between
nonlinks and missing data because positions are determined by
the symmetry of pulls; the device can thus imply the proximity
of two points without imposing direct links. When one builds the
device physically, one can quite literally feel the tensions between the whole and the parts.

We are now extending the device (in simulation) to "realistically" large data sets. Ordinary matrix-based techniques for
these data--anything requiring manipulation of a 700 by 8000 array

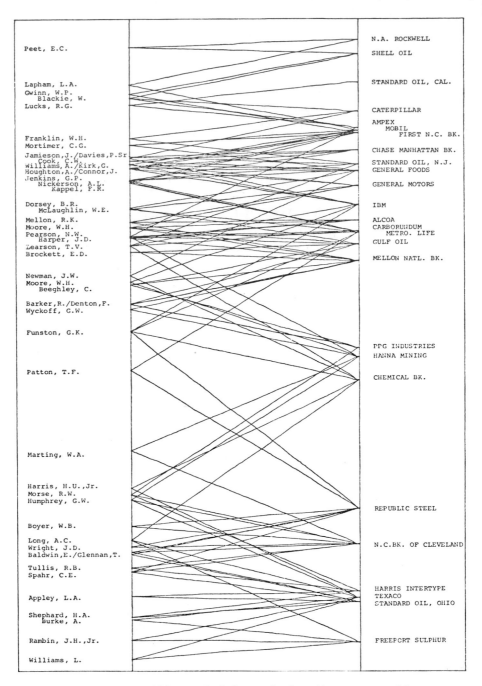

Fig. 5. Frame 320. Labeled graph for 49 persons, 26 corporations, and 124 links.

by formal matrix techniques--would be out of the question. (Network analysts are notorious for exhausting either the accuracy of their computing machines or the capacity of their budgets.) Yet the rubber band model generalizes rather easily, posing conceptual problems, to be sure, but allowing us to formalize and inquire of the formal properties of this large scale social network.

ACKNOWLEDGMENTS

We wish to thank the staff of Project IMPRESS and Edmund D. Meyers, Jr. for their suggestions and generous support of the computations required for this work. We are indebted to Bruce Backa, John Lanzetta, David Miller, Bernard Segal, and Joan Smith for comments on preliminary analyses and on earlier drafts.

REFERENCES

Barnard, Chester I. *The functions of the executive*. Cambridge, Massachusetts: Harvard University Press, 1938.

Breiger, R. L. Duality of persons and groups. *Social Forces*, 1974, *53 (2)*, 181.

Fortune, May-June Directory Issues, 1971.

Levine, Joel, & Roy, William S. Documentation of BARON archive and time-shared data management for the Schwartz and Mariolis data, March 1974 and updates.

Mills, C. Wright. *The power elite*. London and New York: Oxford University Press, 1956.

Russell, Bertrand, *Power*. New York: Barnes & Noble, Inc., 1963. (First published by Unwin Books, London, 1938).

Schwartz, Michael, & Mariolis, Peter. Data archive tapes available through Prof. Schwartz at Dept. of Sociology, SUNY, Stony Brook.

Warner, W. Lloyd (Ed.). *The emergent American society,* Vol. l,
    Chapter 5. New Haven, Connecticut: Yale University Press,
    1967.

Wellman, Barry, & Craven, P. The network city. *Sociological
    Inquiry,* 1974, *43 (3-4),* 57.

White, H. C., & Lorrain, F. Structural equivalence of individuals
    in social networks. *Journal of Mathematical Sociology,*
    1 (1), 49.

Wolman, Benjamin A. *Contemporary theories and systems in psychol-
    ogy.* New York: Harper, 1960.

CHAPTER 18

NETWORK ANALYSIS IN LARGE SOCIAL SYSTEMS:

SOME THEORETICAL AND METHODOLOGICAL PROBLEMS

Edward O. Laumann

Department of Sociology

University of Chicago

Chicago, Illinois

I. INTRODUCTION

For the past 5 or 6 years, my colleagues and I (see Laumann and Pappi, 1976) have been interested in developing theoretical and methodological strategies for studying the differentiation and integration of large-scale, complex social systems. Although formulated during an intensive case study of a community's collective decision-making process, these strategies should prove generally useful in investigating complex social systems that are confronted with the central integrative problem of establishing priorities among competing sets of ends (or goals) which require the expenditure of scarce resources (means), given that the component actors possess competing standards for evaluating these alternatives.

379

"Copyright © 1979 by the Center for Advanced Study in the Behavioral Sciences. Permission for reproduction in any form must be obtained from Academic Press, Inc." ISBN 0-12-352550-0

We have adopted a *freely interpreted* version of the action
scheme developed by Talcott Parsons and his students over the
past 25 years as an orienting framework.[1] Especially helpful are
elaborations of this scheme with respect to the structural and
functional differentiation of societies according to the AGIL
paradigm and the treatment of money, power, influence, and commitment as integrative mechanisms in complex societies (cf. Parsons,
1951, 1960, 1966, 1969; Parsons and Smelser, 1956). The phrase
"freely interpreted" should be emphasized since Parsons' dicta
were not always rigorously followed because they seemed unneces-
sarily restrictive or wrong on substantive grounds or they eluded
efforts to operationalize them.

Our approach assumes wholehearted endorsement of Parsons'
assumption that social systems must be treated as open-ended
rather than closed systems. That is, social systems are analytically distinguishable from their environments, which consist
primarily of other social systems. The systems maintain continuing and essential transactions of needed resources (i.e.,
inputs) and outputs with one another. These transactions serve
two purposes: They can serve to maintain the internal arrangements among a system's components (i.e., its structure); or they
can alter the system's structure. Changes in structure may also
be caused by a variety of intrasystem processes. Parsons also
asserts that structural differentiation of a social system tends

[1]*To be sure, Parsons' approach can be seen to be an important
variant of an emerging "systems perspective" on social phenomena
that has multiple roots in cybernetics, economics, and related
social sciences as well as in the life and physical sciences (cf.
Buckley, 1967; Katz and Kahn, 1966; Sztompka, 1974). We have chosen to follow Parsons' formulations primarily because they are the
most self-consciously articulated with respect to the analysis of
social systems.*

over time to lead to subsystems that perform more functionally specialized roles for the larger system. Moreover, the transactions between the subsystems (which may be treated as systems in their own right) serve to regulate the levels of activities of the subsystems.

Parsons claims that his scheme is analytic and abstract by design and, consequently, a given empirical phenomenon cannot be equated on a strict one-to-one basis to his analytic scheme. In other words, a given empirical phenomenon may be treated in radically different ways, depending on the investigator's analytic purposes in following a Parsonian approach. But to maintain this distinction between the analytic and the real is very difficult in practice especially when Parsons himself has provided so few operational rules to guide the empirical investigator. It is precisely this difficulty of building operational bridges from Parsons' highly abstract formulations to the real world that has led so many of us simply to abandon trying to do anything with the scheme, despite its obvious attractions as one of the few systematically coherent, comprehensive approaches to the study of social systems. I propose to use the scheme as a sensitizing framework that orients us to problems that might otherwise be overlooked.

Because Parsons has tended to mute the discussion of social conflict in the development of his theoretical apparatus, we have found it useful to turn to theorists who are much more explicit in dealing with the sources of structural differentiation in conflicts of interests arising from the division of labor and the unequal distribution of power and authority (cf. Dahrendorf, 1968; Ossowski, 1963; Lenski, 1966; Giddens, 1973; Sztompka, 1974). One might say that Parsons directs our attention to social values as channeling social behavior toward certain ends and to the possibility that these values may be in conflict with one another. The so-called "conflict" theorists, on the other hand, remind us of the importance of real differences of interest resting on the

division of labor (e.g., the class structure in the Marxian sense)
and differential power and influence in accounting for recurrent
conflicts in large-scale complex social systems.

It can therefore be argued that large-scale systems are
usually differentiated on at least two axes or dimensions of potential cleavage and/or social differentiation. The first, which
I call the adaptive axis, refers to the extent and character of
the division of labor in the system that results in a number of
population subgroups who differ greatly from one another in their
characteristic round of daily work activities and the corresponding rewards and privileges associated with these occupational
activities. For societal social systems, this roughly corresponds
to Weber's treatment of the economic class structure. It is here
that discussions of objective interest differentiation have
special relevance.

The second dimension, which I call the pattern/maintenance
axis, refers to the differentiation of the population into subgroups holding distinctive social values regarding the desirable
or ideal states of the social system of which they are members.
The bases for differentiation of value commitments in a population
are varied and may depend on the degree to which given population
subgroups form distinctive groupings that prefer to confine
intimate social interaction among themselves (cf. Laumann, 1973;
Pappi, 1973; Pappi and Laumann, 1975). Two bases for differentiation are, however, especially noteworthy. The first is membership
is what Weber called status groups resting on various ascriptive
membership criteria, such as age, religion, ethnicity, place of
residence, and race. The second is membership in distinctive
population subgroups resting on the division of labor that may
develop distinctive value preferences, for example, a working
class subculture.

II. PRINCIPLES OF STRUCTURAL ANALYSIS

The preceding abstract discussion can be related to networks by observing that the first theoretical and methodological task in studying system differentiation and integration is to devise a replicatable and falsifiable way to answer the question: How is a given social system differentiated? It is obviously logically prior to studying how systems solve the integrative problem. Unfortunately, there can be no unique answer to the question of system differentiation because a system may be differentiated in any number of ways, depending on the questions the analyst is interested in answering. The evident importance of certain bases of structural differentiation in a social system--evident, that is, both to the members and to the observer--reduces the apparent arbitrary nature of the analysis.

Much of what we have been most interested in, then, has to do with what I call social structural analysis. Structure and various descriptive terms about structure, such as hierarchy, dominance, structural differentiation, structural change, power or class structure, and so on, are probably the most popular concepts in the sociological lexicon. Despite the many differences in nuance associated with the term "structure," the root meaning refers to a persisting order or pattern of relationships among some units of analysis, be they individual actors, classes of actors, or even behavioral patterns (cf. Nadel, 1957: 1-19; Levi-Strauss, 1963; Mayhew, 1971; Blau, 1974, 1975). The apparent consensus in the usage of the term masks the unfortunate fact that there is little agreement on the concepts and the methodology whereby one measures or describes given "social structures." But without some way of describing structure, we cannot begin to study the more fascinating problem of structural change.

A. *Elements of Social Structures*

Many of the empirical results we have obtained are based on
new procedures for describing social structures and their principles of organization. These procedures allow us to describe
relations between structures and to account for particular
collective decision-making processes and outcomes. In analyzing
a social system, we identify the individual *actors* (be they actual
persons, corporate actors, or sets of actors) *in* particular kinds
of *social positions* comprising that social system (cf. Parsons,
1951). It is important to bear in mind the distinction between
an *incumbent* and a *social position* inasmuch as an incumbent of
a given social position may simultaneously occupy many other
positions. An earlier formulation of these distinctions further
argued:

> ...At this stage of theoretical development it is impossible
> to relate a given individual's set of unique social positions
> in society (with respect to his manifold role relations
> with specific other family members, neighbors, work
> partners in a particular firm, and so on) to another
> individual's set of unique positions. We are forced
> for analytic purposes to categorize social positions into
> aggregates that hopefully share a sufficiently common core
> of performance requirements so that the positions may be
> treated as more or less equivalent. Consequently, since
> we will be discussing a complex urban social system, the
> individual's set of social positions will be characterized
> categorically, that is, in terms of his group memberships
> and social attributes, such as religious affiliation (in-
> cluding his denomination), ethnic origin, occupation, and
> the like. In short, a person's social position locates him
> with respect to others in the community within some socially
> defined and differentiated domain (Laumann, 1973, p. 3).

A *social structure* is a persisting pattern of social relationships among social positions (see Laumann, 1966). A *social
relationship* is any direct or indirect linkage between incumbents
of different social positions that involves mutual but not
necessarily symmetric orientations of a positive, neutral, or
negative affectual character and/or may involve the exchange of
goods, services, commands, or information (see Homans, 1961;
Parsons, 1951; Blau, 1964). The unit of structural analysis is,
then, the specific relationship obtaining between any pair of
actors, as previously defined. The absence of the specified
relationship between a pair is as theoretically important as its
presence.

B. Postulates of Structural Analysis

In Laumann (1973) the analysis was confined to interpersonal
ties of intimacy. We have achieved a new generalization of this
approach by adopting three postulates.

*Postulate I (Relationship-specific Structures):
There exists a multiplicity of social structures in any
complex social system that arises out of the many possible
types of social relationships linking social positions to
one another.*

Social positions are arranged with respect to one another as a
function of the pattern of social relationships directly and indirectly linking them. Those that would be close together in one
social structure can be "far apart" in another. In short,
relationship-specific structures arrange positions in quite
different patterns of association, and there is no inherent
theoretical reason to suppose that these different patterns are to
be regarded as more or less adequate approximations of *the* "true"
underlying social structure. On the contrary, each structure may
be thought of as reflecting its own logic of social and functional
constraint. For example, the social structure of intimate

association among social positions has no logically necessary
effect on the social structure of political dominance (although
one might anticipate some empirical correspondence between the
two). Note that this postulate does not preclude the formulation
of a theory of structural priority that would hold, as in certain
Marxian formulations, that certain types of relationship structures are more fundamental (in the sense of formative) than
others.

> *Postulate II: (Distance-generation Mechanism):*
> *For any given relationship-specific structure, there*
> *exists a principle of systematic bias in the formation*
> *of relationships between certain kinds of positions and*
> *the avoidance of such relationships between others.*

In other words, we assume that relationships among social positions are not formed on a random or chance basis, but in accord
with some principle of differentiation among positions. When
discussing the distance-generating mechanism for social structures
of intimate association, for example, I argued that:

> Similarities in status, attitudes, beliefs, and behavior
> facilitate the formation of intimate (or consensual)
> relationships among incumbents of social positions.

And conversely, that:

> The more dissimilar two positions are in status, attitudes,
> beliefs, and behavior of their incumbents, the less likely
> the formation of intimate (or consensual) relationships and,
> consequently, the "farther away" they are from one another
> in the structure (Laumann, 1973, p. 5).

I was then able to interpret the relative proximities among
various ethnoreligious groups by pointing to their differentiation
in relative social prestige, socioeconomic status, and commitment
to religiously linked activities.

By Postulate II I am merely asserting that there exists some distance-generating mechanism that arranges the relative proximities of positions for every social relationship. The nature of this mechanism can differ from one type of relationship to another. For instance, the distance-generating mechanism for a structure involving actors' work contacts outside their immediate circles of co-workers need not depend on shared social values, as would be the case for the intimacy structure, but would depend on instrumentally required contacts for the execution of work. Whatever the specific distance-generating mechanism is, it constitutes what I call a *principle of organization* of a social structure.

Postulate III (Structural Contradictions):
Given a multiplicity of relationship-specific structures
with different principles of organization, structural con-
tradictions may occur.

A structural contradiction exists when the relative proximities of social positions in a given relationship-specific social structure are negatively correlated with those of another structure. In other words, positions in close proximity in one structure are far apart in another. When, in a given social system, several functionally significant social structures result in similar arrangements of positions, then the social system is *structurally crystallized*.

Structural crystallization may have serious *negative* implications for the overall functional integration of the system because all of the various relationship structures will tend to place the same positions either close together or far apart. One result would be that disparate positions (i.e., positions some distance from another) would have very limited links to one another through which to communicate and coordinate their respective needs or claims on the system as a whole. In short, a structurally crystallized system tends to be

characterized by groupings of similarly circumstanced positions
with respect to their patterns of forming various relationships,
with the groupings themselves located at some distance from one
another. One can readily see how the postulate of structural
contradictions may be linked to the classic discussions in political sociology of cross-cutting versus reinforcing societal
cleavages and cross-pressures on voting decisions (cf. Lazarsfeld
et al., 1944; Lipset, 1963a, 1963b).

Summarizing, structural differentiation of large-scale complex
social systems has two fundamental implications for system integration. First, structural differentiation is the basis both
of the differentiation of claims for scarce goods, services, and
facilities that system elements make on the social system and of
the differentiation of the means by which they assert these
claims. Second, structural differentiation leads to the differentiation of values that are used by the various system elements
to specify and establish priorities among competing ends or goals.
With these implications in mind, it is possible to discuss the
integrative question: How do social systems set priorities?

Our approach to this question is in the tradition of what
can be termed social choice models. These are characterized by:
(i) their assumption of greater intentionality on the part of the
component actors in their efforts to influence collective (system-
level) decision, (ii) their recognition that component actors may
have greater or lesser impact on the determination of the outcome
of particular collective decisions, and (iii) their willingness
to admit the possibility of a number of component actors acting
in concert to influence such decisions through bargaining and
other political procedures.

Social choice models recognize, at least in principle, the
importance of both the population, the elite, and the significance
of examining the relationships between them to account for system
integration.

We have chosen to work within the broad framework of "social choice" models because they offer a rich range of research questions both with regard to the differentiation of two subsystems, the population and its elite, and their interrelationships. We recognize that in doing so we pay the price of having to work with a very complex model that requires specification of two subsystems, the population and its elite, as well as their interrelationships.

III. AN EMPIRICAL EXAMPLE: COMMUNITY DECISION MAKING

A. Some Background

Given this perspective, the question naturally arises: How can these issues be explored empirically? Research on community decision making is an especially attractive topic for at least four reasons. First, as will become apparent, there are obvious analogues between our theoretical concerns and the sorts of issues that have attracted considerable research on community decision making. We are thus able to build on past research. Second, suitably chosen, the research site can be of sufficient complexity and scale to provide a substantial empirical confrontation of our theoretical distinctions regarding structural differentiation and integration. Third, a site can be selected that will fit current analytic capacities. Finally, the community and its elite is an especially attractive research site since it can be studied by a small research staff with limited budget and time.

B. A Heuristic Model for Studying Community Social Systems

Even a cursory review of the literature on community decision making (cf. Clark, 1968a, 1973; Aiken and Mott, 1970; Bonjean *et al.*, 1971) reveals a number of promising developments. After years of rancorous conflict over the "best" way to study the

subject (cf. Walton, 1966a, 1966b) and the relative merits of
ruling elite and pluralist models of the elite subsystem (e.g.,
Polsby, 1963), investigators have begun to assess alternative
assumptions and strategies in designing new studies. The emphasis
of the 1950s and early 1960s on qualitative case studies,
following the classic leads of Hunter (1953) and Dahl (1961), has
shifted to comparative and quantitative questions in which investigators try to study as many communities as possible, using a
wide range of quantitative data.

    A fairly explicit theoretical model that is quite compatible
with our approach is an open-ended system or input-throughput-
output-feedback model of community decision making (cf. Clark,
1968b, 1968c, 1968d, 1973). Schematized in Figure 1, this
model posits, first, that certain features of communities, including their population size and stability, regional location, age
of community, industrial and economic base, and occupational and
ethnoreligious heterogeneity, act both as inputs by facilitating
and constraining community resources in collective enterprises
and as bases of structural differentiation of the community's
population. Together with attributes of the communities' political institutions, these inputs are, in turn, associated with or
determine certain features of their decision making apparatus,
such as the degree of centralization or diffusion of decision
making (i.e., "throughput" or, the internal organization of the
elite subsystem. Finally, these determine how and which issues
will be brought to decision and with what outcomes (i.e., policy
"outputs" of the elite subsystem), which may, of course, have
"feedback" effects sustaining or modifying the structures of the
community and the elite subsystems and their interface.

    Since "hard" data on inputs and outputs are more readily
available and seemingly less ambiguous than information regarding
the nature of the decision making apparatus itself, the tendency
has been to treat the throughput or "elite decision making core"
as a relatively unobservable "black box" about which only

inferences or approximations can be made. For us, of course, examining this black box in some detail is a central task. We are particularly interested in specifying the nature of social structural differentiation among the rank-and-file members of the community social system.

We believe that coalition formation, resource mobilization, differential activation of persons and corporate groups in different decision making situations, and modes of network formation and degeneration are processes that occur in all differentiated systems in the course of integration, regardless of system scale. By closely observing these processes in a particular system and devising replicatable and falsifiable techniques for doing so, we can gain insight into how they operate more generally and thereby fashion tools of broader applicability.

IV. NETWORK ANALYSIS

A. *General Remarks*

Close examination reveals that network analysis is, at least in part, some rather old ideas that have been refurbished and made more attractive by being combined with sophisticated mathematical and quantitative tools (i.e., sophisticated for sociology and anthropology). The novelty of the contemporary interest lies in its efforts to apply the concept rigorously. Mitchell credits J. A. Barnes (1954) for having raised "...the notion of social network...from a metaphorical to a conceptual statement about social relationships in social situations (1974, p. 280)."

Mitchell has proposed a useful working definition of a *social network* with which to start: "...a specific set of linkages among a defined set of persons, with the additional property that the characteristics of these linkages as a whole may be used to interpret the social behavior of the persons involved (1969, p. 2)." Unfortunately, this definition would not permit a network analysis of social systems of any appreciable size.

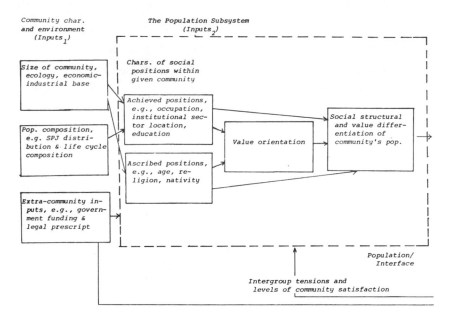

Fig. 1. An input-throughput-output-feedback model for the analysis
         of community decision making systems.

A social network was therefore redefined as a set of *nodes*
(e.g., persons) linked by a set of *social relationships* (i.e.,
Mitchell's linkages) of a specified *type*. In addition, Mitchell's
definition was relaxed in two critical respects:

The first concerns the definition of the nodes. Specifically,
entities other than Mitchell's "real" persons, for example,
corporate actors like business firms or aggregates of persons
sharing a particular attribute like ethnic or class groups, can
act as nodes. Nodes so constructed are called "generalized
social positions." This permits the collection of a number of
persons into a given node and thus reduces the number of nodes to
a manageable number even for very large populations of persons.
The second relaxation of Mitchell's definition concerns the treatment of a social relationship or linkage. What he quite clearly
has in mind is a concrete, observable transaction or exchange.
This notion is obviously unsuited for dealing with large, complex
systems.

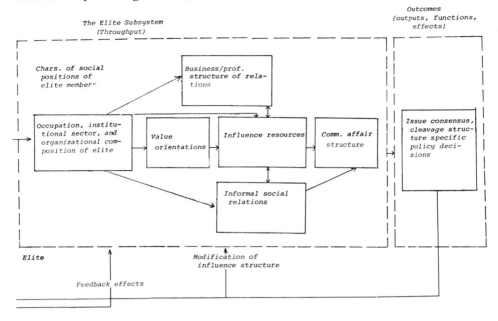

But how is one to infer the presence of links between nodes
that are comprised of complex, nonobservable entities like ethnic
or class groups? One solution is to relativize the notion of a
concrete social relationship, like friendship, work partners, or
marriage, into a stochastic relationship. Consider the "relation"
between two complex entities indicated by the differential likelihood of their constituent elements having the relationship in
question with one another. For example, members of the Protestant
working class (PWC) node may be more likely to marry members of
the Protestant middle class (PMC) node than members of the Catholic working class (CWC) node. Other things being equal, this
suggests that the PWC node is more closely related to the PMC node
than to the CWC node. Once the concept of social relationship in
a network is relativized in this fashion, there are any number of
ways to measure the relative presence or absence of relationships
between nodes.

By adopting these two expedients, the concept of a "relationship" is broadened to include types of relations not normally
considered in person-defined social nets. For example, transactions among corporate actors, such as the sharing of leadership
personnel (e.g., interlocking directorships, cf. Levine, 1972;
Zeitlin, 1974), flows of money, organizational information, and
other forms of organizational support, may become the basis for a
network analysis (cf. Turk, 1973).

The hallmark of a network analysis, as noted in Mitchell's
definition, is to explain, at least in part, the behavior of network elements (i.e., the nodes) and of the system as a whole by
appeal to specific features of the interconnections among the
elements. Network analysis assumes that the ways in which elements are connected to one another, both directly and indirectly,
facilitate as well as constrain the roles performed. For instance,
nodes that are connected to others in such a way that they can
"reach" most of the actors in the system who, in turn, must usually go through them to reach other actors are more favorably
circumstanced to perform mediating and coordinating activities for
the system of actors as a whole than are nodes who are linked to
only a few other, poorly connected actors (cf. Bavelas, 1950).

B. Graph Theory and Blockmodeling Approaches to Network Analysis

Within the scope of network analysis there have been at least
two broad strategies for devising technical solutions for the
analysis of network structure. The first, and by far the most
developed and frequently used, rests upon the mathematical theory
of graphs and digraphs (cf. Harary *et al.*, 1965); while the
second, blockmodeling, was only recently developed by Harrison
White and his associates (1976; Boorman and White, 1976) and rests
on the strategic assumption of structural equivalence (cf.
Lorraine and White, 1971).

The mathematical theory of digraphs is concerned with postulates and theorems relating to "abstract configurations called
digraphs, which consist of 'points' and 'directed lines'" (Harary
et al., 1965, p. v). A graph consists of a set of points
(i.e., our nodes) and connecting lines (i.e., our relationships)
in which the direction of the lines is disregarded. One important
feature of the graph, for our purposes, is its connectedness. A
major technical advance in applying graph theoretic ideas has been
the appearance of computer routines that permit the calculation
of key graph theoretic quantities for large matrices. Still, the
upper limit seems to be about 1000 points (cf. Gleason, 1969;
Farace, 1972; Richards, 1974).

Blockmodeling, in contrast to the graph theoretic approach,
emphasizes blocking groups of points on the basis of their structural equivalence. Here, individuals are treated as structurally
equivalent (i.e., members of a block) when they have similar
patterns of links with members of other blocks. Currently, the
graph theoretic approach uses only one relationship at a time
while blockmodeling provides machinery for examining a number of
relationships simultaneously. We may thus have in hand tools for
developing a theory of relations. Preliminary blockmodeling
analysis of our data by Ronald Breiger (personal communication)
reveals fairly consistent results to those obtained using our own
procedures.

C. Data Reduction Problems

Unfortunately, both approaches are presently limited to
rather small numbers of nodes. Even a path distance matrix for
50 points is singularly complex and it is difficult to comprehend
its essential structure by inspection alone. It is obvious that
some data-reduction procedures are needed to assist the analyst
in describing a large network's structure. Again, two general
strategies for accomplishing this can be distinguished: cluster

analysis and multidimensional scaling. In cluster analysis (cf.
Bailey, 1974), the end result is a set of discrete clusters of
nodes, for example, cliques; while in multidimensional scaling
(cf. McFarland and Brown, 1973; Shephard *et al.*, 1972), the end
result is a spatial solution where the points are mapped as a
function of their proximities into a space, usually Euclidean,
with a minimum number of dimensions. The advantage of multidimensional scaling over cluster analysis is that the relative
locations of all points with respect to one another can be
visualized, provided the solution requires no more than three
dimensions. The spatial portrayal of social structure is quite
appealing, since it is, according to Ossowski (1963, pp. 19-25),
implicit in most conceptualizations of structure.

The nub of the problem in multidimensional scaling is, of
course, to devise plausible estimates of the proximities of pairs
of points. There are usually a number of different ways to estimate these proximities, even with a well defined distance-
generating mechanism. Fortunately, various ways of calculating
proximity estimates for a given structural problem seem to come
up with similar spatial solutions--that is, the solutions are
fairly robust (see Alba, 1975, for a comparison of results with
several alternative estimates of the proximities in the elite
social structures described in Laumann and Pappi, 1976).

Perhaps our most radical innovations have to do with the
research strategy we devised for examining the relationships of
various structures to one another and the causal model we proposed to account for the formation of structures. I have already
noted that one of the limitations of the graph theoretic approach
to network analysis is its inability to handle more than one type
of relation at a time. The postulates for structural analysis,
especially Postulate III on structural contradictions, confront
us with the theoretical necessity of specifying methodological
procedures for comparing and predicting structural arrangements.
The obvious candidate for the unit of structural comparison is

the relationship between a pair of points. Since, for a given
social system, the set of member actors can be specified and this
number implies a determinant set of possible pairwise relationships (in fact, $n(n-1)$ if asymmetric relations are permitted and
$n(n-1)/2$ if only symmetric relations are permitted), and since
the elements of nodes and possible links are invariant across
relationship-specific structures, the possibility of comparing
structures of a given social system is guaranteed by our approach.
The problem is merely one of measuring the characteristics of
these pairwise relationships. The tactic we adopted is to use
the interpoint distances of multidimensional scaling solutions
as structure-specific estimators of these characteristics.
Finally, appropriate modifications of even these assumptions
produced a successful strategy for mapping the pattern of
relationships in a social system comprised of different types
of nodes (e.g., specific persons and population subgroups (see
Laumann and Pappi, 1976, Chaps. 7, 12)).

REFERENCES

Aiken, Michael, & Mott, Paul (Eds). *The structure of community
    power.* New York: Random House, 1970.
Alba, Richard D. Defining proximity in social networks: A re-
    analysis of the Laumann-Pappi data. Unpublished manuscript.
    Bureau of Applied Social Research, Columbia University, 1975.
Bailey, Kenneth D. Cluster analysis. In David R. Heise (Ed.),
    Sociological methodology. San Francisco: Jossey-Bass Publish-
    ers, 1975. Pp. 59-128.
Barnes, J. A. Class and committees in a Norwegian island parish.
    Human Relations, 1954, *7,* 39-58.
Bavelas, A. Communication patterns in task-oriented groups.
    Journal of Acoustical Society of America, 1950, *22,* 725-730.
Black, Max. *The social theories of Talcott Parsons.* Englewood
    Cliffs, New Jersey: Prentice-Hall, Inc., 1961.

Blau, Peter M. *Exchange and power in social life*. New York: Wiley, 1964.

Blau, Peter M. Parameters of social structure. *American Sociological Review,* 1974, *39,* 615-635.

Blau, Peter M. *Approaches to the study of social structure*. New York: Free Press, 1975.

Bonjean, Charles M., Clark, Terry N., & Lineberry, Robert L. *Community politics: A behavioral approach*. New York: Free Press, 1971.

Boorman, Scott A., & White, Harrison C. Social structure from multiple networks. II. Role structures. *American Journal of Sociology,* 1976, *1,* 1384-1446.

Buckley, Walter. *Sociology and modern systems theory*. Englewood Cliffs, New Jersey: Prentice-Hall, Inc., 1976.

Clark, Terry N. *Community structure and decision-making: Comparative analyses*. San Francisco: Chandler Publishing Company, 1968.(a)

Clark, Terry N. Who governs, where, when and with what effects? *Community structure and decision-making: Comparative analyses*. San Francisco: Chandler Publishing Company, 1968. Pp. 15-23. (b)

Clark, Terry N. The concept of power. In T. N. Clark (Ed.), *Community structure and decision-making: Comparative analyses*. San Francisco: Chandler Publishing Company, 1968. Pp. 45-81. (c)

Clark, Terry N. Community structure and decision-making. *Community structure and decision-making: Comparative analyses*. San Francisco: Chandler Publishing Company, 1968. Pp. 91-126. (d)

Clark, Terry N. *Community power and policy outputs: A review of urban research*. Beverly Hills and London: Sage Publications, 1973.

Dahl, Robert A. *Who governs? Democracy and power in an American city*. New Haven, Connecticut: Yale University Press, 1961.

Dahrendorf, Ralf. *Class and class conflict in industrial society.* Stanford: Stanford Universtiy Press, 1959.

Dahrendorf, Ralf. On the origin of inequality among men. *Essays in the theory of society.* Stanford: Stanford University Press, 1968.

Farace, V. Analysis of human communication networks in large social systems. Unpublished paper, Department of Communication, Michigan State University, 1972.

Giddens, Anthony. *The class structure of the advanced societies.* New York: Harper Torchbooks, 1973.

Gleason, Terry C. D.I.P. A directed graph processor. Mimeo. Ann Arbor, Michigan: Institute for Social Research, University of Michigan, 1969.

Harary, Frank, Norman, Robert L., & Cartwright, Dorwin. *Structural models: An introduction to the theory of directed graphs.* New York: Wiley, 1965.

Homans, George C. *Social behavior: Its elementary forms.* New York: Harcourt, Brace, and World, 1961.

Hunter, Floyd. *Community power structure.* Durham, North Carolina: University of North Carolina Press, 1953.

Katz, Daniel, & Kahn, Robert L. *The social psychology of organizations.* New York: Wiley, 1966.

Laumann, Edward O. *Prestige and association in an urban community.* Indianapolis: Bobbs-Merrill, 1966.

Laumann, Edward O. *Bonds of pluralism. The form and substance of urban social networks.* New York: Wiley Interscience, 1973.

Laumann, Edward O., & Pappi, Franz U. *Networks of collective action. A perspective on community influence systems.* New York: Academic Press, Inc., 1976.

Lazarsfeld, Paul F., Berelson, Bernard, & Gaudet, Hazel. *The people's choice.* New York: Columbia University Press, 1944.

Lenski, Gerhard. *Power and privilege: A theory of social stratification.* New York: McGraw-Hill, 1966.

Levine, J. H. The sphere of influence. *American Sociological Review,* 1972, *37,* 14-27.

Levi-Strauss, Claude. Social structure, Postscript to chapter XV. In *Structural anthropology,* C. Jacobson & B. Gruendfest Schoepf, trans. New York: Basic Books, 1963. Pp. 277-345.

Lipset, Seymour M. *The first new nation.* New York: Basic Books, 1963. (a)

Lipset, Seymour M. *Political man: The social bases of politics.* New York: Doubleday, 1963. (b)

Lorraine, Francois, & White, Harrison C. Structural equivalence of individuals in social networks. *Journal of Mathematical Sociology,* 1971, *1,* 49-80.

McFarland, David, & Brown, Daniel. Social distance as a metric: A systematic introduction to smallest space analysis. *Bonds of pluralism. The form and substance of urban social networks.* New York: Wiley Interscience, 1973. Pp. 213-253.

Mayhew, Leon. *Society, institutions and activity.* Glenview, Illinois: Scott, Foresman and Co., 1971.

Mitchell, J. Clyde (Ed.). *Social networks in urban situations.* Manchester: Manchester University Press, 1969.

Mitchell, J. Clyde. Social networks. *Annual Review of Anthropology,* 1974, *3,* 279-299.

Nadel, S. F. *The theory of social structure.* London: Cohen and West, 1957.

Newcomb, Theodore. *The acquaintance process.* New York: Holt, Rinehart, and Winston, 1961.

Ossowski, Stanislaw. *Class structure in the social consciousness.* London: Routledge and Kegan Paul, 1963.

Pappi, Franz Urban. Parteiensystem und sozialstruktur in der Bundesrepublik. *Politische Vierteljahresschrift,* 1973, *14,* 191-213.

Pappi, Franz U., & Laumann, Edward O. Erwiderung auf Bertrams Kritik von 'Gesellschaftliche Wertorienterungen und politisches Verhalten'. *Zeitschrift fur Soziology,* 1975.

Parsons, Talcott. *The social system.* Glencoe, Illinois: Free
Press, 1951.

Parsons, Talcott. *Structure and process in modern societies.*
New York: Free Press, 1960.

Parsons, Talcott. *Societies: Evolutionary and comparative
perspectives.* Englewood Cliffs, New Jersey: Prentice-Hall,
1966.

Parsons, Talcott. On the concept of influence. On the concept of
political power. On the concept of value commitments.
Politics and social structure. New York: Free Press, 1969.

Parsons, Talcott, & Smelser, Neil J. *Economy and society.*
London: Routledge and Kegan Paul, 1956.

Polsby, Nelson W. *Community power and political theory.* New
Haven: Yale University Press, 1969.

Richards W. Network analysis in large communication systems:
Techniques and methods--tools. Unpublished paper, Institute
for Communication Research, Stanford University, 1974.

Shephard, Roger N., Romney, A. Kimball, & Nerlove, Sara Beth.
*Multidimensional scaling. Theory and applications in the
behavioral sciences.* Volume 1. New York: Seminar Press,
1972.

Sztompka, Piotr. *System and function: Toward a theory of
society.* New York: Academic Press, 1974.

Turk, Herman. *Interorganizational activation in urban communities.
Deductions from the concept of system.* ASA Rose Monograph
Series. Washington, D.C.: American Sociological Associa-
tion, 1973.

Walton, John. Substance and artifact: The current status on
research of community power structure. *American Journal of
Sociology,* 1966, *71,* 430-438. (a)

Walton, John. Discipline, method and community power: A note on
the sociology of knowledge. *American Sociological Review,*
1966, *31,* 684-689. (b)

White, Harrison C., Boorman, Scott A., & Breiger, Ronald L.
    Social structure from multiple networks. I. Blockmodels of
    roles and positions. *American Journal of Sociology*, 1976,
    81, 730-780.
Zeitlin, M. Corporate ownership and control: The large corpora-
    tion and the capitalist class. *American Journal of Sociology*,
    1974, *79*, 1073-1119.

CHAPTER 19

NETWORK ANALYSIS: ORIENTING NOTION, RIGOROUS TECHNIQUE
OR SUBSTANTIVE FIELD OF STUDY?

John A. Barnes

Churchill College
Cambridge University
Cambridge, England

I.   INTRODUCTION

Interest in social networks has increased dramatically during
the last 6 or 7 years. Several seminars have been organized on
various aspects of network analysis, of which this is the latest.
I am sure that there will be more to follow. Most of the literature deals with developments, modifications, and applications of
ideas and techniques that have been mooted at earlier conferences
and in published work. The outcome of all this effort will be,
we all hope, a greater understanding of several facets of social
reality. Yet these combined efforts have begun to constitute in
themselves a significant chunk of social reality, and deserve at
least a brief glance, if only so that we may better realize what
kind of collective enterprise we are engaged in. The main thrust
of inquiry in the social sciences ought always to be directed at
making discoveries about the real world, rather than at narcis-
sistically contemplating the internal structure of the academic
ivory tower. Nevertheless, a brief analysis of our domestic

intellectual housekeeping is sometimes called for, particularly
when changes seem to be taking place haphazardly. I hope that
this short chapter in introspection may help us not only to see
our own internal relations more clearly but also to choose more
effectively between alternative strategies of external inquiry.

The basic question I ask is simply: What sort of creature is
network analysis? Is it a new narrow specialism within the social
sciences, or is it a vaguely defined approach to the analysis of
all social phenomena? If it constitutes a specialized, rather
than a generalized, line of thought, then is it characterized by
rigorously defined techniques for generating various measures,
derived at one or more removes from an adjacency matrix? Or is
the diagnostic feature of network analysis an interest in certain
substantively specified social relations: a concern with, say,
friendship, kinship, and face-to-face bargaining rather than with
the state, the law, and other macrosociological phenomena? Are
two or even all three of these criteria needed to embrace the
range of interests grouped together under the same network um-
brella? If so, what relations do these different subspecies of
network analysis have to one another? How long can they travel
forward together without disagreeing about where they should go?
I cannot give a comprehensive answer to any one of these queries
in a single chapter and certainly cannot answer them all. I
shall merely discuss two practical features of network analysis:
(1) how density is measured and, (2) how graphs are delimited --
to see what light they shed on one or other of these queries.

II. SOCIAL NETWORKS

What is the underlying rationale that all efforts to study
networks have in common? Three reviews on social networks
(Barnes, 1972; Mitchell, 1974; Whitten and Wolfe, 1974) concentrate on the scholarly literature of the social sciences, par-

ticularly sociology and social anthropology. We must remember,
however, that writers of many different persuasions--journalists,
novelists, and politicians as well as sociologists--frequently
refer to the existence of a social network. Social psychologists
and political scientists do the same, while natural scientists
and mathematicians have generated a huge corpus of writing on non-
social networks. These popular and multidisciplinary occurrences
of the term indicate that, however specialized and algebraically
rigorous some kinds of network analysis may be, there are also
some quite general ideas which contribute to the notion of networks. The analytical tools of social science must therefore be
refined yet robust enough to stand up to diverse uses, especially
lay usage. This consideration applies as much to the analysis
of networks as to any other branch of social science. If we use
long established words taken from ordinary language, like density,
cluster, balance, and indeed network itself, the technical meaning
we give to our terms ought to be close enough to ordinary usage,
for the propositions we enunciate to stand a chance of remaining
reasonably true even when they are used in lay speech.

As a lay term, "social network" conveys the following set of
ideas: Individuals (or larger social units) are perceived as
being "significantly" in direct contact with many others but not
with all possible others. Indirect contacts, through one or more
intermediaries, may also be significant. An individual may sometimes, if he or she makes an effort, succeed in making direct contact with someone to whom he or she has hitherto been linked only
indirectly; indeed, this is one of the main ways in which individuals make new direct contacts. Intermediaries may facilitate
or obstruct this process of converting contacts from indirect to
direct, or may endeavor to interpose themselves as a barrier or
filter between an individual and a direct contact. Contacts
between individuals may take the form of channels of communication,
or of the flow of resources, or may manifest themselves merely in

the expression of attitudes and sentiments. Whatever form the
contact takes, it may affect the behavior of the individual.
Since every individual has her or his own set of contacts, the
pattern of contacts as a whole affects the behavior of the col-
lectivity and is, simultaneously, an outcome of that behavior.

Most of the occurrences of the term "social network" in social
science that are more than 20 years old, as well as most of the
popular uses of the term, imply no more than the very general and
unquantified ideas just listed. The ideas are uncontroversial
and can scarcely be regarded as testable propositions. They constitute orienting notions and nothing more (Homans, 1967, p. 14).
On the other hand, social scientists in recent years have used
"network" as a precise term and have developed definitions to
generate testable, often quantified propositions. Different
practitioners have tried to propositionalize and quantify network
notions in different ways. In the great majority of instances,
social science references to the social network are still confined to the very general ideas I have listed, and the only
measurement involved consists in counting the number of contacts
impinging on each of a collection of individuals. Indeed, the
use of "personal network" as a technical term for an individual's
direct contacts constitutes a striking case of what we might call
"operationalization by impoverishment." By confining attention
to direct contacts, this definition eliminates the value of the
term "network" as an orienting idea.

III. DENSITY

Indeed, network analysis really begins only when we go beyond
simply counting direct contacts. It is at this point that
measurements become important. For instance, at first sight the
notion of density seems simple enough: the ratio of the number of
links between vertices to the number that would be present if the

graph was complete (Kephart, 1950). It is a measure that can be applied to a directed or undirected graph, and to a first-order zone of an individual or to a graph as a whole, as well as to any intermediate subgraph. Its value ranges from zero to plus one, and its meaning is intuitively obvious. Yet despite this encouraging spread of desirable characteristics, density, as we know, turns out to be a rather poor measure. To calculate density, all links are weighted alike, even if they symbolize very different social facts. This particular distortion could actually be partially overcome simply by constructing a valued graph, with a specified upper limit to the value of a link; the denominator would then be the sum of values for a complete graph in which each link had the maximum value. A more serious objection is that the significance of intermediate values of density is not at all clear. Zero density and a density of unity are easy to understand though rarely found in practice, but the local or global significance of intermediate values varies with the size of the graph as a whole, as Niemeijer (1973) points out, and this limitation is not so easily removed.

Indeed, dissatisfaction with density as a measure illustrates the diversity of interests among network analysts. The density of a graph is obtained by simple aggregation and indicates an average or distributative condition throughout the graph. It is not necessarily a structural property of the graph as an entity. Hence, those analysts who are interested in structural properties of graphs complain that graphs with very different structures may yet have identical densities, while graphs of different size but similar structures necessarily have different densities. The density of a first-order zone, that is, of the subgraph formed by an individual and the others with whom he or she is in direct contact, indicates the state of affairs in the immediate vicinity of an individual but, when second-order contacts are not taken into account, provides a poor overall indication of the individual's

social milieu. Density is therefore an unsatisfactory measure for
those analysts whose focus is the interaction between the individual and the environment.

On the other hand, the larger the zone around an individual
that is used as a basis for calculating local density, the less
the measure of density discriminates between one individual in the
graph and another, since their zones tend to overlap. The right
compromise cannot be found by arguing in terms of graph theory
alone, but only in terms of the social content of the relations
being studied. Thus, for instance, if a relation entails a good
deal of commitment (e.g., coping with an individual contemplating
suicide), a density measure based on first-order zones may well be
correlated with types of behavioral response, whereas if the relation implies a comparatively slight commitment (e.g., providing
electoral support in a political campaign), a density based on a
wider zone may be more revealing. These considerations make density unsatisfactory to analysts who seek to discover regularities
in patterns of social relations that are independent of the cultural content of the relations.

It is of course scarcely surprising that so simple a measure
as density does not meet the needs of every brand of network
analyst, but it is disappointing that it seems to be tailored to
the needs of none. Nevertheless the measure continues to be used
merely because it is easy to calculate. Some kind of distributative
measure, whether it be density or some transformation that takes
into account Niemeijer's objections, is appropriate when the
limits of the graph are arbitrarily or casually defined.

IV. DELIMITING GRAPHS

For practical purposes, the graph we analyze must always be a
proper subgraph of the real social network. In many investigations it is the limited resources of the investigator, rather
than the actual configuration of the social space he is studying,

that determine the size of the graph that is subjected to analysis.
In a hypothetical maximally open society, the number of higher
order contacts of any individual increases exponentially as the
order increases linearly. A snowball sample grows with alarming
speed in a society like, for instance, the United States, where
the average individual is said to "know" about a thousand people
(Lee, 1969, p. 125). Consequently, most investigators give up
at the prospect of identifying and interviewing any of the second-
order contacts and limit the graph to persons about whom reliable
information is available. Only where there is a clear social
boundary in reality corresponding to the limits of the graph is it
meaningful to determine structural properties of a graph delimited
by fiat rather than by observation.

Our measures may tell us all we want to know about the structure of the graph, but this structure may well be merely an artifact of our procedure for delimiting the graph. Furthermore, only
when this boundary encloses a modest number of individuals is it
possible in practice to discover what these properties are.
Bavelas's pioneering studies (1948, 1950) were carried out with
five people in a laboratory and were based on a very restricted
set of data. Conversely, White and Breiger (1974) analyse data
relating to over a hundred scientists and extract structural
features of the graph as entity. In this case the limits of the
graph, apart from the effect of nonresponse to a questionnaire,
seem to be real, embracing all those engaged in a particular
specialism, and the techniques of analysis used are impressively
sophisticated. On the other hand, even with arbitrary limits,
even so unimpressive a measure as density may reveal an interesting
trend. Using between 90 and 100 vertices representing the largest
firms in Britain, and links showing interlocking directorates,
Stanworth and Giddens (1975) show that the density increased
steadily during the period from 1906 to 1970. What is interesting
about their findings is that although the density increased by

40% from one date to another, in quantitative terms it merely
increased from 2.87 to 4.03%. Thus, although the density never
rose to the values often found in artificial and small laboratory
groups, or even in the face-to-face real life groups studies by
Kapferer and other social anthropologists (Mitchell, 1969;
Boissevain and Mitchell, 1973), nevertheless the change in its
value does plausibly reflect a real process of financial and
industrial concentration.

Both the study by Stanworth and Giddens and the analysis by
White and Breiger are based on reported data (directories and
questionnaire replies, respectively) rather than on direct observation, thus avoiding the obvious limitation on the number of
individuals one observer (i.e., one perspective) can cover. More
importantly perhaps, both studies are based on data that are
strictly limited in content, so that replies can be mapped on to
a two- or three-valued scale without distortion, and hence can be
transformed fairly readily. Similar analysis is found in many
field studies carried out by social anthropologists, but with some
of these, the limits of the graph may not have been drawn appropriately.

Consider for example a field situation in Zambia studied by
Kapferer. Kapferer presents an analysis of the interrelations of
43 people who constitute the first-order zone of a selected married couple. Relations are measured on a four-point scale. Kapferer's data-collecting energy was formidable, but even so he
writes that he cannot claim to have included all the individuals
with whom the couple came into contact; presumably he has even
less complete information on the relations between their various
contacts. He does claim to have included all those who met the
husband or the wife "at least three times in the week and spent a
relatively long time in each other's company [Kapferer, 1973,
p. 95]." Obviously all data collection, even of the most routine
kind, involves judgments of relevance and interpretation, and

there is no difference in principle between recoding entries about
company directors in *Who's Who* and deciding who are a wife's real
friends. But in practice there is a difference, particularly with
reference to replicability, so that while conclusions based on
data such as those collected by Kapferer may well be more interesting than those based on *Who's Who*, they must also be viewed as
more tentative, despite the known inaccuracies of semipublic
sources like *Who's Who*.

Because of the way in which Kapferer's graph is delimited, all
his measures, including density, are structural in that they describe its properties as a whole and do not merely report the
averages of values found in its various parts. Hence, the appro-
priateness of the boundaries of the graph has to be scrutinized.
In fact, Kapferer bases his commentary not on the absolute values
of these measures but on how they compare with similar measures
relating to a second graph, based on the contacts of another married couple and constructed in similar fashion. To this extent,
the somewhat arbitrary delimitation of the graphs becomes less
important, for we can make the usual assumption that any distortion introduced by this delimitation affects both graphs equally.
Yet if we wished to compare these two graphs with others pertaining to married couples who lived in cultures where, for example,
"meeting at least three times a week" carried quite different implications, we would again have to question why the boundaries had
been drawn at that level of interaction.

V. MULTIPLEXITY

The concept of multiplexity illustrates the contrast between
the boundaries or sparse areas that occur in the real social network and the arbitrary limits that are imposed by the investigator.
Most social anthropologists concerned with social networks have
adopted Gluckman's term "multiplex" (1967, pp. 19-20) to refer to

links between individuals that serve a multiplicity of interests,
as for instance when A is simultaneously neighbor, workmate, and
mother's brother of B. Multiplex links produce a valued graph,
with values indicating the number of separately recognized interests present in a link, or some more sophisticated measure of
content.

This concern with multiplexity arose, so I infer, from an
earlier mode of analysis current among anthropologists, the so-
called "case history" method. Case histories entailed close observation of a collection of 20 or 30 people, sometimes over a
period of several months, to produce a descriptive study or critical narrative in which each decision made by each actor is discussed in the light of the actor's relations with associates at
the time. Frequently, those associates are people with whom he
or she has interacted with for many years and to whom she or he
is linked in a variety of ways. When well presented, these case
histories provide plausible insights into how face-to-face communities operate. Yet, case histories yield few testable propositions, and those propositions that do emerge from the critical
commentaries are usually in all-or-none form, for example, that A
will choose action X rather than Y next time he has to make a
choice.

The notion of network, and the associated measures like density and span, provide one way of generating quantified statements about the pattern of social relations in a community, pro-
bing for correlations and constructing causal models. But the
greater the variety of interests--kinship, residential contiguity,
ethnic identity, positions in the work force, clientage, brokerage, moneylending, and so on--the harder it becomes to find real
breaks or even sparce patches in the social network. This is
true even when attention is confined to currently activated social
relations. Social anthropologists have, however, rightly stressed
that some kinds of social relations, notably those of kinship,

may remain latent for decades and then suddenly emerge into contemporary significance. Hence, the problem of where to draw the line, of whom to include and whom to exclude, becomes doubly difficult.

The difficulty can be seen clearly in a well-known study, also by Kapferer (1969), of a dispute in the Cell Room at Broken Hill. The 23 individuals whose interrelations he graphs are simply all the Africans who work in the room. European supervisors work in the same room but, for reasons that are not explained, their relations with the African workers are not analyzed. What is perhaps more important is that whereas the individuals necessarily interacted with one another systematically while separating out zinc from zinc sulphate, these relations, which in Homans's terms constitute the external system of the group (Homans, 1951, p. 90), do not all form part of Kapferer's graph. They enter, if at all, under the heading of "work assistance," which, says Kapferer (1969, pp. 212 213), refers "to the practice of some employees assisting others with their specific tasks in the work context," and his data suggest that strictly speaking these (voluntary?) acts of assistance are not part of the external system. The other kinds of relations identified by Kapferer are joking exchanges, personal service, and cash assistance, and it is these four whose presence or absence determines the measure of multiplexity. However, it is clear from Kapferer's narrative that these 23 Africans are involved in joking exchanges, and in relations of personal service, and possibly of cash assistance as well, with many persons in Broken Hill, including their workmates. Yet these links to persons outside the Cell Room are ignored. Hence, although the limits of the graph are set by the external system, the relations specific to that system appear in the narrative account of the dispute but do not enter the formal analysis, while those relations that are analysed are in no sense specific to the work group. Looking at Kapferer's analysis, we cannot avoid wondering whether

there are other individuals outside the Cell Room who have significant links to two or more members of the work group, links
which may well affect the relations of workers to one another.[1]

VI. FIELD STUDIES AND EXPERIMENTAL SITUATIONS

At first sight the work of Kapferer and other social anthropologists who use the same techniques seems to be a valid and
imaginative elaboration of the work done by Bavelas and other
"small group" analysts a decade or more before them. But small
group studies are typically carried out in the laboratory, not in
the real world. The studies are experiments in what has been
called "billiard ball sociology," wherein the subjects who pass
messages to one another and solve contrived problems are treated
as "individuals who are visualised as devoid of biography and
therefore of social experience [Fortes, 1957, p. 160, f.n.1]."
The laboratory defines the limits of the graph unequivocally.
Continued replication is assumed to be a way of cancelling out
the errors that arise because subjects actually have biographies.
Bernard and Killworth (in their contribution to these proceedings)
note that of all the assumptions underlying models of changing
social networks, the assumption of group closure makes the widest
departure from reality.

[1] *I do not mean to imply criticism of Kapferer. I have a high
regard for his work. Of the many writers who have commented on
Bott's study of married couples, he was the first to carry out a
parallel inquiry designed so as to avoid the major logical flaw in
her argument (Barnes, 1972, pp. 21-22). Indeed I have chosen his
study of the Cell Room as my example because it is well known and
widely recognized as a good example of an established genre of
analysis. My comments are directed rather at the general problem
of where to set limits in the analysis of social networks that in
reality do not have any obvious limits at all.*

Field studies, on the other hand, are typically not replicated; indeed they are sometimes nonreplicable in principle as
well as in practice. They are based on the premiss that "biography" is important, that individuals bring into the observed
patch of reality all of their latent roles, their past commitments, loves and hates, histories of previous interactions. Even
though the subjects act for a while under the observer's lime-
light, their lives are not laboratory performances. With these
differences between the field and the laboratory, we could scarcely expect the same mode of analysis to work equally well in both
situations.

The Western Electric Bank Wiring Room may be seen as an intermediate case. White *et al.* (1975) analyze this classic study in
structural terms and draw the boundaries of their graph where
Roethlisberger and Dickson (1939) drew them originally. Although
their mode of structural analysis differs radically from Kapferer's, White and his co-authors seem to base their argument on
assumptions similar to those made (rightly or wrongly) by Kapferer in the Cell Room. The vertices of the Bank Wiring Room graph
are simply the fourteen workers in the Room. Relations between
the workers are analyzed in terms of "Help," "Games," "Like,"
"Antagonism," and "Windows." Only this last category is completely specific to the work situation. Relations of the other
four types must certainly have been paralleled by relations these
workers had with other individuals in Chicago outside the Hawthorne plant, even though the authors refer to "Help" and "Games,"
along with "Windows," as context-specific types of ties. These
extraplant relations are ignored in the formal analysis, though
Roethlisberger and Dickson collected information about the lives
of the workers outside the plant. Most of this information was
left out of their book so that, as Homans (1951, p. 74) says,
other workers would not be able to identify them. Presumably
this information was also suppressed because the authors dis-

covered that it did not bear significantly on the pattern of
interaction within the Bank Wiring Room. If not, the criticism
that they confined themselves unjustifiably to "plant sociology"
has some force (Landsberger, 1958, pp. 81-82). If so, then maybe the heuristic device of treating them as "individuals devoid
of biography" is justified, and it makes sense to look merely at
the interrelations of the 14 workers within the plant.

The decision to ignore relations outside the workplace may
have been taken for different reasons by Roethlisberger and Dickson and by Kapferer, for they carried out their inquiries and
analyses in quite different academic and intellectual surround-
ings--Chicago and Broken Hill are two very different places. We
know from Kapferer's account (1972), as well as from other studies
of urban life in Zambia, that work and nonwork in Broken Hill are
not separate spheres of activity, whereas the chances that the
14 workers in the Bank Wiring Room were all strangers to one
another before they met at work is reasonably high.

VII. GENERALIZING FROM DATA TO REALITY

Networks are interesting but difficult to study since real-
world networks lack convenient natural boundaries. When a network as a whole is impracticably large, the usual procedure is
to arbitrarily delimit a subgraph and treat it as a representative
sample of the whole network. Unfortunately, this procedure is
hazardous not only qualitatively, as in the Cell Room and Bank
Wiring Room examples, but quantitatively as well. The measures
taken on the subgraph may appear to be reliable estimates of
population parameters, but this may not be so. Sample size effects many measures besides density.

As an example, consider two measures used by Levine and Roy
(in this volume) in their study of American business corporations.
They state that 82% of all corporation directors sit on one and

only one board, and that 7.8% (62 out of 797) of the boards of
corporations are not interlocked with any other. These measures
are made, in effect, on a network with 797 nodes (boards of corporations) and 8623 edges (individuals holding directorships),
some pairs of nodes being linked by more than one edge. 797 is
an arbitrary number. It is in no sense a characteristic of
American capitalism, but is merely a limit set arbitrarily by
the editor of *Fortune* magazine (the source of the sampling frame)
because they are, in the opinion of the editor, "prominent." It
is highly unlikely that there is in fact any structural discontinuity between these 797 and the thousands of other "nonprominent"
business corporations. As Levine and Roy say, "The reality de-
cribed by the data knows no natural boundary." We therefore ask
whether the measures, 82% and 7.8% approximate the parameters of
corporate capitalism in the United States, for the substantive
focus of Levine and Roy's interest must be on this "reality" and
not on the perceptions of the editor of *Fortune*. Are the measures
merely a product of the editor's arbitrary decision to include
only 797 firms? If he had been more generous with his space, or
less, would the measures have been significantly different?

The measures do not relate to links between all American corporations, but only to links between the boards of those corporations that form the sample of 797. We do not have information
about the membership of boards of other corporations. For purposes
of discussion, suppose that there is no difference between corporations and directors in the "prominent" and "nonprominent" sets,
in the sense that a sample of 797 nonprominent corporations would
yield a measure of 82% for directors sitting on one and only one
board and 7.8% for corporations not interlocked with any other
corporations in the sample. What happens if we combine this sample with that used by Levine and Roy? If the two sets of directors are disjoint, the measures for the combined sample are un-
altered. But if any singleton director of a prominent corporation

happens to belong to a nonprominent board in the sample, or any
singleton nonprominent director belongs to a prominent board, the
first measure for the enlarged sample is decreased. Similarly, if
any solitary prominent or nonprominent corporation is linked to a
board in the other set, the second measure is decreased. In the
extreme case, in which each director sitting on only one board in
one set sits on at least one board in the other set, and each corporation that is unlinked in one set is linked to at least one
corporation in the other set, then both measures become zero. Even
if there is no essential difference between the two sets of corporations and directors, enlarging the sample is likely to decrease
both measures. Hence, we cannot look upon the measures as estimates of population parameters. Levine and Roy's statement that
82% of directors sit on one and only one board is not true of
American corporation directors as a whole but is strictly limited
to the 797 American business corporations judged by the editor of
Fortune to be prominent. Likewise we can say only that the boards
of 7.8% of *these* corporations are not interlocked with any others
of the 797. Each measure is dependent on the delimited size of
the empirical network for which it is computed.

It may be difficult in practice to enlarge the limits of an
arbitrarily delimited graph, but we can always contract them. In
this example, instead of wondering what measures we would obtain
if the editor of *Fortune* had lengthened the list, we can examine
what would happen if a shorter list had been published. We can
arbitrarily partition the 797 corporations into "more prominent"
and "less prominent" sets, and recalculate the measures for the
network generated by the set of more prominent corporations.
If, as Levine and Roy claim, there is no distinctive elite subset
of corporations in America, we would expect there to be no significant differences between corporations and their directors in
the more prominent and less prominent sets. Since we are con-

tracting rather than enlarging the network on which measures are taken, we would further expect the two measures for the more prominent subset to be *greater* than for the 797 corporations taken as a whole. If the measures for the two networks did not differ significantly, we could infer that there are few or no links between the boards of directors of corporations belonging to different sets. This would seem to conflict with the hypothesis that there is no elite subset.

Alternatively, by drawing yet another sample, consisting of half the more prominent and half the less prominent corporations, we can increase both of the measures. If we allow for differences to exist between more prominent and less corporations in the extent to which they are interlocked with corporations of their own set, and also in the extent to which the members of their boards hold multiple memberships in their own set, the possibilities are more complicated. Levine and Roy have tested their data in this way. We may still say, however, that invariance in the values of the measures despite certain changes in sample size is not evidence that corporations and their directors form homogeneous populations, nor is it grounds for regarding the measures as estimates of population parameters.

VIII. ADVANCED TECHNIQUES

Establishing valid boundaries for formal network analysis has been aided by the sophisticated mathematical techniques now being developed to handle large graphs. Mathematical techniques also permit us to identify, in less haphazard fashion, the limits of the graphs whose structural properties correspond to social facts. Yet this identification still requires empirical evidence about the insignificance of the subjects' links to those excluded from the graph. Individuals can be excluded only after the char-

acteristics of their links with those who will be included have
been investigated. If the investigation reveals that there is
no natural boundary and the total field is impracticably large,
then, mathematical techniques aside, a sample has to be drawn consisting of a graph or network with arbitrary limits, and we are
again confined to statements and measures that are true only of
a delimited graph. I have discussed this matter in very pedes-
trian terms, with reference to Levine and Roy's analysis of business corporation data, but the same topic is treated mathematically and generally by Frank (in these proceedings).

IX. CONCLUSIONS

    Considering how the boundaries of graphs are determined for
purposes of formal analysis, it becomes clear that there are
many varieties of intellectual interest that have converged on
the study of networks. A similar scrutiny of how changes over time
are handled by different analysts, or of whether mismatch between
data and model is met by elaboration or simplification, or whether
or not group properties are reduced to dyadic relations--any one
of these would show that there is at best what Wittgenstein calls
a family resemblance among the various manifestations of network
analysis. Some analysts are interested in microphenomena; in
seeing, for example, how individuals interact with their environment or how married couples adjust their mutual roles in responses
to changes in the interrelations of their friends. Others seek to
identify macrophenomena, the conditions under which cliques or
alliances form, and to examine how stratification is maintained.
I have tried to argue, by showing density to be a poor measure,
that different research objectives call for different measures.
    I hope that it is clear that I do not find much support for
the view that network analysis is particularly appropriate for

the analysis of certain kinds of social relations--voluntary, egalitarian, informal--of which friendship is the paradigm. Any view of the literature on networks should be enough to refute this viewpoint. On the contrary, I think that network analysis has no substantively defined home base. I also have the slightly pious hope that an interest in the cultural content of social relations will be more enduring than an interest in their formal, culture-free algebraic or topological properties. Hopefully, mathematics will remain the ally, but not become the queen, of the social sciences. This leads me to conclude that though diverse substantive interests have for the time being converged on network analysis, it is quite likely that they will continue on their straight-line paths and diverge again in the future.

REFERENCES

Barnes, John Arundel. Social networks. *Module in anthropology 26*. Reading, Massachusetts: Addison-Wesley, 1972.

Bavelas, Alex. A mathematical model for group structures. *Applied anthropology*, 1948, *7 (3)*, 16-30.

Bavelas, Alex. Communication patterns in task-oriented groups. *Journal of the acoustical society of America*, 1950, *22*, 725-730.

Boissevain, Jeremy, & Mitchell, James Clyde. *Network analysis: Studies in human interaction*. The Hague: Mouton, 1973.

Fortes, Meyer. Malinowski and the study of kinship. In Raymond William Firth, (Ed.), *Man and culture; An evaluation of the work of Bronislaw Malinowski*. London: Routledge and Kegan Paul, 1957, 157-188.

Gluckman, Max. *The judicial process among the Barotse of Northern Rhodesia* (2nd ed.). Manchester: Manchester University Press, 1967.

Homans, George Caspar. *The human group*. London: Routledge and Kegan Paul, 1951.

Homans, George Caspar. *The nature of social science*. New York,
    Harcourt, Brace and World, 1967.

Kapferer, Bruce. Norms and the manipulation of relationships in
    a work context. James Clyde Mitchell, (Ed.), *Social networks
    in urban situations*. Manchester: Manchester University Press,
    1969, 181-244.

Kapferer, Bruce. *Strategy and transaction in an African factory:
    African workers and Indian management in a Zambian town*.
    Manchester, Manchester University Press, 1972.

Kapferer, Bruce. Social network and conjugal role in urban
    Zambia: Toward a reformulation of the Bott hypothesis. In
    Jeremy Boissevain & James Clyde Mitchell, (Eds.), *Network
    analysis*. The Hague: Mouton, 1973, 83-110.

Kephart, William M. A quantitative analysis of intragroup rela-
    tionships. *American journal of sociology*, 1950, *55*, 544-549.

Landsberger, Henry Adolf. *Hawthorne revisited: Management and
    the worker, its critics, and developments in human relations
    in industry*. Ithaca, New York: Cornell University, 1958.

Lee, Nancy Howell. *The search for an abortionist*. Chicago,
    Chicago University Press, 1969.

Mitchell, James Clyde. (Ed.) *Social networks in urban situations:
    Analysis of personal relationships in central African towns*.
    Manchester: Manchester University Press, 1969.

Mitchell, James Clyde. Social networks. In Bernard Joseph Siegel
    et al. (Eds.), *Annual review of anthropology*, Palo Alto:
    Annual Reviews, 1974, *3*, 279-299.

Niemeijer, Rudo. Some application of the notion of density to
    network analysis. In Jeremy Boissevain & James Clyde
    Mitchell, (Eds.), *Network analysis*. The Hague: Mouton,
    1973, 45-64.

Roethlisberger, Fritz Jules, & Dickson, William John. *Management
    and the worker: An account of a research program conducted
    by the Western Electric Company, Hawthorne Works, Chicago*.
    Cambridge, Massachusetts: Harvard University Press, 1939.

Stanworth, Philip, & Giddens, Anthony. The modern corporate
    economy: Interlocking directorships in Britain, 1906-1970.
    Sociological Review, 1975, *23*, 5-28.

White, Harrison Colyer, Boorman, Scott A., & Breiger, Ronald L.
    Social structure from multiple networks: Part I. Blockmodels
    of roles and positions. *American Journal of Sociology*, 1975.

White, Harrison Colyer, & Breiger, Ronald L. Multiple networks
    in small populations. I. Blockmodels. Mimeographed, 1974.

Whitten, Norman Earl, Jr., & Wolfe, Alvin William. Network
    analysis. In John Joseph Honigmann, (Ed.), *Handbook of
    social and cultural anthropology*. Chicago: Rand McNally,
    1973, 717-746.

CHAPTER 20

NETWORKS, ALGORITHMS, AND ANALYSIS

J. Clyde Mitchell

Nuffield College

Oxford University

Oxford, England

I. SOCIOMETRY: THE POINT SOURCE

The idea of networks[1] is applicable to many disciplines, in
particular to social psychology, to social anthropology, and to
sociology, but it has received rather different treatments in
these different fields. *Networks* implies different things in
these disciplines and while certain very general and abstract
notions--such as those derived from mathematics, and from graph
theory in particular--might be generally applicable, the substantive issues that relate to social networks influence the particular network features that are germane to the disciplines.

The historical pride of place must go to social psychology,
or rather to that coterie within it devoted to sociometry. Most
of the formal analytical procedures available today arose out of

[1]*There have been several resumés of the history and development of the idea of the social network particularly in relation
to social anthropology (Aronson, 1970; Barnes, 1972; Boissevain,
1973; Bott, 1971; Whitten and Wolfe, 1974; Mitchell, 1969, 1974).*

the efforts of sociometrists 30 years ago to devise simple and
effective methods of revealing the patterns hidden in sociograms.
Similarly, we owe the form and character of the most useful
applications of graph theory to sociometry; as the examples and
illustrations in *Structural Models* (Harary, Norman, and Cartwright, 1965) demonstrate.

Sociometric formulations of social networks differ significantly, however, from those of social anthropological or
sociological formulations (Mitchell, 1969: 22; 1974). The
substantive problems with which sociometrists have been concerned,
such as dominance/submission patterns or prestige and influence
in a specified population, require that the precise nature of
the links between the subjects in the study be defined at the
outset. In social network terminology, the links should represent only one specified content strand. The typical procedure,
therefore, is to ask the subjects to indicate their friendship
choices of other subjects or their choices as leaders for some
particular purpose. The interest of the analyst then switches
to the choice patterns within the population. The analyst then
tries to establish propositions about these patterns and other
social psychological variables. In a sense the social psychologists hold the content of the links constant in their analyses.

The sociological and social anthropological formulations of
social networks, however, differ from the sociometric studies in
two significant ways. First, the data are seldom collected from
defined collectivities using formal questionnaire methods.
Instead they might be collected from respondents in a social
survey, sometimes with a similar restriction about content (e.g.,
Laumann, 1973b), or they may be collected by observation of a
defined group, perhaps supplemented by questionnaires. The second
difference is the more significant: Sociological or social
anthropological interest in social networks focuses on the content of the links. An essential part of the data needed in a
sociological or an anthropological study of a social network

therefore must be the specification of this content. Many of the points of substantive interest to sociologists or social anthropologists emerge from a consideration of coexistence or absence of links of particular kinds.

It should be clear from this that the sociological and social anthropological formulations of the social network are not in any way superior to those employed by the sociometrists, but simply different. The sociometrist's social network is simply not the same thing as a sociologist's network. In what follows I will refer to the notion of social network as employed by sociologists and social anthropologists and will not refer directly to the notions of the sociometrists.

II.   NETWORKS IN SOCIAL ANTHROPOLOGY

Although there is a considerable amount of overlap in both concepts and interests between some social anthropologists and some sociologists, developments relating to social networks differ in each area. In social anthropology, the idea of social networks was first introduced, used purely as a metaphor by Radcliffe-Brown (1952, p. 190) but later as an analytic tool by Barnes (1954) and Bott (1957). The rise of social network studies as a reaction to extreme structural/functional interpretations of social relationships is not as important to this discussion as is the fact that in most of the anthropological studies using social networks the data were collected by intensive fieldwork techniques, frequently through direct observation. This is in keeping with the traditional immersion of anthropologists in the personal relationships of the people whom they are studying and with anthropologists' interest in small scale societies.

The anthropologist refracts particular identifiable strands in aspects of the links among the actors observed into separate strands in network linkages (1969, 1973, 1974). The particular strands identified are determined by the problem under study.

Clearly one basis would be to isolate links on the criterion
of substantive content. For example, the anthropologist may
isolate only the kinship links among actors, or those based upon
ritual performances, and then consider their structure. But a
more fundamental division seems to be between those who choose
structural as opposed to transactional perspectives (Banck, 1973;
Mitchell, 1974). Those who adopt a structural perspective
examine the relationship between behaviors on the one hand and
the morphological and interactional criteria of linkages with
other persons on the other. Typically the focus is on the establishment of normative consensus or the determination of social
status. Bott's (1957) classical study of the relationship between
conjugal role allocation and social networks is an example. For
those who adopt a transactional perspective, the focus is on the
way in which actors engage in exchanges in order to achieve some
end. Typically, the topic of these studies is some sort of
political action. Adrian Mayer's (1966) study of an Indian
local government election is typical. Transactional studies have
close links with the sociological exchange theories developed by
Homans (1961) and Blau (1964), as acknowledged by Kapferer (1969,
p. 182; 1972, p. 4ff), but thus far sociologists' interests have
not followed this.

Anthropologists using network analysis have employed primarily descriptive techniques deriving, no doubt, from their traditional reliance on detailed ethnography. Very few have been
able to, or perhaps felt it necessary to, present their material
systematically, such as in the form of adjacency matrices, which
would permit application of standard graph theoretical procedures.
Exceptions include Harries-Jones (1969) and Kapferer (1969; 1972;
1973), Boissevain (1974), Jongmans (1973). Kapferer (1969) in
particular has presented diagrams (which have provided the basis
for subsequent analysis, e.g., Doreian, 1974, Boissevain 1974)
and sociomatrices of exchange relations among personnel in a
factory both before and at the point of a strike (1974). In

addition he has computed several network measures, which he uses
to support his otherwise descriptive analysis. In particular his
notion of span, which he defines as "The number of links out of
the total viable links between actors...captured by Ego as a result of including specific people within his direct set of relationships (Kapferer, 1969, p. 224), seems particularly appropriate for the sort of analysis he performs.

Wolfe (1970) on the other hand has proposed a scheme to record details on 12 network characteristics. These refer to the
morphology of the links, such as dependence on other links or the
existence of alternative paths: to content, such as functional
differences; to exchange inequalities; and to the context in
which the social relationship occurs, such as an urban or rural
area. The 12 characteristics are coded for each link in the
network and the aggregate of scores over all links compiled into
a "profile" of the network as a whole. This may then be used to
compare networks. So far I have not seen this scheme used in any
substantive analysis.

Jongmans (1973) presents matrices relating to relationships
in a Tunisian village over 11 years. In a manner quite atypi-
cal in anthropology he subjects these data to a systematic analysis of structural balance, an analysis that is intimately integrated with an ethnographic account of the course of events in the
village over 3 years.

Boissevain (1974) provides a detailed ethnographic analysis of
the exchange transactions in the very large networks of two
Maltese people, one of 1751 persons and another of 638. During
the course of his very detailed ethnographic account, Boissevain
makes use of a number of graph theoretic notions such as density
cliques and centrality. In this work there is a pleasing
amalgam of a clearcut theoretical orientation (exchange theory)
applied to a detailed ethnographic account, supported by a systematic quantitative and graph theoretical analysis of the social
network data.

In general, however, social anthropologists have relied upon substantive rather than formal analyses of material relating to social networks. The reasons for this lie presumably in the academic tradition of ethnographic reporting in social anthropology and to the extensive data which would be required to apply formal analytical procedures in this context.

III. NETWORKS IN SOCIOLOGY

The situation in sociology is somewhat different. Whereas in social anthropology the initial impetus for social network analysis took place in the United Kingdom, in sociology the sociometric studies were started by Moreno in the United States in the late 1930s. The borderline between true sociometric studies in social psychology and those conducted within a sociological framework is indistinct. It would be difficult to classify *Personal Influence* (Katz and Lazarfeld, 1955) or *The Acquaintanceship Process* (Newcomb, 1961) as one or the other. In general, however, the notion of the social network does not seem to have caught on in sociology either in the United States or in the United Kingdom.

There have, however, been some studies in which the social network notions have been central, e.g., Caplow (1955), Adams (1967), Katz (1958, 1966), Kadushin (1966, 1968), Nelson (1966), Laumann (1973), Laumann and Guttman (1966), Granovetter (1973), Scheingold (1973), Laumann and Pappi (1973), Wellman *et al.* (1974). On the whole, however, the social network has been used as a general concept rather than as a device for ordering data to facilitate formal analyses.

The studies by Granovetter and Laumann are of particular interest because in their different ways they combine a concern with substantive problems with formal analyses of network material. Granovetter (1973) sets up a set of propositions that state that if a set of people are linked by strong ties, defined as ties of long duration, high, presumably positive, emotional

intensity and great intimacy involving reciprocal services, then
the links among them tend to be interlocked. Conversely, links
involving weak ties, characterized by the opposite set of attributes, are more likely to be radial. Such radial links of weak
ties naturally extend the catchment area for information about
employment possibilities or for the bases for community organization. Granovetter shows that he is familiar with the formal
analytical procedures he might have used; the transitivity model
seems particularly appropriate to the process of job-getting he
is considering. However he does not use it to test his proposition. He argues that his propositions are based on characteristics somewhat different from those assumed in classical structural balance. For example, he uses ties instead of choices and
assumes that strong ties are conducive to transitivity but that
weak ties are not. These modifications do not, however, in
themselves preclude the use of formal analytical procedures
based on the transitivity model.

It seems more probable that in order to test his model
effectively Granovetter would need:

(a) to collect information about the first-, second-, and
higher order stars of the respondents in the study, including an
assessment of the "strength" of the ties in each link in the
stars;

(b) to collect information about the first-, second-, and
higher order zone links of the persons in the star together with,
as before, estimates of the "strength" of the ties in each link;

(c) to elaborate the formal transitivity procedures so as to
enumerate triads involving combinations of strong, weak, and no
links and to compute their incidence probabilities;

(d) to test the departure of observed frequencies of triads
of specified kinds from those expected from random incidence of
links in the three categories of respondents: those who found
their jobs through links involving strong ties, through links
involving average ties, and through links involving weak ties.

That Granovetter did not do this is not surprising. The level
of data collection needed and the skill in modifying the program to achieve the appropriate analysis would be beyond the
scope of most of us--an observation that is germane to the points
I wish to make subsequently.

The analyses that Laumann has conducted have also relied
upon the notion of the social networks (1966, 1973; Laumann and
Pappi, 1973). Laumann's work on urban friends and the nature
of social life in a city (1973) is of particular interest. He
assumes a model in which social networks constitute an intervening
variable between the basic demographic, socioeconomic, and per-
sonality characteristics of individuals and what he calls the
anchorage and crystallization of ethnic, political,and work
attitudes. His social networks have much in common with the
transitivity model: that is, that people involved in social
relationships will tend to share beliefs, attitudes,and orientations and that this will be true particularly if they are involved in interlocking relationships. Of particular interest here
is that Laumann's is one of the few attempts to test some of the
propositions that have emerged from sociological thinking about
social networks. The data he uses were derived from a social
survey in Detroit and the procedure he uses to test the propositions is essentially statistical.

The people in the social networks Laumann studied are the
respondents' "three best friends" as the respondents defined them,
kinsfolk not being excluded from best friends. Personal details
relating to ethnic origin, religious persuasion, age, political
leaning, education, and the extent to which the three friends

knew one another were collected from the respondent. Laumann then computed an index of homogeneity between respondents and their friends and used these indices to compute correlation coefficients with demographic and sociological variables. He also classified the networks of all his respondents into four types of networks ranging from completely interlocking (i.e., maximally dense) to completely radial (i.e., a first order star) and used statistical methods to examine the distribution of these types of networks by social characteristics and their effect on political and social attitudes.

Laumann's results, which to some extent confirm the expectations derived from the general sociological thinking about social networks, are less important here than the connection between the substantive interests of the analyst and the procedures he used to test his propositions. Laumann has a clear formulation of the relationship between the structure of the links in a social network and the behavior (or attitude) of the people involved in those links. They are relationships developed from a priori considerations of the connections between close personal relationships and consensus about beliefs relating to politics, religion, and ethnic values. He also provides one of the few attempts to test these propositions with wide-scale survey data. His procedures are extensive in that he derives fairly general indicators of the characteristics of social networks he wants to examine, categorizes his respondents into equivalence classes in relation to these characteristics, and then proceeds to examine the overlap of these classes with others he defines. His interest is not in the structure of particular networks but rather the molar relationships between characteristics of social networks and other social variables.

IV. THE ALGORITHMISTS

A. *General Remarks*

The pursuit of substantive issues relating to social networks
has been paralleled by, and perhaps overshadowed by, a vigorous
pursuit of formal procedures through which the regularities
implicit in social networks might be made explicit. Each pursuit seems to have disregarded the issues raised by the other.
The need to develop procedures, algorithms in fact, to make explicit the regularities inherent in sociometric data exercised
the ingenuity of a variety of scholars from the 1940s onwards.
The algorithms arose out of the problems defined by sociometrists,
focusing initially on the problem of detecting cliques. These
entailed manipulating adjacency matrices of an order corresponding to the sociograms. The difficulty of effecting these
manipulations before electronic computers became available for
general use, however, constituted a serious barrier to their
widespread use. The expansion of computing facilities in the
1960s introduced dramatic possibilities into network analysis as
well as other types of data analysis. Although manipulation of
sociomatrices to reveal clustering was suggested by analysts in
the 1940s-1950s, they did not achieve wide acceptance because
hand or desk calculators had to be used. Even with computers
commonly available it is only within the last 5 to 10 years that
sufficient interest has developed among sociologists and anthropologists to stimulate practical procedures and some of the more
interesting of these have not yet been published. We are
apparently just at the beginning of a phase of rapid expansion
of analytic capabilities in network analysis.

B. *Graph Theory*

The elementary graph theoretic analytic procedures for social networks include procedures that are able to produce a distance matrix from an adjacency matrix, to determine the strong components of a graph, to produce point centrality indices and similar graph theoretical features from adjacency matrices (e.g., Gleason, n.d.). These measures or characteristics of adjacency matrices refer to some basic feature of the social network but do not in themselves constitute an adequate description of the social network. This can only be achieved in terms of some theoretical perspective and the graph theoretic features measured by these procedures represent building blocks out of which the analyst may possibly erect some structure. Using these notions requires the analsyt to face the difficult epistemological problem of the iso-morphism between the graph theoretic concepts and the substantive concepts, a topic about which there is at present no discussion that I know of.

C. *Clique and Cluster Extracting Procedures*

The earliest procedures introduced by data analysts were de-signed to isolate subsets of actors who were more closely con-nected to one another than to others. The postulate lying behind these clique-detection and clustering procedures is that closely linked actors are likely to act in concert. Actors who are all in direct contact constitute a clique, a set of units in a social network among whom the links are maximally dense.

In reality, however, sets of actors that observers deem to be significant in social action sometimes do not satisfy the strict conditions of a clique. Clusters, that is, sets of actors who satisfy a weakened clique condition, are therefore more practical features of social networks to identify. While clusters may be

significant social groupings, they are more difficult to operationalize in a computer program than the more rigidly defined
clique. This contradiction epitomizes the problem confronting
analysts who wish to use formal methods of network analysis.

There are a confusing variety of clique-detection and
clustering algorithms available. They range from the simple
listing of all the overlapping cliques in a given network, to
sets of units in a social network arranged in increasingly less
tightly linked clusters (see Festinger, 1949; Luce and Perry,
1949; Luce, 1950; Beum and Brundage. 1950; Harary and Ross, 1957;
Coleman and MacRae, 1960; MacRae, 1960; Hubbell, 1965; Spilerman,
1966; Doreian, 1969, 1974; Peay, 1970, 1974; Niemeyer, 1973;
Alba, 1973; and Richards, 1975). These different procedures
involve several different principles and combinations of principles. A number of these were compared for all-round effective-
ness by Lankford (1974), and Roistacher (1974) has described the
mathematical bases of some of them. The problems that derive from
the lack of clear-cut theoretical guidelines have not been re-
solved. Therefore, we cannot develop a specification of what
should be accepted as a cluster. The several different approaches
adopted in the algorithms mean that it is unlikely the same
body of empirical data reveals the same set of clusters when submitted to different clustering programs.

D. Random Net Procedures

Procedures that operate on the basis of random nets demand
more in the way of basic assumptions than those based on density.
These procedures generate a model of what a social network would
look like if the links on it were distributed purely at random.
Biases of a known sort may then be introduced so as to simulate
the actual linkage patterns in the network. The biases are introduced on the basis of some rationale and in effect represent some
postulate about the pattern of linkage in the network (Rapoport
and Horvath, 1961; Fararo and Sunshine, 1964).

Biased nets qualify as true models because they operate upon the basis of postulated parameters with predetermined values. But this makes such stringent demands upon the analyst that they are rarely used to illuminate empirical data in sociology or social anthropology.

E. Transitivity Model Procedures

Procedures based on the concept of transitivity have their origins in structural balance notions, originally due to Heider (1944) and formalized by Cartwright and Harary (1956). These ideas have been considerably elaborated in recent years. Transitivity is a general notion and applies to phenomena wider than the affective orientation of persons in triadic relationships. Davis, in a set of seminal papers (1963, 1967, 1970), has shown how a number of important sociological propositions may be developed from primordial notions of transitivity in interpersonal relations. From these beginnings a set of sophisticated procedures has been developed in which the pattern of relationship in defined groups may be tested against random expectations (Holland and Leinhardt, 1970, 1972; Hallinan, 1974). Emerging from a different strain and employing more sophisticated measurement procedures others (Bernard and Killworth, 1973; Killworth, 1974) have been ploughing parallel furrows.

While the notion of transitivity subsumes that of a clique, in the sense that a clique of n persons may be disaggregated into $\binom{n}{3}$ fully transitive triads, it is clear that the reasoning behind transitivity models is quite distinct from that behind density models and similar results should not be expected to emerge from their application to the same body of material.

F. Structural Equivalence Procedure

Analyses based on these procedures seek to partition a set of
persons in a series of social networks into a number of subsets
such that each subset in the whole contains persons who share the
same "pattern" of social relationships with other persons in the
networks (Lorrain and White, 1971; White, Boorman, and Breiger,
1976; Boorman and White, 1976). These procedures incorporate a
novel feature in that the partitioning is into "blocks" on the
basis of concatenations of different types of social relationships
that the sociologist may have segregated into separate adjacency
matrices for analytical convenience. The relationships among the
blocks may in turn be represented by zero/one matrices that may
then be interpreted as a compact summary of the relationships
among the set of persons in the networks as a whole (see Breiger,
Boorman, and Arabie, 1975). The aspects of the relationships
in personal networks that have been represented in the separate
networks have been qualities of the interaction of the actors,
data perhaps more germane to social psychology than to sociology.
In principle, however, the procedures should be applicable
equally to sociological qualities such as, say, the separable
normative contents in links among persons in a social network.

V. ALGORITHMS AND ANALYSIS

A. Differing Objectives

The existence of these different algorithms, using sometimes
different, sometimes overlapping procedures and assumptions, reflects the current discursive theoretical thinking about social
networks. In effect there is a disparity between the underlying
assumptions and therefore the characteristics of networks taken
to be significant by those interested in network analysis algorithms and those interested in substantive issues. In network
studies, as in other branches of sociological study, there seems

to be a division of labor between those who are seen primarily to
be theorists--or at least those interested in substantive problems, and those who are primarily methodologists--or at least
proficient in the different ways of analyzing given bodies of
data. This typology, like all typologies, simplifies and dis-
torts reality. Many of those who are known as "methodologists"
have usually become so labeled because they have started out on
some substantive problem and in the course of analyzing it have
come to realize the necessity for an improvement over some standard model of analysis. And while most methodologists would
no doubt stoutly proclaim their primary interest in theory, they
face the problem that a useful algorithm must be independent of
the substantive issues in the material to which it is being
applied: In essence data must be decontextualized to make it
amenable to formal analysis. In papers dealing essentially with
ways of abstracting the sociological sense out of social networks
the *procedure*--in extreme cases the *algorithm*--unfortunately
appears to be the be-all and end-all of the exercise.

If we shift our view and examine the substance/procedure
duality as it is handled by those involved essentially in substantive issues then the picture is even less encouraging. The
hard fact of the matter is that as the subject is organized at
present it is a good deal more difficult to acquire the basic
mathematical skills for formal analysis than it is to acquire a
theoretical orientation for sociological analysis. The consequence is that fieldworkers who need to operationalize some
theoretical idea are very badly placed to be able to devise
appropriate procedures to achieve this end. In a sense they may
know what they need to know in order to make some statement in
terms of the set of theoretical concepts with which they are
working, but they do not know how to operationalize it. Ad hoc
procedures devised by ingenious fieldworkers to serve their particular interests are usually open to mordant criticism. Those
with any doubts on the matter should trace the history of the

index of centrality of a social network from Bavelas (1948)
through Beauchamp (1965) to Sabidussi (1966), where the position
seems to be reached that measures that make good intuitive sense
are shown not to measure up to rigid standards of mathematical
acceptability, while the measure that does stand up to mathematical requirements does not seem to be of much practical use.

B. A Case in Point: Multiplexity

The point may perhaps be illustrated by the significance of
the notion of multiplexity in social networks in relation to
current procedures for "analyzing" social networks. From a
sociological point of view the notion of multiplexity presents a
number of interesting theoretical possibilities. Basically the
relationship any actor may bear to any other may, for analytical
purposes, be refracted into various components. Just what sort
of components depends on both the interests of the analyst and the
sort of issues under examination. If the issue is interactional,
as opposed to transactional, for example, one might wish to distinguish the different elements constituting a single relationship between two actors in terms of their different norm-setting
implications for the actors concerned. The analyst may then
interpret the actual behavior of any particular actor in some
specified situation as flowing from the particular concatenation
of elements in the total relationship between actors. The
specifically *social* network, as opposed to dyadic relationships,
emerges when we try to examine the concatenations of contents
in relationships among actors at two and more steps away from
the person assumed to be at the focus of the study. Hitherto
concepts like zone density have proved useful in describing situations of this nature. The first-order zone density anchored on
some defined actor, for example, would be expressed as the ratio
of links of a specified kind among all actors linked directly to
the anchor person to the total possible such links. The

second-order zone density would extend the same notion to people linked to the anchor person by two steps.   To have much utility, however, a measure of density must relate to some specified content of linkage.   One might, for example, refer to the density of kinship links among a set of actors linked to some anchor person, or to the density of links of common occupation.   A measure of *general* density probably would not be useful in sociological analysis.   From a sociological point of view multiplexity should be accorded more weight in the interpretation of social behavior than concepts derived directly from graph theory and commonly used to describe network relationships such as density, reachability, and distance.   These concepts are general concepts, which by their very nature must ignore the content of the links to which they refer: Multiplexity seems to provide one bridge between formal and substantive analyses.

The appeal of the notion of multiplexity may be illustrated by examples of propositions in network analysis that appear to be testable, but that have not yet been tested.   One of these is that multiplex social relationships tend over time to become dense: The more multiplex the relationships are within a given set of persons the more quickly will they become dense.   This is based on the presupposition that if two people interact with a third person regularly in different social contexts then pressures will arise in all three to extend the type of relationships with each other to all three persons.   Co-workers who support the same sports side tend to get jointly involved in other activities more quickly than if they are merely co-workers.   The corrollary of this seems to be that single-stranded relationships tend over time to become less dense so that we would expect social networks to polarize between single-stranded space networks on the one hand and many-stranded networks on the other.

It is true that in the most systematic attempt yet to explore the characteristics of friendship networks and relations to social action, Laumann (1973, Chap. 6) has gone some way towards testing

these notions but he uses correlational rather than causal terms.
He writes: "It is especially noteworthy that interlocking networks are exceptionally likely to be composed of members who are
similar to one another in ethno-religious group memberships,
occupational activities, and political party preferences, while
radial preferences are likely to be more heterogeneous in these
respects (Laumann, 1973, p. 124)." But in fact the causal diagrams he presents (1973, p. 117) show that he thinks the "normative content" of the links of the network determines their interactional characteristics, and these in turn determine its
density. The causal connections between these aspects of the
social network, however, could only be established by examining
the secular trend in the aspects of a given network over time--a
fact of which Laumann is perfectly well aware since he writes:
"In view of the multiplexity of significant relationships reported, there is considerable theoretical and empirical promise
in pursuing a more detailed examination of how these networks
come to be formed and how they function once in existence
(1973, p. 128)."

The notion of multiplexity, however, may be related to other
aspects of network morphology. For example, another proposition
is that actors involved with one another in a variety of different
social contexts will have, by this fact, more extensive personal
investment in one another than if they were involved in only
single-stranded relationships. This is the rationale behind the
difference between *gemeinschaftliche* and *gesellschaftliche* societies, between the small scale rural and large scale urban social
structure, and it has been part of our sociological heritage since
at least the days of Töennies (see for example, Bott, 1957; Barnes,
1964; Mitchell, 1969; Laumann, 1973). Casting this proposition
in terms of abstract entities such as groups or societies
emasculates any attempt to test it due to the confounding effects
of contextual or historical particularity. But it ought to be
possible to operate at a much lower level of abstraction and

examine cohesion or the lack thereof in specified small populations. This will allow delineation of the characteristics of
multiplexity in different links, and, therefore, could provide
at least some test of the proposition. But there are several
impediments to achieving this:

(1) The different aspects of social relationships must be
representable as networks. These aspects of social relationships must be distinguishable and permit representation as distinct links in networks, each of which will refer to one specific
aspect of the relationship and to no other. If this is possible
then the set of relationships can be represented in a total network with discrete lines representing different aspects. This is
no mean requirement for it implies that our conceptual tools must
be sharp enough to dissect one component cleanly from another.
The implication is that multiplexity is essentailly a construct
of the analyst. One analyst's multiplexity is no doubt another's
utter confusion.

(2) Sociological theorizing must be of sufficient sophistication to enable identification of aspects of social relationships
that are worth isolating for an examination of the problem. This
involves difficult epistemological problems, some of which have
been raised elsewhere (Mitchell, 1973). This is a natural extension of notions of the duality between multiplexity and a conceptual framework, in terms of which the component elements of a
total relationship may be separated.

(3) Having achieved both these objectives, information about
all the relationships among *all* in the population must be available to enable the use of systematic methods of analysis. This
involves the previously mentioned problems in data collection.

(4) Following data collection it is necessary to recover the
pattern or patterns in the concatenation of aspects of relations
among all persons concerned, and to spell out the implication
of their combinations--implications that may not be immediately

apparent or obvious to the fieldworker. It is here that the
choice of an appropriate algorithm becomes a matter of some moment, for the algorithm must operate in terms of properties that
are isomorphic with the analyst's concepts. It is at this point
that the lack of isomorphism between the notions underlying substantive analyses on the one hand and the procedures upon which
algorithms are based on the other, comes home to roost.

    (5) The final step is to relate the pattern of strands in
social relationships to some independent criterion of "cohesion."
This could be on the basis of some synchronous indicator as for
example, say, some attitude test but a better measure would be to
observe the same set of actors, over sufficient time for the
polarization or other social relationships to occur.

VI.   CONCLUSION

    The difficulties in testing propositions of this kind are
obvious. In most of the separate steps outlined except perhaps
for the last, which calls for systematic longitudinal studies of
social networks undergoing change, considerable advances have
already been made. What appears to be missing at the moment
are integrated approaches in which propositions are developed
from postualtes out of the conceptual framework informing the
network study: effective and extensive data collection over time
sufficient to observe the structural changes; and finally the
representation of these patterns by analytical procedures that
are compatible with the conceptual framework. In other words,
the essentially unitary aspects of empirical enquiry--substantive
conceptualization, systematic data collection, and extensive
formal analysis of the data using an algorithm consonant with the
theoretical notions underlying the analysis--seem at present
to be becoming dangerously disconnected. My own judgment would
be that the weak link in the chain at present is the current
low level of substantive conceptualization: The data collection

and the formal analysis ought to flow naturally from the conceptual framework. As soon as we are clear about what we want to know, not only will it be relatively easy to say what sort of data ought to be collected but it will also be relatively easy to say what sort of algorithm is needed to carry out an effective analysis.

REFERENCES

Adams, B. N. Interaction theory and the social network. *Sociometry,* 1967, *30,* 64-78.

Alba, R. D. A graph-theoretic definition of a sociometric clique. *Journal of Mathematical Sociology,* 1973, *3,* 113-126.

Aronson, D. R. Editor's Preface in *The Canadian Review of Sociology and Anthropology,* 1970, 7 (4), 221-225.

Banck, G. A. Network analysis and social theory. In J. Boissevain & J. Clyde Mitchell (Eds.). *Network analysis. Studies in human interaction.* The Hague: Mouton, 1973.

Barnes, J. A. Class and committees in a Norwegian island parish. *Human Relations,* 1954, *7,* 39-58.

Barnes, J. A. *Social networks.* Reading, Massachusetts: Addison-Wesley Modular Publications 26, 1972.

Bavelas, A. A mathematical model for group structures. *Applied Anthropology,* 1948, *7,* 16-30.

Beauchamp, M. A. An improved index of centrality. *Behavioural Science,* 1965, *10,* 161-163.

Bernard, R. H., & Killworth, P. D. On the social structure of an ocean-going research vessel and other important things. *Social Science Research,* 1973, *2,* 145-184.

Beum, C. O., & Brundage, E. G. A method for analysing the sociomatrix. *Sociometry,* 1950, *13,* 141-145.

Blau, P. M. *Exchange and power in social life.* London: Wiley, 1964.

Boissevain, J.   Preface in J. Boissevain & J. Clyde Mitchell
    (Eds.).   *Network analysis: studies in human interaction*.
    The Hague: Mouton, 1973. Pp. vii-xiii.

Boorman, Scott A., & White, Harrison C.   Social structure from
    multiple networks: Part II: Role structures. *American
    Journal of Sociology*, 1976, *81*, 1384-1446.

Bott, E.   *Family and social network* (2nd ed.).   London: Tavistock
    Publications, 1971.

Breiger, R. L., Boorman, Scott A., & Arabie, Phipps.   An algorithm
    for clustering relational data with applications to social
    network analysis and comparison with multidimensional scaling.
    Journal of Mathematical Psychology, 1975, *12* (3), 326-383.

Caplow, T.   The definition and measurement of ambiance. *Social
    forces*, 1955, *34*, 28-33.

Cartwright, D., & Harray F.   Structural balance: A generalization
    of Heider's theory. *Psychological Review*, 1956, *63*, 277-293.

Coleman, J., & MacRae, D., Jr.   Electronic processing of
    sociometric data for groups up to a thousand in size.
    American Sociological Review, 1960, *25*, 722-726.

Davis, J. A.   Structural balance, mechanical solidarity and inter-
    personal relations. *American Journal of Sociology*, 1963,
    68 (4), 444-462.

Davis, J. A.   Clustering and structural balance in graphs. *Human
    Relations*, 1967, *20*, 181-187.

Davis, J. A.   Clustering and hierarchy in interpersonal relations:
    Testing two graph-theoretical models on 742 sociomatrices.
    American Sociological Review, 1970, *35*, 843-851.

Doreian, P.   A note on the detection of cliques in valued graphs.
    Sociometry, 1969, *32*, 237-242.

Doreian, P.   On the connectivity of social networks. *Journal of
    Mathematical Sociology*, 1974, *3*, 245-258.

Fararo, T. J., & Sunshine, M. H.   *A study of a biased friendship
    net*. Syracuse: Syracuse University. Youth Development
    Center, 1964.

Festinger, L. The analysis of sociograms using matrix algebra. *Human Relations*, 1949, *2*, 153-158.

Gleason, T. C. *DIP: A directed graph processor*. Center for Group Dynamics, University of Michigan (n.d.).

Granovetter, M. S. The strength of weak ties. *American Journal of Sociology*, 1973, *78* (6), 1360-1380.

Hallinan, M. T. *The structure of positive sentiment*. Amsterdam: Elsevier Scientific Publishing Co., 1974.

Harary F., & Ross, I. C. A procedure for clique detection using the group matrix. *Sociometry*, 1957, *20* (3), 205-216.

Harary, F., Norman, R. Z., & Cartwright, D. *Structural models: An introduction to the theory of directed graphs*. New York: Wiley, 1965.

Harries-Jones, P. 'Home-boy' ties and political organization in a copperbelt township. In J. Clyde Mitchell (Ed.), *Social networks in urban situations*. Manchester: Manchester University Press, 1969. Pp. 297-347.

Heider, F. Social perception and phenomenal causality. *Psychological Review*, 1944, *51*, 358-374.

Holland, P. W., & Leinhardt, S. A method for detecting structure in sociometric data. *American Journal of Sociology*, 1970, *56*, 492-513.

Holland, P. W., & Leinhardt, S. Some evidence on the transitivity of positive interpersonal sentiment. *American Journal of Sociology*, 1972, *72*, 1205-1209.

Homans, G. *Social behavior: Its elementary forms*. London: Routledge and Kegan Paul, 1961.

Hubbell, C. E. An input-output approach to clique identification. *Sociometry*, 1965, *28*, 377-399.

Jongmans, D. G. Politics on the village level. In J. Boissevain & J. Clyde Mitchell (Eds.). *Network analysis: Studies in human interaction*. The Hague: Mouton, 1973. Pp. 107-217.

Kadushin, C. The friends and supporters of psychotherapy: On
    social circles in urban life. *American Sociological Review,*
    1966, *31,* 786-802.

Kadushin, C. Power, influence and social circles: A new
    methodology for studying opinion makers. *American Sociologi-*
    cal Review, 1968, *33,* 689-699.

Kapferer, B. Norms and the manipulation of relationships in a
    work context. In J. Clyde Mitchell (Ed.). *Social networks*
    in urban situations. Manchester: Manchester University
    Press, 1969. Pp. 181-244.

Kapferer, B. *Strategy and transaction in an African factory.*
    Manchester: Manchester University Press, 1972.

Kapferer B. Social network and conjugal role in urban Zambia:
    Toward a reformulation of the Bott hypothesis. In
    J. Boissevain & J. Clyde Mitchell (Eds.), *Network analysis:*
    Studies in human interaction. The Hague: Mouton, 1973.
    Pp. 83-110.

Katz, E., & Lazarfeld, P. *Personal influence*. Glencoe: The
    Free Press, 1955.

Katz, F. E. Occupation contact networks. *Social Forces,* 1958,
    37, 52-55.

Katz, F. E. Social participation and social structure. *Social*
    Forces, 1966, *45,* 199-210.

Killworth, P. D. Intransitivity in the structure of small closed
    groups. *Social Science Research,* 1974, *3,* 1-23.

Lankford, P. M. Comparative analysis of clique identification
    methods. *Sociometry,* 1974, *37,* 287-305.

Laumann, E. O., & Guttman L. The Relative associational con-
    tiguity of occupations in an urban setting. *American*
    Sociological Review, 1966, *3* (2), 169-178.

Laumann, E. O. *Bonds of pluralism: The form and substance of*
    urban social networks. New York: Wiley, 1973.

Laumann, E. O., & Pappi, F. U.   New directions in the study of
community elites. *American Sociological Review,* 1973, *38* (2),
212-230.

Lorrain, F., & White, H. C.   Structural equivalence of individuals
in social networks. *Journal of Mathematical Sociology,* 1976,
1, 49-80.

Luce, R. D.   Connectivity and generalized cliques in sociometric
group structure. *Psychometrika,* 1950, *15,* 169-190.

Luce, R. D., & Perry, A.   A method of matrix analysis of group
structure. *Psychometrika,* 1949, *14,* 94-116.

MacRae, D., Jr.   Direct factor analysis of sociometric data.
Sociometry, 1960, *23,* 360-370.

Mayer, A. C.   The significance of quasi-groups in the study of
complex societies.   In M. Banton (Ed.), *The social anthropology of complex societies.* London: Tavistock Publications,
1966.

Mitchell, J. C.   The concept and use of social networks.   In
J. Clyde Mitchell (Ed.), *Social networks in urban situations.*
Manchester: Manchester University Press for Institute for
African Studies, Zambia, 1969. Pp 1-50.

Mitchell, J. C.   Networks, norms and institutions.   In
J. Boissevain & J. Clyde Mitchell (Eds.), *Network analysis:
Studies in human interaction.* The Hague: Mouton, 1973.
Pp. 15-36.

Mitchell, J. C.   Social networks.   In B. Siegal, A. R. Beals, &
S. A. Tyler (Eds.), *Annual review of anthropology.* Palo
Alto, California: Annual Reviews, Inc., 1974. Pp. 279-299.

Nelson, J. I.   Clique contacts and family orientations. *American
Sociological Review,* 1966, *31,* 663-672.

Newcomb, T. M.   *The Acquaintanceship process.* New York: Holt,
Rinehart, and Winston, 1961.

Niemeijer, R. Some applications of the notion of density. In J. Boissevain & J. Clyde Mitchell (Eds.), *Network analysis: Studies in human interaction*. The Hague: Mouton, 1973. Pp. 45-64.

Peay, E. R. *An iterative clique detection procedure.* Michigan Mathematical Psychology Program Technical Report. MMPP 70-74. University of Michigan, 1970.

Peay, E. R. Hierarchical clique structures. *Sociometry,* 1974, *37* (1), 54-65.

Radcliffe-Brown, A. R. *Structure and function in primitive society: Essays and addresses*. London: Cohen & West, 1952.

Rapoport, A., & Horvath, W. J. A study of a large sociogram. *Behavioral Science,* 1961, *6*, 279-291.

Richards, W. D. J. *A manual for network analysis (using the NECOPY network analysis program)*. Palo Alto: Stanford University, Institute for Communication Research, 1975.

Roistacher, R. C. A review of mathematical methods in sociometry. *Sociological Methods and Research,* 1974, *3* (2), 123-171.

Sabidussi, G. The centrality index of a graph. *Psychometrika,* 1966, *31* (4), 581-603.

Scheingold, C. A. Social networks and voting: The resurrection of a research agenda. *American Sociological Review,* 1973, *38* (6), 712-720.

Spilerman, S. Structural analysis and the generation of socio-grams. *Behavioral Science,* 1966, *11,* 312-318.

Wellman, B., *et al. Urban connections*. Toronto: University of Toronto, Center for Urban and Community Studies, 1974.

White, H. C., Boorman, S. A., & Breiger, R. L. Social structure from multiple networks: Part I: Blockmodels of roles and positions. *American Journal of Sociology,* 1976, *81,* 730-780.

Whitten, N., & Wolfe, A. Network analysis. In J. Honigmann
   (Ed.), *Handbook of social and cultural anthropology*.
   Chicago: Rand McNally, 1974.

Wolfe, A. On structural comparisons of networks. *The Canadian
   Review of Sociology and Anthropology*, 1970, 7 (4), 226-244.

CHAPTER 21

COGNITIVE BALANCE THEORY AND SOCIAL NETWORK ANALYSIS:
REMARKS ON SOME FUNDAMENTAL THEORETICAL MATTERS

Bo Anderson

Department of Sociology
Michigan State University
East Lansing, Michigan

I. INTRODUCTION

The network metaphor, already present in some influential
classical writings, has gotten increasingly entrenched in the
thinking of contemporary sociology and social anthropology. One
reason is that network ideas bridge, both factually and conceptually, two usually disparate areas of inquiry, namely research
on small groups and research on macrounits, such as communities,
associations, formal organizations, regions, social strata,
classes, and so on.

Research on social networks seems to fall into three major
classes. *First,* there are the many case studies of network
anatomy and dynamics. Most of the contributions to a widely
used collection of networks papers fall in this category
(Mitchell, 1969). Events are described and accounted for
("explained") by placing them in a matrix of contacts, obliga-
tions, and other bonds between a set of persons. The theoretical
principles used are ad hoc, or else they remain largely implicit
and uncodified. *Second*, there are the many attempts to develop
formal procedures suitable for the construction and evaluation

of *representational models*[1] of networks. The clique detection
methods belong in this category, and also the recent "block
models" (White, 1976). The methods are algebraic and few, if any,
commitments are made to stated substantive theoretical assumptions. The goal is to represent a network structure in a
parsimonious and intuitively revealing manner, rather than to
explain process. *Third*, a small number of investigators have
attempted to develop *theories* designed to *explain* the events
observed in social networks. In contrast with the abundance of
case studies of networks and the increasing sophistication of network representation methods, the attempts to build explanatory
theories are few and far between. This is quite strange, for
even a casual survey of the social networks literature reveals
many questions that ought to intrigue theorists. Yet, in contrast to the ever increasing sophistication of the formal method
of network representation, the explanatory task has by and large
not been begun. There is one main exception to this dismal
characterization of social network theory, however: Structural
balance theory has been extended to social networks, with some
preliminary success. The purpose of this chapter is to examine
the usefulness of structural balance theory as a tool for the
analysis and exploration of social networks.

[1]*For a characterization of* representational models *(contrasting them with two other classes of models) see J. Berger,
et al.,* Types of Formalization *(Boston: Houghton Mifflin).*

II. BALANCE THEORY

A. *General Remarks*

Balance ideas have been used for studying the clique structures in sociometric networks for some time. These are usually
networks created by an investigator from answers to standardized
questions like "whom do you like to sit next to," or "name the
five persons you most like to be with during recess." These
questions are designed to "tap into" a sentiment, "degree of
liking," and are taken to reflect *both* preferences and overt
behavior. However, it is not very clear how an understanding of
networks of this kind helps when we want to understand such
processes as instrumental exchange networks described by social
anthropologists, students of political organizations, interorganizational linkages, community structures, and so on. The
issue here concerns the relevance of balance theory for general
analyses of social networks. It may be important in some way
but exactly how it helps us understand the emergence, maintenance,
and decay of links between persons in social networks that are
designed for *instrumental* transactions, that is, networks through
which "commodities" like political favors and reciprocations,
business or administrative intelligence, job offers, patronage,
and the like flow, and in which political alliances, community
standing, or political clout are built up, maintained or, as
time goes on, inevitably lost (Anderson and Carlos, 1976; Carlos
and Anderson, 1977) is not yet clear. This question will lead
us to a more general one: What are the reasons why persons sometimes (but not always) prefer balanced states over imbalanced
ones? It is not at all difficult to find examples of how persons
learn to live with, or even prefer, imbalanced triads or larger
structures. At the *same* time, there is no doubt that structural
balance theory has received impressive corroboration in
empirical research. Not only is there data from the Davis *et al.*

research program I will refer to later, but also a variety of
other studies, many of which are, after a fashion, experimental.
For a convenient summary the reader is referred to Webster's summary (Webster, 1975, Chaps. 12-14). The theoretical puzzle
concerns the nature of the processes that lie behind persons'
adoption of balance practices. To put it bluntly, why is
balance theory so empirically successful, even though obvious
counterexamples to its assertions are very easy to find?

B. The Davis, Holland, and Leinhardt Research

In discussing balance theory it is convenient to focus on the
variant of the theory that is used in a series of papers by
Davis, Leinhardt, and Holland (Davis, 1967; Davis, 1970; Holland
and Leinhardt, 1970; Holland and Leinhardt, 1971; Davis and
Leinhardt, 1972; Leinhardt, 1972; Holland and Leinhardt, 1973;
and Holland and Leinhardt, 1974). Their work comprises a coherent research program and analyzes a large body of sociometric
data, using a set of core ideas drawn from the theory of structural balance. (In addition to balance notions, propositions
stated by Homans are used in the research program.) Stochastic
models based on the balance notions fit the data reasonably well.
However, some of the results and theoretical ideas are bound to
appear very strange to persons who study instrumental transactional networks. For instance, in political networks the transitivity idea seems implausible: If A is politically allied with
B and B is allied with C, then A may or may not be allied with
C. Transitivity is certainly not expected to occur as a matter
of course in political networks. In fact, imbalanced triads are
very common in politics: A may maintain excellent and stable
relations with both B and C despite the fact that B and C are
political antagonists. A may even attempt to sustain the antagonism between B and C. If A's power is precarious, then A will
have very good reasons for trying to keep B and C from coming

together. "Divide and rule," that ancient maxim of power politics, surely has to fit into *any* plausible theory of social
structure.

It is a curious fact that much more energy seems to have gone
into the development of the *formalism* of structural balance
theory, for example, the generalization of the structure theorem,
than into the developments of the *substantive* ideas behind the
theory. The result has been an increasing *substantive* sterility.
To remedy this I believe that we need to go back to the kind of
work that Fritz Heider originally did on balance theory (Heider,
1958). There we find a phenomenological method employed in
painstaking analyses of *concrete* situations, attempting to spell
out the principles that underlie the bewildering richness of
insights into how interpersonal relations "feel" or are used in
interaction work, and how slight shifts of emphasis and content
will change the way that any one relation will fit into patterns.
Is it the status value associated with "formal" theory that has
led balance theorists to shy away from the hard work of thinking
about the tricky issues of scope for the theoretical assertions?

As I indicated previously, it is not difficult to find
institutional contexts where the transitivity proposition of
balance theory seems implausible, or where imbalanced triads
persist for a long time and their maintenance is seen to be in
the interests of participating parties. The transitivity principle is of course also violated in many mundane situations.
The *friendship relation* is, in practice, often intransitive: If
A is a friend of *B* and *B* and *C* are friends, then it does not automatically follow that *A* is a friend of *C*. It may of course be
that when *A* encounters *C* for the first time, knowing that *C* is a
friend of his friend *B,* he will feel favorably disposed toward *C.*
Whether or not a friendship will develop from such a favorable
first impression depends on what transactions are added to the
first impression. We have all encountered cases in which some-
body has said, " You *must* meet so-and-so," only to find that we

have little in common with that person, even though he or she
was introduced to us by a mutual friend. It may well be that
most of us carry in our minds a low level program routine that
in the absence of any contradictory evidence, produces an initially friendly impression when we encounter our friends' friends.
This practice of minimal courtesy and friendship loyalty should,
however, not be confused with the establishment of a reliable
link in the social network. The new link is tested and watched
before any one dares to depend on it; this is so the more
instrumentally important the network is. In some cases we even
have higher order rules that tell us to be wary of such initial friendly impressions and their potential consequences. In
some friendships the persons value the exclusiveness of their
relationship and are therefore not likely to easily let others
into it. Friends differ from acquaintances in that they are *not*
merely slots in a grid of social network relations, but are
valued for their personal, *unique* qualities (Paine, 1969). Hence,
when I relate to a friend of a friend, I need to know something
about the perceptions and exchanges that make up this friendship.
My reaction to my friend's friend (or spouse) may even be *unfavor-*
able, although I may *also* well understand and sympathize with my
friend's affection for her, given *his* needs, perceptions, interests and so on. There is nothing strange in the statement: "*I*
don't like her but she is a fine wife for him, and I want the
best for him."

I am suggesting here that structural balance, including the
transitivity principle, should be seen *not* as laws of behavior,
but rather as rules-of-thumb that persons sometimes use when
they construe their life-worlds; they are rules which are activated by factors that the individuals attribute to the situation
at hand, but which *can* be, and often *are*, superseded by higher
order considerations. A politician who bases his power and
influence on a network of alliances cannot often indulge in

balancing practices. He may, of course, deliberately choose to
use the predilections that he *thinks* others have toward balanced
triads if he desires to cement or dissolve relationships among
those others. A manipulation game becomes possible, in which
the participants do not apply the balance preference to themselves, but assume that the others are uncomfortable with
imbalanced relationships.

Davis, Leinhardt, and Holland have assembled a great deal
of data in support of some propositions in structural balance
theory. Their achievement can now be reformulated in a more
precise manner: They have found a set of group situations in
which the participants do seem to use the transitivity rule;
completely missing in their research program, however, is any
attempt to define the scope of this set. Until we know precisely what it is about the situations studied that makes persons
use the transitivity rule, we have not learned very much about
transitivity. We are not dealing with a semantic quibble here:
There is a big difference between saying that we have data from
546 groups corroborating a behavioral *law* of transitivity and that
we have found that persons in 546 groups, because of certain
group features that we cannot yet specify, use a transitivity
rule when they form subgroups. The *size* of the sample is *not*
important, but the specification of those group properties which
when present, make people use this behavior rule is. The fact
that Davis, Leinhardt, and Holland obtain good fits between their
data and their models should lead us to expect that there indeed
are some clear and delineable group characteristics that "acti-
vate" the transitivity rule. But, their findings are entirely
preliminary, because the crucial and unanswered question is:
Precisely what kind(s) of groups were they studying?

It is possible to speculate in a tentative fashion about the
characteristics of the groups that make it *look* like members are
using transitivity and balance rules when they form subgroups.
In a group of children that splits into smaller play groups

during recess, it is easy to see why A may have to select C as a
playmate when C is a close friend of his own friend, B. For, A
knows very well, that if he wants to play with B, then he will
also have to play with C and that if he does not play with C then
B will desert him. The choice of C by A in a sociometric test
is in this case simply a concession to B after A has chosen B.
There is not necessarily any transitive spread of *sentiment* here,
merely a cognitive *recognition* by A of the facts of the situation.
Similarly, if A is inclined to choose C but knows that B is dead
set against C, he may avoid choosing C once he has chosen B. And
A may also at times avoid choosing B if he knows that this means
that he has then to put up with C. Such considerations should be
expected to occur with great ease in groups where by and large
the members see most of the others as *at least plausible* playmates
or companions. Also, the choices made can easily be changed at
short notice, the cliques rearranged, since no significant *resources* are committed. However, if the groups have specific
tasks to accomplish and if there exist rather substantial ability
differences with respect to these among the members of the group,
then we would expect this form of transitivity to occur a great
deal *less* smoothly. Assume that A sees both himself and B as
competent at a task, but thinks C incompetent. Even if B wants
to include his friend C, A may still be upset if choosing B entails having to put up with C. B knows how A feels, and C very
likely, in the end, gets excluded.

Politics is an arena in which a variety of specialized resources and interests coexist, coalesce, and come asunder. The
stakes in outcomes are often high. This affects whether or not
balance rules are used. Assume that A has good relations with
both B and C although the latter two are political enemies. In
this situation B and C may regard A as a useful go-between (a
broker), because they both, however reluctantly, will admit that
they occasionally have joint interests. And A may of course know
that he needs good relations with both B and C in order to obtain

resources that he could not otherwise obtain: They each have something special and unique to offer him. In that situation, both *B* and *C* would think that it would be quite irrational of *A* if he did not maintain good relations with their enemy. And, we can, of course, go one step further: A political entrepreneur or political broker will make it a point to create imbalanced triads. He will deliberately cultivate persons who are not on speaking terms, because he stands to gain from mediating.

In summary, two critical points have been made concerning the current practice of structural balance theory: (1) Balance propositions have erroneously been viewed as candidates for the status of behavior laws. Instead, they should be seen as a set of rules for forming social relationships, used indexically by persons in *some* contexts. Given the context markers, the balance rules, for example, the transitivity rules, will be activated, or they will be suspended and other rules in persons' repertoires will be used. A research problem important for development of balance theory is to specify the context markers that make members of groups use balance rules and the markers that effect their suspension. (2) There has been a failure in balance theory to deal seriously with obvious negative cases. It is easy to find counterexamples to the transitivity rule; any further knowledge about the conditions of activation of this rule will have to come from careful analyses of the positive and negative cases. It is time that we put balance theory back into the phenomenological tradition. This obviously does not mean that we are uninterested in the formal work that has been done; the mathematical analysis of balance phenomena seems, however, to have gained its own momentum and we do not here need to worry about its future.

The phenomenological and substantive analyses should devote much effort to the substantive interpretations of the formal structure that the graph theoretical models have yielded. The structure and clustering theorems (Cartwright and Harary, 1956;

Davis, 1967) spell out the formal relationships between the
graph theoretic balance notion and the partitioning of signed
graphs. In graph theory there exists a *formal* balance theory
that contains theorems that are *analytically* true. The statement that Heider's *psychological* balance can be represented,
in its essential aspects, by a suitable interpretation of that
formal balance theory should, however, be regarded as problem-
atical. We cannot routinely identify the positive and negative
lines in the formal theory with positive and negative "sentiment
relations," and identify the formal balance notion with the
psychological idea of balance or structural tension. Empirical
research has shown that *some* social situations representable by
graphs that are formally imbalanced tend to exhibit features that
indicate that they are also psychologically imbalanced. As already pointed out, other situations may look formally unbalanced
but are not seen to be substantially unbalanced by participants.
It is puzzling that the fine structure of the relationships between formal and psychological balance has been given scant
attention by balance theorists.

Some illustrations from the Davis, Leinhardt, and Holland
research program can serve to explain what I mean by this statement. In one of his papers Davis says:

> Putting it another way, a graph may lack clusters for two
> different reasons: because it contains internal contra-
> dictions in the form of cycles with a single negative line
> and/or because it is incomplete in such a way as to make the
> plus set ambiguous (1967, p. 183).

This is clearly a purely *formal* statement about graphs. Davis
then goes on to say that "this notion leads to some thoughts on
the dynamics of social groups." One thought that comes to his
mind is that "relationships that lie on a cycle with a single
negative line will tend to change in such a fashion as to make

the graph clusterable." On the next page in his article Davis
continues to develop substantive ideas about the effects of
strains in positive or negative lines, reinforcement of signs,
emergence of new lines that are positive or negative (completion
processes), and sign shifts or the disappearance of lines in
graphs.

Davis' discussion deals with the ways in which psychologically balanced or imbalanced structures remain balanced or change
toward balance. To test these ideas we would require investigations of how groups represented by various combinations of
negatively and positively signed lines behave over time. To my
knowledge no such research has been done. The research program
of Davis, Leinhardt, and Holland that relies on cross-sectional
analyses of sets of sociograms contains no such analyses. Yet
it would seem that investigations along the lines indicated
here will be necessary if we are ever going to fully establish
the representation of the concept "structural tension" in the
substantive theory of social structure by the concept balance in
the *formal* balance theory. The representation of a substantive
process by a formal system is obviously not a matter of hand-
waving or fiat. The failure to distinguish the formal from the
substantive balance theory has led to hasty and careless statements and claims. Take for instance the following statement by
Davis (1967):

> In the case of symmetrical sentiments (friends and enemies)
> the Cartwright and Harary balance theorem as Rapoport and
> others have noticed, generates a number of aphorisms regard-
> ing friends and enemies:
>
> (1) A friend of a friend will be a friend, not an enemy.
> (2) An enemy of a friend will be an enemy, not a friend.
> (3) A friend of an enemy will be an enemy, not a friend.
> (4) An enemy of an enemy will be a friend.

The Cartwright and Harary balance *theorem* "generates," of
course, nothing of the sort. Their structure theorem and other
theorems are provable within the formal system; the theorems do
not contain substantive terms like "friend" and "enemy," but
are concerned solely with formal entities called "lines,"
"points," "signs," "cycles," and so on. When we *interpret* a
positive line between points to mean "friendship" or a negative
line to mean "hostility" then we are going *beyond* the formal system. We are making a wager that when the formal calculus becomes
so interpreted it will yield, deductively, certain substantive
results. We are asserting that for every formally imbalanced
graph, all its substantive interpretations, identifying points as
persons, positively signed lines with expressions like "is a
friend of," "likes," etc., and negatively signed ones with "is
hostile towards," "dislikes," etc., will be in states of *psychological* tension. (If we assume that balance theory is *p*-centric,
then any graph has a number of interpretations depending on where
in the graph the point representing the *perceiver* is located.)
To establish the validity of this claim is a tall order and demands a great deal of detailed research.

The confusion between formal and substantive balance also
shows up in a somewhat different way in another statement in
Davis' paper. "It can be shown that the first three propositions
will continue to hold under the clustering theorem." This seems
to imply that the first three propositions can be established by
formal proof. But, obviously, they cannot; they are substantive
propositions and can only be corroborated by empirical research.
The terms "friend" and "enemy" do not have clear-cut meaning, but
as Paine and other social anthropologists have shown (Paine,
1969), there is a good deal of cultural variation in conceptions
of friendships, and certainly more is involved than positive and
negative sentiments.

Substantive balance theory consists mostly of hunches, loosely formulated ideas, and paradigmatic examples; its representation by formal graph theory can obviously not be established by the formal methods of a representation theorem.

III. SENTIMENT VERSUS INFORMATION PROCESSING

The proper domain of balance theories is often said to be sentiment relations. These are taken to be expressed by people's answers to a variety of questions, for example, "Who are your three best friends?" "With whom do you want to work?" and the like. The term "sentiment" suggests that writers have in mind emotions or feeling. It is not very clear what the term "sentiment" contrasts with; in fact, one does not find in the writings of Davis, Leinhardt, and Holland *any* attempt to specify the substantive domain of balance theories. At any rate, I do not believe that we will find out what sentiment relations are merely by looking at the questions that serve as sociometric indicators of those relations. Persons do not answer these questions in a vacuum, but have purposes, activities, and goals in mind. It is information, *relevant* to choices, that is being evaluated and processed by the participants, and some sentiments are taken as admittedly imperfect guides in this process. The balance rule represents *one,* maybe minor, part of the logic by which we process imputations about the tasks, goals, and qualities of other persons that are or might become relevant for our own choices. For instance, if B, whom we have high regard for, tells us that C is a very trustworthy or reliable person, then we are likely to form high expectations about C's moral worth. In some situations, however, we regard such information with suspicion; we ask what were B's motives for recommending C so highly? In many cases we may have few opportunities to obtain any information about C other than that given us by C's friends. Our initial response to C becomes a measure of the trust we have for B, and B, being

aware of this, may hesitate before vouching for C. The more
important B's tie to A is for him, the more cautious he will be
to recommend C to A (the weakness of strong ties). In situations
of imbalance we are confronted by contradictory sets of information, and it may become necessary for us to attempt to harmonize
the contradictions. The balancing operations described in the
literature and shown to exist in experiments reflect the attempts
by persons to reevaluate contradictory information. That balance
principles do not always determine how resolution takes place is
shown by experiments by Berger and Fisek (Berger and Fisek, 1968)
and Tress (Tress, 1971). These experiments show that a "combining" operation is sometimes used when persons are presented
with contradictory but task-relevant information.

Progress toward a fuller understanding of the transitivity
phenomenon should come if we develop our understanding of why
and how persons seek and obtain and make use of information
about others that they obtain second-hand. A deeper understanding of imbalanced states should follow from a more general
theoretical treatment of how people process and evaluate inconsistent sets of task-relevant information about others, as part
of their practical actions.

My student Richard Hurst and I have recently completed a
paper that attempts to show, in a very preliminary manner, how
research procedures available in social psychology can be
adapted to the study of the minutia of the information-processing
logic used by members of small groups. A set of six collective
practices used by groups, when asked to construct decisions
given inconsistent information about the qualificatons of
alleged applicants for scholarships, are identified, and some

(incomplete) experiments are now being run to deepen our understanding of how participants in decisions involving inconsistent
characteristics[2] view the logic they use when reaching decisions.

REFERENCES

Anderson, Bo, & Carlos, Manuel. Political brokerage and network
politics in Mexico. In David Willer and Bo Anderson, *Social
exchange and social networks,* Elsevier 1979.

Anderson, Bo, & Carlos, Manuel. What is social network theory?
London: Sage Publications, 1975.

Berger, J., Cohen, B. P., Zelditch, M., & Snell, J. L. *Types of
formalization.* Boston: Houghton Mifflin, 1962.

Berger, Joseph, & Fisek, M. Hamit. Consistent and inconsistent
status characteristics and the determination of power and
prestige orders. *Sociometry,* 1970, *33,* 287-304.

Cartwright, Dorwin, & Harary, Frank. Structural balance: A
generalization of Heider's theory. *Psychological Review,*
1956, *63,* 277-293.

Davis, James A. Clustering and structural balance in graphs.
Human Relations, 1967, *20,* 181-187.

Davis, James A. Clustering and hierarchy in interpersonal
relations: Testing two graph theoretical models on 742 sociomatrices. *American Sociological Review,* 1970, *35* (5),
843-851.

[2]*Bo Anderson and Richard Hurst, "Formulating Agreements about
Rewards in Small Groups," and also, Nanette J. Davis and Bo
Anderson, "Boundary crossings in social networks: a semiotic
formulation". Both papers to appear in David Willer and Bo
Anderson,* Social exchange and social networks, *Elsevier, 1979.*

Davis, James A., & Leinhardt, Samuel. The structure of positive interpersonal relations in small groups. In Joseph Berger, Morris Zelditch, Jr., & Bo Anderson (Eds.), *Sociological theories in progress*, Vol. 2. Boston: Houghton Mifflin, 1972.

Foster, George M. The dyadic contract: A model for the social structure of a Mexican peasant village. *American Anthropologist*, 1961, *63*, 1173-1192.

Foster, George M. The dyadic contract in Tzintzuntzan: Patron-client relationships. *American Anthropologist*, 1963, *65*, 1280-1294.

Holland, Paul W., & Heider, Fritz. *The Psychology of interpersonal relations*. New York: Wiley, 1958.

Holland, Paul W., & Leinhardt, Samuel. A method for detecting structure in sociometric data. *American Journal of Sociology*, 1970, *70*, 492-513.

Holland, Paul W., & Leinhardt, Samuel. Transitivity in structural models of small groups. *Comparative Group Studies*, 1971, *2* (2), 107-124.

Holland, Paul W., & Leinhardt, Samuel. The structural implications of measurement error in sociometry. *Journal of Mathematical Sociology*, 1973, *3*, 85-111.

Holland, Paul W., & Leinhardt, Samuel. The statistical analysis of local structure in social networks. *Sociological Methodology*, 1974.

Leinhardt, Samuel. Developmental change in the sentiment structure of children's groups. *American Sociological Review*, 1972, *37*, 202-212.

Mitchell, Clyde (Ed.). *Social networks in urban situations*. Manchester: Manchester University Press, 1969.

Paine, Robert. In search of friendship: An exploratory analysis in "middle-class" culture. *Man*, 1969, *4*, 505-524.

Tress, Paul H. *Inconsistent status characteristics and influence: A replication and reformulation.* Unpublished M.A. Thesis, Department of Sociology, Michigan State University, 1971.

Webster, Murray, Jr. Actions and actors: Principles of social psychology. Cambridge, Massachusetts: The Winthrop Press, 1975.

White, Harrison, Boorman, Scott, & Breiger, Ronald. Social structure from multiple networks: I. Blockmodels of roles and positions. *American Journal of Sociology,* 1976, *81,* 4.

CHAPTER 22

ACQUISITION AND MANAGEMENT OF SOCIAL NETWORK DATA

Richard C. Roistacher[1]

Department of Sociology
and Center for Advanced Computation
University of Illinois
Urbana, Illinois

I. INTRODUCTION

Several writers have noted that investigators of social networks fall on a continuum that Clyde Coombs has called rigor versus relevance. At one end are the formal theorists working
largely with directed graphs of their own construction, who are
concerned with theory construction and the proving of theorems.
Most of these investigators come from the social psychology or
sociology traditions. At the other end of the continuum are
social anthropologists conducting studies of social networks in
large group settings in the real world.

The real-world people pose more problems for the data analyst
than do the theoreticians. The theoretician needs relatively
few points in a network, and especially, relatively few isolates.
The field worker, however, may be studying a network of so many
points as to cause considerable problems in data management. Many
of these points may be isolates.

[1]Present address: Bureau of Social Science Research, 1990 M
Street, NW, Washington, D.C. 20036.

The theoretician is generally concerned only with rudimentary
attributes of the points and lines of the graph. Most points have
no attributes, and most lines have no attributes other than
directionality, and sometimes a sign or value. However, the
points in a field worker's network are people or collectivities
who have many important attributes: age, sex, location, etc.
In addition, Gluckman (1967) characterizes people in social networks as having either simplex or multiplex connections. Simplex
connections may be representable by a single value for the relation, while multiplex connections consist of several qualitatively
different relations, each of which takes on a value. Finally,
the field worker may not wish to consider all of the connections
in the graph as occurring at a single time, but may be more
interested in viewing a time series of graphs.

All of these considerations mean that the field worker encounters problems in data acquisition that the theorist entirely
avoids, and encounters problems in data management and archiving
that are largely implicit for the theoretician. In this chapter
I present some approaches and solutions to problems of network
data acquisition, representation, and archiving.

At present, there is relatively little secondary analysis of
social network data, Davis' (1970) work being the most prominent
exception. In the long term, the ideas and the work described
here will hopefully result in a set of conventions for recording
and archiving social network data. Researchers will then be
able to spend the major portion of their efforts in analyzing
social networks, rather than in reformatting data files. Standard file formats will also facilitate the transmission of data
across the continuum, and permit the archiving of data on networks in a way which will facilitate secondary analysis.

II. DATA REPRESENTATION AND FILE STRUCTURE

The most logical place to begin is with a discussion of data
file structures and social network data. Considerations of data
file structure have both logical and temporal precedence over
considerations of data acquisition and management, and even over
the specifics of data analysis procedures. Obviously, only data
that can be represented can be stored in a file, and only data
that have been stored can be analyzed. But file structures also
have an enduring aspect that methods of analysis do not necessarily possess.

For instance, it is possible to analyze the National Election
Survey of 1954 using machines and algorithms that did not exist
at the time the data were collected. However, any contemporary
analysis is largely restricted by the information in and documentation of the original file. Only at his peril does the
computer specialist write programs that cannot read files
produced at some earlier time. The best course of action is
periodically to standardize a set of data structures that are
more than adequate to represent data presently being collected,
but that are not so cumbersome as to hinder data acquisition and
file construction.

This discussion uses some examples of standard files from
survey research and shows how these file structures can be
adapted to data on social networks. Also illustrated are some
extensions of present data structures that are better able to
deal with network data. The generation of new types of file
structures from the original data sources is considered next.
Finally, I will consider some of the strategies of network data
acquisition, including a look at acquiring social network data
from computer networks.

A. File Structures

   1. Rectangular and Matrix Files. The original machine-
readable file was, of course, the punched card, a recording
medium that preceded what we now know as "the machine." The
physical structure of the punched card imposed considerable
limitations on methods of analyzing data. Data items were confined to a single column; extreme measures were taken to limit
records to a single card if possible. Several punched cards
holding data on a single case could be merged, but only after a
considerable amount of collating and cross-checking.

   Most current programs for the analysis of social networks
(e.g., Alba, 1971; Alba and Gutmann, 1971) require the input of
rows of the matrix on punched cards, with the file description
supplied by the user at the time the data are read in. Rows
can almost always be labeled with identifying information, but
the programs have few, if any, facilities for handling lists of
attributes.

   The advent of magnetic recording media allowed the construction of rectangular data files in which data from a single case
occupies a continuous record without any restrictions on the
record's length. This file, which is still the standard structure for analyzing survey research data, can be viewed as a rectangle in which each row is a case and each column a variable.
In its usual arrangement, a single record of such a file contains
a row of the array. The second major type of file used for survey research data is a triangular or square matrix of proximities,
most commonly of correlations.

   These two types of files have been the standard fodder for
data analysis systems since the advent of computers. The major
improvement of such files has been the addition of a machine-
readable dictionary that relates a data item's position in the
record to its name and attributes. Thus, systems using self-
described files require the user to specify only a variable's name

or number, referring to the data dictionary in order to find the variable's position and attributes, such as whether it is categorical or whether identifications of missing data are present.

The matrix file is subject to several processing restrictions that are not relevant to the rectangular file. The rectangular file may be sorted into a different order or subsetted without altering the file's description. For example, if variable 4 is "age" and is identified in the data dictionary as the 11th and 12th character of each record, then this description is true of the file when its records are sorted into any order and is applicable to any subset of records from the file. However, most matrix file descriptions assume that all identity cells are on the major diagonal, making it impossible to sort or subset the matrix file without editing each record in the course of the operation.

Most theoreticians use a matrix representation for networks of interest to them. In many cases, these networks are not stored in any permanent machine-readable form, primarily because they can be transcribed from adjacency matrices with no difficulty. Since the points of the matrix have no attribute except some arbitrary label, they are fully identified by their position in the matrix. However, the needs of the field worker, whose "points" have many interesting attributes, can be satisfied only by a file combining the attributes of a rectangular dataset and a matrix file.

Even though the standard rectangular file of the major statistical analysis systems was not designed to represent network data, these file definitions can be adapted to the purpose. The advantages of adopting standard file definitions far outweigh the disadvantages of their less than perfect format. A machine-readable file description allows for unambiguous (I shrink from saying "error free") transmission of the data format to the analysis program. The description also serves as integral documentation for the file, allowing its identification even if paper documentation has been lost or separated from the file. Finally, the data dictionary serves as both an input and an archival standard, constraining the originator to include sufficient documentation at the outset, and keeping the information in a form that can later be extracted by anyone with access to the same statistical system.

The major disadvantage of maintaining a file of network data in self-described form is that the file can seldom be punched onto cards. If the file or data dictionary records are more than 80 characters long, they will not fit onto a punched card. In many cases, the file or its description will be in binary form, which must be translated in order to be punched. However, the punched card is rapidly losing its primacy as a medium of information exchange. It is far more efficient to maintain and exchange files on magnetic tape than on punched cards. New developments, such as cassettes and floppy disks, will make the exchange of files easier and cheaper.

2. *File Techniques for Network Data.* Standard statistical systems can be used to perform a number of useful operations on network data files, even though these systems have no "sociometric" analysis programs. The following discussion assumes that a clique-finding program has been added to the existing facilities of a statistical system. The file description used in this example is that of OSIRIS III (Inter-University Consortium for Political Research, 1973). This system has several advantages for the handling of network data. Its dictionary is maintained in a file separate from the data, thus allowing use of the data either with or without the dictionary. In addition, the dictionary file can also hold the text of documentation for the network.

Figure 1 illustrates a social network derived from a well-known literary source. Figure 2 shows the data of Figure 1 in what I will call a network file, together with a diagram of the file's machine-readable description. Syntactically, the file

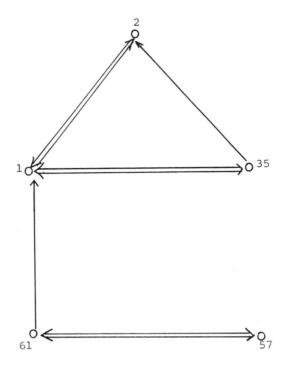

Fig. 1.   Illustration of social network.

is the rectangular data array of the statistical system.   The
first eight variables in each row of the array are a vector of
attributes of a node in the network, together with that node's
row of the network's adjacency matrix.   The file contains an
adjacency matrix as a proper subset, but is free of the standard
matrix file's restrictions on sorting and subsetting.

   This file structure is satisfactory for many network analysis
tasks if three restrictions are observed.   First, records should
not arbitrarily be omitted from the file, whose sort order should
correspond to the column order of the matrix.   Second, the analysis program must be told which columns of the file contain the
adjacency matrix.   Third, the labels used to label the columns
of the adjacency matrix should be chosen so that they can also be

```
VAR    VARIABLE NAME           LOC-    MISS-
NO.                            ATION   ING =

┌─V1   IDENTIFICATION #        1-2      99
│ V2   AGE                     3-5      999
│ V3   SEX                     6        X
│ V4   ID #  1: DOC            7        9
│ V5   ID #  2: S. WHITE       8        9
│ V6   ID # 35: DOPEY          8        9
│ V7   ID # 57: W. QUEEN       10       9
│ V8   ID # 61: A. GHOUL       11       9
│ V9   CLIQUE 1                12
│ V10  CLIQUE 2                13
│ └──────────────────────┐
│                        ↓
└↓              1 1 1 1
  12 345 6 7 8 9 0 1 2 3

  01 274 M 9 1 1 0 1 1 0
  02 017 F 1 9 0 0 0 1 0
  35 291 M 1 1 9 0 0 1 0
  57 039 F 0 0 0 9 1 0 1
  61 999 X 1 0 0 1 9 0 1
```

Fig. 2.   An augmented network data file.

used to label the corresponding rows. The second and third restrictions arise from the way in which the file description is
used. The identification of a row of the matrix is carried in
the data file as one of the variables. Thus, the program can use
the variable "identification number" to order the rows or to
select rows of the matrix. A column of the adjacency matrix,
however, extends across the records of the file, and is identified
by an entry in the data dictionary.

     For example, assume that a file holds identification numbers,
ages, sexes, and the adjacency matrix for a net of five people.
Each record of this file will contain 8 variables: Identification
number, age, sex, and 5 variables corresponding to the contents
of that person's row of the adjacency matrix. The data dictionary
carries, among other things, labels for each of the 11 variables
in the file. A clique-finding program reading the adjacency

matrix from variables 4 through 8 can process the file in two
unusual ways. First, the program, knowing that the matrix has
five columns, also knows that it has five rows, and can extract
the matrix from the file intact. Second, the program can use
the label for variable 4 (column 6) of the file to label results
applicable to row 1 of the file, something not usually done by
statistical programs.

The file can be augmented to carry information about individuals and subsets of the network. One possible procedure is to
augment each individual's record with its own column vector in
the adjacency matrix, thus almost doubling the size of the file.
For instance, the last two variables in the file in Figure 2 were
generated by a program which wrote an augmented version of the
original eight-variable file after finding two cliques. Each
individual's record is now augmented by a string of two 0s and
1s showing the individual's membership in each of the two
cliques. However, for many groups, the number of possible
cliques becomes very large, resulting in extremely long individual
records.

The dual of a file having a record for each individual with
a vector of clique memberships is a file containing a record for
each clique with a vector showing each individual's membership
in the clique. In addition, the record can contain a vector of
the clique's attributes. Files of clique records are usually
easier to generate than files of individual records augmented by
clique vectors. The length of a clique record depends only on
the size of the group and the number of attributes of the clique,
numbers that should remain more tractable than the number of
cliques as size of the group increases. If some cliques are to
be eliminated from the analysis, it is easier to subset the
records of the clique file than to edit the augmented records of
the network files.

The clique file is no longer an extension or augmentation of
the original network file, since each of its records now represents a subset of the nodes of the matrix rather than a single
node. A clique file can be related to its network file only by
specifying the algorithm that generated the cliques. However, it
has the virtue of being a rectangular file that may be sorted or
subsetted freely. Clique files can be generated from network
files by various clique- and subset-finding procedures. The
clique files can then be analyzed with standard survey research
programs to determine the differential characteristics of these
cliques or subsets.

A special case occurs when the set under consideration is the
entire set of nodes of the network. In this case, the membership
vector can be collapsed into a single variable identifying the
network from which the record was derived. Davis' (1970) paper
resulted from an analysis of a set of clique records derived from
a whole set of matrix files. In this case, the basic clique file
consisted of an identifier and a vector of triad counts. Davis,
in a personal communication, said that his life would have been
considerably more placid had his library of sociograms been for-
matted using a standard (machine-readable) data dictionary.

All of the files described up to this point are currently
implemented in existing analysis packages. A network dataset
could be constructed using the file definitions and formatting
facilities of packages such as OSIRIS III (Inter-University Consortium for Political Research, 1973) or SPSS (Nie *et al.*, 1975).
None of the standard versions of these systems presently has any
clique finding or other graph processing routines.[2] However, all
of these systems have well-documented procedures for interfacing
analysis routines into their file handling mechanisms. Thus, the

[2]*However, their factor analysis, multidimensional scaling,
and clustering programs have been used for the extraction of
cliques.*

developer of a network analysis routine will make life easier for
everyone by interfacing new programs into one of the standard
data analysis systems. By doing so, a set of data standards and
documentation conventions will automatically be imposed on the
data, and the author will be saved the trouble of writing many
work-a-day routines for data management.

Existing file structures will handle a network of "simplex"
connections between individuals. However, a network with multiplex connections is best represented as a matrix whose cells are
vectors. Although the network file could be extended so that its
adjacency matrix portion consisted of several columns for each
column of the adjacency matrix, such an augmentation is somewhat
clumsy. A better way to structure such a file would be as a
hierarchy in which a first level data structure is the adjacency
matrix, each cell of which would contain a vector of data
elements.

Such a tree-structured data set can presently be handled by
commercial data base management systems such as Mark IV or System
2000.[3] These systems, however, are extremely complex, have few
analysis capabilities, and are generally unavailable in academic
computing centers. Thus, one of the major tasks in building the
next generation of analysis systems is to develop capabilities to
handle files more complex than rectangles and matrices. Thus, it
may pay to build clumsy rectangular files that will soon be trans-
formable into more tractable forms.

There is currently a project underway to define and implement
a universal "data interchange" file, which will support generalized arrays and hierarchical files, and which will be produced
and read by all of the major statistical systems. General use of
the interchange file should facilitate the archiving and exchange

[3]*The March, 1976 issue of* ACM Computing Surveys *(Vol. 8,*
No. 1) is a definitive review of the present state of data base
management system design and implementation.

of social network data. Roistacher (1976) describes the design
of the data interchange file.

   3. Incident Files. One very nice way to handle large
amounts of data on social networks, especially where data
are gathered over time, is through the construction of what can
be called an incident or cell file. Each record of the incident
file contains the indices of the cell of the matrix and its entry,
either as a scalar or a vector. Incident files contain a record
for each nonempty cell of the adjacency matrix. Like the basic
and augmented network files, an incident file may freely be
sorted or subsetted by record. Incident files are extremely use-
gul where the matrix is sparse or where observations are made
over time. In this latter case, the time of the observation becomes one of the elements in the vector comprising the cell
entry.

   The great strength of an incident file is that it can be extensively analyzed and reformatted using only a sorting program
and an aggregation program. Suppose, for instance, we wished to
find the row sums of the sociomatrix represented by an incident
file. The file is first sorted on the row index so that all
records in row *I* of the matrix are adjacent. The sorted file is
then passed to any of several standard data aggregation programs
(e.g., OSIRIS III's CSUM and AGGREG) that will produce for each
row *I* a record containing the row identification and aggregate
statistics applicable to all records in the file indexed by *I*.

   For example, the aggregated record might show not only the
row sum of the matrix, but also the mean income of those mentioned by *I* and the variance of their ages. Multiple passes of
sorting and aggregation on *I,J* and time can reduce a time series
of observations to a set of cross-sectional matrices by aggrega-
ting *I,J* records with different time periods into a single *I,J*
record.

Even though indices are duplicated on each record, an incident file will be considerably smaller than a social network or matrix file where the network is sparse. In fact, for studies of extended networks, it may be necessary for the observer to create a diagonal for the matrix by inserting I,I records. Otherwise, isolates will not show up in the incident file at all.

One example of the incident file's robustness is that the inclusion of duplicate I,I records does not disturb the file at all. An observer finding a new person who should be included in the study need only enter an I,I record for that person without having to determine whether or not such a record was previously inserted in the file. Barring errors in identification codes, such duplicates will fall out when the file is sorted and aggregated. Roistacher (1976) gives a full exposition of this technique.

B. Data Acquistion

1. Questionnaires and Forms. The standard sociometric questionnaire asks the respondent to list his or her n best friends, coworkers, etc. Holland and Leinhardt (1973) have shown that limited choice sociometric instruments introduce systematic biases into the data which may make the recovery of the social structure impossible. Unlimited choice sociometric instruments that require writing down lists of names are not very popular with respondents. My own attempt (Roistacher, 1974a) to obtain peer ratings from junior high school boys by asking for a written list of friends or acquaintances provoked mutiny beforehand and eyestrain afterward.

A very successful way of obtaining peer rating and network information is to provide each member of the group with a roster of other group members, and to ask the respondent to rate or mark each other person that he or she knows well enough to do so. Roster instruments were successfully used to obtain peer ratings in groups ranging from 100 to over 200 junior high school boys.

The chief disadvantages of roster instruments in collecting data from large groups is that they require extensive preparation, administration, and coding time. Roster instruments often yield a flood of data, especially in networks in which there is a high linkage density or in which, as in some junior high schools, the norm is that everybody knows everybody.[4]

One of the best ways to acquire data in field studies, especially those in which several observers are working at different times, is to build an incident file to which records are continuously added over the course of the observation period. Since records in the file are relatively simple, a record can usually be generated from a short notation indicating who did what and to whom. Incident records can be checked and entered into a file shortly after they are created. Since the incident file is always complete, analyses may be performed while the study is in progress, thus allowing relatively continuous monitoring of the data acquistion process.

2. Data Entry. Small sociometric questionnaires are little trouble to convert to machine-readable form, since each questionnaire will often fit on a single punched card. Large roster instruments require the use of on-line data entry equipment or optical scanning forms if the user is to be spared either inordinate key punch costs or the trouble of creating records from varying numbers of punched cards.

Incident records probably require more keypunching or other data entry time than other forms of network data, but are intrinsically as foolproof as it is possible for data to be. If a study is taking place over an extended period of time, then incident records represent the most effective form of data file,

[4]
Roistacher (1974b) contains a fuller discussion of ranking and rating scales for sociometric instruments.

since the file is up to date at all times. Incident records need
not be entered in batches, but may be added to a file at the
researcher's convenience.

III. COMPUTER NETWORKS AND SOCIAL NETWORKS

Computers are exciting, not only as a tool for analyzing
data, but also as a communication medium. More and more, computer networking is becoming of interest to social scientists.
The Department of Defense's ARPA computer net links 40 computers
in North America, Hawaii, and Europe. However, the major use
of the APRANet is not the transmission of data for computation,
but the transmission of electronic mail among network users.
Computer network facilities allow users to send messages that
are stored and can be read at the recipient's leisure. If
present predictions hold true, computer nets will be an increasingly useful means of tying together, among other things,
"invisible colleges" of scientists.

A current project links a group of criminal justice researchers over the commercial Telenet network, allowing them to
exchange messages, share data, collaborate in the writing of
papers, and request and obtain each other's comments. It is
relatively easy to modify the message transmission program
(subject to the user's permission) to write an incident file
assigning each message a number and indicating its sender, recipient, and time of transmission. Such an incident file would provide a record of activity over the network and could be used to
analyze collaboration among the network's members. Since the
incident file would contain no message text, the intrusion on
members' privacy would be minimal.

In a more comprehensive system, the text of all messages
could be automatically encrypted and a copy diverted to an archive. To insure privacy for the network's users, messages in
the archive would be retrievable only with the permission of the

sender and recipient, who would be the only ones with cipher keys
to their archived messages. Considerable information on the social network could be obtained by analysis of the message incident file. However, the availability of an archive of messages
allows the possibility of content analyzing selected trans-
missions across the network.

IV. CONCLUSIONS

The work of several sociologists has shown that sets of data
on social networks have become valuable resources for secondary
analysis. Anthropologists are making studies of increasingly
large social networks. The development of standard ways to
represent and describe social networks will allow easier transmission and analysis of social network data. In addition, adherence to formatting and documentation standards will help
field workers collect more complete and useful data. Finally,
the advent of computer nets as communications resources for
social networks allows the unobtrusive collection of network
data in forms that are immediately analyzable.

REFERENCES

Alba, R. D. COMPLT: A program for analyzing sociometric data
    and clustering similarity matrices. Columbia University,
    Bureau of Applied Social Research (mimeo.), 1971.
Alba, R. D., & Gutmann, M. P. SOCK: A sociometric analysis
    system. Columbia University, Bureau of Applied Social
    Research (mimeo.), 1971.
Davis, J. A. Clustering and hierarchy in interpersonal relations:
    Testing two graph theoretical models on 742 sociomatrices.
    American Sociological Review, 1970, *35,* 841-851.

Gluckman, M. *The judicial process among the Barotse of Northern Rhodesia* (2nd ed.). Manchester: Manchester University Press, 1967. (Cited in J. A. Barnes, Network analysis: Orienting notion, rigorous technique, or substantive field of study? Paper presented at the Mathematical Social Science Board Advanced Research Symposium on Social Networks, Hanover, New Hampshire, 1975.)

Holland, P. W., & Leinhardt, S. The structural implications of measurement error in sociometry. *Journal of Mathematical Sociology*, 1973, *3*, 85-111.

Inter-University Consortium for Political Research. OSIRIS III User's manual. Ann Arbor, Michigan: Institute for Social Research, 1973.

Nie, N., Hull, C. H., Jenkins, J. G., Steinbrenner, K., & Bent, D. H. *Statistical package for the social sciences* (2nd ed.). New York: McGraw-Hill, 1975.

Roistacher, R. C. A microeconomic model of sociometric choice. *Sociometry*, 1974, *37*, 218-229. (a)

Roistacher, R. C. A review of mathematical models in sociometry. *Sociological Methods and Research*, 1974, *3*, 123-171. (b)

Roistacher, R. C. The data interchange file: A first report. CAC Document No. 207, Urbana, Illinois: Center for Advanced Computation, 1976.

CHAPTER 23

PERSPECTIVES ON SOCIAL NETWORKS

Anthony P. M. Coxon

University College
University of Wales
Wales, United Kingdom

I. INTRODUCTION

Two recurrent themes in this volume relate to "social space" and "conceptions" of networks. Behind these themes lies a set of problems that underlie a good deal of sociometric network analysis: In what sense do networks exist? How do people's behavior, experience, and conceptions of social structure relate to the accounts and explanations we social scientists give? How do partial, restricted, even distorted views of the social environment relate to "the" social structure, if such there be? I do not intend to treat these epistemological issues, but rather take up two more modest, related issues. I contend that a good deal of the confusion and legitimate criticism raised in this field often arises from (i) a cavalier disregard of data-theoretic problems (what other area of sociology virtually writes in the assumption that the data are inherently crude and problematic, but then continues to amass precisely the same

data?) coupled with (ii) a form of methodological monism (in this
case, that one particular representation is most appropriate for
the analysis of the data and the processes underlying its generation).

II.   DATA-THEORETIC PROBLEMS

    Standard, "orthodox," sociometric tests (Northway, 1952)
usually collect what Coombs would term "pick (or order) 3 out of
n" data. The implicit assumptions are that each individual is
able to rpovide reliable information on his or her own micro-
environment, and that the simple fitting together of the micro-
structures provides a single consistent global network--the
sociogram. Later modeling work of Davis, Holland, and Leinhardt
(this volume) (which assumed that the outdegree of a point varied
inversely with its hierarchical status) construed the constant
outdegree demanded by the test as measurement error ("masking")
imposed by the data-collection procedure. Choices made in accord
with the model were still assumed to be veridical, that is, people construed their immediate social environment correctly.
    The early sociometric analysts also assumed, virtually with-
out exception, that the appropriate representation for such
data was graphical, but it is equally interesting to note that
they thought of the graph as being embedded in some way in a
continuous "social space." Contrary to the arbitrary location
demanded by graph theory, they attempted to position points in
a way that reflected such properties as centrality, popularity
bias, and similarity--see for example Northway's (1940) target
diagrams, Bronfenbrenner's (1944) isocontours representing the
probability with which choices received exceeded chance expectation, Chapin's (1950) "signed proximity space" (fixed by the
number of positive, indifferent, and negative choices) and
Mosteller's (1968) use of barycentric coordinates for the same
purpose. Attempts to "encash the spatial analogy" have made

extensive use of multidimensional scaling models, using for input proximity measures either direct pairwise similarity judgments
(Goldstein et al., 1966), or such indices as path length and
density, common contacts at n-removes (Alba and Kadushin, 1970),
and overall discrepancy between percentage distributions (index
of dissimilarity) of choices (Laumann, this volume; Roistacher,
1974).

In such cases, the spatial solution is obtained by assuming
that these (dis)similarity measures represent a (usually monotone) function of euclidean proximity (distance) in "social
space", and well-known Shepard/Kruskal nonmetric iterative
procedures are used to obtain an estimate of this space. This
curt account should not be taken as implicit criticism; in
terms of portraying a good deal of information concisely and
arranging sociometric data in a comprehensible manner, a picture
is worth a 1000 words, as Tukey constantly reminds us. Indeed,
probably the best introduction to simple multidimensional scaling
(MDS) and the meaning of social distance is provided by
McFarland and Brown in precisely this context. Moreover, in view
of the present predominance of the graphical approach in network
studies, the continued use of such models acts as a timely remind-
er of the usefulness of the dimensional and social distance
notions in sociometric analysis.

Nonetheless, the integration of structural information with
spatial representations is rare, and the predominant use of
scaling models in network studies is still chiefly that of data
reduction. The confusion between formal and substantive theory
noted by Anderson (this volume) in the context of balance is also
evident here. At least in the context of studying face-to-face
networks and organizations of moderate size, more attention could
be paid to the "cognitive cost" of obtaining dimensional solutions. This is particularly evident in the context of social
perception and impression formation, which has tended to be
divorced from network studies in recent years, since the

composition function defining a distance model can be interpreted as a combination rule which postulates how (dimensional)
information is combined into overall judgments of personal
attraction, sociometric choice, etc. An example of such an
approach, in much the same tradition as that described by Heider
(this volume) as the "similarity/attraction" model, is the
Davison and Jones (1975) study where the vector (factor) distance
(unfolding) and weighted distance models of Carroll and Chang
(1970) preference mapping are interpreted directly as (imple-
menting) Anderson's (1971) "weighted-sum" model, and two forms
of Byrn's (1971) additive models of personal attraction.

III. ALTERNATIVE REPRESENTATION

One of the more persistent issues in the analysis of social
networks, alluded to in several papers in this volume, is the
"perspectives problem", that is, how different conceptions of the
structure are related to each other. (A single generating structure may be said to underlie [and produce?] the more or less inaccurate perceptions or it may be assumed that the communality
between the conceptions implies a consensual structure). The
most explicit and subtle treatment of this problem has occurred
in the Harvard[1] studies, but some leverage is provided even on
this problem by use of MDS models.

Within the scaling context, the Individual Differences
(INDSCAL) weighted distances model (Carroll and Chang, 1970) postulates that individuals differ in the salience or importance
which they ascribe to the dimensions of the space. Young and
Jones (1972) use this model to some effect to study the micro-
structure of the Thurstone Laboratories over a year's period,
arguing that interpersonal perception is both instrumental to

[1]Reference is to the work of H. White and co-workers.

and conditioned by social interaction. They go on to treat
sociometric choices as the dependent variable of the analysis,
using proximity in a subject's "private space" to predict their
three sociometric judgments with 70% success. (It is incidentally
worth noting that both hierarchy and subgroup structure were dis-
cernible in the dimensional structure). One advantage of the
INDSCAL model is that it many be used equally well to examine the
extent to which *groups* specified on external criteria differ
in their conceptions of their social environment. There is no
reason, for instance, why explicit "structural" characteristics
should not be used to define such groups. It would seem emi-
nently reasonable, for instance, to use point characteristics
(e.g., degree of centrality, weakening/strengthening properties)
and structurally equivalent groups (in H. White's sense) to define groups of this sort, and go on to investigate the extent to
which their conceptions or judgments differ systematically.

But if the fundamental source of information about network
structures is the subjects themselves, and if it is important to
tie concepts back into their phenomenal context, why are subjects
so rarely invited to contribute such information? Why not
credit the subject with his or her own account of the social
structure? Perhaps one reason is that, as we have repeatedly
been reminded, many network processes and judgments are really
evaluations of, or operations upon, the network structure rather
than reports. Since this is so, it is highly unlikely that a
good descriptive representation of a network can be obtained
from the evaluative data normally collected in sociometric tests.

Why not, then, ask the subject to provide an account of his
or her perceptions of the clique structure by inviting him or
her to cluster the group and leave open the explicit question of
how many groups or cliques are recognized. Such direct assess-
ments of sociometric structure correspond fairly obviously to
free-sorting data, and can be analyzed in what are now fairly

well-known ways. A useful aggregate summary of such data is
provided by the "co-occurence," matrix whose entries signify,
(according to differing conventions, Burton, 1975) the frequency
with which individuals i and j are allocated to the same clique
by the "judges." Using the notion of the pairwise intersection
between two sortings, as Boorman and Arabie define a family of
distance measures, allows one to test *in principle* the extent to
which subjects share the same "view" of the sociometric structure.

As an artificially simple example, suppose that the clusterings that each of seven individuals gives is as follows (refer to
Figure 1):

$\underline{p}$:		$\underline{ng}$	$\underline{h(p)}$
A:	{ABC │ DEF │ G}	3	6
B:	{ABC │ DE │ F │ G}	4	4
C:	{ABC │ DEFG}	2	9
D:	{A │ BC │ DEF │ G}	4	4
E:	{AB │ C │ DEF │ G}	4	4
F:	{AC │ B │ DEFG}	3	7
G:	{AB │ CD │ EFG}	3	4

(Note that they differ in the number of clusters which they
recognize, and in the aggregativeness or "height" of their
partition.) From such data, two matrices can be derived:

(i)   *the co-occurrence matrix, $\underset{\sim}{C}$,* (giving the frequency
with which individuals i and j are allocated to the
same group); and

(ii) *the subject distance matrix, $\underset{\sim}{D}$,* (specifying the difference between the partitions of each pair of subjects--in this
case defined by what Arabie and Boorman dub the *PAIRBONDS*
measure (refer to Figure 2):

$$d_{ij} = h_i + h_j - 2h(i \cap j),$$

i.e., the more similar the sortings of two subjects, the
closer the intersections).

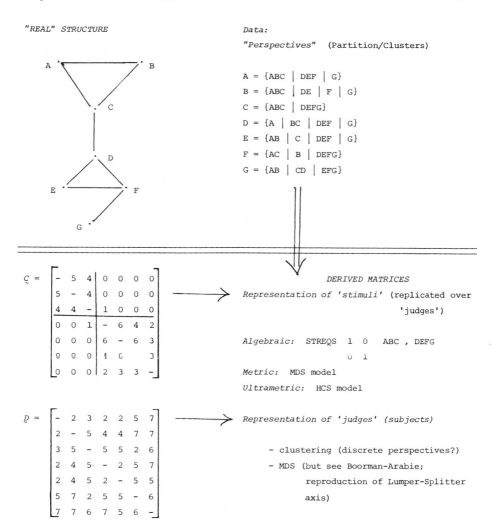

Fig. 1. "Real" Structure and Derived Matrices

	p:	ng	$h(p)$
	A = {ABC | DEF | G}	3	6
DATA:	B = {ABC | DE | F | G}	4	4
	C = {AB | CD | EFG}	3	5

Highly similar clusterings: A and B:

$$B =$$

		ABC	DE	F	G
$A =$	ABC	ABC	–	–	–
	DEF	–	DE	F	–
	G	–	–	–	G

$$h_{(A \cap B)} = 4$$

$$A \cap B$$

$$d_{AB} = 6 + 4 - 8 = 2$$

Highly dissimilar clusterings: B and G:

$$G =$$

		AB	CD	EFG
$B =$	ABC	AB	C	–
	DE	–	D	E
	F	–	–	F
	G	–	–	G

$$h_{(B \cap G)} = 1$$

$$B \cap G$$

$$d_{BG} = 4 + 5 - 2 = 7$$

Fig. 2. Distance Between Clusterings or Partitions
('Height' metric: A–B's PAIRBONDS):

As in the INDSCAL case, and indeed in the analysis of conditional "off-diagonal" data generally, there is a two-fold representation:

- of the nodes of the structure as "objects" of the judgmental process,
- of the nodes as "subjects", that is, makers of the judgments.

There is, of course, no reason why these two sets should be the same, or even overlap; we might be interested in the interpretations which a set of outsiders (sociologists?) has of a group.

But while the matrices are derived from the same data, the information is clearly different. In the sociometric context, the C matrix would usually be used to infer the underlying structure-- if such there be--and it corresponds fairly closely to the conventional adjacency matrix. But the C matrix can equally well be considered as a proximity of similarity matrix, suitable for analysis by the MDS distance model or for hierarchical clustering.

The D matrix by contrast seems more naturally analyzed by non-hierarchical clustering procedures to isolate more or less homogeneous sets of perspectives. In any event, caution is appropriate in interpreting the configuration of subject points resulting from an MDS analysis Arabie and Boorman have shown that, in general, such configurations are not interpretable in terms of proximate clusters, but in terms of projections on to the Lumper-Splitter axis.

It is important to stress again that there is no one simple way of representing these data; indeed there is no reason why the same mode of analysis should be used for both matrices. The C matrix, for example, can be interpreted as a *real-valued graph* suitable for graph-theoretic or algebraic analysis. The entries of the C matrix can be thought of as similar to the results of applying the Breiger algorithm to (0,1) data, and in this example the $\begin{bmatrix} 1 & 0 \\ 0 & 1 \end{bmatrix}$ block structure is clearly evident.

If subjects are familiar enough with the persons involved,
even more complex data can often be obtained. I have used a
hierarchical tree-construction method in this context, which
amounts to getting the subject to perform a Festinger-Katz
clique-detection process upon his or her own cognitive representation of the structure. Once again, distance measures are
available, this time between an individual's trees (Boorman and
Olivier, 1973) to assess the commonality in, and similarity
between, individual conceptions.

IV. CONCLUSION

It would seem, then, that while a dimensional analysis in no
sense competes with graphical and algebraic models of structure,
it can usefully be used both as a data reduction device, and as a
means of tackling recurrent problems of aggregation and composition, social relations, and aspects of commonality and differential conceptions of sociometric structures.

That said, I experience some hesitation in commending such
models, in part because they are de facto limited, along with
many other sociometric procedures, to affective social relations
in fairly small groups. Drawing upon an oft quoted, but rarely
demonstrated, finding of Davis in *Deep South*, sociologists are
fond of stating that perception varies with social distance:
Fine gradations are made around one's own position, and become
cruder beyond a certain point. Whether or not this is so for
social networks is a moot point--not least because it is by no
means clear what "having a conception of a social network" really
amounts to. To be sure, the *notion* of a network has wide
currency and most Englishmen will associate the term immediately
with the "old boy network." However in this, its most common
form, the network is in fact much more like a list-structure (a
filing cabinet of useful contacts) than a spider's net.

Moreover, differential perception in the sense mentioned previously is unimportant compared to differential knowledge of who can be called upon to do what. It is here certainly that anthropological accounts of brokerage and reciprocity through social linkages are most convincing, and at the microscopic level of analysis I for one find egocentric networks more convincing than the constructed, aggregated, form with which sociologists often deal. Differential knowledge and access to knowledge certainly seem to function more like a resource than like systematic distortion of the perceptual accounts; even stars may be competing for network information. The logic of this position may well be to argue that face to face groups have sufficient homogeneity and stability to make the search for common dimensions of social interaction worthwhile. But I should be pleased to be proved wrong.

REFERENCES

Alba, R. D., & Kadushin, C. The intersection of social circles: A new measure of social proximity in networks. *Sociological Methods and Research,* 1976, *5,* 77-101.

Arabie, P., & Boorman, S. Multidimensional scaling of measures of distance between partitions. *Journal of Mathematical Psychology,* 1973, *10,* 148-203.

Anderson, N. H. Interpretation theory and attitude change. *Psychological Review,* 1971, *78,* 171-206.

Boorman, S., & Olivier, D. C. Metrics on spaces of finite trees. *Journal of Mathematical Psychology,* 1973, *10,* 26-59.

Bronfenbrenner, U. The graphic representation of sociometric data. *Sociometry,* 1944, *7,* 283-289.

Burton, M. L. Dissimilarity measures for unconstrained sorting data. *Multivariate Behavioral Research,* 1975, *10,* 409-424.

Byrne, D. *The attraction paradigm.* New York: Academic Press, 1971.

Carroll, J. D. Individual differences and multidimensional
    scaling. In R. N. Shepard *et al.*(Eds.), *Multidimensional
    scaling,* Vol. 1. New York: Academic Press, 1972.

Carroll, J. D., & Chang, J.J. Analysis of individual differences
    in multidimensional scaling via an N-way generalization of
    "Eckart-Young" decomposition. *Psychometrika,* 1970, *35,*
    283-319.

Chapin, S. A three dimensional model for visual analysis of
    group structure. *American Journal of Sociology,* 1955, *56,*
    263-267.

Davison, M. L., & Jones, L. E. A similarity-attraction model for
    predicting sociometric choice from perceived group structure.
    Illinois: Department of Psychology (mimeo.), 1975.

Laumann, E. O. *Bonds of pluralism.* New York: Wiley, 1973.

Mosteller, F. Data analysis, including statistics. In G. Lindzey
    & E. Aronson (Eds.), *Handbook of social psychology* (2nd ed.).
    Reading: Addison-Wesley, 1968.

Northway, M. L. A method for depicting social relations obtained
    by sociometric testing. *Sociometry,* 1940, *8,* 144-150.

Northway, M. L. *A primer of sociometry.* Toronto: University
    Press, 1952.

Roistacher, R. C. A review of mathematical methods in sociometry.
    Sociological Methods and Research, 1974, *3,* 123-171.

Young, F. W., & Jones, L. E. Structure of a social environment:
    Longitudinal individual differences scaling of an intact
    group. *Journal on Personality and Social Psychology,* 1972,
    24, 108-121.

CHAPTER 24

THE THEORY-GAP IN SOCIAL NETWORK ANALYSIS[1]

Mark Granovetter

Department of Sociology

SUNY

Stony Brook, New York

I. INTRODUCTION

In the course of this otherwise excellent conference, and in
my reading of the rapidly expanding literature on "social networks," one nagging question keeps intruding: Where is the
theoretical underpinning for all these models and analyses? I
will argue, here, that most network models are constructed in a
theoretical vacuum, each on its own terms, and without reference
to a broader or common framework. Despite continuing progress,
therefore, the point of diminishing returns is approaching, and
will rapidly overtake us, unless we pay more attention to what I
call the "theory-gap" in network studies.

II. THE THEORY-GAP IN STATISTICAL NETWORK MODELS AND TECHNIQUES

By "statistical models and techniques" I mean principally network sampling and random-baseline models. I will deal with each
of these in turn.

[1]*Revised version of remarks made at the MSSB Advanced Research
Symposium on Social Networks, Hanover, New Hampshire, September 1975.*

A. Network Sampling

It may seem premature to complain about network sampling, a
relatively new area of great potential importance. In any system of more than a few hundred units, the number of possible connecting lines ("relationships") and consequent structural properties becomes so large that no reasonable macroanalysis is
possible without sampling procedures. This explains why network
analysis has, in the past, been typically thought of as a variant
of sociometry, confined as it was to small, closed groups. It
seems possible that network sampling theory will open up the area
of macronetwork analysis in a way similar to that in which the
theory of random survey sampling opened up general macrosociology.

The crucial thing that Ove Frank (1971) and others working on
the technical side of this subject have done is to show that the
problem of sampling from large networks, which I and others had
considered largely intractable, can be attacked with standard
sampling theory methods, such as the use of indicator variables
and inclusion probabilities--though their application requires a
good deal of imagination. In my treatment (1976) of the subject,
I elaborate the theory for the case of sampling network density
and acquaintance volume and attempt to spell out the practical
techniques and applications in a way useful for actual sociological work.

Before we plunge further into network sampling, however, we
need to think through more exactly what it is we want to know
about large networks, and why. Imagine that we had no sampling
difficulty, and that by pressing a button, we could find out anything about the network of the entire United States. The state
of macronetwork theory is now such that it is not clear what we
would want to know. Thus, I will make some general comments
directed at this problem.

First, we should think about whether we can be satisfied mainly with the sampling of average or total properties of large networks. Ove Frank's chapter (in this volume, and to be fair, my own 1976 paper as well!) deals mainly with these. But even what theory we *have* about the subject suggests a need to know about *exact* distributions of various network characteristics and about local inhomogeneities. Exact distributions are necessarily harder to estimate than are their means. Even the *variances* of these distributions are quite hard to estimate.[2] In the case of relatively rare but important network characteristics, the likely large variances will make it difficult to establish acceptable confidence limits from practical sampling procedures.

Certainly there are useful applications of the sampling of average properties (for some examples, see my paper, 1976, pp. 1297-1300). But for the kind of application suggested, for example, by Everett Rogers (in this volume), one would need to know much more detailed network properties. In this case, one would want estimates of the distribution of weak ties, and particularly the extent to which they bridge cliques. Little progress, unfortunately, has been made on this latter type of sampling problem.

My other point is that network sampling has focused more heavily on attributes than on structure; this seems to me true of Frank's chapter which mainly addresses the sampling of node attributes in a network. This would be of great help to the standard survey that tries to infer the attitudes of the population on some subject, or to gauge the level of some individual characteristic such as income, but less useful in estimating

[2]*See Frank's pessimistic discussion on estimating the variance of acquaintance volume, 1971, pp. 109-115, and my further comments on this, 1976, pp. 1301.*

structural properties of the social network. Since Frank's
methods take network structure into account, they are adaptable
to the sampling of that structure. But the implicit theoretical
bias of the chapter is that network sampling has use mainly as
an adjunct to the standard methods of sampling attributes.

B. Random-Baseline Models

Statistically based models of social networks are particularly
prone to carry unstated and sometimes unrecognized theoretical
implications. This point seem especially evident to me in random-
baseline models. At several points in this conference, it has
been proposed that we should accept a finding of structural properties in a graph as valid only insofar as they exceed the structure that would be expected *on some null hypothesis of a random-
graph process*. I argue that such a proposal is fundamentally
atheoretical, and could arise only in a theoretical vaccuum. In
any area of inquiry, null hypotheses can be justified only by some
theoretical consideration. In the theory of sampling, for instance, it is typical to look for effects beyond those expected
at random because the theory *tells* us which effects can be
attributed to the random sampling process itself, and which are
extremely likely to be due only to some other source of variation.
No such justification applies to the use of a random-baseline in
network treatments of an entire relevant population, as in the
two cases I now consider.

I begin with the discussion that ensued at this conference
when Joel Levine described the interlocks he had found among
corporate boards of directors. Scott Boorman commented that
the seemingly short paths between firms, in the network of
corporations, might actually only be those that would be generated
in a random graph, given some fundamental properties of the graph.
In this connection he cited some surprising results on random
graphs from Erdös and Rényi (1961). But I believe that this

criticism could seem potent only in the absence of a theory about the substantive significance of *any* given level of structure.

Levine's response was, in effect, "Who cares how the structure was generated? If it is there, then it has consequences." In general this is the apt response, but its thrust is weakened by failure to specify the consequences of particular configurations. Even if we had a full distribution of the path lengths among corporations in the matrix, we wouldn't know quite what to make of it since we have little theoretical rationale for saying what is a "long" or "short" path, or even what exactly flows through these paths. Furthermore, it is possible that what *causes* a given level of sociometric structure can be of as much interest as the consequences of that structure. In the case of interlocks, the question of whether an observed structure *could* have been generated by some random process speaks to the question of whether any conspiratorial theory of political economy applies (though it cannot settle it).

To sum up: (1) Both the causes *and* the consequences of a structure may be of interest, and are separable issues. (2) If we carry on complex empirical studies of what structure exists in some body of sociometric data but have no detailed underlying theory of what the consequences are of the different types or levels of structure we may *find,* we leave ourselves open to the "Boorman gambit."

Professors Holland and Leinhardt (in this volume) are not merely open to the gambit, they actually make it part and parcel of their model in the form of a "conditioning" procedure. Because the Davis-Holland-Leinhardt family of models constitutes the most important and innovative statistical analysis of small-group structure now available, I think it especially important to subject its theoretical assumptions to examination, as I have done in the past, on somewhat different grounds (1973, pp. 1376–1377). Here, I argue that the procedure of counting as structure *only* that level of structure that exceeds what is expected from a

random graph with the same distribution of mutuals and in- and
out-degrees: (1) gives up in advance the possibility of deciding,
on theoretical grounds, what the significance is of given *levels*
of transitivity and, (2) has theoretical implications that actually contradict the authors' expressed theoretical aims.

The argument about transitivity is essentially the same one
as for the case of path distances among corporations. On the
second point, compare two statements from their chapter: First,
"the lowest interesting level of structure in a digraph is the
level of triples of nodes--the triadic level." Then, "In many
instances, as the level of conditioning increases, what appears
to be structure disappears."

The latter viewpoint, in my opinion, actually gives causal
primacy to the level which, in the former, is said to be less
important. It assumes that any structure found that is consistent with the null hypothesis of a random graph, given these
mutuals and in- and out-degrees, is an artifact of the dyadic
properties. But this reflects, implicitly, a microlevel theoretical prejudice, which contradicts the first statement quoted.
Why is the possibility not allowed for, for example, that the
dyadic level properties are artifacts of the *higher* levels of
structure? Where do these dyadic level properties--the number of
mutual ties and the distribution of in- and out-degrees--*come*
from? In the Holland-Leinhardt paper they are seen as external
exogenous constraints, givens, whose levels are not subjected to
causal analysis, but are explained in terms of individual, personal characteristics. For example, the distribution of in-
degrees is described as resulting from variations in "individual
popularity," that of out-degrees from "individual expansiveness,"
and the number of mutual choices as the result of "friendship."

But if we take the importance of levels higher than the dyad
seriously, and we really think that these are more fundamental,
shouldn't we want to develop the theory in such a way that the
so-called "lower" dyadic parameters could be shown to be the

result of triadic or higher level processes? Instead, this model
says implicitly that the dyadic properties are somehow prior to
the triads and higher level structures. While Holland and
Leinhardt might disavow this on theoretical grounds, the logic of
conditioning the graph on these three dyadic level properties entails this assumption. A great deal of theoretical clarification
would result from an over-time analysis of how these network
structures actually form, but this cannot be extracted from cross-
sectional secondary data. New panel data could shed some light on
this question.

It should be clear that I greatly oversimplify in arguing that
either dyadic properties "cause" higher level ones, or that
triadic and higher level properties "cause" dyadic ones. My
point is simply that the conditioning procedure expresses an implicit theoretical prejudice that ought to be made explicit and
ought to be considered as part of the theoretical backdrop of this
model. The same point arises as for the director interlocks.
Even if a structure is generated by random processes, and this may
indeed be important, how can we say that "what appears to be
structure disappears" once the random model is taken into account?
This implies that we have no coherent theory about why this
"apparent structure" is important, or what level of it has what
effects. "Structure" used in this way, lacks substantive, sociological meaning, since its effects are indeterminate.

III. THE MICRO/MACRO THEORY-GAP:
      SMALL GROUPS, BALANCE THEORY, AND MARKOV CHAINS

A large part of the theory-gap in network models stems, I
believe, from a more general problem in sociological work: the
encapsulation of micro and macrolevel work from one another. I
suspect that much of the atheoretical quality of network models
for small-group structure results from the failure to connect the
groups in question with any larger substantive part of social

life. In Professors Bernard and Killworth's chapter (in this
volume) great stress is put on the importance of prediction in
social science, but relatively less on the question of exactly
what it is we would like to predict, and why. The models they
review, and most other small-group models, including the ones
we have seen here, assume that we want to predict changes in the
group sociogram; but even if we are able to make such predictions,
will these be related in any interesting way to any other level
of social action? Because this question is not considered, the
theoretical content and causal principles invoked seem artificially simple.

Many analysts would agree that the most problematic assumption
of the models is that of no change in group composition over time;
most would also assert that this unrealistic assumption is tolerated because of the great simplification it permits. While I
have no doubt that this is an important motive, I also believe
that the commonness of this assumption reflects, implicitly, the
isolation of microlevel network analysis from other levels. In
order to introduce assumptions about membership changes that
would not be entirely arbitrary, it would be necessary to consider
the social structure in which the small groups were embedded.
Because small-group analysts are usually not concerned with this
larger structure, they find it unnecessary or at least arbitrary
to assume changes: Hence, the unreal aura of stability that
permeates our abstract groups is not effectively challenged.

I will expand on this point by showing how two theoretical
frameworks, those of balance theory and of Markov chains, take on
an entirely different coloration when analyzed outside of the
closed small-group setting.

A.   Balance Theory

Here, as examples, I take some problems that are well known
in political sociology and anthropology, but are not usually
given network interpretations. The first example is from the
extensive literature on "cross-cutting cleavages" (see Truman,
1951; Gluckman, 1965; Lipset, 1960). A cross-cutting cleavage
exists in a population when we have a division along the lines
of one cleavage--say into two religious groups, like Catholics
and Protestants, but also some other cleavage--say village of
residence--that does not coincide with the first but "cross-cuts"
it. That is, all the Catholics do not live in only one of the
villages, but are mixed up with the Protestants within each
village. Let us suppose, for the balance theory analysis, that
individuals who find themselves on opposite sides of both cleavages but nevertheless come into contact with one another, have
relations that are, on the whole, hostile. So, in Figure 1,
individuals B and C, who are split both by religion and residence,
are pictured as being linked by a negative line. Suppose also
that being on the same side of at least one of the cleavages is
enough to generate positive relations, so that A and C, being
resident in the same village, are on good terms despite their
religious differences.

Balance theory tells us that there will be a psychological
strain in this situation and that one of the three lines will be
likely to undergo a change of sign. But outside of small groups,
where likes and dislikes may be based on relatively transitory
personal incidents, it is not so easy to reverse these signs.
Religious and residential differences are reinforced by a host of
institutional and economic constraints. More important, the lines
A-B and A-C in this unbalanced triad are precisely the "cross-
cutting ties" that, according to all discussions, form an essential aspect of stability in political systems. The reason for
this is that person A becomes a structurally induced mediator;

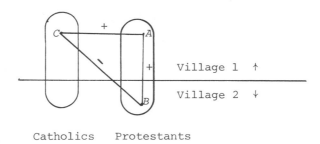

Catholics   Protestants

Fig. 1. Cross-cutting ties.

he has positive ties to both parties who are at odds with one
another, and so has an interest in reconciling their conflict.
This is related to Bo Anderson's earlier point (in this volume)
that a person in *A*'s position may be a political *broker,* who
intentionally maintains ties with people who are enemies, for
his or her own benefit. In the case of Figure 1, the structure
puts the mediator in a rather uncomfortable position; he or she
might just as soon avoid this role, but becomes, willy-nilly, a
mediator. In Anderson's case, the person does it consciously.
But in both cases the overall political context is such that it
is important for various reasons, functional or instrumental, to
maintain this *unbalanced* triad.

   Notice that this particular triad, with one negative line, is
exactly the one whose presence rules out the clusterability of a
graph (Davis, 1967). Robert Abelson pointed out earlier in this
conference that balance and clusterability are, in effect, the
same as cleavage and polarization. In the language of my argument, this is to say that a system without cross-cutting ties
would be completely clustered--polarized into cleavages, all

positive ties within clusters, and only negative ties among them.
Neat as this may seem to balance theorists, it would make a
political situation highly untenable. Battle lines would be
clearly drawn; no one would have any doubt which side he was
on; no one would have an interest in mediation. The resulting
conflict might well then be severe and bitter.

If we wanted to give the discussion thus far a name, we could
call it the "common-ally principle": A is a mediator or broker
because he or she is an ally common to two enemies. This suggests that we might look for a symmetrical "common-enemy principle." This can be found as an important organizing principle
of entire political systems, in the anthropological literature
on "segmentary opposition"--best illustrated by the ideal-type
case described by E. E. Evans-Pritchard in his study of the
Nuer, a tribe of some 200,000 in Eastern Africa. Figure 2a is
a truncated version of a famous diagram from his study, in which
he shows the political/geographical structure of the society
(1940, p. 144). Each geographical unit is pyramidally nested
within larger units. Villages comprise what he calls "tertiary
sections," which combine to make secondary sections, which are
in turn embedded in primary sections, which make up tribes, within the overall Nuer society. The diagram here shows only
villages (A_1, A_2, B_1, B_2) and tertiary sections (A, B).

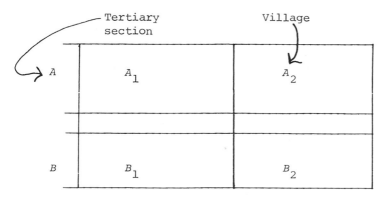

Fig. 2a. Nuer social organization.

Among the Nuer, people in neighboring villages fight a lot,
in part because they are in such frequent contact. Now if it
happens that there is a dispute between someone in Village A_1
and Village B_2, the fact that each village is in a different
tertiary section becomes relevant; there is an aggregation of
loyalties at the tertiary-section level so that people in A_2
join with those in A_1, and those in B_1 with those in B_2. The
dispute escalates, and entire tertiary sections join in combat.
Thus, if person X (Figure 2b) is from Village B_1 and person Y
from B_2, even though they may fight with one another at times,
when their villages are at odds, they also have common enemies,
namely, all those in tertiary section A, of whom Z is a representative. In systems of segmentary opposition (for a general
discussion see Fortes and Evans-Pritchard, 1940, pp. 11-14),
this process repeats itself at each higher level of aggregation.
Thus, members of different tertiary sections may be members of
the same secondary section and have as common enemies all those
in other secondary sections, and so on. The upshot is that any
two individuals (or social units) who might ever have occasion
to fight also know that there are common enemies against whom
they have fought together in the past or will in the future.

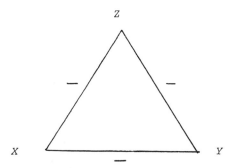

Fig. 2b. Nuer political relations.

Balance theory leads us to expect the common enemy to make one of the ties in Figure 2b positive. In real political life, however, whether among the Nuer or ourselves, there are too many real conflicts of interest between opposed political actors to make them allies simply because they have a common enemy. What happens instead is that the level of conflict is moderated. When X and Y fight, the conflict is not as bitter as it might otherwise be, and there are strict rules about what weapons may be used. As in the case of cross-cutting ties, the unbalanced triad brings moderation into the political system.

What I have shown, then, is that both triads forbidden by balance theory not only exist in macrolevel context, but have similar, stabilizing roles in political conflict. What is seen as "balance" in small groups amounts, in larger structures, to forbidding enemies to have common allies or enemies in conflict situations. In order to change a sign in a small group, it is usually sufficient for an actor to undergo a change of attitude toward another person. It is not necessary for anything about the actual situation to change. In larger contexts, where indirect rather than direct exchanges are the rule (cf. Homans, 1961, Chap. 16; Ekeh, 1974), negative relationships are usually embedded in institutional structures that are not easily changeable. Under these circumstances, triads with one or three negative lines not only persist, but constitute the only practical way to avoid bitter conflict. All this is not to say that I believe balance theoretic predictions for small groups either. Insofar as these groups are not really closed, or there is conflict within such a group that is difficult to erase, some of the present considerations would also apply. But it is in the larger setting that they become particularly relevant.

B. Markov Chains

The point I want to make about Markov-chain models is similar
to that in the preceding discussion of balance theory. Markov
chains have not been prominent in studies of social network structure in the past, but as analysts move increasingly into questions of dynamics and change such models are certain to appear
with some frequency. (Some examples are Holland and Leinhardt,
1977, and Sørensen and Hallinan, 1974.) My argument is that, as
in the case of balance theory, Markov-chain models may be
appropriate for groups that are small and closed, but become
less useful for larger settings.

In order to make this point clearly, it is necessary to
spell out the implicit theoretical assumption of Markov-chain
models. Because Markov models are typically used as a convenient,
mathematically tractable accounting device, the fundamental
theoretical assumption is invariably glossed over--namely, that
the system in question is *shallow in causal depth*. By "depth"
of causation, I mean, in operational terms, how far back in time
one has to go in order to understand what the causes are of
the current state of the system. A Markov model assumes that if
one looks at the system-state immediately previous to the present
one, that is far enough. It may be that the system started
5000 time units ago and that each unit has affected each subsequent one--so that in an indirect sense, there is causal influence right from the beginning; this is a typical representation
of deterministic systems in physics. In the stochastic model as
well, one can run a system through a long time period, in a
simulation, or in closed-form equations, to see whether any
equilibrium point is reached. But the point is that in a
Markov process, any causal influence on the present state of a
system from states earlier than the *immediately* previous one is
necessarily indirect, mediated through this next-to-last state.

Hence, once we know the next-to-last, we need look back no
further since any causal influence from earlier states is summed
up in what we have already found out.[3]

It is too rarely appreciated that the assertion of shallow
causal depth has substantive meaning. In effect, it amounts to
denying the importance of historical factors in a given system.
It is easy to imagine that this is reasonable in many small
groups--as in groups of high school peers that may, in many cases,
form de novo at the beginning of high school and persist no more
than 3 years. This is true a fortiori for artificially created
small groups, in a laboratory setting. But when a much longer
time dimension is introduced and we look at large, fragmented
social systems or networks, the model becomes less appropriate.

Let me mention some data on careers, from my own research
(Granovetter, 1974). If one considers the sequence of jobs a
man holds during a career as a sequence of "states," then a
Markov interpretation would be that the job a man holds at a
given point in time is probabilistically related only to the
one held immediately before. If someone believed in complete
equality of opportunity, he would not even be willing to make
this assumption, but would opt instead for stochastic independence, assuming that each move to a new job depended entirely
on ability, education, or other characteristics that could be
considered appropriate for matching individuals to jobs. Probably no one believes this, but people do tend to think about
career mobility in Markov terms. In my study, I asked how

[3]*In a purely technical sense, Markov models can be extended
in such a way that this assumption of one-step dependence is
generalized to n-step dependence. A purist would have to
specify "one-step Markov models" in this discussion. But for
practical, computational purposes, only one-step dependence is
possible as a working assumption, and it is invariably the one
used.*

individuals got the information that actually led them to move
from one job to another. I found that the source of information
was often a person whom the respondent had met much further *back*
in his career than the job immediately previous to the present
one; the tie to this person was usually one that was weak, infre-
quently activated, and essentially dormant. Career networks,
then, have historicity that has serious consequences for their
operation, in a way that many small groups may not. (For further
discussion, see Granovetter, 1974, pp. 85-92.)

This example is not strictly comparable to most sociometric
Markov models, since the latter predict not information flow,
but rather changes in patterns of sociometric choice. But this
is not different in any crucial way from the case I have described. Since people are channeled into jobs via personal contacts made early in their careers, and since each job one holds
has an important impact on the structure and contents of one's
friendship network, it follows that the pattern of choice is itself dependent on states of the system beyond the immediately
previous one. The Markov assumptions might be valid within a
closed small group over a narrow time span. But the fact that
individuals move into and out of a variety of small groups over
a longer period of time, without, however, ever losing touch
totally with some of the members of groups they have left, makes
these assumptions untenable in a larger setting. To the extent
that a particular small group has flux in membership, is not
entirely closed, and persists over a long period of time, Markov
theory, like balance theory, loses its punch; elements of
historicity become increasingly important.

IV.   CONCLUSION

The overriding concern of these remarks has not been to pro-
pound any particular theory of network structure, or to deny the
value of network sampling, random models, balance theory, or
Markov analysis. I have intended only to insist that all these
models, which on their face seem neutral and innocent of hidden
theoretical assumptions, actually harbor underlying notions of
the nature of social structure. These notions may at times be
exactly those held by the authors of the models, but insofar as
they are genuinely submerged, may actually be at odds with the
theoretical preferences they would have liked to express. The
time has come in the development of social network analysis when
every model that is put forward for serious consideration must
be quite explicit as to the theoretical framework in which it
operates. Without this, it will not be possible to integrate
network analysis into the mainstream of sociological thinking.

REFERENCES

Davis, James. Clustering and structural balance in graphs.
    Human Relations, 1967, *20*, 181–187.
Ekeh, Peter. *Social exchange theory*. Cambridge: Harvard
    University Press, 1974.
Erdös, P., & Rényi, A. On the evolution of random graphs.
    *Proceedings of the Mathematical Institute of the Hungarian
    Academy of Sciences*, 1961, *5A*, 17–61.
Evans-Pritchard, E. E. *The Nuer*. London: Oxford University
    Press, 1940.
Fortes, M., & Evans-Pritchard, E. E. *African political systems*.
    London: Oxford University Press, 1940.
Frank, Ove. *Statistical inference in graphs*. Stockholm:
    Försvarets Forskinganstalt, 1971.

Gluckman, Max. *Politics, law, and ritual in tribal society.*
    Chicago: Aldine, 1965.

Granovetter, Mark. The strength of weak ties. *American Journal
    of Sociology,* 1973, *78,* 1360-1380.

Granovetter, Mark. *Getting a job: A study of contacts and
    careers.* Cambridge: Harvard University Press, 1974.

Granovetter, Mark. Network sampling: Some first steps. *Ameri-
    can Journal of Sociology,* 1976, *78,* 1287-1303.

Holland, Paul, & Leinhardt, Samuel. A dynamic model for social
    networks. *Journal of Mathematical Sociology,* 1977, *5,* 5-20.

Homans, George. *Social behavior.* New York: Harcourt, 1961.

Lipset, S. M. *Political man.* Garden City: Doubleday, 1960.

Sørensen, A., & Hallinan, M. A stochastic model for change in
    group structure. Madison, Wisconsin: Center for Demography
    and Ecology, University of Wisconsin, 1974.

Truman, David. *The governmental process.* New York: Knopf, 1951.

CHAPTER 25

SOCIAL NETWORKS AND SCIENTIFIC IDEAS:
THE CASE OF THE IDEA OF NETWORKS[1]

Nicholas C. Mullins

Department of Sociology

Indiana University

Bloomington, Indiana

This Chapter contains an analysis of a social network in
science. In it, I analyze data collected at   the Mathematical
Social Science Board (MSSB) Advanced Research Symposium on Social
Networks. These data are not from a coherent scientific group
but rather from a collection of scientists whose interests may
overlap. Thus the analysis is a test of a procedure rather than
a contribution to the sociology of science. To provide background
for the analysis, I begin with a brief review of what is known
about the sociology of scientific specialty groups.

(1) Important scientific ideas develop within coherent
groups of specialists. Important scientific ideas are here
defined as ideas that continue to attract the attention of
specialists in some aspect of science for some time (Griffith
and Mullins, 1972).

[1]*Part of this work is supported by National Science Foundation
grant SOC-74-24537. Carolyn Mullins provided editorial services.*

(2) The demographics of science are such that most scientific papers are read on average by only one reader; scientists on average author only one published paper; and most ideas are short lived (Price, 1963).

(3) Most scientists in a specialty group are students of those who started it, or students of students (Mullins, 1972; Griffith and Mullins, 1972).

(4) At some point, a specialty has an intellectual and geographical center, composed of at least three faculty and at least three students. Such centers do not last because of the continuing effects of job, promotion and tenure decisions, and of funding fluctuations (Mullins, 1975).

I. CHARACTERISTICS OF THE SCIENTISTS WHO STUDY NETWORKS

The social scientists who study social networks do not fit these characterizations.

Dating back at least to Simmel (1950) are texts that contain conceptions of social networks similar to those currently used. However, at no time has there been a cluster of scientists at one location who have carried these ideas beyond one project. Instead, there has been a developmental pattern of work stretched out through time and space, connecting a few scientists with similar interests. The work of the following sets of scientists exemplifies this history.

1. Coleman, Katz, Menzel
2. Harary, Norman, and Cartwright
3. Berger, Anderson, Cohen, and Zelditich
4. Davis, Holland, Leinhardt
5. Breiger, Boorman, White

Considering the people at the MSSB symposium as the population to be studied,[2] I shall demonstrate that our interests do not constitute an active specialty. Using techniques for citation and cocitation I will also demonstrate how population definition is done on a more active specialty.

First, the conferees are, on the average, too old to be a coherent specialty group. An active specialty group should have younger members since it is composed largely of new scientists (see characteristic #3). The median age is 44 years--older than the median age of all scientists, 41.2 (Zuckerman and Merton, 1970). In an active biomedical specialty, an average age in the thirties is not unusual (Mullins, 1972). The population under study also shows too even a distribution of ages, and too long a median span--15 years--since the granting of the Ph.D's. Furthermore, the average number of publications indicates that members of this group are more successful than are most members of coherent groups. The mean of 46 papers per person (top of the range, 311; bottom, 3) is quite high for a distribution in a specialty. The top publishers here are as expected, but our lowest have too many publications. The distribution of publications is also not the familiar power curve.

The abnormality is apparent in the average number of publications per year per participant (2.7). At this rate, for a 35-year career, each symposium participant would publish 95 papers--a number equivalent to the production of the most prolific scientists.

Our undergraduate origins also fail to be in keeping with what one would expect. They are quite scattered--only four schools graduated more than one of us.

[2]*Now this is ridiculous. Although Leinhardt has done an interesting and important job of bringing together people, the combination of his judgment and the availability of people for the week the symposium was held are no substitute for a population definition.*

The Ph.D. conferrals are less scattered, but they still constitute a wide selection of institutions and a wide time spread.
The time spread is exemplified by the Harvard group, which contains one Ph.D. conferred in the 1940s, one in the 1950s, and a
cluster of four granted between 1964 and 1970. Four is the
largest number of persons who held a postdoctoral position at the
same institution at the same time, although over time, at least
six persons have been members of the current or past University
of Michigan faculty.

II. CHARACTERISTICS OF NETWORKS AMONG NETWORKERS

I would like now to look at a series of critical networks for
specialty formation.

A. *Teacher/Student Networks*

During the development of a specialty, a few specialists and
their students do similar work. Ultimately, these students and
their students' students constitute the bulk of the specialists
at any time. We, however, were taught by many different teachers.
Table I shows that here is no cluster of graduates from any one
school. We all have had students, but most of our students have
subsequently worked in other areas. This fact reflects the way
in which teacher/student links work. Students learn whatever
their teachers are working on at the time they are in school.
Thus a teacher passes on her/his current focus but not necessarily
her/his entire complex of problems.[3] For most scientists, their
current problem is for all intents and purposes their only problem. However, those with wide ranging interests may find that
none are pursued by their students (e.g., Hilbert's interests in
invariant theory, Fisher, 1967). The small number of students

[3]*A student's strong interest in a problem might also direct
a professor's choice of problem.*

TABLE I. *Institutional Locations of Symposium Participants During the Conferees' Early Careers*

B.A.		
	Chicago	− 2
	Cambridge	− 2
	Swathmore	− 2
	MIT	− 2
Ph.D.		
	Harvard	− 6
	Chicago	− 2
	Oxford	− 2
	Princeton	− 2
	Michigan	− 2
	Columbia	− 2
	Illinois	− 2
Jobs		
	Dartmouth	− 4
	Michigan St.	− 3
	Michigan	− 5
	Harvard	− 4
	Chicago	− 5

who are working on networks, then, is a function of the spotty attention paid by any one of us. Even students who are also interested in many topics usually combine interests different from those of their teachers.

This difference, combined with the fact that most students (like most scientists in general) publish little, deters the development of continuous research programs on networks despite the high quality of individual contributions, and the high status and general activity of interested scientists.

B. Coauthorship Networks

As a group, the aforementioned population publish frequently
and often write with coauthors. There are 261 coauthors for the
31 conferees. However, many of those coauthorships are of papers
that are not about networks at all. Also, contrary to the behavior
of coauthors in coherent specialties, we do not coauthor with one
another's coauthors. I have not examined the data for second-
order connections, (coauthors of coauthors), but such an examination would be unnecessary in normal specialty development.

The lack of coauthor exchange stems from the lack of a single
research focus. In the normal specialty, the work accomplished
at several different geographical centers is similar, although
sufficiently different to maintain some distinctiveness. For
example, path analysts at North Carolina and Michigan can work
together despite slightly divergent approaches because the basic
research program has been accepted.

C. Networks of Acquaintance

Even more important, many of us were unacquainted before the
symposium. That situation is impossible in a coherent specialty.
As Breiger (1976) has shown empirically, relations characterized
as "mutually unaware of each other" only involve recent recruits.
At the symposium, I distributed a questionnaire asking eight
questions. The questions and their marginal distributions are in
Table II. On average, 42% of us were unknown to at least one
other--each person knew the work of just over one-quarter of the
others (answers to questions 2 and 3 overlap).

Ordinarily, a study such as this would end here since there
is little evidence that a more sophisticated analysis of the
sociometric data is needed. However, I pursued it none the less.
By placing the responses to each question into a 42 x 42 matrix
I created eight matrices.

TABLE II. Percentage Positive Responses to Sociometric
Questions

Questions	Percentage positive response[a]
1. *"never heard of his work"*	41.9
2. *"know something of his work"*	27.9
3. *"know his work on networks well"*	28.7
4. *"know him well personally"*	17.5
5. *"teacher of/student of"*	3.2
6. *"colleague of, ever"*	5.6
7. *"colleague of now"*	2.5
8. *"coauthor with"*	1.4

[a] *36 questionnaires, 42 possible responses, 1512 total possible responses. The percentage figures are: P = 100x (responses/1512).*

Some patterns of acquaintance ·connect others to this group. For example, from Frank's paper (1975), I learned that in 1937, J. L. Moreno consulted with Paul Lazarsfeld on sampling in a network; and that Lazarsfeld's students, Katz and Coleman, and a junior colleague, Menzel, also worked on network problems. With Katz, Lazarsfeld himself wrote an early classic network research report (Katz and Lazarsfeld, 1954). However, in any group of scientists, given the sorts of networks in which most scientists participate, we should expect to find ways to connect everyone with everyone else. One fact remains clear: The connections do not estabish that there is a common area. Like elites in all kinds of social organizations, active scientists are connected by ties that may not be recognized by the members as binding them to one another. Certainly that is the case here.

D.   Area Definition and Citation Networks

I used the participants at this symposium as my study population.   There are other ways to define populations.   One technique uses a familiar data source to define current specialty
areas.   The Science Citation Index (SCI) lists current publications and associated citations.   The yearly SCI contains a list,
by author, of cited papers, an of all citations to each paper.
This list has been used by Cole and Cole (1973) and others to
rank scientists; essentially, the more citations the better people are reading and using the work.

The data for the eight matrices was analyzed using the CONCOR
algorithm (Breiger, 1976).   Four blocks of 11, 16, 9, and 6 were
constructed from the 42 participants (including 8 who were observers or staff of the conference).   The pattern of connections
on the first four questions was a full block of ones; that is,
none of the relations produced an interesting pattern of connections.[4]   Symposium participants are not a group, but rather a
collection of persons.

E.   So Networks Are Not a Specialty: So What?

Research on networks has appeared sporadically for 70 years.
We can trace a thin thread of development, never with more than
a few persons working on the topic at any one time.   The pattern
is different from the explosive growth pattern of ideas related
to phage research, or path analysis.   Why?   Basically because
social networks have had little to do with the idea of networks
in the past.   Perhaps symposia such as the one reported on here

[4]*For those who are familiar with CONCOR output, the least
full submatrix was 3% full. All others were over 10%. The identification of those in blocks was not interesting. There was no
grouping by productivity of papers, by discipline, by age, or by
status at the conference. Observers and staff were distributed
to all blocks.*

will produce that common research problem and concentration of interest that leads to a single, strong, well-conceptualized focus.

REFERENCES

Breiger, Ronald L. Career attributes and network structure: A blockmodel study of a biomedical research specialty. *American Sociological Review,* 1976, *41,* 117-135.

Cole, Jonathon R., & Cole, Stephen. *Social stratification in science.* Chicago: University of Chicago Press, 1973.

Fisher, Charles S. The last invariant theorists. *European Journal of Sociology,* VIII, 1967, *2,* 216-244.

Frank, Ove. Survey sampling in graphs. This volume.

Griffith, Belver C., & Mullins, Nicholas C. Coherent social groups in scientific change. *Science,* 1972, *177,* 959-964.

Katz, Elihu, & Lazarsfeld, Paul F. *Personal Influence: The part played by people in the flow of mass communications.* Glencoe: The Free Press, 1955.

Mullins, Nicholas C. The development of a scientific specialty: The phage group and the origins of molecular biology. *Minerva,* 1972, January, 51-82.

Mullins, Nicholas C. A sociological theory of scientific revolutions. In K. Knorr et al. (Eds.). *Determinants and controls of scientific development.* Boston: D. Reidel, 1975, 185-203.

Price, Derek DeS. *Little science, big science.* New York: Columbia University Press, 1963.

Simmel, Georg. *The sociology of Georg Simmel* (Kurt Wolff, trans. and ed.). Glencoe: The Free Press, 1950.

Small, Henry, and Griffith, Belver C. The structure and the scientific literature I. *Science Studies,* 1974, *4,* 17-40.

Zuckerman, Harriet, & Merton, Robert K. Age, aging and age structure in science. In Norman W. Storer (Ed.), *The sociology of science.* Chicago: The University of Chicago Press, 1973.

SUBJECT INDEX

A

Algebra, blockmodeling and, 87-94
Algorithmists, networks and
   clique and cluster extracting procedures, 435-436
   general remarks, 434
   graph theory, 435
   random net procedures, 436-437
   structural equivalence procedure, 438
   transitivity model procedure, 437
Ambivalence, quantitative relationships and, 43-45
Analysis techniques, comment, 110-111
Attitude change, group sentiments and, 225-226
Attribution, social networks and, 11-23
Axioms, new, balance and, 195-198

B

Balance
   clusterability and, 25-29
   cocycles and, 189-192
   conclusions, 47-48
   data and, 198-199
   independent generalizations of, 187-189
   new axioms and, 195-198
   open questions and, 38
      consistency theory, 46-47
      quantitative relationships and ambivalence, 42-45
      stability and, 41-42
      tendencies toward clustering or balance, 39-41
   psychological data and, 192-195
   social networks and, 11-23
   theorems concerning, 29-34
Balance theory
   endurance of, 51-52
   falsifiability of, 52-53
   micro / macro theory-gap and, 509-513
   nonobviousness of, 53
   simplicity of, 53
Blocking, process of, 95-99
Blockmodeling, 85-86

basics
   algebraic approach, 87-94
   available programs and texts, 94
   social networks and, 86-87
conclusion, 112-113
critique and comment on analysis techniques, 110-111
extensions
   on groups other than people, 111
   large data sets, 111-112
glossary of terms, 114-116
network analysis and, 394-395
procedure
   analysis of role structure, 99-110
   process of blocking, 95-99

C

Clique and cluster extracts, algorithmists and, 435-436
Cluster theorem
   transitivity and, 58-59
   triads and, 54-58
Clusterability, balance and, 25-29
Clustering
   basic theorems concerning, 35-38
   conclusions, 47-48
   open questions and, 38
      consistency theory and, 46-47
      quantitative relationships and ambivalence, 42-45
      tendencies toward clustering or balance, 39-41
Cocycles, balance and, 189-192
Community decision making
   background, 389
   heuristic model, 389-391
Computer networks, social networks, 485-486
Consistency theory, clustering or balance and, 46-47
Contact processes, estimation of population totals and, 334-344
Contagion process, randomly constructed biased networks and, 119-124
Control, structural, 202-206
   models, 207-212

QUANTITATIVE STUDIES IN SOCIAL RELATIONS

Consulting Editor: Peter H. Rossi

UNIVERSITY OF MASSACHUSETTS
AMHERST, MASSACHUSETTS